The Smiths
FAQ

The Smiths
FAQ
All That's Left to Know About the Most Important British Band of the 1980s

John D. Luerssen

Backbeat
Books

An Imprint of Hal Leonard Corporation

Published in 2015 by Backbeat Books
An Imprint of Hal Leonard Corporation
7777 West Bluemound Road
Milwaukee, WI 53213

Trade Book Division Editorial Offices
33 Plymouth St., Montclair, NJ 07042

Printed in the United States of America

Book design adapted by John J. Flannery

Library of Congress Cataloging-in-Publication Data is available upon request.

ISBN 978-1-4803-9449-0

www.backbeatbooks.com

Contents

Foreword
The Fifth Smith

I n 1983—when I began my career as guitar player in Aztec Camera—there was a lot of talk about this new band called the Smiths and how great and pioneering and what a huge breath of fresh air they were. Of course, every few years the same thing happens, whether it's a band, actor, or film that the media blows up out of all proportion and starts proclaiming as the new Beatles, the new Bob Dylan, or the new James Dean.

As far back as I can remember, when it came to music, I'd hear or read about how brilliant a new band or songwriter was, and I would be intrigued. I'd look into it, as most people do, and listen to this incredible new talent. Then as now, it was always a huge disappointment when—after hearing them—they didn't live up to the hype.

As such, I chose to ignore most of the talk I was hearing about the Smiths. But when I did eventually listen to them properly, I was truly impressed by what I heard. It was one of the rare times, to my mind, that the hype was justified.

Pop music at that time was saturated with New Romantic bands and cheesy, synth-based, lightweight music. To me, it seemed like the Beatles and even the Clash and songwriters like Burt Bacharach and Brian Wilson were all a distant memory to people who were making popular music.

As a guitar player, there didn't seem to me to be much music around then where the guitar was being used to its potential, or at least inventively. There didn't seem to be anybody around for me who was doing anything interesting with the instrument, except my own Aztec Camera bandmate, Roddy Frame. A huge reason the Smiths appealed to me was because of the constantly inventive guitar playing, as well as the quality of the songwriting. There certainly didn't seem to be a high standard of either around in the early 1980s.

At the start of 1986, I was playing in a band called the Colourfield with Terry Hall from the Specials and Fun Boy Three. I had first played with them in 1984, and the drummer, Simon Wolstencroft, who was a friend of the Smiths, told me Johnny Marr had been asking about me. Basically, the situation was that Johnny wanted to meet up with me in the hopes I might join the Smiths as a guitar player.

At that point, since being in Aztec Camera and playing with the Colourfield, I'd been in the Bluebells for two years and had played with Edwyn Collins and quite a few others. Anyway, it was around this time when Simon had told me

Johnny wanted to meet me, and that I should expect a phone call soon. Fast-forward a few weeks to one Saturday afternoon when the phone rang and it was Johnny asking if I'd fancy meeting up.

We arranged the time to meet and Johnny and his roadie/friend picked me up and drove me to his house. Once we were at his house we were just casually chatting and generally getting to know each other before picking up a couple of guitars. We jammed together for a while and we also played things like "Angie" by the Rolling Stones and a few of other songs, probably "Beast of Burden," as I used to play that a lot around that time. We also played "Some Girls Are Bigger Than Others," "Nowhere Fast," "Bigmouth Strikes Again," and "That Joke Isn't Funny Anymore," as well as a few others.

At one point in the night Johnny told me that they were going to sack Andy Rourke because of his drug problem. I'd already heard from someone else associated with the Smiths that they were going to get rid of him, so it wasn't really surprising to me. In the same conversation, Johnny told me that they were thinking of getting either another guitar player or a keyboard player, although he didn't mention whether it'd be as a session player or a full-time member of the band.

With regards to playing live, it made total sense to me that they were thinking of getting another guitar player in the band. I knew most of their songs would undoubtedly benefit from having two guitars, especially the songs from the new album, *The Queen Is Dead*. Johnny was really nice to me and I really enjoyed meeting and playing with him.

Johnny said that if I was interested I could join the Smiths there and then as a replacement for Andy on bass. It was quite a surprise to me that he was asking me that—not because I was being asked to join the Smiths but because he knew I was a guitar player rather than a bass player. I remember not saying anything to that offer because it really didn't appeal to me, but that was really as far as the conversation went as regards to me joining the Smiths as a bass player. It was never mentioned again.

Just days after that meeting I was asked by Johnny—subject to meeting Morrissey—to join the Smiths as a guitar player. By that time I'd also met both Andy and Mike. The following week, Johnny and I had a meeting with Morrissey in his flat in London and that was it, I was a full time member of the Smiths!

With regards to that bass-playing offer, I'd been making a living as a guitar player since 1983—about the same amount of time as the rest of the Smiths at that point—and it wasn't like I was new to it all. If I'd have felt like I'd been given the consolation prize of being a guitar player that they hadn't planned for, I certainly wouldn't have done it—I was strong-minded enough even at that young age to be willing to leave if I'd felt unwanted in any way. But the fact is, I was now the official fifth member of the band and was told I was as much "a Smith" as any of them and made to feel that way from the second I joined.

Johnny and myself went through a lot of the songs together with him some-times pointing out the way he played a certain guitar part or me giving my own take on another part. Johnny gave me all the albums—including *The Queen Is*

Dead, which hadn't been released yet—so I could start learning all the songs. The first thing I did with the already-released Smiths songs was to learn the parts that Johnny had played on the records so that I'd have a good grasp of all the parts.

The first time we all got together to rehearse was shortly after that at Mike Joyce's house. I didn't know what the situation was with regards to Andy, and as far as I still knew it was just going to be myself, Morrissey, Johnny, and Mike getting together, but when I got round to Mike's house Andy was there, ready to play and obviously still in the band, and it really did sound fantastic, even in rehearsal. We played through various Smiths songs, although Morrissey didn't sing; he just watched and listened.

We knew at that point that the two guitars were going to work. On some of the older songs I'd play a part that was on the record and Johnny would play something new over it, or vice versa, or on something like "The Queen Is Dead" and the other newer songs I'd play my own part. It just seemed to work really well straightaway, without us spending ages making it work. Also at that rehearsal, Johnny had a new song idea that we all put down on tape so Morrissey could take it away and write to it. It turned out to be "Panic," the next single, which we recorded a few weeks later.

At the time I joined the band, with the impending tours approaching, I remember Johnny saying he had been quite nervous about how the Smiths were going to come across in huge venues with just one guitar, so I imagine a bit of weight was lifted now that there were two guitars. There were so many crucial guitar parts on the records that they needed an extra guitar player, so it absolutely made sense asking me to join.

Some people over the years have tried to minimize my role in the Smiths, referring to me as a session guitarist, but the fact is, I was always a full-time member of the band. A lot of groups in the same position might get another guitar player or keyboard player for live stuff or to play on records but not to join the band. My situation with the Smiths was different, and I was in the band for around eight months.

We occasionally rehearsed songs that didn't always make it into the set, such as "What Difference Does It Make?" and "Heaven Knows I'm Miserable Now," which as far as I can remember we only played in America. That song, in addition to "Bigmouth," was another of my favorite songs to play live, along with a few others, as I always loved the guitars on the record and thought it came off great live.

When we played in New York, Mick Jagger and Margot Kidder were at the side of the stage watching us. Back in the dressing room, Mick came in for a quick chat and then Margot—who played Lois Lane in *Superman*—came in, so I was chatting to her for a bit. She asked me why we didn't play "Meat Is Murder," as it was one of her favorite songs, so I told her that that was one song we hadn't actually rehearsed since I joined. The following day we did rehearse it and played it from there on.

Things like that always happen when you're in a band at a certain level. The time I played in New York before that, in 1983, the same thing happened with a pre-fame Madonna, who I ended up going to a party with after an Aztec Camera gig at the Danceteria.

I played in Toronto with Aztec Camera that same year and Christopher Reeve, who played the lead in *Superman*, came to watch us play. So it's quite bizarre that I've been watched by Superman and Lois Lane! Even though I'd been around the world playing in bands for three years, at that point I was only nineteen and was still excited and amused by things like that.

Most of the time before and after Smiths gigs when we were in the dressing room we all got on really well and had a laugh. After one particularly good gig, the five of us had a rock 'n' roll bread-roll fight with crumbs flying. Someone came through the door and just looked at the floor covered in crumbs but was scared to ask what had been going on.

On those U.S. tour dates, as is usual, when you do a soundcheck you occasionally have a jam, and we did that quite a lot. We'd jam through Jimi Hendrix or maybe Neil Young songs, but sometimes Johnny would have a new guitar riff or idea for a song and we'd jam on that. I remember him coming up with this really cool riff that we used to play and then later, when I heard the *Strangeways* album, I realized that it had turned into "Last Night I Dreamt That Somebody Loved Me."

After the final few shows of the U.S. tour were canceled, the last day or two was spent in Miami. Everybody was exhausted by that point, and we flew back to the U.K. on Concorde feeling completely worn out! I think we had a bit of a break and then it was on to the final tour of the U.K.—quite an eventful year all in all!

Craig Gannon
United Kingdom
August 2014

Manchester-born guitarist Craig Gannon is a composer for television and film. In addition to his tenure playing with the Smiths and appearing on the songs "Panic," "Ask," "London," "Half a Person," "You Just Haven't Earned It Yet Baby," and "Golden Lights," he can be heard on Morrissey's well-known 1989 singles "The Last of the Famous International Playboys" and "Interesting Drug." In addition to his work with the Smiths, the Colourfield, the Bluebells, and Aztec Camera, Gannon has also played with the Adult Net, Terry Hall, Alison Moyet, Black Grape, and Roddy Frame.

Acknowledgments

T hank you to my wonderful wife Heidi, for twenty-five amazing years together, and to my lovely children, Meredith, Hayley, and Jack. I love you all.

Special thanks to Craig Gannon for his great foreword and overall help; Morrissey, Johnny Marr, Andy Rourke, and Mike Joyce for the inspiration and music; and my original Smiths posse—Jay Juelis, Dan Yemin, John Kieltyka, Bill Crandall, Bob Kelly, Jim Kulpa, Greg Feldman, Jeff Schneider, Angelo Deodato, Chrissy Bradley, Mary Glynn Fisher, Karen Luka, Teresa Schaefer, Karen Turiel Klein, Bill Boyle, Brian Morris, and Ian Duthie. Plus Doug Heintz, Bill Cort, Dave Urbano, Doug Luka, Pete Martin and Andy Rockman, as well as Nick Catania, Ben Forgash, Kevin Houlihan, Matt Azzarto, Mike Engelhart, Tim Dodd, and Andy Haims.

Much love to my parents, Dave and Pinky Luerssen, siblings Liz Luerssen and Ann Crowther, John Crowther, Jane, Theo and Luke Crowther, David and Caitlin Everett, my superb mother-in-law Marie Garner, besties Tom Jardim and Karen Fountain and Beth and Casey Hoerle, Robert and Anastasia Harrison and Dennis McLaughlain and Yvette Scola, plus Scott and Noreen Singer, Stan and Marci Bandelli, Rob and Kim Hinderliter, Michelle Weintraub, Louis Cowell, Tasneem Baten Carey, Joanne and Stu Turner, Marc McCabe, Jennifer Luerssen and Andrew Tavis, James, Jamie and Andrew Luerssen, Dawn Heintz, Jim and Monica Gildea, Tim Glynn, Bill Garbarini, Jason Karian, Bill Beedenbender, Mike McGonigal, Todd Pearsall, Jenene McGonigal, plus Rob and Colleen Rossi.

Also, thanks to the Hal Leonard/Backbeat Books team, including John Cerullo, Bernadette Malavarca, Wes Seeley, Tom Seabrook, and Robert Rodriguez.

Introduction
Sweetness

A loaned copy of the Smiths' *Hatful of Hollow* was my first significant introduction to the brilliance of Morrissey and Marr. This experience occurred in January 1985, during my junior year at Westfield High School, when a good (but now long-lost) friend of mine, Jay Juelis, turned me on to the band and suggested I tape his copy of the record.

If memory serves, Jay had first heard the Smiths' song "How Soon Is Now?" on WLIR—the Long Island radio station that "Dared to Be Different" by playing alternative music. He wisely picked up the album on import during a trip to our area's best record store of the day, Vintage Vinyl in Woodbridge. One afternoon, I put it on a TDK ninety-minute cassette and began to play it again and again. I was stunned by the depth of their music and mesmerized by the delicate beauty of "Please, Please, Please Let Me Get What I Want" and the shimmering instrumentation of "William, It Was Really Nothing."

I was quickly obsessed with the Smiths, who I immediately rated alongside my favorite bands of the day like R.E.M., Echo & the Bunnymen, the Psychedelic Furs, and the Hoodoo Gurus. I bought the domestic 12-inch pressing of "How Soon Is Now?"—the now-classic song derived from Johnny Marr's instrumental "Swamp"—and played it over and over. I did the same for its flip side, "Girl Afraid," which I had also first heard on *Hatful.*

When a new modern-rock station, WHTG-FM 106.3, emerged as "Your Rock Alternative" at the Jersey Shore and began playing tracks from the band's already-released debut album, *The Smiths,* I knew I had to have it. Then, in the spring of 1985, when Sire Records released *Meat Is Murder,* I not only bought it but also made it the subject of my first published piece—a glowing record review that ran in the WHS newspaper *Hi's Eye.* In doing so, my journalism teacher Walter Clarkson accused me of—gasp—trying to turn our school's weekly into *Rolling Stone.*

Aside from their knack for songwriting, the thing that I loved about the Smiths was the way they began to defy the machinations of the music business. As "The Headmaster Ritual" picked up speed at adventurous commercial and college radio, following the popularity of "How Soon Is Now?," the band was already dropping new and completely unexpected non-LP B-sides like "Shakespeare's Sister."

A year later, only weeks after releasing their landmark album *The Queen Is Dead,* they unveiled the non-LP winner "Panic." The Smiths were a band who thumbed their noses at the traditions of the music business in the greatest of ways.

As a freshman in college, I took to my campus radio station to emulate the DJs on WHTG and spin the records by my favorite bands. The Smiths' brand new non-LP single "Ask" was among the first songs I played on the radio in November 1986, alongside songs by 54-40 ("Baby Ran"), Descendents ("Wendy"), and the Rave-Ups ("Positively Lost Me").

Imagine my surprise, two months later, when I walked into Vintage Vinyl during a weekend back home from Pennsylvania and saw a new Smiths import single for "Shoplifters of the World" with a young Elvis Presley on the cover. I snatched it up before I had even heard it and was amazed by both the A-side and the somber flip side, "Half a Person." Days later, I learned from someone at the radio station that more new songs by the band were forthcoming on the Sire double-LP compilation *Louder Than Bombs*, which was due in March.

That summer, I was back home and working at the Westfield Memorial Pool when I heard on WLIR that—according to reports from England's *NME*—one of my favorite bands of all time would be breaking up before the release of their new single and recently completed album. And when the exceptionally good *Strangeways, Here We Come* was released early that fall, I—like all Smiths fans—hoped that Morrissey and Marr would see the error of their ways and mend fences. Much to our disappointment, it never happened.

To this day, the Smiths can be forever proud that—like no other band since the Beatles—they went out on top. Sure, they've been repackaged in the decades since they disbanded in the summer of 1987, but their recorded output has never been tainted by some cash-grab reunion album and tour (unlike other favorites of the era, such as the Replacements or the Stone Roses). As it stands, the group's four albums, multiple singles, and various compilations are nearly perfect. Take a bow, gents.

John D. Luerssen
Westfield, New Jersey
April 2015

The Smiths
FAQ

Here Began All My Dreams

Morrissey's Childhood

Steven Patrick

Steven Patrick Morrissey was born on May 22, 1959, at Park Hospital in Davyhulme, Lancashire. The second child of Peter and Elizabeth, he would later become known to the music world solely as Morrissey. He was preceded by a sister, Jacqueline, born in the fall of 1957.

Steven has long contended that his mother named him after the American actor Steve Cochran, known for his role opposite James Cagney in 1949's *White Heat*. However, logic suggests Morrissey was named after either his father's deceased sibling Patrick Steven Morrissey or his maternal grandfather, the similarly named Patrick Stephen Dwyer.

Morrissey would later marvel in his 2013 book, *Autobiography*, that his enormous head made childbirth so traumatic for his mother that he very nearly killed her. As a newborn, he had trouble swallowing, and was placed in an intensive care unit at Salford's Pendlebury Hospital. Although his parents were told he probably wouldn't survive, he was eventually released from the unit several months later after undergoing a number of surgical procedures.

Peter and Betty

Peter Aloysius Morrissey, Morrissey's father, was born the second youngest of seven in the slums of central Dublin in November 1935. Soon after, his family relocated to new housing in nearby Crumlin, south of the city. While the accommodation was reasonable, the family lived in poverty amid inferior schools, undesirable scenery, and a lack of decent jobs.

The promise of a better life in England prompted Peter's older siblings to leave Ireland at the start of the 1950s. Mary Bridget was the first to settle in Manchester's predominantly Irish Moss Side neighborhood, where she opened a pet store with her husband, Leo Corrigan. Mary's sister Cathryn Patricia—who wound up marrying Corrigan's brother Richard—followed suit, taking up residency on Stockton Street.

By the mid-1950s, Peter—who had already been working making lampshades and ashtrays—moved in with his sister Cathryn and found a job in Manchester as a forklift truck driver at Richard Johnson, Clapham & Morris in nearby Trafford Park. Before long, he had made arrangements for his younger girlfriend, Betty Dwyer, to leave Crumlin to be near him.

Elizabeth Ann Dwyer, as she was legally known, was also one of seven children raised in Crumlin after her family relocated from their home on Dublin's Pearse Street. In spite of the fact that the Dwyers had once owned real estate in the village of Cashel, County Tipperary, the family's resources had dwindled to the point that Betty needed to quit school at fourteen to work in a local factory sewing buttons.

Two years Peter's junior, Betty was a natural beauty who caught the eye of many men. Following her future husband to Moss Side, she took up with an elderly Manchester couple who lived around the corner from his sister Cathryn's house. Betty soon found work in the warehouse of a blanket manufacturer.

On March 16, 1957, Peter and Mary were married in Manchester's Church of Our Lady of Perpetual Succour. The celebration that followed on Moss Side rolled into the following day's St. Patrick's festivities. While visiting Manchester for the nuptials, Betty's parents and younger siblings were so taken with life in the area of Stockton Street that they themselves would relocate from Dublin within months.

Manchester United

As a young adult, Peter was quite the soccer enthusiast. Upon his arrival in England, he was thrilled by the opportunity to play "association football"—something that was apparently shunned in Dublin at the time—and his talents as a striker for his company team and the local, league-winning pub team were soon evident.

Mr. Morrissey was even given an opportunity to turn his weekend pursuit into a full-time occupation after a plane crash in Munich in February 1958 killed eight members of the Manchester United team. However, Peter's overtime schedule at JCM and the needs of his growing family took precedence over his love of the sport, and despite assurances from friends that he would make the professional squad, Peter put responsibility first and, after mulling it over, decided against trying out for the English League champions.

Harper Street

For several months in 1957, the Morrisseys lived on Henrietta Street, but a lack of space would soon prompt them to move, as Betty was three months pregnant with a girl they would name Jacqueline Mary. Luckily, Peter had just found a better job at the JCM warehouse in the city, and the expanding family wound up settling on Harper Street in Hulme, where they lived until 1965.

Upon baby Steven's arrival home from the hospital after his stay in intensive care in the fall of 1959, he was met with jealousy from Jackie. According to Morrissey, his older sister unsuccessfully attempted to kill him when he was an infant on four separate occasions.

Nannie Dwyer

As children, Steven and Jackie spent a great deal of time in the company of their maternal grandmother, Nannie Dwyer. Born Bridget McInerny of Cashel, Morrissey's nannie was a distinct personality. As a young lady, Bridget had been a promising actress who served as the head of Dublin's first all-female Queen's Theater Revue, until motherhood changed her life's direction.

Bridget and her husband Patrick Stephen (a.k.a. Esty) had eight children: Dorothy, Elizabeth, Patricia, Ernest, Anthony (who only survived nine months), Jeane, Mary, and Rita. As "Nannie," Bridget was the family matriarch. She became a firm but caring force in Morrissey's young life.

Irish Pride

As a boy, Morrissey grew accustomed to being called "Paddy." Such slurs rarely bothered him because of the sense of belonging he felt growing up in Manchester's Irish community.

"We were quite happy to ghettoize ourselves," he told Dublin's *Hot Press* in May 1984. "The Irish stuck rigidly together, and there'd always be a relation living two doors down, around the back or up the passage."

In November 1999, he expounded on the topic to the *Irish Times*, saying, "I was very aware of being Irish and we were told that we were quite separate from the scruffy kids around us—we were different to them. In many ways, though, I think I had the best of both places and the best of both countries. I'm 'one of us' on both sides."

Sandie Shaw

In the fall of 1964, a five-and-a-half-year-old Morrissey experienced his first significant musical moment when Sandie Shaw, then seventeen, took to the BBC TV music show *Top of the Pops* to perform the Burt Bacharach/Hal David composition "(There's) Always Something There to Remind Me."

Shaw—whose career Morrissey would help give a boost in May 1984—lodged her first U.K. #1 single with the song, and Steven was enamored. This marked the beginning of his longstanding fixation with female pop singers. Before his sixth birthday, he would walk into

The picture sleeve for Sandie Shaw's 1964 single, "(There's) Always Something There to Remind Me," which began Morrissey's boyhood fascination with female pop singers. *Eil.com* a Manchester record shop to purchase his very first 45—a copy of Marianne Faithfull's "Come and Stay with Me."

Of the latter, Morrissey told *Jamming!* in May 1984, "I remember it had a profound effect on me, and from that time, I was totally obsessed with popular music."

Queen's Square

The Morrisseys relocated from Harper Street in Hulme in 1965, settling in nearby Queen's Square. Betty's side of the family would soon occupy three row houses in the residential complex, which sat on the edge of the Loreto Convent. The Dwyer clan quickly became friendly with other neighboring families, like the Blows and the Bretts. Steven and his immediate family would remain in Queen's Square until 1969, when the demolition of many old streets and structures in the area prompted their relocation to the Manchester suburbs.

Deaths in the Family

Nineteen sixty-five was a tough year for the Morrissey family. In March, Steven's paternal grandfather Peter died at just sixty-three. Even more devastating was the loss of Betty's beloved dad, Esty, in November. Esty was just fifty-two when he succumbed to a heart attack. His daughter Jeane discovered his body.

Six weeks after Esty passed, Morrissey's nannie was lying in a hospital bed nursing a broken leg when she learned that her only son, Ernie, had died on the way home from his office job. He passed in the street, aged just twenty-four. The cause of death would later be listed as atrophy of the liver.

The deaths of the only Dwyer men, who were buried in the same grave in Southern Cemetery, left a massive void in the family. Morrissey would later reveal that it was a decade before anyone in the family could even mention their names.

Besides sharing a birthday with him, Steven also picked up Ernie's appreciation for James Dean. He was also given the harmonica that once belonged to his cherished uncle.

Losing Her Religion

With the unexpected passing of two of the most important men in her life, Betty Morrissey turned her back on the Roman Catholic Church. Although the church had been central to her for much of her life, her faith offered little comfort in the wake of these heartbreaking losses.

The entire Dwyer clan struggled for answers, as Morrissey explained to *Hot Press* in 1984. "From that point onward, there was just a total disregard for something that was really quite sacrosanct previous to the tragedies."

Despite this lost faith, Steven went ahead with his first Communion at the family's church, St. Wilfrid's, that spring. And, interestingly, Betty's ongoing grapple with God didn't prevent her from giving both of her children strict educations at the local parochial primary and secondary schools.

St. Wilfrid's

Like his sister Jackie and his aunts Jeane, Mary, and Rita before him, Steven was sent to St. Wilfrid's Primary School in Manchester, beginning there in 1964. The school's environs were dark and depressing, and it was widely speculated that the aging institution—which had been constructed from stone in 1842—was haunted.

Steven's teachers' outlooks matched the décor under the direction of Mr. Coleman, the miserable headmaster. Coleman hated children, and his demeanor, coupled with a lack of money and resources, rendered his staff unhappy. In some cases, the teachers became downright mean. Morrissey would describe the school in the pages of *Autobiography* as a "bleak mausoleum" and branded his education there a "secret agony."

Certain occurrences would forever tarnish him. At the age of eleven, for instance, Morrissey was instructed by Coleman to walk a sick student named Patrick Keane to his residence some twenty minutes by foot from St. Wilfrid's while crossing a number of busy intersections. Upon his return to the school, and despite assurances by Steven that Keane seemed perfectly fine, Coleman showed no appreciation and instead called him an idiot for leaving his ill class-mate home alone.

Rather than arrange for an adult to escort the sick child home and look after him, as would be appropriate, Coleman had saddled Morrissey with the blame. "Guilt is astonishingly embedded in Catholic children without them knowing why," Morrissey would explain to the *Guardian* in 1997. "It is a fero-cious burden to carry."

Corporal punishment was also alive and well at St. Wilfrid's during Morrissey's time there. He would later describe Mother Peter as an evil nun with facial hair who beat children for kicks and rivaled Coleman in cruelty. Coupled with the headmaster's ritual, which included regularly hitting young boys (and occasionally girls) with a leather strap in front of their peers, Steven's already growing resentment of Catholicism turned to absolute disgust.

The barbaric environment prompted one hopeless classmate at St. Wilfrid's to snap. Morrissey would later recount how an overweight girl named Bernadette took a leather belt and wrapped it around her neck, threatening to kill herself, as the teacher, Miss Dudley, looked on, evidently compassionless. The disinterested expression on Dudley's face suggested she was waiting for the child to follow through with her promise. For Morrissey and his classmates, it was just another disgusting day at school.

Football's Best

Peter Morrissey had hoped to pass his love of football (or "soccer," to Americans) on to his eight-year-old son by taking him to see George Best, the sport's biggest name at the time, play for Manchester United F.C. at Old Trafford one afternoon in 1967. But Steven became overwhelmed by the sun and the chaos of the massive crowd of 75,000 and fainted in front of his father.

If the excitement of the sport and significance of Best seemed lost on the boy as his dad carried him out of the stadium nicknamed the "Theatre of Dreams" that day, Best would still manage to leave a subtle impact on the future Smiths star. In 1984, Morrissey was chuffed to meet the athlete in a U.K. television studio. He would go on to praise the football legend's intelligence, extraordinary personality, and appreciation of the finer things in *Autobiography*, marveling at how, with Best's ascent, "the old mold of the at-home regular fellow [was] smashed forever."

Peter Pulls Away

Peter and Betty may have started out as young lovers, but as they grew into the complexities of adulthood, it became apparent that they probably weren't the best companions for one another. Mr. Morrissey opted to work the night shift at JCM, which kept him away from his family during the dinner and prime-time television hours that most families spent together during the 1960s.

For another decade, the Morrisseys would keep up appearances, but their children soon came to realize that things were not all right in their parents' marriage. Tensions ran high between the couple, while in the absence of his increasingly distant father, Steven found himself drawn closer and closer to his mother and her love of books.

Fixation on Female Singers

Steven's fascination with female pop artists continued as the 1960s elapsed. Picking up where his interest in Sandie Shaw left off, Morrissey was drawn to Motown artists, plus U.K. teen singers Twinkle and Lulu, who delivered hits like 1964's U.K. #4 "Terry" and 1965's "Leave a Little Love," respectively. He was also fond of global smashes like Petula Clark's 1964 single "Downtown" and Dusty Springfield's "I Only Want to Be with You," as well as Helen Shapiro's impressive run of U.K. hits from 1961 and '62, which he discovered a few years later.

In his fourth year at St. Wilfrid's, Morrissey stood out among the Beatles and Rolling Stones worshippers at school when he brought 45s by Shaw and Twinkle, plus a copy of Susan Maughan's 1962 pop hit "Bobby's Girl," to a school dance. Looking back, he spoke of how he was exhilarated by singers from the era, describing them to *Sounds* in December 1983 as "girls with extreme youth and high spirits who were to boldly claim their patch in a business which was obviously a male domain."

Billy Fury

Morrissey cried when Billy Fury—England's answer to Elvis Presley—died in 1983. Fury, who was discovered working on the docks in Liverpool, had been relocated by handlers to London in the early 1960s, where he was, as Morrissey later explained to *Smash Hits* in June 1984, "styled and forced to make records."

Fury (born Ronald Wycherly) disliked the music business and his career as a singles artist. Morrissey, however, was drawn the singer's hit 45s, including 1961's "Halfway to Paradise" and "Jealousy," '62's "Last Night Was Made for Love" and '63's "Like I've Never Been Gone."

The cover of Billy Fury's 1962 *Hits* EP, which includes the smash "Halfway to Paradise." Young Steven Morrissey became a massive Fury fan after being introduced to the singer by his Aunt Jeane. *Eil.com*

"Billy's singles are totally treasurable," Morrissey would tell the writer Ian Birch, describing how he had discovered Fury through his aunt Jeane. "I get quite passionate about the vocal melodies, and the orchestration always sweeps me away."

Saturday Singles

From sometime in 1965 onward, Morrissey would spend hours each Saturday morning browsing through the racks at the Paul Marsh record shop on Alexandra Road. "Whatever record I could buy was like a piece of my heart," he told Birch.

Early singles he bought included the Righteous Brothers' "You've Lost That Lovin' Feelin'," Jimmy Jones' "Good Timin'," Tony Orlando's "Bless You," the Foundations' "Back on My Feet Again," and the Small Faces' "Lazy Sunday." Just before his aunt Mary left England for the United States in 1968, she took him to Paul Marsh and bought him a gift—"Rainbow Valley" by the Love Affair.

While most boys his age had latched on almost exclusively to Lennon/McCartney and Jagger/Richards, access to the radio and the influence of his older sister Jacqueline helped Morrissey to develop a distinct musical taste from a young age. "I devoured everything," he told the *Face* in May 1985.

Suicidal Thoughts

By 1967, Steven had become obsessed with death—specifically suicide. "I can remember being obsessed with it from the age of eight, and I often wondered whether it was quite a natural, in-built emotion for people who're destined to take their own lives, that they recognize it and begin to study it," he told Len Brown of the *NME* in February 1988. "If there was a magical beautiful pill that one could take that would retire you from this world, I think I would take it and I suppose that's the extremity of the obsessiveness."

Some of these feelings stemmed from what he considered to be an unbearable childhood. Morrissey knew, based on his observations of his classmates, that it was unusual to have these feelings. As he told Elissa van Poznack of the *Face* in June 1984, "The reason I felt strange was because no one else was saying, 'I'm really miserable, I can't stand being nine years old, when are things going to change?'"

Moving to Kings Road

In 1969, Manchester officials moved forward with longstanding plans to tear down a large section of the city's crumbling poor and industrial areas, including the Queen's Square district, where the Morrisseys lived. Taking their cue from his mother's oldest sister Dorothy—who had already moved to the green grass and fresh air of Stretford—Steven's immediate family happily moved to a three-bedroom house at 384 Kings Road.

The semidetached council house had a front yard and a private back garden. With its modern plumbing, electricity, and telephone, plus formal living room, it was quite a step up from the family's previous accommodation.

A Lapsed Catholic

In spite of Betty's ongoing struggle with religion, her children continued their Catholic education after the move. Jackie enrolled at Cardinal Vaughan School, while Steven missed out on being offered a place at a grammar school after inexplicably failing his 11-plus exam in 1970 and was instead enrolled at St. Mary's Catholic Secondary Modern on Renton Road.

Morrissey had already drawn his own conclusions about religion, describing himself at this age as a "lapsed Catholic" to writer Mat Snow in December 1989. "It was at the usual time, ten, eleven, twelve, after being forced to go to church and never understanding why and never enjoying it; seeing so many negative things and realizing it somehow wasn't for me."

Petrified by the statues and other creepy religious symbolism, he imagined how a sensible Christ would want to totally separate himself from the Roman Catholic Church. "I went to severe schools, working-class schools, where they would almost chop your fingers off for your own good," he told *Hot Press* in May 1984. "If you missed church on Sunday and went to school on a Monday and they quizzed you on it, you'd be sent to the gallows."

2

He Kicks Me in the Showers

Morrissey's Adolescence

St. Mary's: Shorts, the "Strap," and Sadism

In the fall of 1970, Steven Morrissey arrived for his first day at St. Mary's accompanied by his mother and wearing the requisite blue blazer and tie. But unlike his classmates, who had opted for long pants, he stuck out by wearing the optional uniform shorts. It was the first indication that Morrissey was different. That notion was cemented each day thereafter as Steven crossed the short railway bridge that separated his back yard from the school grounds for lunch with his mother, while the other kids stayed in school to eat.

According to Smiths biographer Johnny Rogan, just three students from St. Wilfrid's passed the 11-plus exam (which determined the academic road a public would take into his or her teen years) in 1970. Although Morrissey flunked his, putting him on the same path as the other working-class adolescent boys who roamed the corridors of St. Mary's, he was clearly too bright to be in such company.

Amid the suedehead and skinhead Catholic toughs who were his schoolmates, Morrissey easily placed in the top third of his class, although he was often bored by his lessons. Aside from being one of the stronger students, he was a capable athlete who participated in the school's track team. He was also relatively popular among the school's teachers and student body, until a rebellious streak took hold.

Despite being a natural at track and field, he disliked the commitment required of a runner and regularly groaned about the after-school travel it entailed. Steven liked corporal punishment—which was doled out daily—even less. He did what he could to avoid it by keeping a low profile in his early years at Clitherow House, the building at St. Mary's to which he was assigned.

As expected, St. Mary's kept Catholicism front and center, with daily prayer rituals, religious teachings, anti-abortion presentations, and a Friday mass once per month, while a focus on rigidity and discipline was fostered by the headmaster, a veteran army man named Vince "Jet" Morgan. The callous Morgan—who Morrissey would describe in 2013's *Autobiography* as "militantly empirical" in his grey suit and spotless black oxfords—focused mostly on the picayune during his morning inspections. Improperly trimmed fingernails, a smudge on one's dress shoes, or a poorly knotted tie would result in what the boys of St. Mary's called "the whip."

Getting the "strap" across the knuckles or the buttocks in Morgan's office wasn't the only punishment. The misery of the St. Mary's staff was transferred to its students, who endured regular beatings from the faculty. If the staff were unhappy with the despicable environment, miniscule pay, and the headmaster's lack of educational background, this in no way excused them from treating the boys of St. Mary's as human punching bags. According to Smiths biographer Tony Fletcher, a metalwork teacher routinely beat his pupils on their bottoms with a wooden stick, while a female instructor smacked the back of their calves with a similar implement.

The cruelty and depravity didn't stop there. In his memoir, Morrissey writes of one gym teacher who was obsessed with homosexuality and enjoyed taunting the students about whether they were or weren't gay. And following physical education class each day, this peculiar teacher would insist that the boys participate in a communal shower. Morrissey would also relay how a different P.E. instructor at the school made a homosexual advance toward him when he was fourteen. The incident occurred inside the teacher's office, after he inspected Steven's injured wrist.

As an upperclassman, Steven was on the receiving end of headmaster Morgan's attention and found himself one of a dozen called out for daily floggings, although by this time he was less upset about his own treatment than the cruelty Morgan delivered to the smaller boys who stood alongside him in line for beatings. Six lashes to the rear end from the headmaster's thick leather strap rendered many of the smaller underclassmen unable to walk. When the depraved Morgan changed his routine, multiple thwacks to the back of the hand would leave them unable to clench a fist.

Elsewhere in his book, Morrissey describes his experience at St. Mary's as "five confined years that will answer no purpose." Morgan, he writes, "busies himself day after day with the beatings of small boys. And it goes on, and on, and on, and on—leading nowhere, achieving nothing. . . . Each day is Kafka-esque in its nightmare. The school offers nothing at all except a lifelong awareness of hate as a general truth. Encouragement is not on any curriculum."

Michael Foley

Morrissey took secret pleasure in watching his classmate Michael Foley stand up to Morgan. Tired of the daily brutality, Foley confronted his abuser, telling him to "fuck off." Surprisingly, despite this act of rebellion, there is no suggestion from Morrissey, in his memoir, that Foley was expelled, as one might expect.

Steven would befriend Foley for a while, remembering him as a handsome kid who had his way with the ladies. Michael even encouraged Morrissey to join him in his Saturday job working on a bread van. But after reporting to work at 6:30 a.m. just once, Morrissey decided he preferred sleeping in on the weekends and ditched the job.

Vegetarianism Begins at School

Before Morrissey was yet a teen, he turned vegetarian after watching a television documentary about how farm animals were raised. He soon found the smell of meat in the St. Mary's cafeteria hard to take, lamenting the "daily waft of dead pig and foul fish" in *Autobiography*.

Speaking to Dan Matthews in an interview for People for the Ethical Treatment of Animals in September 1985, Morrissey explained how he made the choice to stop consuming meat when he was eleven years old. "My mother was a staunch vegetarian as long as I can remember," he told Mathews, who would go on to become the organization's vice president. "We were very poor, and I thought that meat was a good source of nutrition. Then I learned the truth."

Ironically, in 1973, Morrissey's aunt Nellie—unaware of his staunch feelings about vegetarianism for several years—asked him if he had ever considered being a butcher. At first, he was stunned at his father's sister's question, until he realized she was never informed of his position on animal rights.

Taking the Stage

When Morrissey was eleven, he was cast in a local community-center production of a play called *On Dartmoor*. In the role of Ulrick, a petulant child who could be heard but not seen, Steven shouted down to the stage from an imaginary bedroom, showing promise as he elicited laughter and applause from the crowd.

Pleased with his own performance and the audience's reaction, Morrissey—like any son—sought approval from his father after the play. But Peter was not pleased with his son's effort. Steven was heavily discouraged from pursuing any further roles by Mr. Morrissey, who cruelly informed his son that his performance was an embarrassment.

Unhappy Family

By 1970, Peter and Betty had grown further apart. Although their marriage would drag on for several more years, the love and companionship that gave impetus to their teenage romance had long disappeared.

Jackie found herself in tears over her parents' quarrels. Constant negative comments about Steven's artistic and literary interests had already damaged the boy's opinion of his dad, pushing him closer and closer to his mother. By now, according to a 1985 Morrissey interview with journalist Nick Kent, his father regarded him as a "complete fruitcake."

Joys at home were had when Peter was at work or off watching Manchester United at the pub. In his absence, Betty, Jackie, and Steven would gather around the television to watch thought-probing movies like 1955's *Blackboard Jungle*, starring Glenn Ford, or 1967's *Up the Down Staircase* and *To Sir with Love*, which starred Sandy Dennis and Sidney Poitier, respectively.

Lillian's Gang

Around the time of his twelfth birthday, Morrissey was taken under the wing of a tough yet sweet sixteen-year-old girl named Lillian, who protected her neighborhood gang of boys and girls who roamed the streets of Stetford from outsiders.

Handsome and tender but nonthreatening, Steven was well liked by the girls. This earned him trouble one day in the form of a jealous boy named Leslie Messenger, who challenged him to a fight. Morrissey did more than defend himself: he surprised everyone by knocking his oppressor to the ground, much to the glee of onlookers. But in spite of the brief thrill he experienced by sticking up for himself, Steven felt uncomfortable about fighting. From then on, he avoided getting into further altercations.

Immense Isolation?

Although Morrissey would use the media early on in his career to portray a tragic, lonely childhood and to sound off about his meager upbringing, there were some obvious embellishments. Speaking to *ZigZag* in February 1984, he would tell writer William Shaw, "It was just a time of immense isolation." Of course, ample evidence that he had friends now exists to counter this claim.

It is well documented by biographer Tony Fletcher that Steven had alliances with people like Foley, Paul Whiting, and Ian Campbell. He vacationed with classmate Jim Verrechia's family to North Wales, went to school dances, and regularly hung out with neighborhood kids. He also seemed to have plenty of money for records and paperback books, despite the suggestion in early interviews that he grew up deprived. "'Tragic' makes me sound like I was a part-time axe murderer as a six-year-old child," he clarified to Shaw. "I was raised in dire poverty. We never had money for socks or anything, and I think that had a great influence on me."

Steven's Bedroom

Aside from his days spent at St. Mary's, much of Morrissey's pubescent years on Kings Road elapsed in his small bedroom in the company of books—largely by choice. He owned many American paperbacks and was drawn to assorted feminist titles, which he purchased at the nearby shop Grass Roots on Newton Street.

Steven's record collection also continued to grow with 7- and 12-inch vinyl purchased at Manchester shops like Robinsons Records, Rare Records, Piccadilly Records, and Virgin Records. His walls were adorned with pictures of his favorite rock acts and photos and posters of the late movie star James Dean.

James Dean

Morrissey's fascination with James Byron Dean began when he was still in primary school, after he caught a television broadcast of the actor's best-known film, *Rebel Without a Cause.* Dean, of course, died when his Porsche 550 Spyder crashed in Cholame, California, on September 30, 1955.

Morrissey found himself intrigued by Dean's life story, and explained to *Smash Hits* scribe Ian Birth in 1984 that researching the actor was "like unearthing Tutankhamun's tomb." Steven was deeply impressed by Dean's drive, which saw him leave behind his life on an Indiana farm to move to California and later New York in pursuit of acting.

Describing Dean's "constant uneasiness with life," Morrissey marveled at how his hero was disinterested in the stardom that followed his role in *East of Eden.* "He was still incredibly miserable and obviously doomed," he told Birth. "That kind of mystical knowledge that there is something incredibly black around the corner— people who feel this are quite special and always end up in quite a mangled mess."

The Dean pictures taped to his bedroom wall couldn't help but feed Morrissey's fashion sense. In '84, he spoke fondly of the actor's image to *Undress* writer Iain Webb, opining that he "looked perfect persistently" and "could wear an old rag and he was still quite stunning."

"Soldier Blue"

When Canadian pop/protest singer Buffy Sainte-Marie took to *Top of the Pops* in 1971 to deliver her U.K. #7 hit "Soldier Blue," Steven Morrissey was hooked. The fact that even the conservative BBC aired the single's anti-war commentary was highly unusual for the times.

In keeping with his appreciation for female singers, Morrissey bought the 45. When he flipped it over, he found himself captivated by "Moratorium," an even more controversial number. As the Saskatchewan-born Canadian-American Cree vocalist sang of a dungaree-wearing girl holding a sign that read, "Fuck the war— bring our brothers home," Steven felt empowered.

"Get It On"

That same year, Morrissey got caught up in the rollicking guitar charge of T. Rex's chart smash "Get It On" on *Top of the Pops.* The

The U.K. sleeve for T. Rex's landmark single "Bang a Gong," the first of many hits of 1971 and '72 that earned the devotion of an adolescent Steven Morrissey, who went to see the Marc Bolan–fronted band live at Manchester's Belle Vue Theatre in June 1972. *Eil.com* group had a quick succession of blockbuster singles like "Jeepster" (U.K. #2 for six weeks), "Telegram Sam," and "Metal Guru" (both U.K. #1), but the Marc Bolan–fronted foursome's appeal went beyond their contagious music.

Morrissey was excited by Bolan's feminine image, which included wearing makeup and blouses and was quite controversial for 1971 and 1972. In fact, Steven was so fond of the group's glam-rock approach that he begged his mother to let him see the band live. She agreed, and the thirteen-year-old went by himself, wearing a purple satin jacket, to the band's gig at Manchester's Belle Vue Theatre on Hyde Road on June 16, 1972, having been dropped off in front of the venue by Peter and Jackie. The band's electrifying performance of their hits was met with screams and pandemonium. Bolan left Morrissey amazed, stunned, and forever hooked on pop music.

4th Place Race

At St. Mary's, Steven found a niche for himself in sports, which gave him a sorely needed confidence. He was a fine runner and even wound up representing the school in a 400-meter race at Stretford Stadium, where he finished in a respectable fourth place. Of course, Peter was standing at the finish line as his son came in, ready to take him down a notch. With Morrissey's legs covered in mud and his body wet from the day's rain, Peter felt it necessary to point out the obvious—he didn't win!

Still, Morrissey's athleticism gave him the confidence to rise above his father's hurtful remarks. "[It] made me act in a somewhat cocky and outspoken way—simply as a reaction against the philistine nature of my surroundings," he told the *Face* in May 1985.

Like his dad, Steven's schoolmasters weren't content to let him have any glory either. Despite his skill and love of track—specifically the 100-meter dash—he was overlooked by his coaches. "It became a slow but sure way of destroying my resilience," he told Nick Kent in that interview. "They succeeded in killing off all of the self-confidence I had."

Four Eyes

Not long after his thirteenth birthday, Steven's vision had deteriorated to the point where he was regularly squinting. Because of the stigma attached to boys who wore glasses—that they were nerds—he held off on getting them until he could no longer avoid his mother's insistence.

"If you wore them you were a horrible green monster and you'd be shot in the middle of the street," he joked to *Star Hits* in 1985. Of course, his black National Health spectacles would ultimately become part of his image, but in the early 1970s they were absent of style.

Despite his glasses, Steven's athletic status kept him from being bullied by his peers at school. "I was never picked on, never pushed around and that's that," he explained, to the surprise of readers of the aforementioned publication's "20 Questions" column.

Wilde Boy

As her children grew up, Betty Morrissey's love of books led to her becoming a librarian. And, with her encouragement, Steven was introduced the works of Thomas Hardy and Oscar Wilde. She handed him the latter's complete works at a young age and suggested they contained all he would need to know about life.

Morrissey became deeply taken with Wilde, whose works would go on to have a remarkable sway over the teen. It didn't stop with *The Picture of Dorian Gray* and *The Importance of Being Earnest*; Steven read everything he could about Wilde's life of prestige, privilege, and controversy.

Morrissey continued to identify with Wilde—who shared his Irish heritage—for many years, although he acknowledged they had little common ground. "It's a total disadvantage to care about Oscar Wilde, certainly when you come from a working-class background," he told Birch. "As I blundered through my late teens, I was quite isolated, and Oscar Wilde meant much more to me. In a way, he became a companion. If that sounds pitiful, that was the way it was."

Morrissey's use of flowers onstage from the Smiths' earliest performances onward were perhaps his most obvious tribute to his favorite writer. It is well known that Wilde had a long-standing passion for flowers, especially white lilies.

"All the Young Dudes"

Morrissey found Mott the Hoople's David Bowie–penned U.K. #3 smash "All the Young Dudes" electrifying enough to share with his father after he brought the glam-rock single home in the summer of 1972. Unfortunately, there was no common ground to be had with Mott, as his father—who preferred country music singers like the Louisiana-born Faron Young—ducked out of the room, repulsed.

When school began that fall, Morrissey was given a chance to share his love of the Ian

The cover of David Bowie's 1972 U.K. #10 hit "Starman." Morrissey won a copy of the track's parent album, *The Rise and Fall of Ziggy Stardust and the Spiders from Mars*, in a *Sounds* magazine contest that took place around the time of its June 6 release. *991.com*

Hunter–fronted band with his St. Mary's classmates. After a young priest became bothered when Steven appeared bored with the day's classroom topic, he asked Morrissey what in life sparked his interest. "Mott the Hoople," Morrissey proclaimed proudly, enlightening those who were still unaware that his musical tastes were superb.

"Starman"

Morrissey shifted allegiances from Marc Bolan to David Bowie in the summer of 1972. After watching the latter on the television that June—replete with his spiky hair and a sparkling jumpsuit—the thirteen year-old became captivated by "Starman," which would become Bowie's first U.K. Top 10 single since "Space Oddity" ascended to #5 soon after the Apollo 11 moon mission in 1969.

Steven was quick to enter a *Sounds* contest for Bowie fans and won a copy of his new concept album, the iconic *The Rise and Fall of Ziggy Stardust and the Spiders from Mars*, around the time of its release on June 6. After devouring the album—which included such brilliant songs as "Five Years," "Moonage Daydream," "Suffragette City," and "Rock 'n' Roll Suicide," Morrissey backtracked to discover *Hunky Dory*, *The Man Who Sold the World*, and *Space Oddity*.

Bowie's flamboyant TV performance of "Starman"—in which he and guitarist Mick Ronson snuggled up to each other as they played—came just six months after the singer proudly informed *Melody Maker* readers, "I'm gay, and always have been." While the broadcast and ensuing publicity shocked many, the fact that Bowie had a wife and young son at home only fed into the controversy over his sexual proclivities.

It translated into big ticket sales to kids like Steven Morrissey, who excitedly caught Bowie's *Ziggy Stardust* tour on September 3, the second of two nights at the Hardrock Village Concert Theatre in Stretford. Hours ahead of the show, Morrissey camped out to see if he could catch a glimpse of his high-heeled rock hero as he stepped out of a black Mercedes-Benz for his mid-afternoon soundcheck. Steven, in his St. Mary's blazer, managed to touch Bowie's hand and give him a personalized note, and was thrilled beyond belief when David kindly accepted it.

Anthony Morris

Morrissey's best friend as a boy was Anthony Morris, the son of Betty's friend Eunice. With their blue eyes and similar build and complexion, people often mistook them for brothers as they roamed the halls of St. Wilfrid's and played together in the Moss Side complex where Morris lived.

Not long after Morrissey turned fourteen and made evident his appreciation of ambiguous rockers like David Bowie, however, the narrow-minded Anthony dumped his longtime friend. Morris cited Steven's "queer" taste in music as the main reason for the severed friendship. Morrissey was brought to tears by Anthony's cruel remarks.

Of course, deep down, Steven soon realized that he liked being thought of as peculiar by others. "I was delighted when I was a secondary school," he told Alex Needham of the *NME* in 2004. "I thought, 'Well, however you are I don't want to be like you, so if you think I'm unbalanced then I'm delighted.' That really stayed with me."

Feminist at Fourteen

At fourteen, Morrissey discovered a paperback called *Men's Liberation* by a gay activist named Jack Nichols. The book—according to his 1985 interview with Kent—completely changed his outlook on women. He embraced Nichol's central message that humanity has confused our attitudes about sex roles. Morrissey embraced Nichols' philosophy that regardless of whether one is male or female, they should be able to adopt any mannerism they choose without being ostracized. This train of thought aligned nicely with the androgynous rock 'n' roll he was embracing at the time.

Virginity Lost

As the child of attractive parents, Steven was quite handsome, and his looks earned him the attention of girls. It helped that he was sensitive, bright, and—unlike most teenage boys—had more on his mind than getting laid. These attributes made him all the more desirable to young women, even though he was becoming aware that he was less and less interested in these heterosexual pursuits.

Morrissey lost his virginity at some point in 1972, according to an interview he gave to *New Musical Express* in February 1987. "It was in my early teens," he revealed, "but it was an isolated incident, an accident." When probed for more information on the event, he told the U.K. music weekly, "I've got no pleasant memories from it whatsoever." Details about where or who have been kept private.

For a time, Morrissey would invite a crew of girls into his bedroom each week to listen to the BBC broadcast the week's top hits on Radio 1. Despite his ability to attract females, however, nothing romantic was happening in his room. As for his thoughts on women, Morrissey dismissed their vaginas—which he refers to as "Bermuda Triangles" and "honeypots" in *Autobiography*—as "nothing but a mangled jungle of tangled hair presented as the jackpot payoff." According to his book, at this age, while he liked the company of girls, he much preferred the regular company and secret intimacy of his friend Edward Messenger to any shot at intercourse with the opposite sex.

Roxy Music

On November 9, 1972, Morrissey returned to the Hardrock to catch the Bryan Ferry–fronted group Roxy Music. They were supporting their self-titled LP, which had been released that June, and the subsequent non-album smash "Virginia Plain" (U.K. #4), which had followed in August.

Before the show, Morrissey conversed briefly with Roxy's Andrew MacKay as the saxophonist played pinball in the venue lobby. It wasn't until Morrissey was in the front row that he learned the up-and-coming American opening band, the New York Dolls, had been forced to cancel. Just three days earlier, that group's drummer, Billy Murcia, twenty-one, had died suddenly from an accidental drowning after passing out at a party. Panicked friends had put Murcia in a bathtub, where he asphyxiated, despite attempts to revive him.

After the concert, Morrissey, Michael Foley, and some female friends followed Roxy Music to Manchester's historic Midland Hotel. The Roxy devotees were clearly unwelcome, and met with harsh resistance from the staff. When a tough-talking acquaintance of Morrissey's named Hazel Bowden cursed out security, hotel employees took out their frustrations with her on Foley, who had said nothing. Michael caught several punches in the face. Morrissey, meanwhile, took off for the exit, escaping unscathed.

Despite this incident, Steven's loyalty to Roxy Music continued into 1973. After skipping class to catch the band at Preston Guildhall that spring, Morrissey—nearly fifteen—copped to doing so when one of his St. Mary's teachers asked the reason for his recent absence. Not long after Mr. Barry punished him for the infraction, Morrissey learned Ferry's favorite meal was veal. This disturbed the fourteen-year-old considerably, and his fascination with Roxy Music began to wane.

Yellow Hair

Around the time of the second Roxy show, Morrissey had his hair dyed by Kath Moores, a friend of his who also had a keen ear for glam rock. When he showed up in class with a bright yellow streak that ran from the front left corner of his head to the rear right, he caused quite a stir.

One teacher at St. Mary's, Miss Power, took exception to the unorthodox hairstyle and attempted to embarrass Steven in front of his classmates. It had the reverse effect, however, and with much of the student body tuned in to David Bowie, Steven became famous throughout school for his unique look.

Drummer Bummer

Around the time of his fifteenth birthday, Morrissey imagined himself as a drummer in a rock 'n' roll band. He managed to buy a drum kit, but despite his energy for the instrument, the Morrissey home proved too small to fit the set, which took up all of the available space in his bedroom.

In spite of Steven's already encyclopedic knowledge of pop, he had none of the musical inclinations of his main inspirations, Roxy Music's Paul Thompson and Bowie's Spiders from Mars drummer Woody Woodmansey. He had already failed in his attempts to play guitar, and his parents, sister, and neighbors were quick to inform him that he was also a disastrous drummer.

Foul Adolescence

Although he continued to catch his favorite performers, like Lou Reed at the Palace Theatre on September 25, 1973, with friends like Bowden and Moores, Morrissey would long contend that his teen existence was a downer. Or, as he later wrote, life was "foul" and "unspecial." He would however acknowledge the value he found in his life in isolation—his escape into music, novels, and films.

"I think if I'd led an acceptably frivolous teenage life I wouldn't be singing in [the Smiths]," he rationalized to *Sounds* writer Bill Black in November 1983. "I'm sure if you have a great time and get everything you want, all the friends you want, then you tend not to be so ambitious. If you're deprived of certain things it makes you very resilient and you kick very hard for what you want."

Anji Hardy

In his mid-teens, Morrissey's appreciation of music led him to meet and become friends with Anji Hardy during one of the many concerts he attended at the time. Anji was also a New York Dolls fanatic, but she lived in Haslingden, which was some twenty miles north of Manchester.

According to Morrissey, Hardy lived with her Scottish mother in a large but noticeably empty house. Because of the distance between them, he could only visit her occasionally, by bus. Their strictly platonic friendship was strengthened by lengthy, laughter-filled phone calls.

Sadly, Anji learned she had leukemia when she was just seventeen. When she explained to Steven that she had just six weeks to live, he at first thought she was joking. Coming to terms with her imminent death and losing his dear friend left Steven understandably devastated at this impressionable age. He sought solace in his books and his ever-growing record collection.

3

Throw Your Homework onto the Fire

Johnny Marr's Early Years

Here's Johnny

Future Smiths guitarist Johnny Marr was born John Martin Maher on October 31, 1963, in Ardwick, Manchester. For his first nine years, Johnny was raised at 12 Hayfield Street in the vicinity of Hyde Road, not far from a number of once-thriving industrial plants. Later, his family moved to Brierley Avenue, also in Ardwick, where Johnny began attending St. Aloysius Primary School.

John and Frances

Johnny's parents, John Joseph Maher and Frances Patricia Doyle, had moved to Manchester from the small town of Athy in County Kildaire, Ireland, in 1962, when they were still in their teens and married that same year. His father was one of five children who had emigrated with his family around the time, and his mother—who had thirteen brothers and sisters—was joined in Ardwick Longsight by most of her clan.

"My parents and their mothers and sisters—about five families in all—all moved within two streets of each other in Manchester," Marr told *Musician* in 1989. "They were all really young; my parents were like seventeen when I was born."

Young Johnny would never be lonely. As the Maher and Doyle siblings married and had children of their own, there were always family parties with plenty of drinking and uninhibited behavior, including music and singing. Just as his mother had relied on her siblings, Johnny would do the same when his younger sister, Claire, arrived in late 1964.

"My sister is eleven months younger than me, which is known as having an Irish twin," Marr explained to the Smiths fan site www.askmeaskmeask.me in 2012, describing himself as a sensitive and quiet little boy who was very close to his sibling until their teens. "I grew up in an environment that was intense. It was intensely religious, intensely Irish, intensely musical, and intensely young."

Johnny recalled spending a lot of time hanging out with his young mother and her cousins and friends at the age of five or six. "They were enjoying a sort of liberation after coming from little villages in Ireland," he continued. "It was very working class and very Irish. There wasn't a lot of money around, but it was a lot compared to where they'd left."

As one of the older children, it wasn't uncommon for Johnny to be put in charge of the younger ones when they gathered in his parents' home. As was customary at the time, the Mahers proudly represented their Irish Catholic heritage with an obligatory portrait of late U.S. president John F. Kennedy, a hero to his people thanks to his political accomplishments.

Musical Upbringing

Around the time Johnny came into the world, the Beatles had U.K. music fans in hysterics. Manchester bands like the Hollies followed suit, and that group's Everly Brothers–influenced sound appealed to the Mahers—especially John, who had been a devout fan of Americans Phil and Don Everly, the legendary duo behind 1950s smashes like "Bye Bye Love" and "Wake Up Little Susie."

As an infant, Johnny was also exposed to country and western music in addition to pop and rock at home. His father's appreciation of records by Jim Reeves, Eddie Arnold and Hank Williams was equaled by his mom's love for pop music in general, including the Hollies and the Beatles. Marr would later recall his mother playing an Everly Brothers 45 about fifteen times in a row.

Dusty Springfield's 1963 smash "I Only Want to Be with You" left a mark on Baby Johnny. "[It] was the soundtrack to all of the '60s to me, really," Marr told *Pitchfork* writer Mark Richardson in April 2012. "It played at pubs and christenings, there would be cover versions on TV shows, or if you went to parties, people would play it on a 45. That sound was very evocative of my early childhood and it never went away. I always thought a person would have to be made of stone to not react to that record. I still love it; I never didn't."

The Guitar

When Johnny was just four or five, he discovered a wooden toy that resembled a guitar hanging in a store window in Ardwick. After convincing his mother to buy it for him, he painted it white and glued beer caps to it so that it would look like an electric.

As he clutched his pretend instrument, Johnny stood on a chair in front of the radio for two-to-three hours each afternoon. Frances would clean the house and leave him to his own devices, watching as he obsessed over music and memorized every song that came out of the stereo.

Before long, Johnny had a real guitar and real rock 'n' roll dreams. "A lot of people probably thought I was a cocky little shit," he told John Crace from the *Guardian* in February 2008, "but even as a kid I had this sense I was going to make a career in music. My parents were musical obsessives and they taught me not so much to listen to music as to analyze it." Every Christmas, he would get a better guitar. "Finally, I got one that was big enough to make a proper sound," he told Crace. "And after I could do that, I never wanted to do anything else."

Later, Marr worked a paper route and saved up his money to buy a used three-quarter-size, Stratocaster-shaped Vox. Along the way, his father—who had been skilled on the accordion—taught Johnny to feel his way around that instrument, too, and helped him master the harmonica.

"Jeepster" by T. Rex was the very first 45 that Johnny Marr, age eight, owned. Already taken with the track, he saw the single in a bargain bin in a furniture store, of all places, and asked his parents if he could have it. *991.com*

"Jeepster"

When Johnny turned eight, around the time his baby brother Ian arrived, his parents gave him the money to buy his very first 7-inch single. Already quite familiar with "Jeepster" by T. Rex, he found the 45 in a bargain shoebox in a furniture store and knew he had to have it. "Those thunking guitar riffs were so great!" he told www.pitchfork.com's Mark Richardson.

Marr was also taken by the product's hand-drawn art of an insect designed to represent Fly, front man Marc Bolan's vanity label with EMI. On the paper label of the flip side, "Life's a Gas," there was a full-color picture of Bolan, with his Les Paul guitar, and his trusty sideman Mickey Finn on bongos. "My first lightning bolt came from Marc Bolan," Marr told Will Hodgkinson from the *Guardian* in June 2004. "When I heard that record, I heard magic."

Nine-year-old Johnny continued to be loyal to Bolan, and was equally stunned the following year by "Metal Guru." Speaking to Martin Roach about the T. Rex hit in 1994's *The Right to Imagination and Madness: An Essential Collection of Candid Interviews with Top UK Alternative Songwriters*, Marr would describe hearing it for the first time. "It was a feeling I'll never forget—a new sensation. I got on my bike and rode and rode, singing this song. It was a spiritual elevation, one of the best moments of my life."

T. Rex instantly became the first band Marr could call his own as he watched Bolan perform on *Top of the Pops* that spring. And even if Johnny would eventually discover that the main riff to "Jeepster" was nicked from Howlin' Wolf, it was Bolan's music that sustained his interest in guitar playing at this young age. "I was already trying to hold some chords down on the guitar," he explained to Richardson. "I was very serious about it. I had a crummy acoustic that took a lot of love and dedication to play, but I never had to be told to practice. I never had a lesson."

Learning Mott's "Dudes"

Marr had no idea that Mott the Hoople's "All the Young Dudes" had been written by David Bowie when he first became fixated with the song in 1973. "It was almost mystical to me," he told *Ink 19's* Gail Worley of his obsession with the track in 2003. "To get technical about it, I wondered where the 'magic spot' was—this split second of magic. I realized it was on the line [sings] *'Carry the new-ews'*—the chord change goes from a major chord to a minor chord. That experience coincided with me actually putting chord changes together on the guitar."

Johnny went on to relay his desire to not just play the guitar lick but the entire record—including the piano, organ, and string parts. "That whole 'glob' of sound—for want of a better word—*that dramatic slab* was what I was trying to get out of my little supermarket acoustic guitar."

Marr's interest in music continued to broaden as he stayed glued to the radio and treated himself to a new single each week. Spinning his purchases of records by the likes of Bowie, Sweet, Gary Glitter, and Roxy Music over and over, Johnny would dissect the songs, teaching himself to play the pieces he could figure out.

Confident in Wythenshawe

Nineteen seventy-three was also the year that the Maher family was forcibly relocated to the Manchester suburbs of Wythenshawe, as part of the ongoing "slum clearance" of five areas. The timing was ideal, following the arrival of baby Ian, as Johnny's parents realized that the suburban setting of Churchstoke Walk would be a better environment for their growing family.

Marr was enrolled in Sacred Heart Roman Catholic Primary School, where he could forgo the uniform he had been required to wear at St. Aloysius in favor of clothing of his own choosing. For Johnny, this meant baggy pants or jeans, V-neck football jerseys, and a two-tone "Budgie" jacket—which gave him something of an exotic look.

"I'd already started playing the guitar, and because I'd come from the inner city I was already pretty into my clothes," he told www.askmeaskmeask.me. "My relationship with my sister was quite important. The two of us looked a lot alike. We arrived in this suburban town that had a reputation for being pretty tough, but the place we'd come from, Ardwick, was much, much tougher, so it was like arriving in Beverly Hills for us."

Johnny used the opportunity to reinvent himself and explore his keenness for fashion. His unique presence and obvious musical ability left an impression on his new schoolmates and neighbors in south Manchester. With the opportunity to start over, Marr felt free to be outspoken and confident. He became known as the vibrant new city kid who played guitar—it gave him a cool identity and a newfound popularity.

Musical Friends

By the time he turned twelve, Johnny—who had since moved on to St. Augustine's Grammar School on Altrincham Road in the fall of 1975—was ready to start his own band. "I was always the one to instigate it," he told *Musician*. "I was fairly boisterous."

Unfortunately, these early groups never lasted more than a few months. The other players would show up for weekly jam sessions looking to have fun, but Marr took it more seriously. Recognizing the need for songs, he took a crack at songwriting and never looked back.

With Johnny having previously enjoyed the uniform-free environment of Sacred Heart, forced conformity didn't sit well with him. He endured the Catholic teachings, but when it came time for homework, he usually ignored his obligations or did the bare minimum in favor of spending time down at the West Wythenshawe Youth Club, where he could interact with classmates, talk to girls, play games, or participate in activities like rock climbing and roller skating. "West Wythy," as the kids called it, also held a Wednesday night disco, where pop artists like Abba were played alongside funk acts like the Fatback Band.

Here, Marr made friends with some older boys from Brookway High School, who were impressed with his musical knowledge and ability. His new pals—Robin Allman, Dave Clough, Barry Spencer, and future Cult co-founder Billy Duffy— were all heavily into rock 'n' roll, and most of them also played guitar.

Even at twelve or thirteen, Marr recognized the importance of playing with musicians who were better than him as a means to develop his chops. He first got his chance when he went across the street to Allman's house during a band rehearsal that also included Duffy in 1976.

Billy described Johnny as "very alert, smart, and inquisitive for his age" in an interview between the friends for www.billyduffy.com. The Cult guitarist recalled feeling paternal toward Marr at the time, even selling him his first amplifier, a used Falcon 15. "Coming to a band's rehearsal and behaving inappropriately would have been very awkward, but Johnny just fitted in," Duffy explained. "It's fair to say that Johnny had an insatiable appetite for observing what was going on, asking the right questions, and hanging out with the right crowd."

Duffy was a big fan of the Who's Pete Townshend, Bowie guitarist Mick Ronson, Free's Paul Kossoff, and the New York Dolls' Johnny Thunders. Allman was hooked on Neil Young and Television's Tom Verlaine. Johnny loved Rory Gallagher. As Marr told Duffy, "It was like a salon for aspiring young guitar players; encouraging and competitive in a good way, very funny too."

Holidays in Kildare

The Mahers continued to take pride in their Irish heritage, and the family would return to County Kildare with their children on vacation. Summers were spent visiting with friends and family, which opened Johnny's eyes to the vast, green outdoors of Ireland and exposed him to the drinking culture and the music.

Johnny was especially keen on a hip uncle who sported Beatle boots and strummed a Gibson acoustic guitar. He was also stunned by some of the drunk behavior of his parents relatives and acquaintances, and would later recount a time when a few of the men went racing down country roads at night, intoxicated, with their headlights off!

In the Maher family, such behavior and conversations were rarely off limits, as the kids were typically spoken to as if they were adults. The arguments and personal sagas of their parents' friends and extended family were always out in the open. "There was a lot of very grown-up conversation around me all the time," Johnny explained to www.askmeaskmeask.me in 2012. "The language was very colorful, and the drinking was even more colorful . . . as was the dancing. In that order."

Struggles with Dad

While Johnny always got along splendidly with his mother, he and his father began to struggle to communicate with one another around the time he turned eleven. Mr. Maher was something of a quiet personality, but he tried to relate to his son's love of music by sharing one of his favorite records, by American country artist Emmylou Harris, when Johnny was thirteen.

Although Marr wasn't nearly the fan of country that his parents were, he cited the gesture as one of the most memorable and touching moments of his mostly awkward relationship with his dad to *Musician* in 1989. For while they obviously loved each other, they were regularly at odds. "My old man had nothing to do with me until I was famous," he said. "Which I swore, before I was famous, I'd never forgive him for. . . . Probably if I didn't have that ongoing battle with my father I would never have had the desire to prove myself."

Discovering the Stones

Dave Clough's collection of singles and albums included several by the Rolling Stones, who by 1976 had long since become the world's biggest rock band. When Johnny finally took the time to appreciate and subsequently dissect their hits, the band clicked for him, and he realized that Keith Richards was the kind of guitarist he could identify with.

Such was the case with "Gimme Shelter," which first saw release on the Stones' iconic 1969 album *Let It Bleed*. Johnny heard it one afternoon as he goofed off with his musical friends and was enlightened. Marr was stunned by the way his hero could take a basic guitar line and make it distinctly his own.

He ran out and bought the 1971 compilation album *Gimme Shelter*, a rare Decca-pressed LP that included some of the greatest Stones songs to date. He kept coming back to that one particular track.

"When my parents went out, I would turn all the lights off, lay down in the dark on the floor, and take the speakers from off the shelves and put them next to my ears—like the world's biggest headphones," he told Worley in 2003. "The record would play continuously until I just completely zoned out. That's transcendence for you, and no one's gonna tell me any different."

If it's little surprise that Johnny would rank Richards' instrumental break on "Gimme Shelter" as "the greatest guitar solo ever" in a June 2007 *NME* feature, by November 2012, he was calling the band's 1965 single "(I Can't Get No) Satisfaction," his favorite Rolling Stones song. Pressed to comment on the eve of the band's fiftieth anniversary tour, he told the *Daily Telegraph* that the song was "as perfect a Stones record as it gets. It's a bratty riot that showcases a true punk guitar riff and stomping drum beat. . . . Mick Jagger's vocal performance takes the whole thing to another level altogether."

The Beatles

While Johnny dismissed the Beatles for much of his early life, by the time he turned fourteen, he could no longer resist the charms of the Lennon/McCartney songbook. While his friends were obsessing over punk and new-wave bands like the Jam, Stranglers, and Boomtown Rats, Marr found himself largely disinterested. Instead, he splurged on the Fab Four's "Red" double LP, *The Beatles 1962–1966*. He was blown away by the guitar playing on "A Hard Day's Night," later telling *Guitarist*, in 1985, that "Lennon's hand is like a pump." He was also reminded of how much he loved the harmonica by its presentation on "Love Me Do."

Taking a cue from his sister Claire, who had already started delving into the music of the 1960s, Johnny found himself caught up in classic Motown records. "Retro was new when I invented it," he joked to *Ink 19*. "This entire ocean of amazing music opened up."

As for the Beatles, the "Blue" album came next, as he became mesmerized by "I Am the Walrus," which pushed the boundaries of pop music. "It's completely anarchic and beautiful," he told Worley. "I very rarely would use the word 'genius' but it's a genius piece of work, and genuinely trippy, you know? I don't think anything's really quite surpassed it."

Skipping Punk

Johnny was barely thirteen when punk rock began its ascent in the U.K. Too young to hit the clubs where the movement was taking shape, he somehow found himself appreciating folk/rock artists like Richard Thompson and Pentangle instead, as well as the blues guitarist Rory Gallagher.

Marr was taken with Gallagher's 1975 album *Against the Grain* and his anti-image. When Gallagher played the Manchester Free Trade Hall in 1976, Duffy and his mates snuck Johnny in by prying open the venue's doors with a broken car antenna.

Pentangle was another touchstone for Johnny, who was mesmerized by guitarist Bert Jansch's fingerpicking. If it was Duffy and Allman who turned Johnny on to Jansch's playing, his appreciation of the guitarist became a virtual obsession after he caught a Pentangle concert on television when he was fourteen. Describing the performance to the *Guardian* in 2004, Marr explained, "This was the era of Deep Purple and Led Zeppelin, and I got the impression that Pentangle regarded those bands as utter lightweights musically, physically, philosophically, and lyrically."

Johnny also loved Nils Lofgren, an acrobatic guitarist and Maryland native who got his start playing alongside Neil Young when he was only seventeen. After fronting the band Grin, Lofgren went solo with an eponymous album in 1975, which Marr loved. And then there was Young himself, whose 1975 LP *Tonight's the Night* left an ineradicable mark on the future Smith. In fact, it was his proud appreciation of Young that first earned Johnny the attention of a kid at St. Augustine's named Andy Rourke.

4

Young and Alive

Johnny and Andy Align

Neil

Defying St. Augustine's uniform policy, Johnny Marr showed up at school with a massive four-inch button promoting a certain Canadian rocker's 1975 album, attracting the attention of one Andy Rourke. "I was wearing a Neil Young *Tonight's the Night* badge, and he came up to me and said, 'I'm really into Neil Young,'" Marr told *Musician* in September 1989.

Like Johnny, Rourke was a guitar-carrying music nut. Andy was heavily into West Coast rock music, thanks to the influence of his older brothers, and Johnny was all ears as he sought to absorb all the sounds that he could. With their shared passion for music, the pair became fast friends.

Andy Arrives

Andrew Michael Rourke was born in Manchester on January 17, 1964. The Smiths' future bassist was the third of four boys born to Michael Rourke and Mary Stones. Alongside older brothers Christopher and Phillip and younger sibling John, Andy was raised in a comfortable four-bedroom house on Hawthorn Lane in Ashton-upon-Mersey.

The Rourke boys came from part-Irish, part-English heritage. Their father's family had settled in England around the turn of the twentieth century, while their mother was of pure British stock. As a teen, Michael had planned to join the priesthood, until he met Mary, and they married before they reached their twenties. Mr. Rourke then pursued a career in architecture instead.

Beatles, Stones, and a Real Guitar

Exposure to Mary's favorite groups, the Beatles and the Stones, nurtured Andy's love of music. As a young boy, he was given musical Christmas gifts, beginning with a plastic trumpet, followed by an electric toy organ and finally a plastic guitar. When an unsatisfied Rourke complained to his parents that real guitars were made from wood, they relented. His very first official acoustic guitar arrived a few weeks later, on the occasion of his seventh birthday.

Soon after, Andy was enrolled in lessons, which gave him feel for the instrument. Amazingly, he found himself able to play along with many of his mother's records. After mastering all of the songs on a compilation of Beach Boys hits, he began to teach himself the songs he heard on the radio.

Glam Kid

Alongside his mother's steady diet of established British rock bands, Andy—through his older brothers' tastes and his own keen ear—established some new favorites. Like many kids in the U.K. in the early 1970s, Andy was drawn to Slade. The Noddy Holder–fronted group landed a stag-

As a youngster, future Smiths bassist Andy Rourke was drawn to glam rock, especially the hits of the Noddy Holder–fronted Slade. "Mama Weer All Crazee Now"—shown above and released in August 1972—was one of their many #1 U.K. singles. *Eil.com*

gering six #1 hits between 1971 and 1974, including "Coz I Luv You," "Take Me Bak 'Ome," "Mama Weer All Crazee Now," "Cum on Feel the Noize," "Skweeze Me, Pleeze Me," and "Merry Xmas Everybody."

The glam band Wizzard—who had massive U.K. hits in 1973 with "See My Baby Jive," "Wall of Sound," and "Angel Fingers"—were another one of Rourke's favorites in his early years. He also liked Suzi Quatro—who supported Slade on their 1972 tour—and was drawn to her hits from the same era, including "Can the Can," "48 Crash," and "Devil Gate Drive."

A Catholic Education

Unlike older brothers Christopher and Phillip, who went to the high-caliber secular secondary schools St. Ambrose and De La Salle, respectively, Andy's lack of focus in elementary school nearly landed him at the undesirable Stretford Grammar, until Mary pleaded with her priest. With Andy now in possession of a credible reference from his religious leader to offset his iffy academic background, the aforementioned Monsignor McGuiness accepted him at St. Augustine's.

From a proximity standpoint, the school was hardly convenient. The seven-mile commute took an hour or more by bus, with multiple transfers to

Wythenshawe from Ashton-upon-Mersey—quite taxing for a boy who was still several months from turning twelve.

Mary Leaves Home

Less than a year after securing Andy's enrollment at St. Augustine's, Mrs. Rourke announced that she was leaving her husband and family. Hired as a nanny for an American millionaire, Mary Stones moved to the Mediterranean island of Majorca, where she soon became involved with the man.

Back on Hawthorn Lane, the abandoned Rourke boys weren't just mourning the absence of their mother, they were stuck fending for themselves during the bulk of most workweeks. Michael worked for a roofing company based in Sale, which required regular business travel.

In the early stages of this transition, Andy fought often with Christopher, who had developed a steady habit of smoking marijuana. Within a year, however, the arguing ceased when Andy, who was barely a teenager, began using the drug himself.

Andy Befriends Johnny

Andy's troubles at home prompted him to act out at St. Augustine's midway through his first year. As a corrective step, the twelve-year-old Rourke was reassigned—along with fellow troublemaker and future Smiths roadie Phil Powell—to Adrian Jessett's class. It was here that he first met Johnny Marr.

According to an interview Marr gave to the *Face* in 1985, he had been originally asked by the school's headmaster to keep an eye on Rourke, who he described as "this posh kiddie with a chip on his shoulder." If they were initially weary of one another, a shared appreciation of music helped forge a solid bond. Before long, they arranged to play their guitars in the St. Augustine's practice room during lunch breaks.

"I was a hippie, hair down my back, listening to Neil Young and folk music," Andy told *Q* in March 2006. "Johnny was the same. We were the misfits at school."

Jamming

Although Rourke had taken lessons and started playing the guitar earlier, Marr made up for his lack of formal training with his quick ability to grasp and process the Neil Young songs they were working on. "I would show him everything I knew," Rourke told Smiths biographer Tony Fletcher. "But then the next week he'd have taken it to a whole new level."

The following year, the pair started rehearsing at Marr's with a friend named Marc Johnson. Jamming on numbers from Young's songbook, Johnny soon grew disappointed with Johnson, who wasn't taking their efforts nearly as seriously as he and Andy. Marc got the boot.

Paris Valentinos

Back down to a duo, Johnny and Andy set their sights on forming a band. They soon aligned with two older kids Marr had known from the West Wythenshawe Youth Club and arranged a rehearsal.

It helped that fifteen-year-old bassist Kevin Kennedy had an amplifier, while his friend Bobby Durkin had his own drum kit, and a practice space at his parent's house. When Durkin's mom complained about the noise, the drummer asked his father to see if they could jam at a space inside the social club he ran for the nearby Sacred Heart Roman Catholic Church.

The priest agreed to let them use the church hall on one condition: Johnny, Andy, and Kevin would need to play acoustic guitar during Sacred Heart's Sunday afternoon "Folk Mass" each week. In exchange for strumming along with the choir on numbers like "Kumbaya" and "Peace Perfect Peace," the Paris Valentinos were given ample rehearsal time to work out covers like Thin Lizzy's "The Boys Are Back in Town," Tom Petty's "Breakdown," some Rolling Stones staples, and a pair of songs by Marr's beloved Rory Gallagher.

A Better Place on Bass

It was apparent from the outset of their friendship that Johnny had influence over Andy. So when Marr suggested that Rourke and Kennedy change instruments, Andy didn't like it, but he went along with it. Even though Rourke had always imagined himself a guitarist, he quickly found out that Marr was on to something. He did have a knack for the bass.

The heavier, four-stringed bass somehow gave Andy—who by now had long hair and sideburns—a new sense of purpose. This feeling was bolstered by the fact that his older brother Phil already owned one—he played it in a different band for a spell—which he had at his disposal much at the time. So, with Marr's encouragement, Andy threw himself into the bass with full force.

The Paris Valentinos worked hard on their repertoire throughout the 1976–77 school year. Those efforts finally came to fruition that June, when the quartet were hired to play their first and only gig at a Benchill street party celebrating the Queen Elizabeth's Silver Jubilee.

As an aside, it's worth mentioning that Paris Valentinos member Kevin Kennedy would eventually rise to fame as an actor on *Coronation Street*, in the role of "Curly" Watts. Debuting in 1983 at the age of twenty-two, he remained on the long-running U.K. soap opera for twenty years.

Marr Goes to Shows

Under the supervision of older friends like Clough, Allman, Phil Fletcher, and his role model, Billy Duffy, Johnny, just thirteen, began attending local rock shows. On March 4, 1977, he saw Uriah Heap at the Free Trade Hall, with support from U-Boat, the new band of one-time Spiders from Mars guitarist Woody Woodmansey. A week later, on Friday, March 11, he watched T. Rex play the hits of his youth with openers the Damned at the Manchester Apollo.

On June 8, Marr was witness to one-time Mott the Hoople singer Ian Hunter perform with one-time Bowie guitarist Earl Slick at the Free Trade Hall. It was here that he first became friendly with Andrew Berry, a kid with dyed-red hair who he had recognized from the West Wythenshawe youth club.

Johnny and his friends rarely paid for tickets. Security was fairly lax, especially at the Free Trade, and the boys had figured out how to pry open a side door and sneak into shows when no one was watching.

In June of '78, Johnny, now fourteen, traveled to Knebworth, where he caught one of his favorite up-and-comers, Tom Petty, as part of a diverse bill that included American new-wave outfit Devo, commercial rockers Jefferson Starship, and headliners Genesis.

Sex Pistols

With the Buzzcocks by now putting modern Manchester music on the map, Johnny had started playing catch up with punk rock. He favored the Sex Pistols for their explosive music and controversial approach, even if they had already self-destructed by the time he caught on.

This didn't keep Marr from citing Pistols front man Johnny Rotten as "the coolest rock star in the world ever" and heralding him to *NME* in June 2007 for representing "the pure essence of the original idea of rock 'n' roll." Johnny's assessment of the Pistols' singer was that he looked cool and had a persona that was equal parts streetwise and intellectual, while Rotten's voice during his band's 1976–77 heyday, he added, was "as primal, as confused, as transcendent as a rock 'n' roll vocal can get."

Discovering James Williamson

One afternoon in 1978, Marr summoned Billy Duffy, keen to share a blistering new riff he had written. "I said, 'It's my superb new masterpiece that no one else can play!'" Johnny told *Pitchfork*'s Mark Richardson in April 2012. When Duffy explained that it sounded exactly like "Gimme Danger" from *Raw Power*, Marr was irritated that someone had come up with the song first. But he was also curious.

Once Duffy had introduced him to the album, Marr was hooked. Thirty-five years after he first heard it, *Raw Power* remained one of his all-time favorites. "Just looking at the sleeve, you get a whole story of not only that record, but what rock 'n' roll should be in a fifteen-year-old's life: sexy, illicit, uncommercial, exciting, druggy," he told Richardson. "I wanted to sign up for all of that."

At the core of the album's allure—in addition to Iggy Pop's raw vocals and rebellious stance—was guitarist James Williamson's playing. Over the course of the next twelve months, Marr taught himself every one of Williamson's parts from the album.

Patti and Steve

Billy Duffy and Howard Bates, the bassist in Manchester's Slaughter & the Dogs, brought Johnny—who loved *Radio Ethiopia* and was already into American bands like the New York Dolls and Iggy & the Stooges—to see Patti Smith at the Apollo on August 31, 1978.

"It was on the *Easter* tour," Marr remembered to *NME* in June 2007, proclaiming it the best gig of his life. "I was fourteen and I saw rock 'n' roll as an alternative way of living played out in front of my every eyes and ears. It was pumping, exciting, and poetic too. It was like a doorway into another world opening up and it never closed. From that night on, things in my life were different."

It was at this seminal gig that Duffy introduced Marr to a friend of his named Steven Morrissey. Marr had heard much about the front man of the short-lived Nosebleeds and outspoken Dolls and Patti Smith follower from Duffy. Yet Johnny's first meeting with Morrissey was disappointing, with the latter displaying—as he would tell Tony Fletcher—"utter non-interest."

5

Sixteen, Clumsy, and Shy

Morrissey Makes the Scene

The New York Dolls

A year after they canceled as openers for Roxy Music, Morrissey finally got to see the living, breathing New York Dolls when the reconstituted glam-rock band appeared on *The Old Grey Whistle Test* on November 26, 1973. While his parents were not impressed with David Johansen and his cohorts as they mimed "Jet Boy" on the BBC music program, Steven was mesmerized by the electrifying display.

The band's fusion of pop flamboyance and tough noise lit a spark inside the fifteen year old, who promptly plunked down £2.29—the equivalent of about $5.50 at the time—at Piccadilly Records to buy *New York Dolls*, their Todd Rundgren-produced debut LP.

"They were as important to me as Elvis Presley was important to the entire language of rock 'n' roll," Morrissey would later explain, as he read everything he could about the band in publications like *Circus* and *Melody Maker*. The Dolls were all-accepting. They embraced homosexuals and—while clearly heterosexual themselves—proudly dressed in drag. "I never saw them as being remotely fey or effeminate," Morrissey told the *Face* in 1985. "They were characters you simply did not brush aside, like the mafia of rock and roll."

"Jerry Nolan on the front of the Dolls' debut album is the first woman I ever fall in love with; the hussy-slut positioning of the legs is playmate call-girl, and the pink drum kit just might be a rock 'n' roll first," Morrissey confesses in *Autobiography*. "The Dolls were a social unit, great fun, grave fun, salty and completely off the deep end," he continues, equating Johansen's attitude, the excess-plagued lead guitarist Johnny Thunders and the detachment of guitarist Sylvain Sylvain and bassist Arthur Kane as "the opposite to polite and antiseptic."

Morrissey played "Frankenstein" for his St. Mary's literature class and even brought the sleeve of *New York Dolls* into school so that he might attempt to paint a replica of it. His art teacher, Miss Power, found the cover disturbing. She took it from Steven's desk, held it high in front of the class, and chastised him for owning it. Proclaiming the sleeve to be perverse, Power maligned the band's members for dressing in drag to appeal to other men.

Of course, this did nothing to stunt Morrissey's fixation with the Dolls, which would continue long after he left St. Mary's Secondary Modern in 1975. Between 1974 and 1976, he hoped to raise the group's profile—and his own as a budding journalist—by writing letters about the band to music papers like *New Musical Express*. In December 1975, for instance, in a letter to *Sounds* credited to Steve Morrissey of Kings Road, he wrote of how the Dolls had influenced modern acts of the day like Bruce Springsteen, the Tubes, Kiss, Aerosmith, and the Dictators.

Before long, Morrissey began his own unofficial New York Dolls fan club and began corresponding with likeminded followers of the band around the globe. This made him happy, and gave him something to cling to that was outside of rock's mainstream.

"I always liked the Dolls because they seemed like the kind of group the industry couldn't wait to get rid of," he explained to *Melody Maker* in November 1984. "And that pleased me tremendously. I mean there wasn't anybody around then with any dangerous qualities so I welcomed them completely."

Wild *Horses*

One Saturday in December 1975, Morrissey wandered into the Macclesfield branch of Boots, a pharmacy that also sold albums. Here, he found a U.S. pressing of Patti Smith's *Horses* on sale for £5 amid the hit albums of the day. Steven—who had just read back-to-back reviews of the album in the *NME*—snatched up the record.

Back home that night in front of the fireplace, Morrissey was transfixed by the record's contents and equally amazed by how this androgynous singer appeared to be the antithesis of a pop star. Writing of the experience in his 2013 memoir, he marveled how Patti was "the cynical voice radiating love; pain sourced as inspiration, an individual mission drunk on words . . . unfulfilled as a woman, impotent as a man, [she] cut right through."

Morrissey had been captivated by Smith's blunt truthfulness and her ability to reinvent the idea of what a female rock singer could sound like. Although he went on to describe *Horses*—which is now regarded as one of the finest rock debuts of all time—as "part musical recording and part throwing up," the album restored his faith in rock music.

Gabba Gabba Hey!

On April 23, 1976, four punk pioneers from Queens, New York, released their debut album, *Ramones*, which contained future classics like "Blitzkrieg Bop," "Beat on the Brat," and "I Wanna Be Your Boyfriend." But while Steven soon learned of the band through the U.K. music papers, it took him a while to actually give them the time of day.

Morrissey was inclined to dismiss the band because of his loyalties to the New York Dolls, whom he still felt deserved to conquer the world. In a letter published in the *Melody Maker* on July 24 and headlined "Ramones Are Rubbish," he

THE ELECTRIC CIRCUS - MANCHESTER
on
SUNDAY, 22nd MAY, 1977
at 8.00 p.m.
THE RAMONES
plus
Talking Heads
Tickets £1.50

N° 0486

A ticket stub for an Electric Circus double bill of
the Ramones plus Talking Heads from May 1977.
Morrissey attended this concert. *MDMarchive.co.uk*

wrote, "The Ramones have absolutely nothing to add that is of relevance or importance and should be rightly filed and forgotten." Yet when he finally heard the Ramones' crudely contagious album with an objective ear, its brilliance could not be denied. And he sensed it was a historic turning point. Joey, Johnny, Dee Dee, and Tommy "slapped the face of the world," as he acknowledges in *Autobiography*.

"I was 100 percent wrong," Morrissey told *Billboard* in October 2012. "Three days after writing that Ramones piece, I realized that my love for the Ramones would outlive time itself."

When he went to witness the Ramones' first Manchester performance with Talking Heads at the Electric Circus on May 22, 1977, he was completely blown away. He liked them so much, the next time he caught the band—at the Lyceum in London—he brought his older sister Jackie along.

Phoning Jones

According to *There Is a Light That Never Goes Out*, Morrissey was purportedly flipping through the U.K. music weeklies in early 1976 when he came across a classified ad that read, "singer wanted." On a whim, he supposedly picked up the phone and called the London guitarist named Mick Jones, who had placed the announcement, to ask about the position. Another version of the story speculates that Morrissey—who had apparently started playing drums by this point—applied by letter for a job as the new group's kit man, despite living nearly 200 miles away.

In either case, it would have been hard for Jones to seriously consider the typically shy Morrissey, as he lived hours away from this fledgling group. Future Clash guitarist Jones had already spent much of 1975 playing in the proto-punk band London SS before leaving to form a new band with bassist Paul Simonon. Not long after Morrissey's inquiry, the group recruited 101'ers front man Joe Strummer as their mouthpiece and Terry Chimes on drums (soon supplanting the latter with Topper Headon).

Raw Power

By the age of sixteen, Morrissey had also belatedly discovered the charms of *Raw Power*, the third album by the Stooges, who had since been reconstituted as Iggy & the Stooges. The record's David Bowie connection—he mixed the album—was played up in the U.K. music papers around the time of its release in 1973. While Iggy Pop's friendship with Bowie helped earn him some notoriety—they began collaborating by 1976—the disc's proto-punk approach meant that radio ignored it even as discerning rock fans embraced it.

Describing his appreciation for Iggy's early work, Morrissey told the *Daily Telegraph*'s Michael Deacon in 2011, "His initial appearance and contribution were so fantastic and so extraordinary." Of course, music from the fringes appealed to Morrissey, who had grown disgusted with Bowie after witnessing the Thin White Duke at Wembley for his seventeenth birthday. The guttural and provocative Iggy, however, was an inspiration. He was shirtless and all muscle with his lipstick and silver leather trousers. Morrissey was left awestruck after he finally witnessed the Stooges—flanked by guitarist James Williamson—tear it up in concert. The man born James Osterberg invented the stage-

A copy of an original flyer for the historic gig at Manchester's Electric Circus on December 9, 1976, that featured the Sex Pistols, the Clash, Johnny Thunders' Heartbreakers, and local band Buzzcocks. It was at this show that Morrissey first befriended one of his dearest friends, Linda Sterling, a.k.a. "Linder." *MDMarchive.co.uk*

dive right before Steven's very eyes, grunting and writhing through primeval rock songs like "I Wanna Be Your Dog" and "Your Pretty Face Is Going to Hell."

Uncovering VU

Although Morrissey had seen Lou Reed live in 1973, it would be another couple of years before he would delve into the man's earliest work with the Velvet Underground. These records have had a tremendous and lasting influence over the singer ever since he bought them at the age of seventeen. In fact, he would still count *The Velvet Underground & Nico* (1967) and *White Light/White Heat* (1968) among his top thirteen favorite albums of all time when asked to compile them for music website the *Quietus* in 2010.

In *Autobiography*, Morrissey compares the band's front man and lyricist Reed with the greats of the literary world. Citing Reed's artistic vision, he champions VU's "harsh expressionism," adding, "You will understand their meaning to be far greater than whatever seems logical during their lifetime."

In the wake of Reed's passing in October 2013, Morrissey—who became friends with him later in life—spoke of the VU brainchild's sway over him. "He had been there all my life," an official statement read. "He will always be pressed to my heart. Thank God for those, like Lou, who move within their own laws, otherwise imagine how dull the world would be."

The Sex Pistols

On June 4, 1976, Morrissey was in the audience to watch a landmark concert at the Lesser Free Trade Hall in Manchester, where the burgeoning punk group the Clash opened for the Sex Pistols. The show, which also featured Manchester's own punk group Buzzcocks (formed by Howard Devoto and Pete Shelley for that very gig after they recruited the other bands to come north from London to perform) is now considered one of the most revolutionary concerts of all time.

After spotting a leaflet promoting the event on Peter Street the afternoon of the gig, a curious Steven elected to attend. Inside, future Manchester luminaries like Joy Division front man Ian Curtis, his bandmates Bernard Sumner and Peter Hook (who would also later form New Order), Mark E. Smith of the Fall, and Tony Wilson—a Manchester TV personality who would go on to found the city's legendary Factory Records—all stood side by side. They were each among the four dozen people who witnessed what would become widely known in the punk community as "The Gig That Changed the World."

Morrissey wrote about the show in a letter to the *NME* the following week, describing how the "bumptious Pistols in jumble sale attire had those few that attended dancing in the aisles." He also added that it was "nice to see that the British have produced a band capable of producing atmosphere created by the New York Dolls and their many imitators."

His allegiance only grew when he discovered that the Pistols hated everyone but the Dolls. "I thought they were fantastic," Morrissey told Deacon. "I always loved them." Of course, it made sense that the group's original lineup of Johnny Rotten, Steve Jones, Paul Cook, and Glen Matlock had something of a blind loyalty to David Johansen's band. After all, their manager, Malcolm McLaren—who had been a King's Road clothier—had been affiliated with the Dolls and even aided them with their outlandish fashions.

In 2013, and with nearly four decades of hindsight, Morrissey reflected on the Sex Pistols—who he would observe in concert twice more in 1976—as something different and something socially significant. "Their immediate success [was] an exhilarating danger to behold," he writes, in *Autobiography*, recalling the controversy that followed the band everywhere after the release of singles like "Anarchy in the U.K." and "God Save the Queen."

Slaughter & the Dogs

Morrissey returned to the Lesser Free Trade Hall on July 20 to catch the Sex Pistols once more. This time, the Johnny Rotten–fronted foursome shared a bill with a local punk band, Slaughter & the Dogs. Founded by singer Wayne Barrett and guitarist Mick Rossi and named for both Mick Ronson's *Slaughter on 10th Avenue* and David Bowie's *Diamond Dogs*, the Wythenshawe band got its start playing songs from *Ziggy Stardust*, plus numbers by VU and the New York Dolls, in local clubs before turning to originals.

Slaughter had been in the studio that year with rising producer Martin Hannett to track their first demo, which included the songs "Cranked Up Really High" and "Love, Speed, and Beer" and became a fixture of the Manchester scene. They would eventually sign with Decca Records and release the popular single "Where Have All the Boot Boys Gone?" in 1977. Although Steven had no way of knowing it at the time, in 1979, after Barrett quit the band, he would get one of his earliest opportunities behind the microphone, briefly working with Rossi.

Staten Island and CBGB's

Shortly after the second Sex Pistols gig, Morrissey traveled to the United States to visit with his mother's sisters, Patti and Mary, who had settled in New Jersey and Staten Island, respectively. To his recollection, Aunt Mary, her spouse, and Steven's cousins, Matthew and Erin, lived in a surprisingly rural, swampy area of Staten Island on a property that was inundated with toads.

The memorable arrival of Hurricane Belle put fear into Morrissey during his visit that August. Instead of evacuating, as local authorities suggested, the family boarded up the house and hunkered down, only to discover that the toads had survived the storm.

Trips to the beaches and Manhattan tourist spots also formed part of his journey to America, but what Steven was most interested in was traveling down to the Bowery to visit the already notorious punk club CBGB's, which had recently launched the careers of two of his latest favorites, Patti Smith and the Ramones.

Steven's excursion to the venue resulted in one of his biggest thrills, when he encountered Sparks singer Russell Mael outside the venue and asked to have his photo taken with him underneath the club's iconic awning. Morrissey had become a bona-fide fan of the Los Angeles–based experimental duo, which also included Russell's brother Ron, after first hearing them on the radio at home in the U.K. From there, he had gone on to explore albums like 1974's *Kimono My House* and 1975's *Indiscreet*. At the time of their meeting, the Maels had been in New York, putting the finishing touches to their sixth long player, *Big Beat*, which was produced by Rupert Holmes (later of "Pina Colada" fame) at Manhattan's Mediasound Studios and released by Columbia Records that October.

I Found a Job

Upon his return to England in August 1976, Morrissey—who had spent the past year at Stretford Technical School—learned that he had passed three of his four O-levels (the subject-based qualification that was part of England's General Certificate of Education until 1988), which meant that he was eligible for an entry-level job with the Civil Service. He lasted just two weeks in his position, however, before he deemed it intolerable and resigned.

Steven next landed work at Yanks, a damp record store on Oxford Road, where he operated the register for a few months that fall. Despite his love of records, the large unheated basement shop—piled with endless stacks of crappy U.S. cutouts—wasn't exactly Morrissey's ideal arrangement. After he was mugged and left bloodied one November night by some area thugs after closing up the shop, he was officially done with Yanks.

By 1977, Steven was again working—this time at the Inland Revenue, as a filing clerk. Although he dreamed of a better life and thought about returning to the United States after he had saved up enough to make a new start, it didn't take long before he began to loathe the monotony of the job. He pushed his luck by reporting to work in his Ramones T-shirt. Of course, the "Gabba Gabba Hey" shirt blatantly defied the Inland Revenue's formal dress code. After being called in to a meeting with the chief inspector about his questionable judgment, seventeen-year-old Morrissey resigned.

This didn't serve him well when he showed up at the Stretford Job Center in search of a new assignment. Here he was given a severe tongue-lashing from one of the office women for having the audacity to resign from a perfectly good job. She further chastised him for showing up to their meeting looking unkempt before denying his request for unemployment. Instead, Steven was commanded to take a job cleaning canal banks.

Ignoring that order, Morrissey instead wound up reporting to the Stretford Sorting Office of the Royal Mail. Once there, however, he failed the physical and psychological tests, losing his shot at one of several vacancies available at the time. With little left to choose from, he accepted a job at Bupa Hospital in Whalley Range, but after a few weeks of shaking post-op surgical gowns free of their medical waste, he was understandably disgusted and quit.

A year or so later, after spotting a sign in Cross Street salon for a stylist, Morrissey applied for the vacancy. Although he had no training, the establishment's owners gave him a shot anyway—and soon lived to regret it. Steven was jobless once more.

Befriending Linder

On December 9, 1976, at another famed Manchester Sex Pistols show at the Electric Circus that also featured the Buzzcocks, the Clash, and Johnny Thunders' Heartbreakers, Morrissey first met Linda Sterling, the girlfriend of Howard Devoto. Linder—as she was better known—was a fixture on the Manchester scene who had grown up in Liverpool but studied art at Manchester Polytechnic. Her talents would famously be displayed on the sleeve art for the Buzzcocks' classic '77 single "Orgasm Addict," which memorably features an iron in place of the head on a naked female torso.

Morrissey had come to the show to meet Thunders and his former New York Dolls bandmate Jerry Nolan, two of his rock 'n' roll heroes, but his interaction with the two disinterested Americans left him hollow. Luckily, he then came upon Linder, who he had first seen from afar at the Pistols' Lesser Free Trade Hall gigs earlier that year. They hit it off splendidly, which made the night all the more special, considering Steven's disappointing meeting with the ex-Dolls.

Morrissey and Linder would begin a weekly ritual of meeting at Kendals rooftop restaurant and nurture a friendship that would last for the next four decades. Linder—who would soon front her own band, Ludus—would at some point during a future lunchtime gathering ask Steven if he was still ill, thereby prompting the future Smiths song of the same name. For a while, she was a unique if disregarded presence on the largely male Manchester music scene.

Peter Leaves Home

On December 23, 1976, after years in an increasingly strained marriage, Peter Morrissey left home, moving in with his sister Patricia. Steven's longstanding allegiance to his mother and the Dwyer clan had been unwavering as he gave up on his father and all but ignored him during his final year at home. When the split was finalized, Betty reverted back to her maiden name.

In *Autobiography*, Morrissey dismisses his father's disappearance as something that occurred "amidst loud assumptions that he has other lives elsewhere." Nearly three decades earlier, he spoke of the divorce to the *Face*, revealing that it had been coming for many years. "Realizing that your parents aren't compatible gives you a premature sense of wisdom that life isn't easy and it isn't simple to be happy."

Morrissey's bond with Betty grew stronger than ever as she fully supported her adult son during the next few years as he struggled to keep a job, suffered from depression, and stumbled through his musical pursuits. Despite his eccentricities, deep down she was proud of her son. He was an independent thinker who was highly intelligent, very well read, and a feminist at a time when that movement was still in its infancy.

Bolan Bummer

In March 1977, T. Rex were in Manchester to perform at the Apollo, with support from punk band the Damned, and Morrissey had the opportunity to meet his former hero, Marc Bolan. Although he had long outgrown the band that had once wielded hits like "Bang a Gong (Get It On)," front man Marc Bolan still held a special place in his heart, as T. Rex were the first rock group he had ever seen live.

Inside the lobby of the city's Midland Hotel, he asked the curly haired Bolan for an autograph. The aloof T. Rex front man—who was touring in support of his final album, *Dandy in the Underworld*—declined the request and walked off.

Six months later, Bolan was killed when the purple Mini 1275GT driven by Gloria Jones—the mother of his son Rolan—hit a chain link fence and collided with a sycamore tree.

Celibacy

By his late teens, Morrissey had become dismissive about sex. Speaking of his celibacy to journalist Bill Black in November 1983, he described it as "an involuntary decision" that stemmed from low self-esteem. "I remember for a long time feeling totally charmless and unhandsome," he continued, acknowledging that he was not alone. It was a point he would make on the Smiths' 1983 debut, as he crooned of how the hills were alive with *celibate cries* on "These Things Take Time," while cunningly referring to *The Sound of Music.*

Sounds Off

Morrissey's letters to the likes of *NME, Melody Maker,* and *Sounds* had become so regular that he twice had the distinction of having two letters published in the same issue of the same publication. His thoughts on Patti Smith, the New York Dolls, the Ramones, and the Sex Pistols eventually earned him a job interview.

Sounds had been looking for a writer, and, upon receiving Morrissey's application, editor Alan Lewis invited him down to London. While Steven's hopes were high on the train ride back up to Manchester, they were dashed when he received a letter of rejection by mail a week and a half later.

Fanzines and Maker

Despite that disappointment, Morrissey continued to write about music, sending letters to the London music weeklies and contributing to Xeroxed U.K. fanzines like *Kids Stuff, Alternative Ulster,* and *Next Big Thing.* He penned articles on the New York Dolls for both in 1977 and even considered starting up his own publication on the band. Although his writing efforts didn't earn him any money, he did manage to strike up friendships with a handful of Dolls-obsessed pen pals.

Among them were Brian Young, guitarist in the Belfast punk band Rudi, and a London musician named Tom Crossley. Another Londoner, sixteen-year-old James Maker, actually sought Steven out at some point in 1976, phoning Manchester directory assistance to track down his phone number after Morrissey had placed an ad in the back of *Sounds* in search of Dolls acetates.

Through their letters and phone contact, Maker and Morrissey became friendly. By the summer of '77, James was invited up to Manchester for a weekend visit. Steven would also visit James—a handsome homosexual lad one year his junior who worked at a London travel agency—at his parents' home on a number of occasions.

During that first visit to Manchester, not long after they had properly met, the new friends were chased through Manchester's Piccadilly Gardens by a pack of homophobic hooligans. Morrissey escaped a thrashing, but Maker was pummeled by seven toughs until an elderly couple intervened. From this experience was forged a bond that lasted several years. In fact, James Maker would appear onstage alongside his friend at the very first Smiths gig.

Simon Topping and Nico

Morrissey found another friend in Simon Topping, a Flixton-based lad who had just gotten out of school and lived with his parents and sister. Unlike Steven, Simon rode a motorbike, but they had a shared fondness for Nico, and together they would hang out at Betty's house on Kings Road and listen to *Chelsea Girl*.

Unfortunately, after meeting Steven, Topping's mother did not approve of their friendship. As Morrissey suggests in *Autobiography*, Mrs. Topping was concerned that he might be a homosexual. She was worried that her Simon might be tempted into an alternative lifestyle, and had determined that Steven was a bad influence. As a result, their friendship was over. Walking home depressed and alone, Morrissey contemplated suicide before taking solace in the sad charms of Nico once more. "If I had access to a high place, I'd [have] jump[ed] from it," he confesses of this incident in his 2013 book.

If the model-turned-singer born Christa Päffgen in Cologne in 1938 reminded Morrissey of Topping, her pensive voice somehow managed to lift him out of his sadness, and would remain important to him always. A decade later, his voice would have that same effect on misunderstood teenagers and young adults.

"The Nico net caught me early," Moz would write in his liner notes for the 2003 compilation album he curated for the *Under the Influence* series. "Her voice equaled the sound of a body being thrown out of a window—entirely without hope, of this world, or the next, or the previous . . . I am in love." A decade later, in his book, Morrissey revealed that he continues to treasure her four albums, despite their downhearted content.

Ironically, Nico would relocate to Manchester in the early 1980s. Sadly, however, her beauty dwindled as she descended into the throes of heroin addiction. She died after suffering a heart attack while on a bicycle in the Spanish resort of Ibiza in July 1988. She was forty-nine.

Buzzcocks

Alongside Slaughter & the Dogs, Manchester's Buzzcocks became local favorites on the Lever Street punk scene that Morrissey frequented. Saturdays were spent hanging around at Virgin Records, talking with kindred spirits and perusing a bulletin board that encouraged bands to come together and hang flyers promoting their upcoming shows.

As Morrissey thumbed through the latest punk records, the Buzzcocks' three-song *Spiral Scratch* EP stood out. Produced by Martin Hannett, it included anthems of the movement like "Breakdown" and "Boredom," which quickly spoke to Morrissey.

"Quite intellectual in their way, but delivering very fast pop music, and that was quite new to me," he said of the Buzzcocks, during an August 2008 guest DJ stint on KCRW's *Morning Becomes Eclectic.* "I thought they had a very cranky intellectual edge, which I really welcomed, because I was tired of pop music being seen as rather vain and . . . rather foppish."

Steven was standing inside the store wearing a New York Dolls T-shirt when another local music snob, Phil Fletcher, first introduced himself. Before long, Steve and Phil had begun attending punk shows at venues like Collyhurst's Electric Circus, Chorlton's Oaks Hotel, Rafters on Oxford Street, and others.

As '77 elapsed, Morrissey's presence at concerts by bands like the Buzzcocks, Ramones, Talking Heads, and the Jam—coupled with his vast knowledge of music—earned him acceptance from Fletcher's friends. Among them were the local musicians Steve Pomfret and Billy Duffy.

Oh Joy

Before Joy Division ever took shape, future members Peter Hook, Bernard Sumner, and Ian Curtis were frequently seen hanging out in the same Lever Street circles as Morrissey. By May 29, 1977, when they made their live debut in Manchester under the preliminary name Warsaw, supporting the Buzzcocks and Penetration at the Electric Circus, the group's singer, Curtis, and Morrissey had already become acquainted.

Curtis lived with his grandmother on Milner Street, not far from the Kings Road home Morrissey shared with Betty and Jackie. Ian had become aware of Steven's literary and musical passions and shared some of his earliest poems and lyric drafts with him by telephone. Or, as Morrissey explains in *Autobiography,* Curtis called "to test my palette of words."

Coronation Street

Morrissey's appreciation of the long-running U.K. soap opera *Coronation Street* may have originated with the program's opening credits, which pan over the rooftops of the area of Manchester where he had lived as a baby. Steven had even witnessed the Granada TV production shooting an exterior scene with actress Violet Carson, who played the character Ena Sharples, near a friend's home.

His appreciation of the show would—according to Simon Goddard's *Mozipedia*—find him camped outside the Granada Studios at various points during his youth, waiting for autographs. Actress Julie Goodyear (Bet Lynch) was pleasant; Bernard Youens (Stan Ogden) wasn't.

Steven began writing his own scripts, replete with character and plot suggestions, which he sent to the show's producer, Leslie Duxberry. They began a correspondence. Morrissey was encouraged to submit a proper script and wrote a treatment about the appearance of a jukebox in the Rovers Return, which led to a debate between the young and old about punk rock. His script was not picked up, and Duxbury suggested he explore a different creative avenue.

"They were probably a little too adventurous for the *Street*," Morrissey told *Record Mirror*'s Eleanor Levy in September 1985. "Naturally, the storylines were rejected. I think there were a couple of divorces in there somewhere. A few deaths . . . the odd strangulation thrown in."

Morrissey's fascination with the show would follow him to stardom. In May 1985, he interviewed the show's matriarch, actress Pat Phoenix, who played Elsie Taylor, for *Blitz* magazine. In turn, she appeared on the sleeve of the Smiths' single "Shakespeare's Sister."

Wanting to Sing

After six years of attending rock shows, Morrissey had firmly decided that he wanted to take the stage as a singer in his own band. Despite his shyness, he had seen enough people in the punk movement doing it that he felt confident he too might be able pull it off. He even placed an ad in *Sounds*, announcing his plan of launching a "Manchester-based punk band" and hoping to find kindred "Dolls/Patti fans." Nothing ever came of it.

After touting himself as a singer, Morrissey finally got his turn behind the microphone when he got up the courage to answer an ad on the bulletin board at Virgin that had been placed by Billy Duffy and Steve Pomfret. He was invited to practice at the latter's home in Wythenshawe. Simultaneously, he answered an ad in *NME* posted by a sixteen-year-old Manchester lesbian named Quibilah Montsho. He envisioned all of them playing together as one unique musical force and tried to bring them all together in the fall of '77. Things did not gel as he had hoped.

The Nosebleeds

In addition to the Buzzcocks, the Manchester punk scene's other bright hope in 1977 was Ed Banger & the Nosebleeds. It featured front man Ed Garrity—a former roadie with Slaughter & the Dogs—a guitarist named Vini Reilly, bassist Peter Crookes, and drummer Phillip "Toby" Tomanov, who sold 10,000 copies of their debut single "I Ain't Been to No Music School"/"Fascist Pigs."

When Garrity and Reilly quit the band—supposedly following a dispute over money—Duffy stepped in on guitar. He recruited Morrissey as his singer. Despite his nerves and lack of self-confidence, Steven found himself in the group's rehearsal space in early 1978, working through songs with Duffy, plotting gigs, and embracing his new role with all his might. He was transformed from an uncertain young adult into a seemingly assured new front man for the group Duffy suggested they either call Hearts Go Bop or the Politicians. Steven offered up the names T-Shirt and Stupid Youth as alternate suggestions.

With plans to carry on as a new band, the quartet were hired to open for Magazine—the new band led by ex-Buzzcocks member Howard Devoto—at the Ritz on Whitworth Street on May 8, 1978. Without a name, the group were introduced as the Nosebleeds and performed five songs, including a cover of the Shangri-Las' "Give Him a Great Big Kiss" and the Morrissey/Duffy originals "Toytown Massacre" and "(I Think) I'm Ready for the Electric Chair."

Much to the group's surprise, the Nosebleeds were heralded by Paul Morley in the *New Musical Express*. Despite incorrectly listing him as "Steven Morrison," Morley praised the singer as "a front man with charisma" and a "minor local legend . . . aware that rock 'n' roll is about magic, and inspiration."

Morley went on to write that "only their name can prevent them from being this year's surprise." Sadly for Morrissey, after just a few more gigs, the band split up. While Morrissey and Duffy remained friendly, Billy decided that the band had no real future for him. Within a year, the talented guitarist would move to London to pursue his music career.

Bedroom Depression

The end of Morrissey's short-lived tenure fronting the Nosebleeds left him deeply depressed in the weeks following his nineteenth birthday. Speaking to Elissa van Poznack of the *Face* in July 1984, he confessed to spending three or four consecutive weeks in his hot cramped bedroom that summer with the shades drawn. In the company of his typewriter, his books, his records, and his James Dean pictures, he actually worried about whether he would ever leave the room. He became reliant on sleeping pills, and things grew incredibly bleak until he decided he was going to try to find a way to live with and cope with his despair.

"It just seemed suddenly that the years were passing and I was peering out from behind the bedroom curtains," he told *Melody Maker*'s Allan Jones in '84. "It was the kind of quite dangerous isolation that's totally unhealthy." Elsewhere, he revealed that he had contemplated suicide on more than one occasion. "It really got to the point where I was so angry and yet I was really very ambitious," he admitted to *City Life*, in its spring 1984 issue. "I was prepared to kick very, very hard."

Meeting Marr

Despite his fragile mental state, Morrissey did manage to leave the house on August 31, 1978, to catch the Patti Smith show at the Manchester Apollo. It was at this show that he made conversation with Duffy, plus Mick Rossi and Howard

Bates from Slaughter & the Dogs, outside the venue. It was also here that Billy introduced Steven to his young friend Johnny Marr. Alas, the conversation, according to Morrissey's recollection, was brief.

Steven was actually talking with another local music junkie named Philip Towman when they first spoke. Johnny marveled at Morrissey's funny voice, which didn't exactly elate him. It would be another three years before they met again.

Rocky Mountain Low

In November 1978, after several more months confined to the house, Morrissey left Manchester to make a fresh start. Again, he went to stay with his aunt Mary, who had since relocated to Arvada, Colorado, a suburb of Denver. His sister Jackie went with him.

While Jackie assimilated quickly, landing a job within weeks of their arrival, Steven was not so successful. If his appreciation of music by U.K. new-wave outfits like the Jam and Public Image Ltd. didn't made him an outsider with the Bruce Springsteen and Led Zeppelin worshippers his own age, his pink tie sure did.

His applications for jobs at the local Target store and a large grocery chain were both declined. And when his ad in the local *Rocky Mountain News* seeking local musicians to play with went entirely unanswered, it prompted Morrissey, still only nineteen, to return home to Manchester after just seven weeks.

6

Now, Today, Tomorrow, and Always

Johnny and Angie

Crashing at the Rourkes'

With the demise of the Paris Valentinos, Johnny sought out other players. After he jammed with friends like David Clough and Robin Allman, the latter began talking up Marr, still only fourteen, to Chris Sievy, who fronted local band the Freshies. While he didn't get a gig in that group—likely because of his age—Johnny was becoming increasingly well known around Manchester for his guitar playing.

He and Andy continued to hang out, and with Mr. Rourke often gone, Johnny slept at his house a lot during 1978 and '79. "We were like brothers," Marr told fan website www.askmeaskmeask.me. "It was Andy and his three brothers and me and Angie."

Angela Brown

One Friday afternoon in early 1979, Marr trudged through the snow to his part-time job at a certain Wythenshawe supermarket only to learn he was being fired. In truth, he had seen it coming—he was arrogant, unmotivated, and lacked focus for anything but his music.

If Marr is to be believed, he was pelted with eggs by his co-workers near the loading dock as part of his discharge. En route home, the embarrassed teen stopped off at his friend Danny Patton's house. Sensing Johnny could use some cheering up, Patton asked his mate to go to a party with him, lending him a shirt and jacket for the occasion.

It was here that Johnny met Angela Brown, a petite, brown-eyed vegetarian girl who would become the love of his life. They were stunned to learn that they shared birthdays—she was exactly one-year younger than he.

Despite their different backgrounds—Angie's family was far more middle-class than his—they soon became a perfect and virtually inseparable fit for one another. They both wore eyeliner, they shared a strong fashion sense, and they loved rock 'n' roll. "From the first minute I saw her," Marr told Tony Fletcher, "I wanted to be with her all my life."

Football Skill

In addition to his musical abilities, Johnny was quite the athlete in his early-to-mid teens. At St. Augustine's, he played for the first football squad. He also played for Brooklands Athletic, a local Sunday team in which he trained alongside future stars of the sport like David Bardsley (later of teams like Watford, Oxford United, and Queens Park Rangers) and Gary Glissett (who played with Crewe Alexandra, Brentford and Wimbledon).

Marr was an accomplished player, at one time recruited by Nottingham Forest and Manchester City, where he played for their junior team. "I had trials for Forest," he told *ShortList* in February 2011. "But I wasn't good enough to be a professional footballer. I just wanted to dick about. I could run pretty fast, so I was a tricky winger. Still am."

While it's forever debatable whether Marr really wasn't good enough, his deepest interest lied in music. He much preferred hanging with Angie and Andy listening to records. Besides, he didn't really care for the company of professional footballers. They were, as he explained to Fletcher, "too macho."

The Perfect Fit

With Angie in his corner from such a young age, Marr was undistracted in his musical pursuits. She was the ultimate girlfriend for sixteen-year-old Johnny—she gave him her full support and, if that wasn't enough, she could roll a great joint.

It helped that they had similar musical tastes. Angela loved the New York Dolls, the good Rolling Stones albums like *Beggars Banquet, Let It Bleed,* and *Sticky Fingers,* Iggy's *Raw Power,* and Jimi Hendrix. She was completely happy to sit in Marr's room for hours, thumbing through music and fashion magazines, keeping him company while he noodled around on his guitar.

Angie and Andy and Johnny

With many teenage romances, best friends usually come second—when they aren't ditched altogether. But in Marr's case, that never happened. He encouraged Angie and Andy to become friends, and they hit it off from the start.

They all liked the same music. They each shared the same taste in clothes. And they all genuinely liked each other's company. Most importantly, there was no jealousy over Johnny. Brown filled one role and Rourke filled another.

In between jam sessions at Andy's, the unsupervised house became the young couple's home away from home. Rourke—a thrill seeker who was often quite stoned—gladly lent them his father's bedroom so they could be intimate when they wanted.

Rock 'n' Roll Truants

In the fall of 1977, St. Augustine's morphed into a public high school and was renamed St. John Plessington. Its open enrollment led to a lowering of standards and the departure of its best teachers. Rourke and Marr were looked upon as misfits who dressed the rock 'n' roll part before they regressed into serious truants.

At this stage, Marr felt it was important to dress as if he was in a band, even when he wasn't. "Most people at school must have really loathed me because I went around telling people that I was going to have a #1 album," Johnny told *Melody Maker* in August 1985. "Yes. I was an obstreperous cocky little upstart. [I was] interested in playing with a group and nothing else."

This outlook didn't exactly endear Marr to the teachers that stayed on. Neither did his propensity to cause trouble, or the fact that he and his pal Rourke came and went as they pleased. Although they continued to be habitual truants in their last few years at school, officials never got around to expelling them, even though they barely attended at all during their final year. In the mornings, Johnny would pretend to head off to the bus stop, where he would meet Andy. There they would await Marr's parents' morning departure to work. Once the coast was clear, they would go back into his home on Churchstoke Walk and play music all day.

Sister Ray

In the summer of 1979, fifteen-year-old Johnny was asked to join the Wythenshawe group Sister Ray, fronted by area eccentric Clive Robertson. Sister Ray took their inspiration from Lou Reed's first band, the Velvet Underground, with their name obviously coming from the closing track on the band's classic 1968 album *White Light, White Heat*.

Johnny replaced co-founding guitarist Alf Henshall and rehearsed with the band in Whalley Range. He only lasted for one gig, supporting the aforementioned Freshies at the Wythenshawe Forum, before moving on.

Robertson, bassist Alan Gooch, and dreadlocked drummer Bill Anstee were all "speed freaks," as Marr told Fletcher, while in Johnny Rogan's 1994 book *The Smiths: The Visual Documentary*, the guitarist remembered them as "a bunch of vagrant, biker nasties." The other members were considerably older than Marr and had a sordid history, and a little bit of local notoriety, because, as Johnny told Rogan, "the singer was crazy."

White Dice

Not long after Marr extracted himself from Sister Ray, he was approached by an older friend, Robert Allman, with an offer to play music with him and a classically trained keyboardist named Paul Whittall. Johnny—who was just turning sixteen—recommended Andy Rourke on bass and helped solicit former Paris Valentinos drummer Bobby Durkin.

Throughout late 1979 and during the first few months of the new decade, the quintet, now named White Dice, set about perfecting the American-sounding soft-rock formula that Allman—a locally respected songwriting talent who drew on the likes of Tom Petty, Neil Young, and the Fairport Convention and aspired to become a professional musician using a similar approach—wanted.

White Dice practiced religiously at TJ Davidson's rehearsal rooms in Manchester in the space directly under the rising local group Joy Division around the turn of the decade. The facility was "a bit rough," as Marr would tell John Robb in his 2010 book *The North Will Rise Again*. "The health and safety inspectors used to come down all the time."

Regardless, when bands didn't pay the rent, the landlord used to break in and steal their equipment, prompting Johnny to guard his by sleeping in the ramshackle room on more than one occasion.

Visiting Duffy

Around the time Marr turned sixteen, he started taking regular trips to London, where he would crash with Billy Duffy, who was playing guitar in the band Lonesome No More and working in a clothing shop. Johnny sought excitement beyond what Manchester had to offer and figured out a way to sneak on to the train and travel down to the big city, where he would latch on to Duffy, whether Billy liked it or not.

It wouldn't be uncommon for Marr to forgo school on Friday to make his way south for the weekend. He would return the following Monday or Tuesday and tell his parents he had been at Rourke's all weekend. Because he spent so much time at Andy's anyway, Mr. and Mrs. Maher would be none the wiser.

So Long, St. John Plessington

During their tenure in White Dice, Johnny and Andy were officially set free from St. John Plessington in the spring of 1980, but not before Marr failed his O-levels. Rourke's atrocious attendance disqualified him from taking his altogether.

Andy set a short-term goal of earning enough cash to buy a bass amp and worked for Snap-On Tools in the second half of 1980. Johnny, on the other hand, was upset with the fact that he had failed his exams. His parents encouraged him to go back to school and stressed that—should he go on the dole—they would kick him out.

Marr enrolled in the West Wythenshawe College of Further Education, which was located in the same building where he spent many of his early teen nights, to study drama. His outgoing personality landed him in a position of power when he was voted the president of the student union.

So It Goes

Although Johnny and Andy had started to be drawn to new-wave bands like Japan, the Cure, and Siouxsie & the Banshees, White Dice was Allman's band. And they had little problem following Rob's lead, on the understanding that working under Allman's direction seemed promising and might even turn profitable—especially after White Dice earned the attention of London's F-Beat Records, the new label founded by Elvis Costello's manager Jake Riviera.

The group had somehow managed to win a demo contest with a song they had recorded crudely around a boom box. Upon hearing the submission's four-part harmonies, Riviera contacted White Dice and invited them to record with producer/performer Nick Lowe—fresh from his biggest hits, "So It Goes" and "Cruel to Be Kind"—in his London home studio in April 1980. The group—which by this point featured drummer Craig Mitchell, who supplanted Durkin—tracked a six-song demo at Lowe's house: five originals co-written and arranged by Allman and Marr, plus a cover of Tom Petty's "American Girl."

If high points of the trip included Johnny being asked to play Costello's Rickenbacker in the studio and Johnny and Andy getting a look at Lowe's wife Carlene Carter in her negligee, the end result of the journey was daunting. Riviera called Allman at home, as Rourke told Fletcher, and told them the songs lacked "that spark or edge" that F-Beat was looking for.

Although the rejection did not sit well with Allman, White Dice tried to stay optimistic, resolving to continue on for just a little while longer. Andy's brother Chris even took over management duties, booking the band's first live gig and getting them some publicity. White Dice played their first and only concert in late 1980 at the Squat off Oxford Road in Manchester. Unfortunately, the gig was abysmal. Allman had started drinking to combat his nerves and wound up blowing the performance.

By January 1981, White Dice had officially and understandably split. But over two decades later, the band's bassist looked back fondly on their year and a half together. "We were a great band, we had harmonies and keyboards," Rourke explained in the 2002 Granada TV documentary *These Things Take Time: The Story of the Smiths*. "Good times. Exciting times."

New Direction

Although White Dice had crapped out, Johnny's experience of playing in the band and working with a talent like Nick Lowe made him all the more driven to succeed. He had already changed his last name, insisting in his final year at school that his teachers address him as Marr, as opposed to Maher—in part for fear that he might be confused with Buzzcocks drummer John Maher.

Johnny's parents respected and shared his passion for music. His dad actually wound up becoming a local country-music promoter around the time Johnny turned sixteen, and it gave them some common ground that hadn't previously existed. "We never had any communication before that at all, and it was a major breakthrough," Johnny told *Guitarist* in 1985. On rare occasions, they even listened to some of the same artists.

While supportive of Johnny's decision to pursue music as a career, John and Frances were concerned about their son. He was a free spirit—a wild child who was idealistic and extremely energetic. Johnny was also opinionated and, when it came to the guitar, extremely determined to get things right. "After the White Dice ended, I cut myself off from all my old mates in Wythenshawe," he told the *Guardian*'s John Crace in February 2008. "I wanted to rethink my music, my style, everything. I wanted to form a band that played the kind of music I was hearing in my head."

While the kids around him were still very much into successful modern acts like the Jam, the Clash, and Elvis Costello, Johnny remained drawn to folk music and New York bands like the Talking Heads and Patti Smith. He had also finally become enamored with the sounds of the Beatles, the legendary and pioneering Liverpool rock band he had dismissed for the first seventeen years of his life. Without the influence of his musical mentors, Johnny was free to call his own shots and feeling optimistic.

Andy Tries Heroin

At the same time, early 1981 was a hard time for Andy Rourke. Without White Dice, he wasn't sure what his future might hold. In the absence of a positive adult role model, he found himself experimenting with harder drugs. His father continued to be gone most of the time on business, which allowed his older brothers to increase their drug dealing from just marijuana to other drugs like heroin. With smack in ample supply, Andy gave it a try.

"When I was seventeen or sixteen, I just started dabbling with [it]," Rourke admitted to the *Daily Beast* in October 2013. Because he never liked needles, smoking heroin became his preferred method of ingestion, followed by snorting it.

When Marr learned of Rourke's descent into hard drugs, he pulled away from his best friend for the longest duration since they had first met. It would be several months before Andy—who seemed aimless and had trouble holding down a job—would hear from Johnny.

Learning from Lennon

Marr maintained his focus on music and quickly discovered that he much preferred being the only guitarist in jamming situations. He knew that when he finally got his next band off the ground, he would want to pursue it with that approach. As he neared eighteen, he became more and more interested in what he would eventually describe as a "greedy" style of guitar playing, with which he would fill in the spaces of a song with melody.

Johnny found himself drawn to John Lennon's rhythm playing around the time of the late Beatles co-founder's murder in December 1980. Although Marr had been prone to block them out before—mostly because they had been omnipresent from the time of his birth in late 1963—he now finally allowed himself to enjoy the Fab Four.

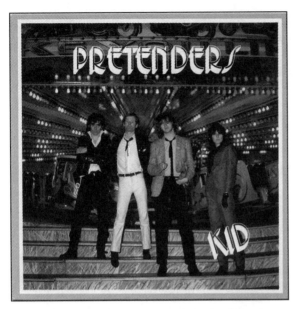

Johnny Marr was drawn to the sounds of the Pretenders and was especially fond of guitarist James Honeyman-Scott's playing on this 1979 single, "Kid." For many years—well into his time in the Smiths—Marr would warm up in rehearsals by playing the track's guitar solo. *Author's collection*

Aside from the fact that they had ushered in musical and social revolutions during their heyday, Marr was simply stunned by George Harrison's Rickenbacker playing on "Ticket to Ride," while Lennon's guitar work on *A Hard Day's Night* was even more influential.

The Great Pretenders

Marr also found himself taken by the Pretenders, a popular U.K. group fronted by Ohio-born singer/guitarist Chrissie Hynde. As a guitarist, Johnny was drawn to the playing of the band's jangling axe-man, James Honeyman-Scott, and later cited him as the last significant influence on his fretwork before he decided to launch his own pop group.

Of course, a decade later, he would find himself briefly playing guitar in Hynde's band. "The first time I played 'Kid' with the Pretenders, I couldn't believe it," he told *Guitar Player* in 1990, before acknowledging that Honeyman-Scott's solo was one he would play every day for years as he warmed up.

Passion for Fashion

In the spring of 1981, Johnny moved out of his parents' house on Churchstoke Walk. He had learned from a friend about a room for rent in the attic of a big Victorian house in Bowdon, Altrincham, which was not far from Wythenshawe. His landlady was Shelley Rohde, a Granada television news anchor who had been one of the first female reporters assigned to Moscow in the 1950s before covering the Hungarian Revolution. As a divorcee in the 1960s, Rohde had gone on to become a columnist for the *Daily Mail* and also wrote a biography of the artist L. S. Lowry. At the time, Rhode resided with her four children, Gavin, Christian, Daniel, and Michelle.

Marr found a part time job in the Manchester city clothing store, Aladdin's Cave in the Arndale Center, working alongside Angie. The goth-rock clothier soon evolved into Johnson's, serving a modern clientele that included fans of the

Pretenders and the Jam. A subsequent line known as La Rocka was also launched by the owners to accommodate fans of the era's rockabilly revival.

Soon after that, Angie was lured away to work as a receptionist (and occasional model) for the city's Vidal Sassoon salon. Marr also shifted to another store, Stolen from Ivor, where he became a buyer, using the role to arrange free clothes for himself and Angie. Johnny job-hopped again, successfully interviewing for a position at X-Clothes, which was opening up a new store on Manchester's Chapel Walks.

In addition to having a keen sense of style, Johnny was musically astute and helped program the music in the store. On his advice, goth acts like Siouxsie & the Banshees and the Cure could be heard alongside Liverpool's Echo & the Bunnymen, Scottish pop acts like Aztec Camera, synth-pop acts like Depeche Mode and Soft Cell, offbeat U.S. acts like the Cramps and, of course, local heroes New Order—just up from the ashes of Joy Division following the suicide of singer Ian Curtis the previous year.

Disaffected Youth

During Marr's time at Stolen from Ivor, he was hired to appear on a recurring local television program after the casting director spotted him at work. The show was designed to focus on teenage unemployment in the area, and Johnny was asked to appear alongside around a hundred jobless young adults.

At first, Johnny questioned why he was being requested for the show. After all, he actually had a job. The show's representatives explained to him that they wanted someone who looked like he did. So, once a week for eight weeks, Marr was paid £35 and provided lunch by Granada in return for appearing on the show. In addition, his employer at the shop gave him a free outfit for each broadcast in the hopes that he might draw in customers.

Surprisingly, Marr was hesitant to speak up on camera, and only made one comment during his eight weeks on the short-lived series. He would eventually admit that he was only really interested in his paycheck—and his free suit.

7

Oh, Hello!

The Microphone or the Typewriter

Slaughtered

Back from his unsuccessful attempt at life in Colorado by early 1979, Morrissey was solicited that March on Billy Duffy's recommendation to join Slaughter & the Dogs, who were looking for a replacement singer after Wayne Barrett quit. Steven was already acquainted with guitarist Mick Rossi and bassist Howard Bates and passed the band's audition, but the following month—after the group traveled to London to audition their new singer for Decca Records—he was removed from his duties.

Slaughter's remnants—including Duffy—relocated to London as the Studio Sweethearts and recorded the single "I Believe," with Rossi on vocals. But fans should take note that unreleased Decca demo recordings of "I Get Nervous," "Peppermint Heaven," "The Living Jukebox," and the Nosebleeds holdover "(I Think) I'm Ready for the Electric Chair" with Morrissey on vocals do apparently exist.

Curiously, Morrissey makes no mention of this early career failure in *Autobiography*. It clearly serves as a matter of significant embarrassment to him, as he would tell author John Robb, "Local history has me down as an ex-member of Slaughter & the Dogs, which is ridiculous, but I find that any details about me from this period are generally believed by whoever wants to believe them."

Managing a Certain Ratio

Granada Television host Tony Wilson launched Factory Records in late 1978 as a means to help Manchester bands get off the ground and fill his own pockets. For the company's first release, *A Factory Sample*, which came out that December, Wilson and his then partners Alan Erasmus and Peter Saville gathered material by local acts like Joy Division, the Durutti Column, John Dowie, and Cabaret Voltaire.

Nineteen seventy-nine saw singles by A Certain Ratio and the Liverpool band Orchestral Manoeuvres in the Dark emerge from Wilson's label. The latter's "Electricity" became a bona-fide hit, prompting Virgin Records to buy out the duo's contract. That summer, Joy Division released their debut album, *Unknown Pleasures*, which put Factory on the map.

Frustrated by his inability to have success as a singer, Morrissey aligned with A Certain Ratio in the hope of finding another way into the music business. ACR—who were readying the material that would wind up on their December 1979 Factory cassette-only release *The Graveyard and the Ballroom*—blended elements of funk with krautrock influences like Can and Kraftwerk to craft a distinct sound.

Morrissey—who had rekindled his friendship with ACR singer Simon Topping—very briefly collected the band's pay during early gigs, including a January '79 show at Band on the Wall. But after months of trying to help the band—including writing a fawning article about the group for the fanzine the *Next Big Thing*—his relationship with Topping began to crumble. His van ride to Liverpool for A Certain Ratio's gig at Eric's in August 1979 would be his last.

Learning from Ian

The milestone of turning twenty was extremely difficult for Morrissey, not least because Margaret Thatcher, whom he loathed, was elected prime minister that same month. He had no foreseeable future and was depressed at how life was shaping up for him. As he watched Joy Division's ascent during 1979 and into early 1980, he thought front man Ian Curtis had it all. But, soon enough, his and everyone's thoughts about Curtis' existence would drastically change.

On May 18, 1980, Curtis hung himself at his home in nearby Macclesfield. He was just twenty-three and left behind a wife and a baby girl, his shattered bandmates, and a legion of stunned fans on the same day he was due to depart for Joy Division's first U.S. tour. The posthumous release of the song "Love Will Tear Us Apart"—which peaked at #13 in the U.K. singles chart the next month—offered an enduring reminder of what the world lost.

If Morrissey took anything from Curtis' suicide, it was that his death was a waste. Should he ever find his way to pop stardom, he decided, he would embrace his role, if not cherish it. There was nothing he wanted more.

Harvey Goldsmith Entertainments
with the
New Manchester Review
present

MAGAZINE

PLUS SPECIAL GUEST
JOHN COOPER CLARKE
AND
THE NOSE BLEEDS

THE NEW RITZ
Whitworth Street, Manchester

Monday 8th May 1978

Tickets: Pandemonium, Black Sedan, Virgin, Hime & Addison, and Paperchase.

A flyer promoting the Nosebleeds' May 1978 gig, with new singer Morrissey, supporting Magazine. The band's show was held at the New Ritz on Whitworth Street in Manchester, and although the performance was short, it earned high praise from *NME* writer Paul Morley. *Author's collection*

Living with Linder

In the three and a half years since they first met, Linder Sterling had become Morrissey's closest female friend. She also became his roommate in 1980 when he moved in to her home at 35 Mayfield Road in Whalley Range. Sterling had continued to thrive as an artist in the time since she and Morrissey first met, designing the cover of Magazine's first album, *Real Life*, and working with U.K. writer Jon Savage on his now-iconic fanzine the *Secret Public*.

Because Steven and Linder spent so much time together, often taking long walks through Moss Side, there was speculation from those who knew them that they might be a couple. As she would describe it in a 2010 *Interview* piece with Morrissey, it was "just the two of us together, but very alone at the same time, extremely intimate but very separate."

Their friendship was strengthened by the fact that both of them were avid readers, specifically of suffragette literature. They would consume the same titles and then spend time discussing them inside and out.

To pay the rent, Morrissey worked briefly in the hospital where his estranged dad was also employed. Meanwhile, Linder's avant-garde band Ludus played around Northern England and began to attract a following after the release of records like the EP *The Visit* and the subsequent single "My Cherry Is in Sherry." Both were issued via Richard Boon's Manchester's New Hormones label, the one-time home of the Buzzcocks.

Record Mirror

Life for Steven at this stage wasn't nearly as gloomy as he would later claim in mid-'80s magazine interviews. Aside from his close relationship with Linder, there was encouragement from his mother—who supported him morally and financially whenever she could—that he might have found his calling as a music journalist and critic. Morrissey had even held on to the idea of writing a book on the New York Dolls and continued to work at it, but by 1980 there was minimal interest in David Johansen's long-defunct band.

Building on his desire to write about pop music, Morrissey persistently approached leading music papers like *NME* and *Melody Maker*, but they dismissed his story pitches. An editor at the former reportedly turned him down five times, prompting Steven to seek employment with the lesser-known *Record Mirror*. There, in a turn of good luck, he was hired to review Manchester concerts.

While Morrissey was happy with the notoriety that came with the position, he was displeased with the way his editors chopped up his coverage of concerts by everyone from London glam revivalists Wasted Youth to Iggy Pop. Covering the latter's gig at the Manchester Apollo in a review that ran on July 18, 1981, Steven callously thrashed his former hero. "Iggy . . . Dear Iggy!" he wrote. "Always there when we . . . don't quite need him." Elsewhere Morrissey added, "Everyone screams so loudly that they probably didn't hear Iggy's dire vocals, and the doleful heavy metal bash coming from his new band."

Lost Play

In October 1980, Morrissey heard that Tony Wilson was considering expanding beyond his record company interests into publishing, which prompted Steven to send him a play he had written. Two months later, after returning from visiting family in the U.S. during Christmas 1980 and learning that he hadn't gotten a reply, Morrissey fired off a scathing letter to Factory, asking Wilson if he would please return his work.

Wilson never did. "He wrote a short, fantastic short play about eating toast," Tony told *Mojo*'s Johnny Black in 2004. He lost it. That same year, Wilson claims Morrissey told him he was going to be a famous singer. "I said, 'Steven, write your novel.' I thought there was no way he'd make a pop star."

Vox Humana

Also in 1980, Morrissey—perhaps on Linder's recommendation—recorded a crude demo, which he sent to former Buzzcocks manager Richard Boon at New Hormones. The tape started with a spoken apology from Steven for the poor sound quality of his *vox humana*.

Morrissey explained that there was someone asleep in an adjacent room before beginning his a cappella rendering of two songs. As Boon would later explain to the *Face*, one of the performances was an original that would become the future Smiths song "The Hand That Rocks the Cradle," but sung to a different melody. The second entry was, rather ironically, a Bessie Smith song called "Wake Up Johnny."

Pen Pals

In October 1980, Morrissey had begun corresponding with a mustached teen named Robert Mackie, after responding to a classified ad that the Glasgow-based music fan had placed in *Sounds*. The correspondence lasted fourteen months, during which time Steven sent letters during his visits to the U.S.A., where he pretended he was an American and suggested he was going to launch a band he was calling Angels Are Genderless.

According to Fletcher's book, Morrissey announced to Mackie in his letters that both he and his girlfriend Annalisa were bisexual, and that he hated sex. He also extolled the virtues of celibacy and wrote of his unwillingness to work a full-time job. When he found out his eighteen-year-old pen pal had a full-time job, Steven criticized him before disclosing that he had seen a staggering sixteen David Bowie concerts in his young life.

Morrissey and Mackie's main common interest was their love of the Velvet Underground. At the time, singer Nico was actually living in Manchester, suffering through a heroin addiction and being managed by Alan Wyse, a local promoter who rented office space in the New Hormones offices. As a result, Steven would eventually run into her at the label's offices, where Linder's band Ludus remained under contract to Richard Boon.

Steven and Robert's friendship fizzled after Mackie came to visit Kings Road one weekend. Although their correspondence picked up after several months of silence, it had completely run its course by early 1982.

Babylon Books

In early 1981, Steven Morrissey's first book-zine, titled *New York Dolls*, was published by the small local Babylon Books, owned by John Muir. The forty-eight-page tome spoke to the importance of the Dolls, whose arrival signified the end of the 1960s, or, as Morrissey wrote, "their unmatched vulgarity dichotomized feelings of extravagant devotion or vile detestation."

While he later dismissed his allegiance to the band as a mere teenage fascination, here he describes watching the band on *The Old Grey Whistle Test* as his "first real emotional experience," confesses to wearing his own "self-designed" Dolls T-shirts, and recalls how his teachers worried that he might show up for school in drag. "The Dolls gave me a sense of uniqueness, as if they were my own personal discovery," he attests in the book, which he dedicated to his old friend James Maker.

A Bland Jelly-Baby

At times during his tenure at *Record Mirror*, Morrissey's journalistic ethics came into question. He praised Billy Duffy's band Lonesome No More, describing them as "alarmingly proficient" and "oozing with great possibilities" while "possessing the spit and polish of even the most well-oiled . . . " He also heralded the Cramps—whose U.K. fan club, the Legion of the Cramped, he had co-founded—by calling them "the most important American export since the New York Dolls."

But when he championed Linder's band in a review of their August 1981 performance as openers for new chart favorites Depeche Mode, he went too far. Morrissey condemned DM's latest hit "New Life" as "a bland jelly-baby" while writing of Ludus, "Theirs is a name destined to be in everyone's mouth . . . their music offers everything to everyone. Linder was born singing and has more imagination than Depeche Mode could ever hope for."

It's never been clear if Morrissey's editors at *Record Mirror* had any knowledge that he and Linder were best friends and housemates at the time the piece ran, but his dismissal of Depeche Mode's palatable techno-pop was destined to alienate the paper's young readers. It was his last byline for the publication.

James Dean Is Not Dead

In the wake of the reasonable popularity of his New York Dolls book, Babylon's owner John Muir asked Steven to write another book sometime in 1981. This time out, he decided to pay tribute to James Dean, whose pictures adorned the walls of his Kings Road bedroom throughout his adolescence. Titled *James Dean Is Not Dead*, the short book shared its title with a 1979 poem he'd written about the star in which he imagines the late movie actor is still alive. Unlike the poem, Morrissey's second foray into publishing was a fairly accurate story of the *East of Eden* and *Rebel Without a Cause* star's life and death.

Morrissey writes of Dean's desire to make it on his own terms in Hollywood, while exploring "gossips of his bisexuality." He also suggests that the actor made a series of porn movies that Warner Bros. Studios covered up. Curiously, the book wasn't properly published until 1983, after the Smiths had achieved some notoriety. Morrissey expressed his frustration over project's eventual emergence in the wake of his own fame.

"I hate it, it's a cash-in," he told Elissa van Poznack the following year, griping about the way the project had been packaged to appeal to his fans, replete with a recent photo of him on the back cover. "I'd rather leave the book, if it can be called such a thing, in the past."

Exit Smiling

While Babylon's publisher Muir held off on releasing *James Dean Is Not Dead*, Morrissey submitted his third book, which he'd actually written first. Penned in 1979, the seventy-two-page *Exit Smiling* was initially rejected by Muir, who left it unpublished until 1998. The fourteen-chapter project focused on Morrissey's favorites of the cinema—specifically B-movie talents that he would describe in the tome as "some of the screen's also-rans." It was presented in the Courier New font of his cherished typewriter and celebrated the lives and accomplishments of obscure actors like Pier Angeli and Mamie Van Doren, as well as future Smiths record-sleeve stars like Terence Stamp and Rita Tushingham.

When Muir finally released *Exit Smiling*, as another obvious cash-grab, in September 1998, its run was limited to just 1,000 copies. Each came with its own unique numbered certificate of authenticity. Opposing the book's publication, Morrissey released a statement through his then-label Reprise Records explaining that the release of his "essay" in book form was "very much against my wishes, and I ask anyone who has any interest in me not to buy it. . . . Please do not think that this book is any way sanctioned by me."

Morrissey would also explain that he was unable to stop publication of this or his previous Babylon releases because he had accepted £50 from Muir in 1978 as an overall payment. "I have never been offered any royalties," he continued, "I did not consider the essays to be worthy of publication in book form, and found the final designs to be tatty and embarrassing."

No Devoto

At one point in early 1981, Morrissey hatched the idea of writing a book about Howard Devoto, the co-founder of the Buzzcocks, who went on to success with

Magazine. Although he had called Devoto's voice "very irritating" and his lyrics "often plain bad" in a 1978 fanzine review, he had since become a loyal fan of Magazine's records, specifically 1980's *The Correct Use of Soap*.

Unfortunately, Devoto—who was Linder's ex-boyfriend but didn't actually meet Morrissey until 1985—wasn't interested in being interviewed for such a project. Without his subject's cooperation, Morrissey's plans for the book were dead.

8

Shoplifters of the World

Johnny Finds His Way

Spector, Motown, Disco, and Funk

Johnny Marr discovered Phil Spector's classic records after hearing Patti Smith's version of the Ronettes' "Be My Baby" in the late 1970s. Spector's work with famous girl groups like the Ronettes and the Crystals—not to mention his efforts with Ike & Tina Turner, the Beatles, and the Ramones—opened the guitarist's mind.

"When I got into him it was just the end for me. Fantastic!" he told *Total Guitar* in May 1995. "I always said that I could relate to Phil Spector more directly than guitar players—like your Jeff Becks or your Eric Claptons. I never wanted to be a guitar soloist."

Johnny was hooked on the idea of a succinct, moving, three-and-a-half-minute single. Spector paved the way for Johnny's appreciation of classic soul singles, which he began devouring. By this time, the budding guitarist hadn't uncovered a contemporary group that excited him, so he began collecting Motown singles by acts like Marvin Gaye, the Supremes, the Four Tops, the Isley Brothers, and the Jackson Five. He also devoured hits crafted by classic pop songwriters like Leiber & Stoller (including Elvis Presley's "Hound Dog" and "Jailhouse Rock," Ben E. King's "Stand By Me" and "Spanish Harlem," and the Drifters' "On Broadway") and started thinking of himself as a serious songwriter.

Encouraged by Pete Hunt at Discount Records in Altrincham to open his ears to a variety of styles, Marr also found himself taken with disco records. He picked up the 1977 hit "Shame" by Evelyn Champagne King and was drawn to the stylistic guitar playing of Chic's Nile Rogers, citing that band's 1978 smash "I Want Your Love" as a touchstone. If the latter was itself an interpretation of Bo Diddley's classic beat, it's little surprise that Johnny once described the latter's 1957 "Hey Mona" as the root of all dance music.

Johnny's appreciation of the dance sound dated back to Hamilton Bohannon's 1975 U.K. smash "Disco Stomp." As he told *Ink 19* in May 2003, "It had this overstated, choppy rhythm. It wasn't this vibrato as such, but I found the rhythm totally infectious and I was nuts about it." His love of funk

The sleeve for "Yum Yum (Gimme Some)," the 1975 single by the Fatback Band that first lured Johnny Marr toward the funk genre. With his old friend Andy Rourke, Marr formed his very own funk band, Freak Party, in 1981. *Eil.com*

stemmed from the Fatback Band's modestly successful '75 single "Yum Yum (Gimme Some)," which also had an extravagant guitar line that made him want to dance.

Freak Party

Alongside his employment at X-Clothes, Marr set about launching his own funk-influenced dance band with Rourke in 1981. Inspired as much by Nile Rodgers as the rising success of Manchester bands like A Certain Ratio and New Order, Johnny reunited with Andy—who seemed to have cleaned up his act—and local drummer Simon Wolstencroft in a new group, Freak Party.

The trio rehearsed at Decibelle Studios, which was located in a converted cotton mill on Jersey Street in Ancoats, where they auditioned potential singers. Over the course of several months, the trio perfected their instrumental sound and even managed to demo two vocal-free numbers, including one known as "Crak Therapy," with an aspiring studio engineer named Dale Hibbert.

Still, Freak Party's future was briefly in jeopardy when Tony Wilson—already aware of Johnny's reputation as an exceptional musician—came into Marr's place of employment one afternoon in the fall of 1981 to ask if he wanted to join Section 25, a local band he was managing. Section 25 were headed out on a European tour as the opening act for New Order, but after some lengthy deliberation Johnny declined Wilson's offer. Following his experience with White Dice, he would no longer serve as anyone's hired gun. Music wasn't merely a paycheck—it was his passion.

All the same, Freak Party were in trouble, and heroin was to blame. Rourke had begun to rely on smack again and Marr's patience was being tested once more. Beyond the poisonous environment on Hawthorn Lane, where Rourke's older brothers had graduated to hardcore dealers and users, the drug was approaching epidemic levels throughout Manchester in the early days of the Thatcher era.

After Marr witnessed a pair of friends shooting up one evening after a Freak Party rehearsal, he decided he wasn't having any of it. He had to leave Andy behind, sacrificing Wolstencroft—who would join the Fall in 1986—in the process.

Although Marr and Rourke would reunite within a year, at the time Johnny wasn't clear if their paths would ever cross again. Interestingly enough, when asked for his version of why Freak Party broke up in a March 2006 interview, Andy made no mention of his heroin use or its role in the band's split. Explaining the group's dissolution to *Q*, he simply said, "We never found a singer and Johnny got bored with it."

Art Bust

Before Freak Party disbanded, the group had been practicing one night at Decibelle when the local police kicked down the door to the trio's rehearsal space. They pushed Marr—who had been playing his Les Paul—up against the wall and handcuffed him. The four officers arrested him on "fencing" charges after he tried to sell stolen art for a friend. Coincidentally, the drawings in question were by L.S. Lowry, the famed Manchester and Salford artist whose biography had been written by Marr's landlady.

Marr had been pressured by an acquaintance to introduce him—as he would later relay to www.askmeaskmeask.me—to "this dodgy guy." Although he didn't have any real contacts in the criminal world, he used his resourcefulness to make an introduction. "I found out who the local contact was in the underworld who specialized in these kinds of matters and put Mr. X with Mr. Y and all shit broke loose," he told the fan site.

The infraction was so serious that it threatened to keep Johnny away from Angie for six to eight months. But when the case went to court, everyone involved but Marr was sentenced to prison. "The judge," as he told Fletcher, "sentenced me to embarrassment and stupidity." The court recognized that Johnny had not made the introduction with any hope of profit, but only to "get this guy off my back."

Spinning at the Exit

With Freak Party over, Johnny and Angie sought excitement elsewhere, and they found it in Manchester's nightclubs. Because of their reputations in the city's fashion community, they were welcome in booming night clubs like the newly opened Exit and the established gay spot Devilles.

At the former, Marr was thrilled to discover that Andrew Berry, a friend from his West Wythenshawe neighborhood, was manning the DJ booth, spinning disco obscurities by Hamilton Bohannon in between new records by the Human League. Eventually, Marr found his way into the booth with Berry, who was moonlighting from his hairdressing job in the club opened by flashy Mancunian promoter John Kennedy. After late nights spinning records—including many culled from Johnny's diverse collection—it wasn't uncommon for Marr to crash at Andrew's apartment on Palatine Road, not far from Factory Records and near the center of the action.

Together, they dug deep into their crates of vinyl, plotted out their shared sets, and brought underground New York disco and hip-hop records from the likes of Lovebug Starski—who had just dropped "Positive Life" with the Harlem World Crew—the Sugar Hill label roster, and more to the Exit's audience.

Matt Johnson

During a trip to London, Pete Hunt had befriended a rising musician named Matt Johnson, who had just released a well-received album, *Burning Blue Soul*, on 4AD Records. When Johnson revealed to Hunt he was in the throes of assembling a new band he was calling The The, the Discount Records manager suggested he follow him back to Manchester so that he might meet Marr, who had long been one of his favorite customers.

An introduction was made while Marr was on duty at X-Clothes, and Johnson was thrilled to learn that Johnny was already well aware of his album. They hit it off and jammed together at Hunt's place over beers and speed before heading out to the local nightclub Legends to hit the dance floor.

Matt was stunned by Johnny's confidence and musical prowess, later telling Fletcher, "he had that young gun-slinger vibe." Although Johnson asked Marr to join his group, Johnny wasn't convinced they had the same musical goals. Matt was pursuing experimental music like Wire and Cabaret Voltaire, whereas Johnny's interests were still steeped in classic pop. They parted as good friends, leaving the door open to future collaborations.

Joe Moss

One afternoon in early 1982, Marr had wandered out of X-Clothes and into the competing clothier next door, Crazy Face, during his lunch hour. Marr introduced himself to the store's proprietor, Joe Moss, as a frustrated musician.

Moss had opened the shop as a satellite of his Stockport enterprise on Chapel Walks, having ascended from his initial operation at Eighth Day, a popular craft exchange, earlier in the decade. It was here that Moss had his first success by making and selling loon pants, which he branded "Crazy Face," after the 1970 Van Morrison song.

When the pants took off, Moss and his partner implemented a manufacturing operation. Moss profited further by distributing his wares to London boutiques. Crazy Face became its own clothing line, and the stores followed suit.

Although Johnny was fond of the fashions Moss sold, he was mostly captivated by the timeless music he played. Unlike the trendy gothic rock and new-wave records that were X-Clothes' mainstay, Crazy Face dared to play the kind of timeless music—including blues, soul, vintage rock, and jazz—that spoke to Marr.

Johnny and Joe became friends, and despite their significant age difference—Marr was just nineteen, while Moss was married with children—the former began to show the latter how to play certain songs on the guitar. Moss was in awe of Johnny's ability. "I'd known guitarists from '60s Manchester bands, and I'd never heard anything like this kid," he told *Mojo* in June 2004. "My bloody tongue was hanging out."

Joe and his wife, Janet, entertained Marr and Angie Brown at their home in Heaton Chapel, where Moss exposed the aspiring guitarist to his vast record and book collections, serving as a father figure and confidante. "Joe was a huge influence on my whole musical ethos at the time," Marr also told *Mojo*. "He was someone whose opinion I really respected."

9

The Songs That Saved Your Life

Marr Calls on Morrissey

Johnny Comes Knocking

Throughout early 1982, Marr focused on writing completely structured songs over mere riffs. He revealed to Joe Moss his desire to find a singer and songwriting collaborator to finalize his tunes with the ultimate hopes of forming a band. He brazenly approached Pete Shelley, who had just disbanded the Buzzcocks, about working together, but the former punk star—who had just dropped the synth-pop winner "Homosapien" on the world—declined his offer.

While Joe was supportive and knew Johnny would eventually make the right connection, it wasn't until Marr thought about the time that Billy Duffy had introduced him to Steven Morrissey at a Patti Smith show that the idea of a viable partner truly clicked. Johnny recalled a day—months after their unspectacular introduction—when Billy had shown him some of the lyrics that the short-lived Nosebleeds vocalist had written.

These recollections gave Johnny the idea of cold-calling Morrissey—who himself had long been writing and thinking up vocal parts—to see about a possible musical alliance. After discussing the idea with Joe for several weeks, Marr convinced himself to move ahead. He hatched a plan to bring a mutual friend, Steve Pomfret, to Steven's home on King's Road for the meeting.

Marr dressed like he was already a star in his faded Levi's, biker boots, and a fresh quiff hairstyle, courtesy of Andrew Berry, as he and Pomfret took the lunchtime bus ride to Morrissey's place that May. They knocked on the door and Morrissey—wearing a vintage cardigan—answered.

Ironically, the visit came at a time when Morrissey had all but given up on the idea of singing in a band. "It was very strange for me because I had tried to do it for a very long time," he explained on the interview album *Ask Me, Ask Me, Ask Me*, which was recorded in 1984.

Steven's first impression of Marr was that he resembled the actor Tom Bell, who played Blackie in the 1961 British crime thriller *Payroll*. Johnny told Morrissey that he was unhappy with the state of modern music in 1982 and wanted to change it. They talked briefly about when Duffy first introduced them, before Johnny, now eighteen, pulled out his guitar and began to show off his abilities.

Stunned by Marr's musical talent, Morrissey, four years his senior, couldn't help but wonder how he managed to arrive at his doorstep. "It was an event I'd always looked forward to and [had] unconsciously been waiting for since my childhood," the singer told *Melody Maker* in September 1987. "I'd hung around for a very long time waiting for this magical, mystical event."

Both were excited at how well and how quickly they hit it off. Marr would describe this first meeting as "the attraction of opposites" in the August 3, 1985, edition of *Melody Maker*. Johnny was stunned to discover Steven's neatness, his massive collection of books, and his unique sense of humor. If Marr was still largely obsessed with rock 'n' roll—something his potential musical partner had outgrown—they shared so much common ground, in terms of '60s pop influences, that they knew they had to make a go of things.

When Johnny left, he had in his possession a cassette of Morrissey singing an original song, "Don't Blow Your Own Horn" without accompaniment. The hope was that he might build some music around it. Meanwhile, Pomfret stood mostly silent, bearing witness to the earliest interactions between Morrissey and Marr. At the time, there was little way he could know he was in the company of the two men who would evolve into the greatest songwriting partnership of the 1980s.

Partners

While Marr was ready to get started that instant, the pair parted with the reassurance that Morrissey would call him to firm up plans to try writing together. When Johnny received that phone call at work the next afternoon, he knew this wasn't going to be the false start he had initially worried it might be.

When the singer arrived at Marr's place in Bowdon a few days later, Johnny was completely certain they would make a go of it. "He was very aggressive," Morrissey told *Hot Press* in May 1984. "I could see this was someone who was going to get things done quickly."

Johnny's plan was to try to write a song or two and see if the pair had a proper creative connection. Although Marr was unsuccessful at structuring a tune around Morrissey's idea for "Don't Blow Your Own Horn," the pair weren't discouraged and moved along to work on something else. Steven fused some lyrics he had already written to an existing musical piece of Johnny's, and their first official collaboration, titled "The Hand That Rocks the Cradle," emerged.

Thrilled that they had put a workable song together with minimal effort, they kept at it and tried to perfect another. When Johnny came up with a guitar line on the spot, Morrissey tried out lines from another poem in his notebook. The end result was "Suffer Little Children," which—despite its somber depiction of Manchester's Moors murders of the mid-'60s—also left Steven and Johnny elated. Not only had they finally found each other, they found a way come up with some really great material on their first try. A creative alliance was forged.

Single Thoughts

That same fateful day that they wrote "Suffer," long-term *Coronation Street* disciple Steven was thrilled to discover that Johnny's landlady was *the* Shelley Rohde. As he marveled at the framed, autographed pictures of the show's stars adorning the walls of her home, he had a great idea.

Morrissey imagined that when the time came for Marr and him to release a single, they could utilize vintage photos of entertainers. It was here that the notion for a unique and in most cases obscure cover star to adorn each of the band's ensuing singles took shape.

That evening, Johnny and Steven also decided that they would form a band to present their songs, and that each member would dress similarly onstage and in publicity photos. The plan was to seek out a label like Rough Trade—the London home to groups like Aztec Camera and the Fall—to release their records.

Morrissey and Marr also spoke about writing for other acts and envisioned themselves as a modern-day Leiber & Stoller. They decided that their shared appreciation of Sandie Shaw made her an ideal first choice to approach to test this approach. The pair would ultimately assist in her comeback.

Steven and Angie

When it came to Johnny's longtime girlfriend, Angie Brown—who had been with him in her Volkswagen Beetle that memorable morning to pick up Morrissey at the Altrincham train station—the aspiring front man immediately realized that the young couple came as a package deal. Not that it mattered, as Angie and Steven hit it off and developed a friendship all their own.

Morrissey appreciated how she avoided—as he later put it in *Autobiography*—"the Girlfriend Syndrome" that strained and severed other bands like the Beatles. Brown's impartiality and ability to put what was best for the Smiths ahead of her own agenda was—as the singer would attest—"honorable" and "far superior to the commonplace and dreaded musician girlfriend."

Songwriting with a Purpose

Although the plan to deliver their songs as a band was a key concept from the outset, writing quality numbers that were different from the status quo was at the core of what Morrissey and Marr set out to do. "We both felt the need to react against what we'd been hearing over the past X years. Basically, we had a lot of gripes." Johnny explained to Bill Black from *Sounds* in 1983. "If you're happy with the music you're making and the music around you then you're going to be complacent, boring and safe."

The idea was to write a catalog of songs that were inspired by the music of the '60s, when music fans went to the shops to buy singles that they would prize.

Without appearing as revivalists, Johnny and Steven hoped to restore an element of preciousness to pop music.

It helped that they were both equally committed to songwriting and got a charge out of working together. Although Morrissey's vocal tunes were often completely different from the music Johnny was writing, when they put it together, the outcomes were unpredictable and exhilarating. Or, as Marr enthused to Black, "It's joyous, the way we work together."

Attraction of Opposites

Morrissey and Marr's shared commitment coupled with the way they complimented one another—perhaps the ideal example of the attraction of opposites—was downright magical. Their working relationship made Johnny—who already had the woman of his dreams in his corner—complete. His admiration for and ability to confide in Morrissey, and vice versa, became a huge reason they were able to triumph artistically right from the start.

"There's an unusual aspect to both our personalities that we both understand," Marr told Tony Fletcher. "It's about having a knowing of this vision of something that you can do and something that you can be, which is a really big part of you."

They became reliant on one another, and their bond was so strong that they would each later quantify it as love. Not that they were *in love* with one another, but the intensity of their relationship and the need for one another ran extremely deep. They even made each other mixtapes, which—as Marr would point out to *Pitchfork*'s Mark Richardson in 2012—was something "you do with people you love," explaining their connection was "about passion, imagination, escapism, idealism, desperation."

Morrissey conveyed his feelings about their bond to Nick Kent in 1985 and revealed how Marr provided him with "this massive energy boost," adding, "I could feel Johnny's energy just seething inside me."

Friends

Although Johnny was the far more outgoing of the pair in the earliest days of the Smiths, Morrissey was hardly a recluse. The aspiring vocalist had a number of friends at this stage. He may have kept discerning company, but he was fairly social, and introduced the guitarist to his close friends like Linder, Richard Boon, and James Maker.

Johnny would remember Morrissey's pals as likeable, artistic, and engaging. When Marr introduced his own friends, like Andrew Berry, to his new musical partner, Steven seemed very quiet at first, but over time he came out of his shell.

The Name

In need of a suitable name, Morrissey suggested calling their band the Smiths. And, when neither managed to think of anything better, the name stuck. They both liked the fact that it has no stylistic connotations and possessed a certain timelessness that harkened back to bands like the Who, the Kinks, and the Byrds.

"The name doesn't mean anything, it simply serves its purpose," Steven told *i-D* in late 1982, for the magazine's February 1983 edition. "I think it's very important not to be defined in any one category. Once you're defined you're limited and musically that petrifies me."

Explaining this concept further, the singer told *Record Mirror*'s Graham K. Smith and Dylan Jones in September 1984 that it was a reaction to the long band names like Echo & the Bunnymen that were popular at the time. "I wanted to get rid of all that kind of rhetorical drivel and just say something incredibly basic," he said. "The Smiths to me sounded quite . . . um . . . down to earth."

Pomfret out, Hibbert In

With a number of songs now written, it became obvious to Morrissey and Marr that they would need a bassist and drummer—what the former would describe to McCormick as the "basic utensils"—to present their songs properly as a band.

Although Pomfret initially served as a second guitarist, out of obligation, during the earliest rehearsals in Bowdon, it quickly became clear that Johnny wanted to be the only guitarist in the Smiths. On bass, Marr recruited Decibelle Studios' own Dale Hibbert, then twenty-one.

Although Hibbert was fronting his own band, the Adorables, he saw such promise in Marr that he put his own group on hiatus. Early on, Hibbert learned that he shared some commonalities with Morrissey—they both worshipped the Velvet Underground, and they were both vegetarians. After band practices, he would often give the singer a ride home on the back of his motorcycle.

One of the first songs they attempted with Hibbert in the fray was a cover of "I Want a Boy for My Birthday," which was originally recorded by the early-'60s New York group the Cookies in 1963. Ahead of their first practice, Johnny gave Dale a cassette of the Goffin & King song, which he'd recorded with Morrissey on his TEAC Portastudio, to learn.

Meanwhile, the Smiths went without a permanent drummer in their earliest months while they continued to seek their ideal kit man.

The Hacienda

On May 21, 1982, the Hacienda nightclub and music venue opened its doors in Manchester. A joint venture between New Order, their manager Rob Gretton, and Factory Records owner Tony Wilson, the club was a regular hangout for Marr—and to a lesser extent Morrissey—that summer.

Andrew Berry was a regular fixture in the DJ booth after he had been lured away from a competing club called Berlin, and his close friend Johnny was welcome alongside him at any time. Part of Andrew's arrangement with the

Hacienda's owners allowed for him to run his own hair salon, Swing, out of the venue's dressing room during the day.

Morrissey also turned up regularly with Linder and hung out with the likes of Cath Carroll and Liz Naylor, a pair of lesbian feminists who steered the ill-fated band Glass Animals and ran the local zine *City Fun* out of Boon's New Hormones headquarters.

Carroll and Naylor were ultimately tapped by Boon to manage Ludus, who were at the peak of their run, having released two LPs (*The Seduction* and *Danger Came Smiling*) plus an EP (*Completement Nue Au Soleil*) in 1982. With Linder at the helm, Ludus continued to push artistic boundaries with its music and presentation.

An invitation to the opening night of the Hacienda, held on May 21, 1982. During the summer that followed, both Marr and Morrissey were regulars at the nightclub launched by the members of New Order, their manager Rob Gretton, and Factory Records' owner Tony Wilson. *MDMarchive.co.uk*

At their November 5 gig at the Hacienda that year, Linder wore a meat dress, under which she revealed a large strap-on dildo. As she delivered songs like "Vagina Gratitude" and "Bloody Chamber," her managers handed out pornographic pictures wrapped in raw meat.

The controversial exhibition—which was a reaction to the fact that the Hacienda regularly showed pornography—proved to be the final Manchester performance by Ludus. Three months later, Linder's longtime loyal friend Morrissey—who had just made his live debut at the nearby Ritz four weeks earlier—would take the stage with Marr at New Order's venue for the very first time.

A Delicate Bloom

While it has never been publicly known if Marr knew or even cared about Morrissey's sexual proclivities at this stage of their relationship, according to Liz Naylor, "Steven was a lot more of an active gay man than he ever let on."

Speaking to Tony Fletcher, both Carroll and Naylor explained there were times at the height of their friendship when Morrissey would become sulky. He might even shut down on his friends, especially if he didn't agree with a remark.

Steven may not have had much money, but it wouldn't keep him from allowing extravagance into his life. At times in 1982, he was known to blow through a substantial portion of his unemployment check in wine bars, hanging out with hairdressers from Vidal Sassoon.

All the same, flagrant homosexuality found little acceptance in early-'80s Manchester. If Morrissey was an extremely private person, then as now, Naylor believed he harbored feelings of confusion, fear, and uncertainty about his place in the world, just as she and Carroll did about their lesbianism.

Although he felt comfortable enough to make campy remarks with his friends, he never felt comfortable enough to confide with them seriously about his intimate affairs with others. "There was a part of Steven that we never saw, a part of him that had personal relationships with people," Carroll told the Smiths' biographer. "I think we got the sense that behind that wall was some stuff that wouldn't be quite so easy to deal with."

It wasn't until a 1986 interview with *Melody Maker*'s Len Brown that the singer gave his first public indication that he might have led an alternative lifestyle. "The gay scene in Manchester was a little bit heavy for me," he confessed after several years of ambiguity, before adding, coyly, "I was a delicate bloom."

In Search of an Image

If the gender-bending Cookies cover seemed a curious choice to Hibbert, it made sense when he learned that Johnny and Steven were toying with the idea of playing out as an overtly gay band. From a marketing standpoint, Soft Cell, Culture Club, and Yazoo's Vince Clarke (formerly of Depeche Mode) had already proven that gay imagery in pop music could be well received.

Although Marr had experienced his share of the thriving and exciting gay nightlife of the day in the company of his friends Berry and John Kennedy, he wasn't homosexual. Neither was Hibbert, who had a daughter with his girlfriend. And although it seemed likely that Morrissey might be gay, he was in no way ready to carry the torch as a gay star. On the singer's insistence, the band dropped the idea of being a "gay band" and instead decided to take a more fashionable and artistic approach to the pop market that might appeal to a broader audience.

Hibbert was given a haircut by Berry and a rockabilly-inspired fashion makeover that included vintage jeans and bowling shirts to better align him with his bandmates. That fall, the trio participated in a photo shoot in Manchester. The photos would be included in a promotional kit that the band was putting together to help market themselves to clubs, labels, and writers.

10

If the People Stare, Then the People Stare

The Smiths Solidify

Decibelle Demo

After a series of rehearsals with Hibbert at Marr's place, the Smiths moved forward with plans to record their first official demo at Decibelle, Hibbert's place of employment in the early days of August 1982. Because Morrissey and Johnny had yet to settle on a drummer, the guitarist solicited Freak Party's Simon Wolstencroft to participate in the session.

Wolstencroft had not met Morrissey before he came in to track versions of "Suffer Little Children" and "The Hand That Rocks the Cradle." The eight-hour overnight session in the eight-track studio was notable in that it marked the rare occasion of Johnny singing backing vocals on the latter song, while the ending of the former included creepy laughter from Morrissey's friend Annalisa Jablonska.

"Suffer"—which Steven had written about Manchester's notorious Moors murders, when Ian Brady and Myra Hindley murdered five children between 1963 and '65—was decidedly unique. Marr upped its spookiness by adding a snippet of schoolyard children at play and layering it with a waltzing piano part he recorded on his landlady's piano.

In Search of a Drummer

With the Decibelle demo in place to solicit live gigs and pursue a recording deal, the Smiths needed a permanent fixture on drums, as "Funky Si" Wolstencroft had no interest in the band's somber musical approaches. He also couldn't stand Morrissey.

Drummer Bill Anstee—who had previously played with Marr in Sister Ray and in another band with Hibbert—jammed with them too, but he wasn't the right fit either. He disliked the music and especially Morrissey's lyrics and singing style. He told Fletcher, "I would have had a total personality clash with Morrissey if I'd stayed around."

A former St. Mary's classmate of Morrissey's named Gary Farrell—who had played in a band with future Easterhouse members Ivor and Andy Perry—was also approached. Although Steven had once been friendly with Gary, he had Marr look him up and hand over a copy of the Decibelle demo for consideration, but Farrell didn't care for the songs.

Hibbert's drummer in the Adorables didn't make the cut either. A fourth candidate, Guy Ainsworth, tried out at the band's new rehearsal spot inside Spirit Studios on Tariff Street, where Dale was now working after being offered a partnership. But Ainsworth sensed there was tension between Morrissey, Marr, and Hibbert and decided he wasn't interested in that kind of working arrangement.

Joyce Joins

At the time of his audition to play drums in the Smiths at Spirit Studios, Mike Joyce knew Johnny Marr through his Chorlton flatmate Pete Hope, and had previously been aware of him through his work at X-Clothes and as a member of the local music scene. Joyce had also met Dale Hibbert a few years earlier, when both were part of the Manchester Musicians Collective—a movement that allowed for experimental, avant-garde, punk, and new-wave bands to come together and perform for a broader audience than they might otherwise draw individually.

As a teenager in the late 1970s, Joyce had played drums in local punk band the Hoax. He was still eighteen months into his stint with his second band, the Belfast-by-way-of-Manchester punk outfit Victim, when Hope told him that Marr was looking for a drummer for his new band.

Joyce sensed that Marr was destined to be a star. He already knew he was a great guitarist, and he had the look down pat with his biker boots, faded jeans, and white polo-neck shirt.

Joyce was unfamiliar with any Smiths songs when he dropped in to play a new original—"What Difference Does It Make?"—and the aforementioned Cookies number as part of his tryout for the band. It's important to note that Joyce couldn't have taken his audition too seriously, as he had taken a handful of psychedelic mushrooms before he even walked into the room.

"I started playing," he told *Mojo* in August 1997. "I was looking around at Morrissey and I saw this dark figure in a long overcoat, kind of walking stealthily around the room. By the time we finished, I was pretty out of it."

Joyce was tripping by the time he stepped out from behind his drums. Equally intrigued and intimidated by Morrissey, and thrilled by the sound of the band, he decided that, if asked, he would quit Victim and join the Smiths. He later told some friends that he thought the group was fantastic and might be the next big thing. He remembered telling Hope, "I think they could be the next Psychedelic Furs!" and explained to *Mojo*'s Johnny Rogan, "That was as big as I could see then. I thought that was huge."

Elsewhere, in 2008, Joyce spoke again about his first impressions of Morrissey and Marr, remembering how Johnny looked cool with his quiff haircut and a three-quarter-length jacket. The eccentric singer in the room was a little harder to figure out. "I didn't really get Morrissey at all," he told music blog *All in the Game.* "I hardly spoke to him; just furtive glances, nothing more than that."

Just the same, Joyce made a strong impression, and Marr quickly offered him a spot in the band. Mike asked for a day or two to think about it, but soon made his mind up after Johnny played him their Decibelle demo. "I thought it was the best thing I'd ever heard, both musically and lyrically," he told *Record Mirror* in '84. Although he still needed to give notice to Victim, he knew being asked to join the Smiths was "a once in a lifetime opportunity."

When he ran into Johnny and Angie at the Gallery days later, at a gig by Australian favorites the Church, Joyce was sure he was making the right decision. At nineteen, the drummer—who had named his kit "Elsie"—had already outgrown punk. Marr's band offered him a chance to grow musically and to try something new. He told Johnny he was in, although he continued to play in Victim as well for several months.

Mike Joyce

Michael Adrian Paul Joyce was born on June 1, 1963, in Chorlton-on-Medlock in inner-city Manchester to Irish parents—his father came from Galway and his mother from County Kildaire. He was the youngest of four boys and a girl who lived in one of the old terraced houses near the landmark Holy Name Church until 1970, when the family moved to a council estate in Fallowfield, south Manchester.

If the indoor plumbing was a step up, the house was still crowded for a family of seven. Like Marr's friend Andrew Berry, Joyce attended St. Gregory's Grammar school, where he could often be found pounding out rhythms on his wooden-topped desk. Mike petitioned his parents for a drum kit, but it wasn't until his oldest brother left home that there was enough space in his bedroom for the teenager to keep a secondhand set. In spite of the noise, his mother was actually relieved, because Michael had already worn a hole in the family's sofa by continually practicing on its cushions with her knitting needles.

Mike selected a red kit, just like his hero John Maher from the Buzzcocks, after witnessing the band play live in 1978. He was so taken with the band that he had all of their records, including bootlegs, and once even knocked on front man Pete Shelley's door.

By the end of the '70s, Joyce had left school and moved out of the family home. While still a teenager, he lived first in Hulme and then Whalley Range before settling in the bohemian enclave of Chorlton-cum-Hardy, where he lived with roommate Hope until sometime after he joined the Smiths.

The Hoax

Mike drew heavily on the Maher's style when he first aligned with the Hoax in March 1979. This fledgling punk group consisted of vocalist Ian Chambers,

The sleeve for *Only the Blind Can See in the Dark*, the four-song EP by fledgling punk band the Hoax—featuring drummer Mike Joyce—that was released in December 1979. *Boredteenagers.co.uk*

guitarist Andy Farley (a.k.a. Jeremy Fox), bassist Steve Mardy (a.k.a. Socks), and Joyce. In October of that year, the quartet recorded a four-song EP at Rochdale's Cargo Studios titled *Only the Blind Can See in the Dark*, which featured the tracks "Oh Darling," "We All Hate Myself," "Take It Easy," and "Storm Trooper." That lineup lasted just nine months before Chambers quit in December 1979, just prior to the record's release, after falling out with Mike over a girl.

The group carried on, with Fox assuming lead vocals, and in January 1980 the band—now a trio—returned to Cargo to track an eight-song EP titled *So What*, which was eventually released that June. Boasting the originals "Rats in the Cellar," "Some Say," "Nice Girls," "Ich, Habe Keine Spur," "Radio D.J.," "T.V. Addict," "Rich Folk," and "Schizophrenia," the EP—like its predecessor—was pressed for the group's own Hologramme Music label in a limited run of 2,000 copies.

Fox, Socks, and Joyce carried onward, releasing a four-track 12-inch EP titled *Quite in the Sixpennys* in late 1980. It featured the tracks "ANTOK," "One in a Crowd," "Out You Go," and "Locked Out." Then, following a short tour of Belgium in early 1981, Joyce was recruited to play in Victim.

Victim

Formed in Belfast in 1977 by Bowie worshipper and Jam fanatic Wes Graham (bass/vocals), Victim went through a variety of lineups before solidifying around guitarist Joe Zero and—after a high-profile tour supporting the Damned in 1979—settling in Manchester, where they signed with TJM Records.

Despite the release of singles like "Why Are Fire Engines Red?" and "The Teen Age," Victim floundered with management and membership shifts. In early 1981—after the addition of drummer Mike Joyce—they finally got down to recording new demos and perfecting a lengthy, experimental rendition of the T. Rex classic "20th Century Boy."

Outside of Victim, Joyce also kept busy providing drum lessons throughout Manchester, although it had more to do with keeping occupied than it did with need. According to Johnny Rogan's book *Morrissey and Marr: The Severed Alliance*, Joyce had received a substantial settlement in the prior year for injuries he had incurred in an earlier car accident.

In May 1982, the group embarked on a U.K. tour, which included high-profile shows in Liverpool and London, as well as a local gig at Portland Bars, but by the summer of 1982, Mike was considering his options beyond Wes and Joe. It wasn't until November—three months after his audition for the Smiths—that Joyce informed the other members of Victim that he was leaving. Mike had just been in the studio with Graham and Zero, recording the songs "Cause or Consequence" and "The Bluff Brigade" for a planned single. The news was not well received, and the single was never issued. Victim were over.

Supporting Blue Rondo

The Smiths took the public stage for the first time on October 4, 1982, at the Ritz on Whitworth Street, as the supporting act for Blue Rondo à la Turk—a London-based jazz-inspired pop ensemble fronted by Chris Sullivan. The gig was promoted by Berry and his partner John Kennedy and billed as "An Evening of Pure Pleasure." In addition to the live bands, the event also featured a fashion show, a drag artist, and a nearly nude dance ensemble.

Morrissey, Marr, Joyce, and Hibbert followed a Latin jazz DJ named Hewan. They were introduced by Morrissey's old friend James Maker, in French, to the sounds of Klaus Naomi's "The Cold Song." Maker then danced alongside the band in drag—complete with ladies' shoes—while shaking maracas and a tambourine through the Smiths' set.

While Maker's exhibitionist streak could have overshadowed "Suffer Little Children," "The Hand That Rocks the Cradle," "I Want a Boy for My Birthday," and a new original, "Handsome Devil," he wasn't permitted to leave the chalk circle that Morrissey had drawn on the stage, and the Smiths' short, sharp set stood on its own. Fearing Blue Rondo's audience would be unreceptive, Marr charged the band up, and they took the stage with an aggressive approach, despite being apprehensive.

"I was pretty nervous," Marr told *Mojo* in June 2004, admitting in a subsequent interview that he had knocked his guitar out of tune on the way to the stage. "I counteracted it with heaps and heaps of attitude. I knew we were gonna be one fairly confusing prospect for the audience. . . . I knew there was nothing around like us."

There were some other awkward moments during the show. Because the support band was forbidden to alter the headliner's stage setup, Morrissey was required to crouch in order to sing into a microphone that was set too low, while Rourke pounded right through the skin of his snare drum. When he asked to borrow a snare from the headlining act, he was snubbed, leaving him to play without this key piece of kit.

Just the same, the gig was impressive. Marr's musicianship was instantly memorable, and Morrissey's stage presence was as massive as it was unique at that introductory gig—at least as far as Joe Moss, the group's acting manager, was concerned. Moss praised Johnny afterward and gave him a massive boost of confidence while encouraging him to make some subtle changes to the group that would have lasting effect. By the time of the Smiths' second live performance, Hibbert would no longer be in the fold, while Maker was on borrowed time.

Dancing Dale Gets the Boot

Although Morrissey was initially fine with his friend Maker's ancillary antics, Dale Hibbert's performing style did not sit well with the singer, who didn't want a dancing bassist taking attention away from his stage. In his opinion, the rhythm section of a group should be replaceable. Even if they hadn't exactly conveyed it to the others in their budding outfit, it had been established early on by the partners that he and Marr *were* the Smiths.

Hibbert was out of the Smiths by the end of 1982. Because of his domestic situation, his full-time studio-engineering job, and his partnership at Spirit, he wasn't going to be in a position to tour—an essential part of the Smiths establishing themselves as a successful band. Furthermore, he wasn't used to following someone else's lead. Speaking to Fletcher nearly thirty years after he parted with the Smiths, he admitted that the thought had crossed his mind that Marr had only asked him to play bass in the band because he had access to a studio for practice and demo purposes. All the same, Dale preferred the idea that he was sacked because his bass playing was inferior.

i-D

As a result of the gig supporting Blue Rondo, the Smiths were interviewed by *i-D* in late 1982 for the magazine's February 1983 issue. It was their first real press feature, and it focused on the band's Manchester presence, their return to a basic sound, and—undoubtedly because of Johnny's day job—their fashion sense.

Marr spoke of how the Smiths were different because they were forgoing technology—as opposed to most modern U.K. bands—in favor of real musicianship. In reverting back to the formula of guitar, bass, and drums, he said, they were unique. "[Synthesizers] will never replace the real thing. You don't get any depth or real sounds."

Elsewhere, Johnny opined that being in a young band in Manchester provided better opportunities than one might get in London. With the successes of Joy Division, New Order, and other, lesser-known groups, there was a greater opportunity to remain original and avoid becoming part of short-lived trend.

Of course, as an elementary and orderly guitar outfit, the Smiths had planned all along to serve as the antidote to synthesizer bands like Soft Cell, OMD, Depeche Mode, and the Human League. In line with their traditional instruments and their simplistic moniker, the group's straightforward but innovative sound was deliberate.

The group's presentation was also uncomplicated: Levi's, polo shirts or button-down shirts, cardigan sweaters, and black Oxford shoes. When asked for his take on fashion, Steven explained how style had more to do with attitude than fashion. "You can't become stylish—either you are or you aren't," he said. "But you can become fashionable. You can go out and buy [clothes], but if you wear it badly it means nothing."

Rourke Returns

Andy Rourke had been working at a Trafford Park lumberyard when Marr stopped over for a visit on the back of Hibbert's motorbike in late '82. As the two talked privately, Dale had little knowledge yet that Johnny was hoping to replace him with his old friend.

Johnny and Andy had been estranged for a year, and Rourke was thrilled when Marr called him and offered him the opportunity to play with the Smiths. As much as Johnny had also wanted to reconnect with Andy, his phone call had a purpose: after just one gig, the Smiths had been offered a demo deal with a major label. The bassist jumped at the opportunity.

The Drone Demo

Following the Ritz show, and with a copy of the Smiths' Decibelle Demo in hand, a college friend of Marr's named Tony O'Connor, who had just gotten a job as a junior A&R representative with the massive record label EMI, helped the Smiths land a demo deal with the London-based company. Morrissey accompanied him to a hastily arranged meeting, where they played the songs for the department's head, Hugh Stanley-Clarke. Much to the band's surprise, the label financed a demo in a proper recording studio.

"I got a phone call from Johnny saying they were going to do a demo at Drone studio in Manchester and did I fancy coming down," Rourke told *Q Classic* in March 2006. "I went down and we recorded 'Handsome Devil' and 'Miserable Lie.' I was winging it. I didn't know the songs at all."

The "Drone Demo," as it would become known to fans, was recorded in December 1982 and marked the first recorded effort by the Smiths with their proper lineup. Along with the songs cited by Rourke above, a third track—an early version of "What Difference Does It Make?"—featured a low-sung vocal by Morrissey. Additionally, the reverb-laden early rendition of "Miserable Lie"—replete with alternate lyrics—clocked in at seven minutes, and was played in a higher key to accommodate the singer's natural range.

Unfortunately, the final results were too offbeat to sustain the interest of EMI. If the musicianship was impressive, Morrissey still hadn't completely found his voice. At times his vocal delivery seemed to lack confidence; he sounded uncertain, and was presented in a lower than ideal pitch. As a result, the Smiths' three-song recording was rejected in early 1983.

Moss Signs On

As Morrissey, Marr, Joyce, and Rourke entered 1983, Hibbert's Spirit Studios was no longer an option for rehearsing. Joe Moss happily stepped up and offered Johnny a sizable space in a large room above a third Crazy Face location on Portland Street in central Manchester, at no charge to the band. According to Morrissey, this arrangement allowed the band to hone their craft and build their confidence. "It is here that we are free to re-order the universe," he wrote of their practice space, some thirty years later, in *Autobiography*.

Moss was now officially acting as the group's manager—with Morrissey's blessing. He helped them to acquire a P.A. for rehearsals and gigs, set about getting a van for touring, and lured Marr away from X-Clothes to run his basement store on Portland Street. Joe also opened his home to Johnny, who moved from Rohde's into the Moss family house.

These arrangements all served Johnny well. Inside the shop he had the phone at his disposal for store and band business, while Moss—who was as much of a father figure as an adviser—got him to work on time. After Marr locked up the shop each night around 5 p.m. he would meet his bandmates by the freight elevator, where they would ride up to the fourth floor and play into the night.

Practice Makes Perfect

In response to some of the flaws in their first show, Joe, Johnny, and Morrissey decided that it made the best sense to wait until everything had been perfected before they played out again. Inside the Smiths' practice room, Marr's guitar prowess meshed ideally with Joyce's powerful drumming and, now, Rourke's thumping bass work. Following his involvement in the Drone recordings, Johnny had officially recruited his old pal for the bassist's spot in the group. In Marr's eyes, it was a role Andy was destined to fill, and he was now sure he had the right musicians in place to bring his band back into the light.

Atop their musical foundation, Morrissey would cultivate his own innovative vocal style. In his 2013 book, he defines the opportunity to front this band as "a gift from Jesus." They worked persistently together, eliminating any kinks in originals like "Still Ill."

As the band perfected their approach, Marr was content to be Keith Richards to Morrissey's Mick Jagger. Johnny understood that there was something noble about being the propeller that gave the Smiths flight. His philosophy—as he relayed it to *Pitchfork* in April 2012—was to "be appropriate to the song, be interesting, and be a great guitar player—but none of that showboating shit."

Morrissey recalled going from pessimistic closet case to an enthusiastic front man in rehearsals and, later, as he took the stage. "Suddenly, life was close to me," he remembers, in his book. "As I belted out 'Miserable Lie' with the full of my body, I no longer felt like an overgrown forget-me-not."

First Impressions

It took Steven quite some time to open up to Andy and Mike during this early stage. At practices, Rourke and Joyce remember him as pretty shy, if not aloof. When he wasn't singing, he would stand patiently in a dark long overcoat, his nose in a book.

"Morrissey was at the far end of the room pacing up and down, looking at the floor with the microphone in his hand, like a caged bear," Joyce told *Q Classic*. "It weirded me out. He didn't really speak to me, just looked over and said hello. Johnny was the go-between. He did all the communication."

While Rourke had complete faith in the music, he wasn't so sure about Johnny's eccentric choice of vocalist. Although he liked the lyrics, he had qualms with Morrissey, and their shared bus rides home from practice only added to his doubts. Having a normal conversation with the singer was impossible. They had little in common; Andy was five years Steven's junior, and Morrissey's balance of shyness and arrogance left the bassist with nothing to do but count streetlights.

Despite this early awkwardness, Morrissey knew that the four members of the band looked good together, but sometimes his eccentricities and Marr's steely focus became too much for both Mike and Andy, who each nearly quit on occasion, only for Johnny to go after them and convince them to stay. Eventually, Andy used his sense of humor to connect with Morrissey. His ability to cut through tensions would become essential to the Smiths.

Together, they were a remarkable force, where tough musicianship met with the peculiar ferocity of Steven Patrick Morrissey. As Joe Moss told *Mojo* in June 2004, "It was just immediately stunning. It felt unique."

Prolific Partners

With each successive cassette of music that Marr handed off to his singer at practice, Morrissey would return with words to match. Johnny continued to be surprised and pleased with his front man and thrilled by his originality. Together, they were quite prolific, working up the compositions that would ultimately define their auspicious debut.

"He was so unorthodox, and he really had his own style," Marr told *Musician* in September '89, citing Morrissey's wit, insight, uniqueness, and dedication as they tweaked early numbers like "These Things Take Time," "Jeane," and "What Do You See in Him?"

"Hand in Glove"

During a family visit one Sunday in January, Marr picked up a guitar at parent's house in Wythenshawe and started playing the riff that would become "Hand in Glove." Afraid he might forget it if he put the guitar down, he played it over while Angie drove her VW to Morrissey's.

Brown told him to toughen it up and give it more of a Stooges vibe. When he arrived unannounced, Morrissey joked that he didn't have an appointment. Marr put the tune to tape, left it with the singer, and went home. Steven finished the intensely personal but remarkably universal love song that same night in just under two hours.

When they came together to play it, it was immediately liberating, and it remained one of Morrissey's proudest accomplishments some two years later. "It was to be our first record and it was important to me that there'd be something searingly poetic in it, in a lyrical sense, and yet jubilant at the same time," he told *Star Hits* in 1985, citing it as his favorite lyric yet. "They're two extreme emotions, and I wanted to blend them together."

The Smiths Take Manhattan Sound

Ahead of his band's second live show—and their first with the lineup that would define the Smiths until their demise—Marr got in the ear of everyone who knew him as "Johnny from the shop" to make sure they turned out. X-Clothes and Crazy Face loyalists like Factory's Tony Wilson, music writer Jon Savage, New Hormones' boss Richard Boon, regular customers, friends, and acquaintances were all asked to come out to see his new band at Manhattan Sound, an underground disco he frequented, for their Tuesday night performance.

At weekends the venue—located in the cellar of a building around the corner from the shop—catered to a gay clientele, but on Tuesdays the promoter, Rick Stonell, booked aspiring bands for his "Quando Club" night. On January 25, 1983, about three hundred or so local music fans paid one pound each to watch this historic Smiths gig unfold.

Before the performance, Marr threw up with nerves. Then the band blew everyone away.

Wilson and his Factory denizens dropped in on the show, which was a warm-up for the group's next gig at the Hacienda, and placed the Smiths alongside another local group named Foreign Press. Although there was no stage, no drum riser, and no monitors, practice had served the band well. Their performance—which included the original songs "Handsome Devil," "The Hand That Rocks the Cradle," "What Difference Does It Make?," "What Do You See in Him?," and "These Things Take Time"—was considered exceptional by many in attendance, with Wilson telling *Mojo* in 2004, "I was blown away. It was fantastic."

The Smiths had vastly improved in the months since their live unveiling with Hibbert. Image-wise, Johnny assumed a rockabilly look, while Steven sported the quiff with which he would soon become synonymous. During "Miserable Lie," the gig's finale, Morrissey surprised everyone—including his bandmates—by pulling confetti from his pockets and letting it fly into the air. It was an unexpected visual that resonated with the audience, which also included a handful of music business executives that Moss had invited up from London. "As soon as [Morrissey] went on he became something different,"

Rourke remembered to the *Guardian*'s Dave Simpson in January 2012. "It took your breath away."

Things looked incredibly promising for the new foursome that night, with Morrissey ally and *City Fun* fanzine scribe Cath Carroll praising his "dreamily affected baritone." The only hiccup would be blamed on a video crew that had been brought in to film the event, with unfortunate results. Things went upside down with the shoot's lighting, which glared blindingly against the establishment's mirrored walls. Wisely, Moss demanded that the crew scotch the lights just a few numbers into the Smiths' eight-song set.

Maker was again with the band to introduce them onstage and provide his dancing routine, but with Morrissey serving as the focal point, his old friend's presence was unnecessary, and he was relieved of his duties thereafter. As an aside, it's interesting to consider that the Spring Gardens venue had been showing pornographic films in its adjacent lounge as the Smiths conquered Manchester.

Rourke and Marr and Moss

Andy and Johnny picked up where they left off as friends in the Smiths' newly solidified lineup. While Morrissey was Marr's writing collaborator, it was Rourke who kept Johnny happy at practices and performances. "He could switch my intensity down," Marr told Fletcher, explaining how the bassist kept him grounded. In turn, Johnny raised Andy up, bolstered his confidence, and kept him from falling back into the drugs that had affected their friendship in the past.

Johnny's lone requirement of Rourke to remain in the Smiths was that he kept himself free of drugs. For Andy, that was easier said than done. Marr could tell by looking into his old friend's eyes that he had in fact been using during the earliest days of the band. Johnny called him out on it, expressing his frustration. But instead of booting Andy out, he confided in Moss—and only Moss—unwilling to share Rourke's addiction with Joyce or Morrissey. He made it clear to Joe that he loved Andy and wanted to keep him in the band.

Moss offered to open up his home, setting up a makeshift apartment in his basement, where the bassist was able to dry out and keep himself free of temptation. As a result, Rourke was able to stay off of heroin for a while and focus on the band without distraction. The Smiths gave him a purpose and a future. He would be forever grateful for Joe's generosity and willingness to try to help.

Flowers for the Hacienda

When the Smiths took the stage at the Hacienda on Friday, February 4, 1983, Morrissey stepped onstage holding a bouquet of flowers and informed the audience, "We are the Smiths, not Smiths." This stemmed from the confusing way the group had been billed on posters advertising them as the support act for headliners 52nd Street—a local multicultural funk band that had recently signed to Factory Records.

"The thing to be in 1983 is handsome," the front man told the crowd before the band capably plowed through their show opener, "These Things Take Time." At the song's end, the singer thrashed the bouquet against the stage floor, creating a memorable spectacle inside the cold warehouse club that trumped the confetti of a week and a half earlier. "What Difference Does It Make?" was offered at a slower pace than became its trademark and incorporated alternate lyrics ahead of "Handsome Devil," "Jeane," and the aforementioned "What Do You See in Him?," which would re-emerge a few months later as "Wonderful Woman." "Hand in Glove" was also rendered with a noticeably slower pacing, and the set concluded with "Miserable Lie."

Fashion-wise, the band was suitably groomed by Andrew Berry, who gave them each "quiff" hairstyles, which combined the pompadour and the flat-top and was derived from the French term "coiffe." Morrissey took the stage in a woman's extra-large blouse, with beads, that he had bought at the outsize clothing shop Evans. All eyes were on the singer, who writhed around on the floor and yodeled unexpectedly with a gladioli coming from his pocket. "It was theatrical, quite balletic," Rourke told Simpson in 2012. "None of this was rehearsed. I remember watching the faces of the people at the front. It was just shock: 'What the hell is this?'"

Clearly it was showmanship. *NME* writer Jim Shelley agreed, publishing a review of the show in March that heralded their confidence and live strength. Shelley compared the Smiths to acclaimed modern bands like Magazine, Josef K, and the Fire Engines, insisting, "The four Smiths were proud and powerful, pale and angular, a formidable and inventive force . . . The Smiths should soon be capable of reaching the greatest of heights!"

The cost of admission for this now-legendary performance was only £1.50 in advance or £2.50 at the door.

Dismissed by Factory

Although Tony Wilson had complimentary things to say about the Smiths in hindsight (as evidenced by his remarks above, from 2012), at the time, he and his Factory partner/New Order manager Rob Gretton rejected the band's first demos. When Wilson shared his opinion of the Smiths with Morrissey around this time, he criticized Marr's musical approach, comparing his Rickenbacker sound to the Byrds and knocking "Hand in Glove" for being too similar to Bowie's "Rebel Rebel." For "Steve the Nutter"—as Wilson had long described the eccentric scenester—the feedback felt hurtful and disconcerting.

This One Is Different— Because It's Us!

Signing to Rough Trade

Oh, Hell

The Smiths were booked to open for Richard Hell & the Voidoids at Rafters in Manchester on February 21, 1983. New York punk icon Hell, best known for his single "Blank Generation," had gotten his start with Television, and was now touring in support of his second studio album, 1982's poorly received *Destiny Street*.

Inside the Oxford Street venue, the Smiths delivered a succinct but charismatic set that left an impression on a local singer named Tim Booth. Booth was the front man for the upstart band James, who would sign to Factory Records and have modest success in the 1980s before going on to fame in the early 1990s with massive U.K. hits like "Sit Down" and "Laid." Booth was left awestruck by the Smiths' performance and just how confident and prepared Morrissey and Marr seemed for the next phase of their career.

Strawberry Studios

Following their rejection by EMI and subsequent dismissal by the powers that be at Factory, the Smiths picked themselves up, dusted themselves off, and kept at it. With the undeniably strong "Hand in Glove" in their back pockets and the financial support of Moss—who fronted them £250—the band booked studio time at Strawberry Studios in Stockport on February 27 to record the track as a possible first single.

Musically, the session was remarkable, with Marr's chiming Gretsch guitar and piercing harmonica lines meshing superbly with the crack rhythms of Rourke and Joyce.

Unfortunately, at the completion of the ten-hour session with Chris Nagle— Strawberry's house engineer and a frequent collaborator of Joy Division producer Martin Hannett—Morrissey was displeased with his vocal performance.

A week later, the singer returned to the studio to perfect his part, and by the time the song was mixed, with its unorthodox fade-in opening, the men of the Smiths had an outstanding A-side under their belts. A live rendition of

"Handsome Devil," taken from the soundboard at the group's recent Hacienda show, was given to Nagle for preparation as its B-side.

For Joyce, this session would remain one of the high points of his time in the Smiths, even though it was one of their earliest milestones. "Morrissey said his life began with recording that song, and it was like that for me," the drummer told *Q Classic* in March 2006. "When we listened back to it at Strawberry Studios, it was like we'd put into practice everything we'd learnt so far. I was thinking, 'Fuckin' 'ell, 'ow good are we?' If the band had split up right then, it wouldn't have mattered. We'd made one of the all-time great records."

Approaching New Hormones

With their proposed single in hand, Morrissey and Marr approached early supporter Richard Boon, who had managed the Buzzcocks, Ludus, and the Beach Club, and owned the Manchester label New Hormones. Unfortunately, their timing wasn't ideal.

Boon informed them that his record company was about to go under. As much as he loved "Hand in Glove," he would have to say no to the Smiths. But before he did so, he gave the group some advice, which follows below. Ironically—and unbeknown to the band—Boon would soon move to London to work as the production manager at Rough Trade, where he would have a significant involvement in the group's future.

Portland Street

In the event the Smiths' label pursuits proved unsuccessful, Marr and Moss—on Boon's advice—had a backup plan. They would press up copies of their debut single under the imprint Portland Street, replete with a picture of Moss's residence on the record's label.

Although this approach would require Johnny and Joe to assume marketing and manufacturing duties, it was a challenge both would be up for, if necessary. But after members of the Smiths traveled to London to cold call the aforementioned Rough Trade label, this alternate course of action wouldn't be required.

Simon Edwards

One Friday afternoon in March 1983, Johnny Marr hopped on a train to London with plans to visit Rough Trade Records. In doing so, he hoped to secure either a proper record deal for the Smiths, or—at the very least—a distribution agreement for their self-issued single. It was on Richard Boon's recommendation that Johnny and Morrissey should see Simon Edwards at Rough Trade, although it was actually Rourke who traveled south with Johnny for the weekend trip.

Edwards was the man in charge of sales and distribution for both Rough Trade and its profitable distribution arm, the Cartel—a record distribution business that thrived by helping companies like Factory get U.K. hits like Joy Division's "Love Will Tear Us Apart" and New Order's "Blue Monday" into the hands of record buyers.

Despite the fact that they had arrived without an appointment, dropping Boon's name was all Marr would need to do to get a quick meeting in Edwards' office. Edwards wasted no time playing "Hand in Glove" on his office stereo. He was immediately pleased with its unique but likable presentation—specifically the harmonica part—and offered the Smiths a distribution agreement. Marr was glad to hear that was an option, but he was pushing for a record deal and asked if he could see Rough Trade's owner, Geoff Travis. Edwards told him Travis wasn't around and that he would have to come back the following week.

Inflammable Material, the 1979 album by punk band Stiff Little Fingers, was Rough Trade Records' first major success. The label's first LP release, it reached #14 in the U.K. album charts and sold an unexpected 100,000 copies. *Eil.com*

Geoff Travis

Geoff Travis launched the Rough Trade record label in 1978, two years after the start of his successful London record store of the same name. Travis already had a chain of shops in the works by the time he was inspired to press his own records after the French punk act Metal Urbain sought him out and asked him for help in getting their music out.

With the help of customer-turned-employee Steve Montgomery and business partner Richard Scott—also the brainchild behind the Cartel—the company put out singles by Sheffield's Cabaret Voltaire, Belfast's Stiff Little Fingers, Birmingham's Swell Maps, and the London acts the Monochrome Set and Subway Sect in quick succession during its active first year. Then, in 1979, Rough Trade had a massive, unexpected triumph when SLF's album *Inflammable Material*—the company's first long-player—peaked at #14 in the U.K. charts, selling over 100,000 copies and making it a force to be reckoned with.

Alongside the Cartel's lucrative operations, Rough Trade continued to thrive into the early 1980s with up-and-coming bands like Scritti Politti and Aztec Camera. But by 1983, Scritti Politti's contract had been bought out by Virgin, while the success of Aztec Camera's single "Oblivious" meant they too might be leaving the label for a bigger, better deal. All this meant that the label was in need of new talent, and the Smiths couldn't have landed on the Rough Trade doorstep at a better time.

Not that Travis made it easy for Marr, who was asked to come back another time by a secretary and could have very easily followed instructions. But the guitarist suspected he might be being given the slip and found his way back into the building through an open loading bay. Finding his way to Geoff's office with Andy beside him, he waited until the Rough Trade boss was alone and introduced himself.

"I'm in a band from Manchester and you won't have heard anything like this," Marr told Travis, according to a May 2013 interview with the *Daily Mail.* "That's what just came out! Anyway, he was pretty gracious, gave me the brush-off—but he took the tape." The following Monday, back in Manchester, Travis called Joe Moss at the phone number on the cassette. He explained that Rough Trade was interested in releasing "Hand in Glove," and a formal meeting with the group was set.

If Morrissey had been absent from the initial meeting with Travis, the singer was well aware of the company's accomplishments to date and had been in favor of aligning with Rough Trade or a label of its ilk. Long before the band actually formed, the singer "knew how he wanted the group to be perceived," Marr told *Record Collector* scribe and future Smiths biographer Johnny Rogan. Rough Trade was a credible and accomplished independent company with a vast reach—the perfect solution for leveraging the Smiths.

Rock Garden

As luck would have it, Joe Moss had arranged for the Smiths' first-ever London gig to be held at the Rock Garden on March 23. It was an opportunity for Rough Trade's founder and owner to witness his potential new signing in a live setting. The band were erroneously billed as a quintet in an advertisement that might have been penned before the exit of dancer James Maker and described the Smiths' guitar-pop sound as "difficult to pigeon-hole." They were supported by a local band called Two Chances.

Travis was amazed by the group's live show. "I see Morrissey onstage as pretty much a revelation at the Rock Garden," he marveled to *Rough Trade: Labels Unlimited* author Rob Young in 2006. "Because he was fully formed. Dancing about, it was great. Then again, I remember some people were going, 'I'm not sure about this lot.' But you have to have that kind of ridiculous belief. If you take a consensus of opinion, you've had it."

Travis also couldn't help but think he was on to something substantial after he read the remarkably positive review of the Smiths' Hacienda gig from the month before that ran in that morning's *New Musical Express* ahead of their London debut. Rough Trade's head honcho was also given copies of press clippings from *i-D* and *City Fun*, which made clear that Morrissey and Marr weren't only praiseworthy—they were capable of handling themselves in front of journalists, too.

As Travis' colleague Mike Hinc stood alongside him, he watched as his friend appeared astonished by the Smiths. Geoff's tells meant only one thing—he had to have them on his label. After the show, Travis approached Joe Moss. He told him that he no longer wanted to release a mere single by the Smiths. He wanted to sign the group to a multi-album contract.

All Trade Booking

During Johnny and Morrissey's first meetings with Travis, it was recommended that the band align with All Trade Booking, a concert-booking firm that he was affiliated with that was run by Mike Hinc and Nick Hobbs. If this might have been a conflict of interest, it also seemed logical. After all, the agency's office was in the Rough Trade building on Blenheim Crescent, and it handled clients like Nick Cave's group the Birthday Party, Edwyn Collins' rising pop band Orange Juice, and the Andrew Eldritch–fronted goth outfit Sisters of Mercy.

Hobbs and Hinc were seeking new clients for their stable of touring artists, and Travis introduced Mike to the Smiths when Morrissey and Marr returned to London in April to master "Hand in Glove" for release. As indicated above, Hinc had already seen the band and had previously been tipped about them by his friend Mike Pickering, the soundman at the Hacienda, who had already sent Hinc a cassette of their recent gig for consideration.

In fact, Hinc had already played the Smiths' Hacienda cassette for both Eldritch and Aztec Camera's Roddy Frame, and both gave resounding approvals. In the meantime, Hobbs—who handled All Trade's European gigs—had also somehow gotten a copy of the band's EMI demo from a contact who knew a friend and sometime roadie for the band named Ollie May.

Long-term Contract

Although there had been no competing label interest when Morrissey and Marr sat down to sign with Rough Trade in April 1983, there were two things that made Travis' company a perfect fit for the pair at the time. The first key factor—which was and still is quite rare in the music business—was that Geoff's deal with them allowed for a 50/50 split of profits from record sales.

If that financial philosophy wasn't enough, Rough Trade was supportive of the Smiths' frugal outlook. The band's stance was spearheaded by Morrissey and—as Marr told Rogan in *Record Collector*—they insisted on "not spending money on bullshit and complete nonsensical things and not being extravagant."

In the presence of Rouke and Joyce, who according to Morrissey were there merely to observe, with drummer Mike signing the document as a reliable witness, Johnny and Morrissey officially signed to the label on April 29, 1983, at which time they received an advance of £3,000. Exactly three months later, an equal amount was disbursed to the pair for sales of the single. The singer and guitarist had since established their own enterprise, Smithdom Ltd., for band business.

When asked by *Sounds* in June 1983 if the label was the ideal choice for quick stardom, Morrissey defended their allegiance to the company. "What we want to achieve CAN be achieved on Rough Trade," he emphasized, confidently adding, "If people want to buy the records, Rough Trade will supply them. No problem."

Despite the connotations of being an indie band, Morrissey was already thinking globally. "I don't really understand what being an independent group means," he continued to Dave McCullough, citing "lesser people" like the Fall. "I don't share their attitude, so I wouldn't want the Smiths to be considered in any particular category."

12

The Good Life Is Out There Somewhere

The Smiths Ascend

Steven Is Dead

With the release of "Hand in Glove," Steven Morrissey ditched his first name for good. Weeks after he started insisting that everyone around him call him by his last name only, the sleeve for the Smiths' debut single asserted he was now known solely as Morrissey. As he would later relay to Nick Kent, he extracted Steven from his name because throughout his life he preferred the way he felt when people addressed him by his surname. In his mind, Steven was dead, although the name would stay in place for legal purposes.

"When the Smiths began, it was very important that I wouldn't be that horrible, stupid, sloppy Steven," he told Elissa van Poznack in July 1984. "I needed to feel differently and rather than adopt some glamorous pop star name, I eradicated Steven which made perfect sense. Suddenly, I was a totally different person."

Legally Marr

Around the same time, Johnny legally changed his last name from Maher to Marr. While he was concerned that it might hurt his parents' feelings, as a musician on the verge of stardom, it just made sense over constantly having to explain he had a different last name.

In truth, Johnny had made the decision years earlier when, at fourteen, he discovered another John Maher from Manchester had risen to popularity as the Buzzcocks drummer. From then on, he told everyone to call him "Marr" even though it had yet to become authorized.

"That shows you how determined I was to make my living as a musician," the guitarist told www.askmeaskmeaskme.com, following on the heels of the glam, punk, and new wave artists who had altered their monikers for the stage. "I changed it legally as soon as I could afford it; I changed it when the Smiths started."

An early publicity still of the Smiths—Andy Rourke, Johnny Marr, Morrissey, and Mike Joyce—shot in late 1983 by photographer Eric Watson. *Author's collection*

Smithdom Ltd.

In May 1983, Morrissey and Marr established the company Smithdom Ltd. as a means to earn income and transact business. As the sole and equal partners, the pair collected songwriting and recording royalties for themselves and performance fees and royalties for themselves, Rourke, and Joyce.

While the group's financial arrangements seemed acceptable to all members on the eve of their first single, the arrangement of Smiths business would result in a tumultuous legal battle in years to come. In 1996, the group's drummer sued famously for unpaid royalties. More on that later.

Pulling Peel and *Sounds*

On May 6, the Smiths took the stage between headliners the Sisters of Mercy and support act the Laughing Clowns at the University of London Union. The gig came courtesy of Mike Hinc, who plugged the band in as a late replacement for a group called Babluna.

With one week to get the word out about "Hand in Glove," Rough Trade's promotional consultant, Scott Piering, brought John Walters, a BBC producer who worked alongside the legendary DJ John Peel, with him. The show, which launched with "You've Got Everything Now" and included "Handsome Devil," "Reel Around the Fountain," and their forthcoming single, left a significant impression on Walters, who asked the band to come to London during the third week in May to record a session for Peel.

Journalist Dave McCullough's review mirrored Walters' approval. The *Sounds* scribe—whom Piering had also invited to the gig—would soon observe how the Smiths "blew nobody headliners Sisters of Mercy off the stage."

Piering

Scott Piering was a San Francisco–born music industry veteran who had previously served as an independent concert promoter in the 1970s, putting on shows in a market dominated by Bill Graham for the likes of Bob Marley & the Wailers at a time when they had been ousted as the opening band on a Sly Stone tour. An allegiance with Island Records' Chris Blackwell stemmed from this arrangement and led to Piering promoting a U.S. tour for the reggae act Third World, who were then managed by Richard Scott.

After a short stint managing the Cramps in New York, Piering was lured to Rough Trade to assist with publicity and promotion efforts at the dawn of the 1980s. Rough Trade's money woes forced Piering to launch his own publicity firm, Appearing PR, where he worked for the company on a project-by-project basis. He also picked up Factory Records as a client and represented the company's biggest band, New Order, and their massive hit, "Blue Monday," which became the biggest-selling U.K. 12-inch single of all time.

"Hand in Glove" Hits the Shelves

May 13, 1983, was a historic day for the Smiths. It marked the release of the band's first single into record shops throughout England. Somewhat controversially, its blue-and-white sleeve featured a picture of a bare-assed model facing away from the camera to the right of the band's name and the song's title. The image was a Jim French photograph selected by Morrissey from *The Nude Male*, a book by Margaret Walters. He had decided that the image was an essential artistic statement, and that it was destined for the cover of "Hand in Glove."

If the visual was a brave, even eclectic one for a rock band to place on the sleeve of their debut single, Morrissey was adamant that it wasn't a gimmick. It was, in fact, the singer's way of defying expectations of gender and transcending boundaries. "I wanted to even the balance out," he told McCullough, soon after the single's emergence. "It's crucial to what we're doing that we're not looking at things from a male stance."

When Rourke's father saw the cover, he was "mortified," the bassist told writer Simon Goddard. "He said to me, 'that's a bloke's bum,' and I said, 'yeah,' but when he asked me why I just didn't have an answer for him."

Surprisingly, the image did little to negatively affect sales, and radio responded quickly. Thanks to Walters' support, both Peel and fellow DJ David Jensen picked up on the song, which was played almost nightly on BBC's Radio 1 throughout June and July 1983. The single, replete with a note of gratitude to Joe Moss inscribed on the sleeve, quickly sold out of its initial pressing of 6,000 copies.

Despite the exposure, "Hand in Glove" somehow failed to crack the Top 50, stalling at #70. It continued to sell steadily for the next eighteen months, however, and remained a fixture on the U.K. independent charts.

Making Friends with the *NME*

The day after "Hand in Glove" was released, the *NME* highlighted the Smiths' "Crisp Songs and Salted Lyrics." The coverage came courtesy of Morrissey's old friend Cath Carroll, who was now writing for the paper, and here delivered a highly favorable piece on the group.

Delivered in Q&A form, the profile allowed for the singer to emphasize the importance of communicating with one's audience, the need for quality pop songs like those that had been written by '60s collaborators Goffin & King and Leiber & Stoller, and his desire to control packaging and artwork.

"This is our product," Morrissey told Carroll, revealing the band's plans for a full album to follow soon. "We haven't come this far for some stranger to step in. We're not hollow musicians."

Extolling the band's abilities, Marr took the opportunity to thrash the many modern acts of the era that were utilizing technology to mask their inferior skills. "We can all play our instruments really well," Johnny explained. "Limited musicians cover up by using synthesizers."

Camden Electric

Mike Hinc booked the Smiths as the support act for popular Mancunian post-punk band the Fall at London's Camden Electric Ballroom on May 21. The Fall, fronted by Mark E. Smith, were supporting their sixth and most recent album, *Room to Live* (a.k.a. *Undilutable Slang Truth!*), at the time.

The London gig came just three days after the foursome's aforementioned Peel session, which is outlined below, and which yielded the first recording of "What Difference Does It Make?" That song was the turning point in the night's set after the band fumbled through "Accept Yourself."

Although the Smiths rendered an iffy version of "Reel Around the Fountain" later in the show, forceful versions of "Hand in Glove" and "Handsome Devil" bookended "The Hand That Rocks the Cradle," a tune that the band would record for their debut album, despite abandoning it from future live shows after this gig.

By the conclusion of their finale, a spirited take on "Miserable Lie," Morrissey, Marr, Rourke, and Joyce had won over the room. In spite of their missteps, the audience's enthusiasm sent them off on a high.

Peel Session

The Smiths' first Peel Session aired on May 31, 1983, two weeks after it had been recorded with BBC engineer Roger Pusey. The fifteen-minute set comprised four previously unreleased songs: "Miserable Lie," "What Difference Does It Make?," "Handsome Devil," and "Reel Around the Fountain."

It was an electrifying time for Marr, who remembered how he still "had a whole lot of romanticism about being in a band and being involved in music" when he spoke to the *NME*'s Dave Haslam in June 1989. "Morrissey in some ways never had that. If we were traveling down to London overnight, to do a Peel session or something, we'd all be excited. Morrissey would just try to make sure he got some sleep and he'd make sure we'd stop on the way for a proper meal."

Two years earlier, in 1987, Peel had discussed the band as part of the BBC radio documentary series *Peeling Back the Years*. The world-famous DJ credited his producer for helping to uncover the group, before explaining that he "liked the fact that I was hearing words being used in popular songs that I wasn't used to hearing."

"[It] pleased me as much as anything else," Peel continued. "And [Morrissey's] voice was not a voice that you could immediately trace back to somebody else. I mean, he wasn't trying to be Marc Bolan or he wasn't trying to be Jim Morrison again. [The Smiths] just arrived from nowhere with a very clear and strong identity, you know. And that is always attractive."

The recordings from the Smiths' "Peel Session" were eventually released on the successful 1984 *Hatful of Hollow* compilation. While the members of the band would never actually meet the revered radio personality to thank him for the career boost during their time together, Morrissey would get the opportunity to meet Peel before his death in 2004.

Handsome Stars

In addition to his live review, London-based *Sounds* scribe Dave McCullough also wrote a one-page feature on the band for the publication's June 1 issue. In the piece, titled "Handsome Devils," he predicted fame for the attractive foursome, citing Marr's red Rickenbacker "machine gun" and Morrissey's penchant for hilariously personal lyrics, while pondering whether Travis' company had the reach to "make this exceptional new group the stars they can very likely be."

"I tremble at the power we have, that's how I feel about the Smiths," Morrissey explained. "It's there and it's going to happen." Asked about his sexuality, the singer admitted an interest in the topic, suggesting that every one of his songs was about sex and proclaiming himself as "a kind of prophet for the fourth sex." Morrissey told McCullough how he was bored with "sexual segregation" and expressed his hope that people would abstain as part of his "new movement of celibacy."

If Marr mentioned a fondness for the Ramones in passing before arrogantly touting his band's own greatness by suggesting that "there is very little good music around except the Smiths," it was the once shy Morrissey who dominated the conversation. When he wasn't listing his favorite feminist writers—Molly Haskell, Marjory Rose, and Susan Brown-Miller—or ignoring an inquiry about child molestation, he took to dismissing popular synthesizer bands of the moment, including Heaven 17 and New Order.

All the same, there was an undeniable camaraderie, confidence, and chemistry between the members of the Smiths in the article's accompanying photo shoot. In the respective photos, Joyce and Rourke hug, as do Morrissey and Marr, the former clutching an armful of gladioli. When asked about the importance of the flowers, the vocalist explained how he first utilized them at the Hacienda in response to the venue's sterile environment, and that he continued to do so because he "wanted some harmony with nature."

Miner's Disaster and Fighting Cocks

The Smiths embarked on their first stint of headlining shows in early June 1983, beginning with a disastrous "Miner's Gala" gig at Cannock Chase in Staffordshire on the 2nd. Following obscure acts like A Dog Named Ego and Shambolic Climate, plus speeches by union officials and Labour Party politicians, the band took the stage to a crowd of mostly intoxicated men who didn't care much for Morrissey's performing style. While the band got through several songs, including the debut of "Wonderful Woman," they were soon booed and pelted with bottles, cans, and cups from the audience, which forced the show to end sooner than planned.

The next night, at Birmingham's Fighting Cocks, the Smiths fared considerably better. Despite the heat, the crowd—which had come to the small venue to see the rising Smiths—was receptive to material like the set opener "You've Got Everything Now" plus upbeat renditions of "What Difference Does It Make?" and "These Things Take Time."

Chewing the Cud

The Smiths went back to support status on June 4, opening for a band called the Decorators. Despite their billing, the band's Peel Session broadcast and McCullough's coverage in *Sounds* made them the larger draw as they took the stage at the Brixton Ace in London.

Although performances of "Accept Yourself" and "Reel Around the Fountain" were plagued by sound problems, a review of the show by writer Gaye Abandon that ran in a late-June issue of the *NME* gave the band's six-song set "full marks" and described how the Smiths "graze plaintive prickly pastures but chew the cud with simple pleasing intensity . . . and yes, they're handsome devils."

Some of those sound problems were blamed on Mike Joyce, who was making mistakes in the live set that night, including ending one song too soon in front of a number of important onlookers. These gaffes were in fact witnessed by Rourke's drummer friend Wolstencroft, who had since begun to play in the Colourfield with former Specials and Fun Boy Three front man Terry Hall.

During a shared ride home to Manchester after the show, Rourke suggested that Joyce's days might be numbered if Wolstencroft wanted another shot at the spot. Of course, while his bandmates might have considered making this change at the time, Mike ultimately managed to adapt his punk-influenced playing style to fit the Smiths, and his position would remain unchanged.

The Renault

With an uptick in touring planned to maximize the Smiths' rising popularity, Joe Moss bought the group a Renault van with dual cargo doors. To better suit the group, and to allow for sleeping in the vehicle when absolutely necessary, the rear seats were removed, and mattresses were put down.

In addition to the band and driver/manager Moss, the entourage on early trips included roadie Ollie May and, at times, Angela or Andrew Berry. Then, in June '83, Grant Cunliffe—a.k.a. Grant Showbiz—became another permanent fixture in the van when he was hired as the Smiths' sound engineer.

Showbiz

Cunliffe was first introduced to the Smiths backstage at the ULU show by Piering and Travis, who were both well aware of his studio production work on records for the Fall—including their 1979 independent-chart-topper *Dragnet*—and regular efforts as their soundman. Showbiz was also a veteran of the experimental rock group Here & Now, had started the cassette label Fuck Off Records, and even ran a recording studio known as Street Level.

Grant was drawn to the Smiths' originality and, after witnessing them onstage, was very interested in working with the group. "They were amazing," he told music blogger Julie Hamill in 2013. "They were like the Beatles and the Stones in that they had a complete identity, language, style. They had Andrew Berry's haircuts, very important about the hair. They had their top collars done up, beads, jackets . . . and they looked unlike anything I had ever seen before. They used words like 'handsome' and 'charming.' Words that I hadn't heard . . . sort of Dickensian."

Showbiz and the Smiths hit it off. Easygoing Moss had one key instruction for their new sound guy: make Morrissey's voice as loud as the rest of the band! In doing so, the already-experienced musicians in the band—who needed little direction—were properly equalized with their singer. It made a significant difference to the already great band's performance.

In turn, the already-established producer relished the opportunity to serve as the group's live soundman, hitting the road to see the places he wouldn't otherwise see.

Headlining the Hacienda

With Showbiz in tow, the Smiths returned to Brixton Ace with a newfound assurance on June 29. With his band sandwiched between London upstarts Flesh for Lulu—who would become best known for 1987's "I Go Crazy"—and headliners Sisters of Mercy, Morrissey was pleased to discover he had a few bona-fide fans in attendance and expressed his gratitude to these "cheery charmers."

The next day, the Smiths joined Aztec Camera—who had become one of the U.K.'s biggest pop successes of the year—for a gig at Warwick University in Coventry. A well-received headlining performance at the Midnight Express in Bournemouth followed on July 1 before the band returned home for another Hacienda show, this time as headliners. Ahead of the group's performance, they recorded another BBC Session featuring all new songs tracked for the "Kid" David Jensen's show, which aired right before John Peel's on the evening of July 4.

During the special, which featured Radio 1 studio versions of "These Things Take Time," "You've Got Everything Now," and "Wonderful Woman," the singer dismissed his hometown. "I don't really feel any kinship with the place," Morrissey told Jensen, who catered to a broader and arguably more devoted rock audience than Peel. "It's just somewhere that I just so happen to live. It doesn't mean a great deal to me. And I'm sure I'll leave very soon—when I'm rich."

If the Smiths' singer was only partially joking, it didn't matter. That remark didn't alienate the more than 2,000 kids who flocked to the Hacienda on the night of July 6 to catch the band during their ascent to stardom. Onstage, Morrissey clutched a bouquet of flowers, which he shook up and down to Joyce's drum work during the opener, "You've Got Everything Now." Later in the set, the band dedicated "I Don't Owe You Anything" to Richard Boon.

For Moss, the turnout was a clear sign that the band was going to be massive. "There were 2,400 people there, and thousands more standing outside, unable to get in," he told the *Guardian* in January 2012. "I remember Morrissey was already doing the shirt-wearing. I'm standing behind these two guys. After one of the songs, part way through, one guy turns and goes, 'You've got to admit, they're fucking great, these guys.' And the other guy goes, 'But his fucking shirt's shit!' If ever there was an exchange that sums up Manchester—that's it."

Sold Out in London

Word of the Smiths spectacle continued to spread thanks to the continued Radio 1 support. When the foursome returned to London's Covent Garden on July 7 for a sold-out show at the Rock Garden, the heat inside the venue prompted Morrissey to tell the audience "You'll have to bring your swimwear next time," before the band broke into "These Things Take Time." A handbill for the gig likened the band to Magazine, the Velvet Underground, and the Stooges' *Raw Power*, while inside, *Sounds* reviewer Johnny Waller was taken aback, pronouncing them as "effortlessly brilliant."

The crowd was equally delighted with the nine-song set, calling the Mancunians back to the stage for an encore of "Accept Yourself." When a second encore was demanded, Morrissey and Marr huddled together, perplexed with what to do. They had already played their latest single. A few more seconds passed before the singer returned to the microphone to jokingly scold the crowd for disturbing the peace. From there he kidded them that they would need to suffer through "Hand in Glove" for a second time. In doing so, the Smiths were met with resounding cheers.

Him

Alongside her *NME* piece on the Smiths, Cath Carroll wrote a quickly suppressed feature on Morrissey for the August 1983 issue of *Him*, a gay publication. In the article—which the band's camp curiously sought to bury almost immediately after it emerged—Morrissey seemed happy to utilize the publication for exposure, even though he insisted he was not homosexual.

"He never wanted to represent himself as a gay band or a gay man or even as a bisexual man or whatever he might have been," Carroll later told Tony Fletcher. In spite of these denials, the Smiths' vocalist was adamant that the use of a naked man on the cover of "Hand in Glove" was necessary as a means to exploit the male body. In doing so, he claimed he was righting the wrongs for all the women that had been demoralized for so many years. "Naked men should be splashed around the Co-op," he insisted to *Him*.

Of course, that article, coupled with Morrissey's continued celibate cries, was hardly representative of the whole band. Marr, Joyce, and Rourke were all heterosexual men with girlfriends. At the same time, they recognized the effectiveness of their singer as he spoke to a growing legion of fans that—as outsiders—identified with the Smiths music.

13

The Low Life Has Lost Its Appeal

Off the Dole and on to the Radio

Five-album Deal

Geoff Travis knew Morrissey and Marr had the songs to support a full album, not to mention the determination to make a good—if not great—record. When he approached them with a long-term contract, they were pleased to know that the man behind Rough Trade had that kind of faith in them as artists and musicians.

Despite the success of "Hand in Glove," and contrary to previous reports, the Smiths did not have a number of major-label A&R scouts sniffing around that summer with the hopes of signing them. There was some major-label interest, but Rough Trade's dedication to the group and the already-established relationship made working with the label a no-brainer.

The five-page contract between Morrissey and Marr and Rough Trade was finalized on June 24, 1983. As with their debut 45, the extensive deal also allowed for an almost unheard-of 50/50 split of profits in the U.K., plus a 75/25 breakdown in the Smiths' favor for the rest of the world. It also included a guarantee for three albums over three years that could be extended to five albums over five years.

Rough Trade also conceded that Morrissey and Marr could have the final choice over producers to work with and allowed them the option to release their recordings through another record label five years after their contract expired if they so chose. The contract included a clause that ensured that either side would have the option to end the agreement if they were dissatisfied. Upon signing, the principal members of the Smiths were advanced approximately £4,000.

It was only days after the Smiths signed that EMI executive Hugh Stanley-Clarke and CBS's A&R head Muff Winwood came inquiring enthusiastically about the Smiths at their aforementioned Brixton and Warwick University gigs, respectively. Joe Moss told them both they were too late.

Off the Dole

Not long before "Hand in Glove" began to sell, Morrissey and the other eligible members of the Smiths stopped signing on for unemployment benefits from the

The Smiths–Mike Joyce, Andy Rourke, Johnny Marr, and Morrissey–photographed on September 7, 1983, by *NME* photographer Kevin Cummins. *Kevin Cummins/Getty Images*

United Kingdom's Department of Health and Social Security. Although they had yet to earn any money from record sales, being on unemployment "became too dangerous," as the singer explained to van Poznack in 1984.

"Of course, the DHSS feel that if you've made one record you're just an enormous international massively rich person," he added, revealing that he did not yet have his own personal bank account. "Even if your record's 38 in the independent chart and you owe your record company £30,000."

Tate Hired

July 1983 found the Smiths entering London's Elephant Studios with producer Troy Tate to get started on their already-announced Rough Trade debut. Tate, who was also signed to the label as a solo artist at the time, was hastily chosen on Travis' recommendation.

Early word on the sessions was positive. "It's been quite a magical communion," Morrissey told Kid Jensen's listeners that month, speaking of their preliminary work at the studio in the Docklands area of Wapping. Perhaps prematurely, the voice of the Smiths promised an album release by September.

Tate had gotten his start in music playing guitar in the Cheltenham punk outfit Index, releasing the 1978 single "Jet Lag"/"Total Bland" before aligning with ex-Rezillos members in the short-lived Shake. In late 1980 he joined the Teardrop Explodes, playing alongside their eccentric singer Julian Cope on the album *Wilder* before releasing a solo single, "Lifeline," in 1982. Tate followed this with his Rough Trade debut, "Love Is . . . ," the following year before jumping to Seymour Stein's Sire for two proper LPs, 1984's *Ticket to the Dark* and '85's *Liberty*.

In May, well in advance of their check-in at Elephant, the Smiths recorded a number of songs in rehearsals above the Crazy Face warehouse, which they presented to the producer so that he could get a feel for their sound. When they finally hit the studio to record with Troy in July and August, the work was prolific. By the time they were through, they had tracked more than a dozen songs, including "The Hand That Rocks the Cradle," "You've Got Everything Now," "These Things Take Time," "What Difference Does It Make?," "Reel Around the Fountain," "Hand in Glove," "Handsome Devil," "Wonderful Woman," "I Don't Owe You Anything," "Suffer Little Children," "Miserable Lie," "Pretty Girls Make Graves," and "Jeane."

Tate Fired

Although Tate and the band had gotten along splendidly, upon completion of the sessions that August the original version of the Smiths' eponymous long-player was deemed unsatisfactory the following month, specifically by Morrissey and Travis. It didn't take long for Marr to see their point.

If the decision to scrap the project after two months of work was expensive, it was also necessary. Marr and Morrissey both agreed that Tate's efforts sounded unpolished—more like a demo than a proper album. It was not how they wanted to project themselves to the world.

"It was a weird period for us," Marr told Hugh Felder in *Sounds* in February 1984. "We were going into the studio for a lengthy spell for the first time and we were a bit worried about what might happen to our sound."

While things didn't work out between the Smiths and Tate, Johnny insisted there was never any animosity. "We were just really sorry to hurt his feelings," Marr would tell *Record Collector* in 1992. "It was a professional decision and he took it very badly. He'd got himself wrapped up in it, and understandably so."

Charming Men

Throughout August, the Smiths played a series of well-attended gigs for an increasing number of new fans who had likely been exposed to the group through the BBC's repeat airings of their Peel and Jensen performances. A show at the Lyceum in London on August 7 was the lone exception that month as the quartet supported fellow Mancunian Howard Devoto. Here the band was met with respectful yet mostly disinterested applause from a crowd waiting to hear from the headliner.

Two nights later, at London's Camden Dingwalls, things were much different. The foursome were in the company of their own fans, playing a rousing eleven-song set to a packed and enthusiastic crowd.

"We're the delicate Smiths . . . hello!" Morrissey announced, quite obviously, to the audience. Their mid-set rendition of "Reel Around the Fountain," which had been a favorite of Peel's, even found loyalists singing along to the lyrics of the unreleased song, having likely taped it from the radio. As with past shows, the band played "Hand in Glove" twice at both London shows, and at Dingwalls they also performed "Handsome Devil" twice.

After strongly received mid-month gigs at the Warehouse in Leeds and the Gala Ballroom in Norwich, the Smiths returned to Dingwalls on August 30, supported by another up-and-coming Manchester band named Easterhouse, which featured Morrissey's one-time neighbors, the Perry brothers. The sold-out London audience rapturously greeted the Smiths, appreciating the group's best- and lesser-known numbers with enthusiasm. Curiously, Morrissey would introduce "Reel" to the crowd as the band's forthcoming single. "This is our new record, which you will buy," he told them, revealing plans that would ultimately change. (The Smiths' second offering would of course be "This Charming Man.")

This concert marked the live debut of "Pretty Girls Make Graves," but the addition of new material to the live set still didn't keep the band from serving up a second take on "Hand in Glove" as an encore. At this point, the event became chaotic, as fans invaded the stage, prompting Morrissey to yell, "Decorum! Decorum!" He soon lost his microphone in the madness, forcing the band to leave the stage as the houselights came on to the sound of Dusty Springfield's "Wishin' and Hopin'."

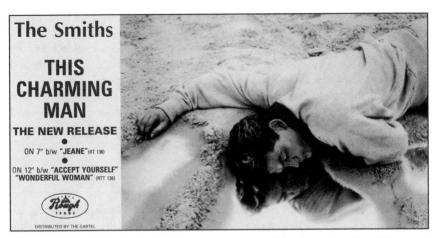

A promotional poster for the band's second single, "This Charming Man." Released in England on October 31, 1983, the song became the Smiths' first U.K. Top 30 hit. *Author's collection*

When the audience refused to leave, and with a sense of order—and Morrissey's microphone—back in place, the Smiths came back. The served up a second shot of "Handsome Devil" on this historic night, which affirmed that from this point on, the Smiths were stars—if only in London.

Finding Porter

John Porter had been working as a contract producer for BBC Radio when he was asked in August 1983 to produce the Smiths for Jensen's show. Porter—who held a pedigree as one-time bassist with and producer for Roxy Music, and had helmed Japan's influential 1979 LP *Quiet Life*—wasn't initially slated to work with the group at Maida Vale studios that day, but after meeting Marr in the break room beforehand, the guitarist pushed to have him record the band.

If Marr was awestruck by John's resume, he was equally pleased with Porter's focus that day on guitar sounds—including the juxtaposing of electric and acoustic instruments. Geoff Travis was also happy with the results of the eight-hour session for Jensen, and when he began to have doubts about Tate's recordings in late summer of that year, prior to severing ties with him, he asked Porter if he could get his opinion of some rough mixes.

John agreed, and after he listened to the master tapes of the fourteen or so songs at London's Regent Sound, he came back to Geoff with his feedback—and he didn't sugarcoat his thoughts. "I said, 'There's a lot to my ear that needs to be redone here,'" Porter recalled to *Mix* in September 2010 of his consultation. "To be quite candid, I didn't think it was very well-recorded. A lot of it was out of tune and out of time."

High Praise

By mid-summer 1983, when Morrissey and Marr sat down with two reporters from the fanzine the *Underground*, their confidence was at an all-time high. "We want to influence people," Johnny explained. "Get them off of their backsides . . . and inspire them to form groups of their own and play honest, direct music that comes from the heart."

This ambition wasn't lost on the publication. Neither was the band's importance. "The Smiths are the most important band since at least the Sex Pistols," the *Underground* argued. "What other band has come out fighting, totally honestly and taken on the shit, head on and beaten it?"

Here Comes the *Sun*

Following the popularity of the Smiths' initial Peel and Jensen sessions, the group returned to BBC Radio 1 on August 25 to track four more songs for the latter. Having just shelved the Tate version of their debut—which they had planned to name *The Hand That Rocks the Cradle*—the band cut versions of "Accept Yourself," "I Don't Owe You Anything," "Pretty Girls Make Graves," and "Reel Around the Fountain" as a means to continue to spread the gospel via the Beeb while their debut album was still in limbo.

However, on September 5, the members of the Smiths awoke to a completely unexpected controversy in the popular tabloid newspaper the *Sun*. In a sensationalized story by entertainment writer Nick Ferrari, Morrissey and his mates were the subject of the headline, "'BAN CHILD-SEX POP SONG' PLEA TO BEEB."

Although Ferrari had interviewed the band, he cited McCullough's *Sounds* article on the Smiths from months earlier and took—out of context—a quote of Morrissey's in which he said, "I don't feel immoral singing about molesting children." Ferrari also suggested that the BBC—ahead of that evening's planned Jensen broadcast—was considering banning the band from its airwaves altogether.

Ferrari's story took shape after another *Sounds* scribe, Gary Bushell, who had a serious disdain for the group—and McCullough, for that matter—accused them of being sexual deviants in his column. After some fact-checking, cooler heads prevailed at the BBC. Morrissey was vetted after making it completely clear to McCullough in the same story that he absolutely did not condone child molesting and that he himself had "never molested a child."

It was only because of the possible negative reaction from the *Sun*'s four million readers that Porter's radio-session production of "Reel Around the Fountain" was withheld from broadcast, purely as a precautionary measure. But while the remaining three songs aired on Jensen's show as planned, the damage had been done, and Morrissey especially felt reviled and confused.

Singled out for no apparent reason, the Smiths went on the attack, asking Rough Trade to approach both papers for retractions. They also threatened to take legal action for defamation.

Speaking to the *NME* that month, Morrissey said he felt like "bait" for Ferrari's story. "We were completely aghast," he told David Dorrell. "We really can't emphasize how much it upset us because obviously it was completely fabricated." Marr called Ferrari's article a "hatchet job" to Dorrell, explaining how his poor little brother, Ian, then eleven, had been hassled by his classmates and teachers after the story ran.

Peel Back

Despite the unwanted negative attention, the BBC continued to back the Smiths by asking them to record a second Peel session on September 14. Four all-new songs—"This Charming Man," "Back to the Old House," "This Night Has Opened My Eyes," and "Still Ill"—were recorded for broadcast on the DJ's September 21 show.

As soon as the Smiths had been vetted, the BBC press office issued a brief statement of support. "The *Sun* got it wrong again," they informed the media.

14

You're the Bee's Knees

The Smiths

n the September 3, 1983, issue of *Melody Maker*, Morrissey spoke enthusiastically to Frank Worrall about the Smiths' forthcoming debut album,
asserting that "anything we produce is wonderful" and that "we've done
everything right and it will show." Yet privately, Morrissey's excitement for the
Smiths' work with Troy Tate had waned substantially—especially after John
Porter evaluated the recordings and told the band and Geoff Travis that, in his
opinion, nearly everything needed to be fixed.

By the time the *NME* announced, in its September 24 issue, that the album
was still imminent—and that a North American distribution agreement had been
reached with Warner Bros. imprint Sire Records—the brakes had been put on
the record that had been initially promised as *The Hand That Rocks the Cradle*.

Yes, Sire!

With the ever-growing buzz about the Smiths in Manchester and London, Geoff
Travis had proof of what he had believed all along—the group was viable and
had massive potential. With the right business partners, he knew he could break
the band worldwide and profit from them in the process.

Travis was also aware of Sire Records' history as an American label that took
chances and thrived through its distribution deal with music industry power-
house Warner Bros. Geoff's own proven reputation with Rough Trade meant
that he could pick up the phone to request a meeting with Sire head Seymour
Stein. And that's just what he did.

Sire Records was the first significant label to embrace punk, power pop, and
new wave—the music that would ultimately give way to what would be generally
classified as alternative rock. The company released a staggering number of
groundbreaking albums by the Ramones, the Flamin' Groovies, Talking Heads,
Richard Hell & the Voidoids, the Saints, the Dead Boys, the Undertones, the
Pretenders, Madness, Echo & the Bunnymen, Soft Cell, Depeche Mode, Yaz,
Madonna, and Modern English between April 1976 and mid-1983.

In Travis' mind, a distribution deal with Sire was not only a slam-dunk—it
was the best possible way for the Smiths to crack the U.S. market. And, after

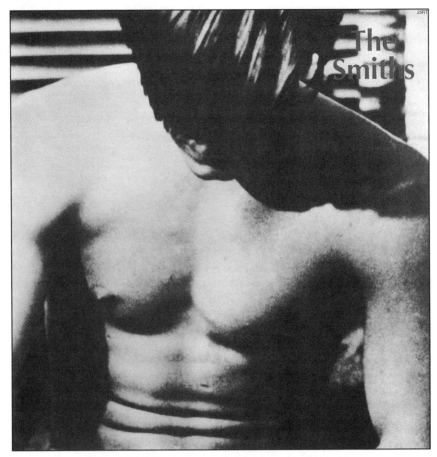

The album cover for *The Smiths* features a cropped still of actor Joe Dallesandro taken from Andy Warhol's 1968 film *Flesh*. *Author's collection*

hearing the band's demos and in-progress recordings with Tate, Stein felt the same. In late August, Geoff flew with the band to New York to cement a deal with Sire Records.

The arrangement was a little complex, however. Instead of actually signing the Smiths directly to his label, Stein signed a deal with Rough Trade and Morrissey and Marr to license the Smiths music in North America. With Rourke and Joyce looking on as simple witnesses once again, the singer and the guitarist signed its deal with Sire.

Five weeks later, Stein flew in from New York to catch the Smiths' show at London's ICA on the Mall on October 5. As the band played a brief but killer set, featuring "This Charming Man," "Handsome Devil," "Hand in Glove," and "What Difference Does it Make?," among others, Stein was mesmerized.

"I was quick to notice that this band has two superstars," Stein told *Rolling Stone*'s website in 2005. "Johnny Marr is a very integral part of the Smiths. I did think Morrissey's lyrics were just amazing, great poetry. They're timeless. I said to him, 'If you had been around at the beginning of the nineteenth century, you would have been a star, but your name would have been Lord Byron.'"

Following a business lunch at a vegetarian restaurant in London's Notting Hill the next day, Stein introduced Morrissey, Marr, Travis, and Joe Moss to Steven Baker, the man who would become their main contact at the label in the U.S.A.

Producer John

Early suggestions that John Porter might remix the album gave way to him being commissioned to produce the Smiths' just-penned next single, "This Charming Man," for an October release. The success of that session made it obvious to Travis that the group would be better off starting from scratch, with Porter producing.

On a shoestring budget, the Smiths were booked into Matrix Studios with John, where they tracked a preliminary version of "This Charming Man," plus "Accept Yourself," "Still Ill," and "Wonderful Woman." These four tracks were cut for just £500. The speed of the session was also helped along by Marr, who quickly bonded with Porter and was receptive to his many suggestions, including forgoing playing his Rickenbacker on the single in favor of a 1954 Fender Telecaster. On John's recommendation, Johnny implemented a capo to change the key, which helped him to better accompany Morrissey's vocal range.

This was more than a teacher-student relationship, though. Porter would later compare it to the younger brother–older brother kind of musical mentoring. Johnny and John worked into the night to get the tracks exactly the way they wanted. They also began hanging out, with Porter—who had married Keith Richards' one-time girlfriend Linda Keith—sharing stories from his past as they smoked pot together.

Working at Pluto and Eden

Porter had proven himself to the Smiths—most obviously to Marr—by the time the group moved on to Pluto Studios in Manchester in October 1983. It was here where they recorded much of the remainder of the group's eponymous first album, on the cheap, in just six days, working with engineer Phil Bush.

At the time, Pluto was a busy mid-level studio owned by Keith Hopwood, who had been a member of the 1960s pop band Herman's Hermits. The facility's bread and butter came from the radio and television jingles that Hopwood wrote and arranged during the days. At night, Pluto's 24-tracks catered to bands and counted noteworthy clients like Cabaret Voltaire and the Clash, who recorded their 1980 single "Bankrobber" there.

On the heels of the Pluto sessions, John Porter brought the band down to Eden Studios in London for overdubbing and mixing with house engineer Neill King. Travis was able to finance the extensive vocal and guitar overdubbing that

Porter oversaw that month thanks to an influx of money resulting from a newly signed distribution deal with Sire/Warner Bros. for North America.

From inside the vocal booth at Eden, Morrissey insisted that only Porter and King be allowed in the adjacent control room as he tracked his parts. Inside the darkened studio, with his back to them, the Smiths' front man sought privacy as he sang his heart out. At the time, he was insistent that—save for a small amount of delayed reverb here and there—his vocal parts remain free of effects.

Personality Clashes and Click Tracks

As work on the album, now re-titled *The Smiths*, progressed, it became evident that Morrissey disliked Porter. As Rourke would later convey to Fletcher, these feelings stemmed from the singer's belief that his vocal parts weren't being given the attention he felt they deserved. He may have also been jealous of Johnny's budding relationship with the producer.

Andy—like Johnny—looked up to Porter because of John's successful tenure in a band he always admired, his amicable demeanor, and their shared interest in the bass. Porter, in turn, liked Andy's musical instincts and ability. If the producer also liked Mike Joyce, he struggled with the drummer's style and approach. Porter had a bias against punk musicians, considering them to be typically unskilled. In order to get Joyce's parts right, John insisted that they record him to a metronomic "click track" in order to compensate for his inconsistent playing.

Not So "Charming"

Joyce's imperfect drumming on "This Charming Man" during the Smiths' sessions at Matrix led to an extensive editing session at Eden, with Porter trying to ready the song for single release by cherry-picking Andy's best parts and splicing them together. When Travis heard this version—later known as the song's "London" mix when it ultimately surfaced on a 12-inch single—he was displeased and insisted that the group start again on the song.

The Smiths returned to Stockport's Strawberry Studios—where they had tracked "Hand in Glove"—with Porter producing in the company of engineer Chris Nagle. Porter initially programmed the drums electronically in the hope he could relieve Joyce of the stress of building the track's rhythmic foundation. From there, John layered Rourke's bass, Marr's guitars, and Morrissey's vocals atop his Linn drum arrangement. Next, Mike came in to track drum parts. And, thanks to Porter's vision, he did so in just one take.

The end result of this unusual production approach was an astoundingly strong sounding pop song. In its final, exemplary version, "This Charming Man" was ready for the airwaves and seemed destined to be a bona-fide hit. And, within several weeks of its official release as a U.K. single via Rough Trade on October 28, 1983, it was.

This Charming 45

The musical alignment of Marr's jangling guitar lines, Rourke's buoyant, Motown-inspired bass work, and Joyce's upbeat drumming was augmented by Morrissey's vulnerable presentation of his shameless, sexually ambiguous lyrics on the Smiths' second single. Upon its release, the undeniably great song made a respectful showing in the U.K. singles charts, where it peaked at #25 in late 1983.

It was backed with "Jeane"—a likable holdover from the Tate sessions—on the 7-inch single, while the 12-inch vinyl release of the single added "Accept Yourself" and "Wonderful Woman," both of which had been cut with Porter at Matrix. The artwork for both formats featured a still frame of French actor Jean Marais, in a photograph extracted from Jean Cocteau's 1950 movie *Orphée*.

Morrissey told writer Karen Swayne around the time of its emergence that the single contained deliberate language. "People aren't used to thinking in a very charming or handsome way," he told the *No. 1* scribe, explaining his reason for using positive albeit increasingly obsolete words in song. In the singer's estimation, the art of conversation was dead, and his was a counter to the language of the times that "totally erodes the heart" and had been the norm.

Long after the initial success of the song—which finds a bicyclist with a punctured tire flirting with a charming man after being offered a ride home—Morrissey explained that the lyrics were meant to be humorous, in a deadpan way. Much to his frustration, however, that element was overlooked. Instead, writers would focus on what he would call "this 'festive faggot' thing" in an interview with the *NME* in February 1984. "People listen to 'This Charming Man' and think no further than would anyone would presume. I hate that angle. I hate it when people talk to me about sex in a trivial way." Elsewhere, he would reveal that the crux of the lyrics represented a time in his life when he lacked money to buy fashionable clothes to wear out on the rare occasion he might have been invited to a party or event.

"This Charming Man" was heralded by *NME* writer Paul Morley, who called it "accessible bliss," cited it as "unique and indispensable," and dubbed it "one of the greatest singles of the year." As an import release, the single wound up in the hands of *New York Times* scribe Robert Palmer, who described it as "sparkling, soaring, superlative pop-rock" and wrote of how it was "proof that the guitar-band format pioneered by the Beatles is still viable for groups with something to say."

Oasis guitarist/songwriter Noel Gallagher became a fan the first time he heard the song. "Everything made sense," he told *Uncut* in 2007. "The sound of that guitar intro was incredible. The lyrics are fuckin' amazing, too. People say Morrissey's a miserable cunt, but I knew straight away what he was on about."

In time, U.K. music fans followed suit. In 1992, after the Smiths' catalog had been sold to Warner Bros., "This Charming Man was reissued as a single and peaked at #8 in the charts. In the years since, the track's legacy has only grown. In 2008, *Mojo* writers placed it at the top of its list of the "50 Greatest U.K. Indie Records of All Time." Popular U.S. band Death Cab for Cutie recorded a cover of the song on its 1997 demo, *You Can Play These Songs with Chords*. Canadian indie-pop group Stars also released a version of the song in 2001, and New York punk band Skaters tracked their rendition in 2014.

Five More Facts About "This Charming Man"

1. Released several months ahead of *The Smiths*, this successful single was curiously left off of initial U.K. vinyl pressings of the album, although it was included as the sixth track on the U.S. version of the LP, which was issued via Sire Records in 1984. U.K. cassette copies of the album did include the song as a bonus track.

2. Johnny Marr claims he assembled the music for this song in only twenty minutes in September 1983 on his TEAC 3-track tape recorder. He told *Guitar Player* in 1990 that the song was penned for the Smiths' second John Peel session on the same evening he came up with the musical parts for "Still Ill" and "Pretty Girls Make Graves." He later confessed that he became jealous when he heard Aztec Camera's "Walk out to Winter" on Radio 1, and his competitive urges spawned the tune.

3. Marr told *Select* in December 1993 that there are fifteen guitar tracks on "This Charming Man," including Porter's aforementioned 1954 Telecaster, three tracks of acoustic guitar, and a backwards guitar with extensive reverb. There is also a distinct guitar line heard near the end of the chorus that he recorded as he dropped knives with metal handles on the same Telecaster while it was plugged into his Fender Twin amp and tuned to an open chord. Contrary to popular belief, though, Johnny does not play a Rickenbacker guitar on this recording.

4. Morrissey extracted the line "A jumped-up pantry boy who never knew his place" from dialogue he heard in the 1972 homoerotic cult film *Sleuth*, which starred Laurence Olivier and Michael Caine. The film was based on a play of the same name that stemmed from the 1945 Henry Green novel *Loving*.

5. In December 1983, François Kevorkian—a dance music producer who had reworked songs like Yazoo's "Situation," Tin Tin's "Kiss Me," and U2's "Two Hearts Beat as One"/"New Year's Day"—remixed the song for New York clubs. When Travis heard it, he released the mix in the U.K., with Morrissey's approval. After it was issued, however, the Smiths' singer decided he disliked it. When questioned about it in interviews, he suggested it was released against his will and asked fans not to buy it. As a result, Rough Trade quickly deleted "This Charming Man (New York)" from its catalog.

"Charming" Flip Sides

While "This Charming Man" stood out, its B-side and 12-inch bonus tracks would become a cherished part of the group's recorded legacy. In years to come—especially after the group's demise—Smiths loyalists would dig deep and cling on to every lyric and every shimmering guitar line in their canon.

"Jeane"

Treasured by fans for years, this song—apparently about living in squalor in the throes of a failed relationship—is one of the most underrated songs from the band's early days. Upbeat and contagious, it somehow managed to avoid being formally released on any subsequent compilations—of which there were several—to languish as the flip side of the original 7-inch for "This Charming Man."

The thumping, contagious, and captivating tune, coupled with Morrissey's falsetto, defies its desperate lyrics. Penned in late 1982, the track is the lone officially sanctioned recording from the group's July/August '83 sessions with Troy Tate. The following year, acclaimed singer/songwriter Billy Bragg began covering it.

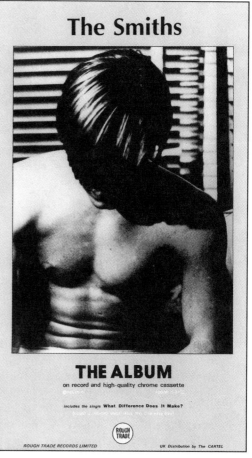

The Smiths

THE ALBUM
on record and high-quality chrome cassette

Includes the single **What Difference Does It Make?**

ROUGH TRADE

ROUGH TRADE RECORDS LIMITED   UK Distribution by The CARTEL

A promotional poster for *The Smiths*, which was serviced to record shops throughout England by Rough Trade in tandem with its release to help drive awareness and sales. *Author's collection*

"Wonderful Woman"

When asked by Simon Goddard about this song, Morrissey explained that the pensive number was "quite tongue-in-cheek" and revealed how the subject was "an incredibly vicious person" but added that he still found himself drawn to her. "All the things that she wanted to do, nasty as they were, were completely forgivable due to whatever reason," he explains, in the book *Songs That Saved Your Life*. "It's all metaphysical."

The song started out with different lyrics under the title "What Do You See in Him?," before Morrissey rewrote it in the spring of '83. The Smiths first tracked it with producer Dale Griffin for broadcast on Kid Jensen's July 4 show. The version that appeared on the 12-inch single of "This Charming Man" was recorded in September of the same year with John Porter at London's Matrix Studios.

"Accept Yourself"

Recorded alongside "Wonderful Woman," this song appears to have been written by Morrissey to himself as a means of encouragement. The singer's message—regardless of how peculiar or dull he perceived himself to be in the lyrics—was to embrace life and acknowledge the person he was.

Ironically, at the time, Morrissey wasn't embracing this notion of freedom, although the song—which matched Marr's guitar with the front man's lyrical thoughts—suggests he wanted to. Despite the fact that the answer to his problems appeared right before him, he would not or for some reason could not open his eyes.

The Smiths

Long before they became the most important and influential indie band of the 1980s, the Smiths were a promising and determined guitar group with a record deal, an unconventional lyricist/front man, and a wunderkind multi-instrumentalist. With an agenda of stomping out the synthesizer-driven new-wave merchants of the day, they gathered with John Porter, after an unfortunate false start with Troy Tate, to craft a lasting debut.

Following completion of *The Smiths* in November, but in advance of its release on February 20, 1984, Marr would call the album "phenomenal" in an interview with *Sounds*. Promoting the record in that article the same month, Johnny cited Porter as the "perfect studio technician for us."

Upon hearing the final mix of *The Smiths* that December, Morrissey disagreed. He shared his views with the band before telling Porter and Travis that, in his opinion, the album wasn't fit for release. Regardless, Rough Trade pushed forward with plans to issue the final product, reminding the singer that they had already invested £6,000 in it.

Although it would be three decades before Morrissey shared his official thoughts about working with Porter on the debut, when he finally did so, it was with contempt. In *Autobiography*, Morrissey complains of how John "failed everyone" with *The Smiths*. He blames Porter for stripping the Smiths of their forcefulness, removing all of the swagger from their sound, and turning the group's songs into something he deemed tepid and "sanitized."

The commercial and critical response to the debut album would soon contradict the singer's notions of the record. *The Smiths* peaked at #2 in the U.K. album survey in its first week of release.

"Reel Around the Fountain"

From a sequencing standpoint, there were clearly more immediate choices with which to launch *The Smiths* than the mid-tempo song that was banned by the BBC that fall, following unproven media allegations that Morrissey condoned pedophilia. But if the six-minute number lacked the roar of a typical album-starter, "Reel" was certainly poignant, alluring, and, perhaps, a little dark.

Morrissey would soon relay to *Rolling Stone*'s James Henke that "Reel Around the Fountain" was about the loss of innocence one feels after one's first sexual experience. He would also attribute the lines, "I dreamt about you last night, and I fell out of bed twice," to the 1958 Shelagh Delaney play *A Taste of Honey*.

Fans of Delaney were critical of Morrissey's use of the dialogue in the song. Speaking to the *NME* in 1986, the singer complained how he had been "whipped persistently for the use of that line," before declaring that "at least 50 percent of my reason for writing can be blamed on Delaney."

Musically, Marr claims the song's lilting melody stemmed from him trying to play the Jimmy Jones R&B hit 'Handy Man,' which James Taylor had covered in the 1970s. Johnny had first discovered the song on a jukebox during a vacation when he was about thirteen. He was reminded of it again when he heard it while he was working one morning in Crazy Face with Moss.

"It was in the air," Marr told *Mojo* in October 2012. "When I tried to play it, this string of strange chord changes fell from my fingers."

By the time they recorded the song with Porter in October 1983 at Pluto, the Smiths had already tracked it twice in BBC sessions, and again, unsuccessfully, with Tate. Despite it becoming a definitive part of the group's catalog, Porter was never completely happy with how it turned out. In a 1994 interview with *Q*, the producer said, "I don't think they ever really captured it. I always wanted to have another go at it."

"You've Got Everything Now"

Written in April 1983, this upbeat four-minute number originally clocked in at over six minutes. It was first recorded in June of that year, with former Mott the Hoople drummer/producer Dale Griffin, for the Smiths' first Kid Jensen appearance.

Morrissey would later reveal on BBC2's *Oxford Road Show* in 1985 that the lyrics were a look at his former classmates, many of whom had settled into well-paying jobs and had bought homes and cars at a time when he was still living at home with his mother and struggling to find his path in life.

During overdubbing and mixing sessions for the track at Eden in November '83, John Porter brought in his friend, Roxy Music keyboardist Paul Carrack, to play Hammond organ on the song. At the time, Carrack was best known for his lead vocals on the respective Ace and Squeeze hits "How Long" (U.S. #3, 1974) and "Tempted" (U.K. #41, 1981).

"Miserable Lie"

Originally titled "(Love Is Just a) Miserable Lie," this emotive track starts off in a pensive state in its verse and gives way to a cathartic, punk like chorus. Dating back to the summer of 1982, "Miserable Lie" is one of the very first songs penned together by Morrissey and Marr.

In his lyrics, Morrissey addresses his decision to become celibate, unable to cope with his own physical commitment failures. Speaking to McCullough on the subject, he supposed that because of his feelings, he was "unnatural in the general scheme of things." Although he never went further into specifics during interviews, the line in which he suggests his lover laughed at his genitals is devastatingly honest.

"Pretty Girls Make Graves"

Inspired by Jack Kerouac's 1958 novel *The Dharma Bums*, the Smiths' skiffle shuffle provided the foundation for Morrissey's subtle lyrics about his inability to respond to an attractive but promiscuous woman's advances. Rounded out by his crooned refrain, the song's tack—ambiguous as it might have been—was truly original for the day.

To his credit, Morrissey never actually revealed his orientation in songs such as this, reckoning that to do so would risk alienating a portion of his fan base. But he does address sex and relationships on "Pretty Girls Make Graves," while confessing to losing his faith in womanhood. Despite leaving his female attractor unsatisfied in the song, he acknowledges feelings of jealousy and confusion after she begins to lust after another man.

Morrissey penned this song in tandem with "This Charming Man" in August of 1983, and hoped to release this unforgettable number as a single from the album. After meeting with resistance from Travis, however, those plans changed. Note: the song features backing vocals by Morrissey's friend Annalisa Jablonska.

"The Hand That Rocks the Cradle"

As mentioned elsewhere, Morrissey once sang an early draft of these lyrics without accompaniment on a demo tape he sent to Richard Boon in 1980. It is also significant as the first original song completed by Morrissey and Marr after establishing their partnership in the spring of 1982.

Featuring a play on words from James Joyce's *Ulysses*—"Over the Stones, rattle his bones, he's only a beggar who nobody owns," which also surfaced in Shelagh Delaney's 1960 play *The Lion in Love*—the song also incorporates lines from Al Jolson's 1928 song "Sonny Boy." There is evidence that the title stemmed from a 1917 dramatic film of the same name about birth control.

There are several possible interpretations of "The Hand That Rocks the Cradle." Morrissey revealed in a 1985 *Melody Maker* interview that it was inspired by a relationship he had had that "didn't really involve romance," but he never went into detail. Fans have speculated that it might relate on some level to the relationship between Morrissey and his then-estranged father. There also seems to be a connection to experiences with an overbearing, suffocating mother.

And while it has also been suggested that it could in some way be about child molestation, there has never been any confirmation from the singer one way or the other regarding its meaning.

"Still Ill"

For Morrissey, "Still Ill" was a deeply personal realization that his old dreams and freedoms were dead and, perhaps, the ultimate deliberation over his sexual persuasion. As the protagonist of the song, he finds a lover and winds up with sore lips after they kiss under an iron bridge.

Unsatisfied with the pressures of adulthood and aggravated by the Thatcher era's insistence that all able bodied people must seek work, Morrissey felt out of place in early 1980s England, without love and marginalized by the world around him. Acknowledging that the grand old days when he was left to his own devices to spend his youthful days with someone who meant the world to him had long since passed him by, he sings "Still Ill" with yearning and desperation. Ideally served by Marr, Rourke, and Joyce's punchy pop arrangement, Morrissey's aching vocal delivery finds him pondering whether the body rules the mind, or vice-versa.

"Still Ill"—which was written for the band's second Peel session—is also the singer's way of subtly asking himself cryptically if he is still gay, at a time when homosexuality was widely seen by many as an illness.

"Hand in Glove"

The Smiths' first single was rerecorded with Porter in October 1983, but when Morrissey declared that he was dissatisfied with that rendition, and with studio time starting to run out, he and Marr elected to have the producer remix the original Strawberry Studios recording for the LP. In doing so, John raised the drum volume, pushed the bass part down in the mix, and increased the separation between the vocals and the guitar parts.

In a 1984 interview with *Jamming!* in advance of the album, Morrissey spoke of his dissatisfaction with the lack of attention the song had received to date. "It should have been a massive hit," he asserted. "It was so urgent. . . . It really was a landmark." He hoped that its presence on the album might someday elevate it to anthem status.

It was yet another Smiths song to reference playwright Shelagh Delaney, lifting the line "I'll probably never see you again" from *A Taste of Honey* and *The Lion in Love*. Elsewhere, the song paraphrases the 1974 Leonard Cohen tune "Take This Longing," and may have possibly borrowed its title from the 1947 Ngaio Marsh novel of the same name.

In celebration of the single's thirtieth anniversary, Marr was asked by the *NME* in 2013 what his favorite Smiths lyric was. He replied that it would probably be all of this song, because, he explained, "It's such a statement of love and friendship and has a sense of going forward. And it has a kind of genuine spirit about it."

"What Difference Does It Make?"

The hard-driving "What Difference Does It Make?" began as a thirty-bar instrumental sequence without verses, as John Porter revealed to *Mix* in a September 2010 article about the song's germination. "It was just this thing that started and went," the producer explained. "Morrissey would sing, and whenever he didn't sing they would just carry on and then he would sing again."

If the song lacked structure at the outset, once Porter suggested that Marr add an introductory riff, "What Difference Does It Make?" had an identifiable start. Multiple guitar parts were layered over throughout each successive part of the song until it ended up with fifteen or more different tracks of six-string instrumentation. In addition to Marr's own instruments, Porter lent Johnny many of his acoustic, semi-acoustic, solid-body, and electric guitars as they crafted a captivating arrangement.

The song—which became the Smiths' third single upon its January 1984 release—is also augmented by a backward piano part and the sound of little kids playing in a schoolyard. Mike Joyce's crashing cymbals and Andy Rourke's thumping bass round out the recording, building an ideal anchor for Morrissey's falsetto vocal line at the conclusion of the track.

"I Don't Owe You Anything"

Morrissey sings of stolen wine, a knowing glance, and lustful anticipation on this lilting love song, which he and Marr penned in April 1983 with their debut album in mind. The track started as an upbeat, seven-minute number that was reworked into the slower, shorter version heard on *The Smiths*. As with several other numbers on the record, Paul Carrack plays Hammond organ. Porter first produced the song for the Kid Jensen show in August before tracking the official version at Pluto in October.

"Suffer Little Children"

Morrissey had already penned the lyrics to this controversial song, written about the Moors Murders, when he brought it to Marr in late May of 1982. This definitive version initially featured a piano coda similar to the original, which was first tracked at Decibelle in August 1982, until it was eliminated during mixing sessions for the record.

The song's somber, Joy Division–esque presentation—which coined the now-famous phrase "Oh Manchester, so much to answer for"—instead features a lengthy fade and clocks in at five and a half minutes. As with "Pretty Girls Make Graves," it features supporting vocals by Jablonska.

The title refers to a biblical phrase found in both Luke 18:16 and Mark 10:14, in which Jesus condemns his followers for rejecting a group of children. Topically—and quite controversially—the song focused on Ian Brady and Myra

Hindley, who abducted and murdered five children between 1963 and 1965 around Manchester. After the children were lured from streets in close proximity to where Morrissey lived as a boy, several of their bodies were buried north of the city on Saddleworth Moor.

As a child, Morrissey regularly heard his relatives talking about the case and was made aware by them that he could have very well been a victim. As an adolescent, this prompted him to read about the gruesome killings in Emlyn Williams' semi-fictionalized 1967 book *Beyond Belief: A Chronicle of Murder and Its Detection.*

In the lyrics, Morrissey refers to the murder victims and their evil killers by name, which prompted relatives to object after the media elected to sensationalize the song in 1984. In doing so, *The Smiths* was banned from sale for a time by some U.K. retailers. In several interviews conducted in late 1984 and early 1985, the group's vocalist expressed his confusion and frustration with the fact that certain local and national newspapers would write a story judging him and disfiguring the song without asking him to comment on it. When the *Daily Mail* actually asked for his remarks, he shared with them that he wrote the song as a tribute and that he had since become friendly with some of the victim's parents, including Ann West, the mother of Lesley Ann Downey. As a result, they didn't print the story. As he told *Jamming!* in December 1984, "That really upset me."

Later, Morrissey acknowledged that such a reaction was clearly a case of distorting the truth to sell newspapers. "It really reflects the absolute and barbaric attitudes of the daily press," he told *Melody Maker* in its March 16, 1985, edition. "In essence they were just really saying how narrow-minded and blunderous they were. . . . Some of the reports were so full of hate, it was like I was one of the Moors Murderers, that I'd gone out and murdered these children. . . . It was incredible."

In 1986, he told *Spin* how he was portrayed in the media as a "hideous Satanic monster" and expressed his desire to continue to raise awareness of the crimes. "We don't forget the atrocities of Hitler, do we?"

Flesh

The album's cover art was chosen by Morrissey, who selected a carefully cropped frame of actor Joe Dallesandro from the 1968 Andy Warhol film *Flesh.* Morrissey would later explain to the *Face* the following summer that it was with this movie that he "succumbed to the whole Warhol thing."

Mike Joyce relayed quite hilariously to *Select* in April 1993 how Marr came to him with the concept for the cover. "'It's a picture of a bloke going down on another bloke.' So I'm like, 'Great! Fan-ta-stic! Hey, mum, look what I've been doing the last eight months!'"

Picking up the story in the March 2000 issue of *Mojo*, he explained, "Very cleverly, [Morrissey] didn't tell me the picture was going to be cropped. I could imagine my parents going, 'Well, that's nice, Michael.' The local priest, all my relatives . . ."

The photograph of Morrissey found on the inner sleeve of the LP was shot at an early Smiths gig in London by photographer Romi Mori, who would go on to join the Gun Club on bass in 1986.

Release and Reception

"I really do expect the highest critical praise for the album," the Smiths' front man told *Record Mirror*'s Andy Strikes for the paper's February 11, 1984, issue, calling the LP "a signal post in music." And, for the most part, his assessment of the band as being different from "the rest of the clatter" was met with positive marks when music critics got their hands on the debut.

For Morrissey and Marr, the idea was to make profound music, along the lines of memorable and powerful singles like the Sex Pistols' "God Save the Queen" or the Plastic Ono Band's "Give Peace a Chance." And not only would *The Smiths* have an immediate effect on popular music in the U.K., it would have a lasting impact on the world.

Even so, early reviews were mixed. *NME* critic Don Watson focused on the Smiths' main mouth, writing, "What Morrissey captures above all is a notion of despair reflected perfectly in the lackluster sound of his cohorts, a death of the punk ideals that [he] quite old enough to have been closely involved in." And he championed the singer's wit and "sensitivity to deal in despair without resorting to preaching in desperation."

Stateside, Kurt Loder praised the album in *Rolling Stone*, insisting, "This record repays close listening," and denoting Morrissey's painful "memories of heterosexual rejection and homosexual isolation." Although Loder felt that the singer's voice "takes some getting used to," he concluded, "*The Smiths* is surprisingly warm and entertaining." *Creem* writer Robert Christgau wasn't entirely convinced, grading the album B- and knocking Morrissey's "hypersensitivity as a spiritual achievement rather than an affliction."

High Fidelity critic Wayne King saw little of worth in the record. "Forget the music, a watered-down cop of the R.E.M./Echo and the Bunnymen style of jangly, 'new psychedelic' guitar/bass/drums," he wrote. "Ignore singer/songwriter Morrissey's canny self-promotion. . . . Instead, focus on a quotation from 'Reel Around the Fountain': 'Fifteen minutes with you,' the singer tells us, recalling the particularly apt Warholian dictum about stardom and the quarter hour, 'well, I wouldn't say no.' When it comes to *The Smiths*, I would."

The Smiths debuted at #2 in the U.K. album charts, surprising everyone. Much to Morrissey's dismay, it was kept from #1 by the Thompson Twins' synth-pop favorite *Into the Gap*, which was anchored by the global pop smash "Hold Me Now." The singer explains his frustration in *Autobiography*, noting how longtime friend and ally Richard Boon—who had since aligned with Geoff Travis as an employee of Rough Trade—informed him at the time that the band would have likely reached #1 in the chart, were it not for delays in the label manufacturing the cassette version of the album.

Legacy

Over time, *The Smiths* began to gather increased acclaim in the media, although it would take more than just a couple of years before its legacy was established. Upon word of the band's split in August 1987, *NME* scribe Danny Kelly was still unimpressed, reassessing the quartet's debut negatively. "The frenziedly-awaited debut LP disappoints," he wrote, "thanks to elephants-ear production (grey and flat), and ludicrously overblown expectations."

By 1989, perception of the record had finally started to shift, as *Rolling Stone* ranked it as #22 on its list of the top 100 albums of the 1980s. Later, in 2012, it ranked at #473 on the magazine's list of the "500 Greatest Albums of All Time."

Uncut's Stephen Dalton got it right by naming it "the coming of age of a major songwriting duo and a highly original new voice in pop" in his 1998 four-star re-evaluation. Then, on the album's thirtieth anniversary in February 2014, *Billboard* gave it a grade of 93 out of 100, with writer Chris Payne opining, "College rock and indie rock already existed (albeit in their early stages) when the Smiths hit in 1984. But after their John Porter-produced debut made its mark, those entire scenes would never be the same."

In Hindsight

By August 1985, Marr was acknowledging that he was no longer "madly keen" on the Smiths' debut album, confessing to *Melody Maker* that "a lot of the fire was missing on it," while listing tracks like "Still Ill," "Suffer Little Children," and "Hand That Rocks the Cradle" as worthwhile contributions. At the time it was being made, Marr would later explain, he was still learning from John Porter how to make a proper album and it wasn't until people around him began to point out its weaknesses that he lost enthusiasm in the end product.

Despite his concerns over the production, he told *Select* proudly, in December 1993, "I didn't think it was the best debut of all time, I just thought it was the best record out at the time. I know it's a great collection of songs. It became the norm to criticize it. People echo what they've heard in the press." In a January 1997 interview with *Guitar Magazine*, he blamed the Roland Jazz Chorus amplifier for a lot of his dissatisfaction with the record. "That's the fuckin' prime suspect," Marr contended. "Hey man, it was the '80s! They sounded fine to the player, but I think they failed out front. There seemed to be [a] big hole in the sound."

In an April 1994 *Q* interview, Morrissey acknowledged that he was baffled by *Rolling Stone*'s assessment of the record as a hidden gem in the band's catalog. Recalling the story of how he told Travis and Porter that it wasn't good enough, he stressed, "The Smiths' first album should have been so much better than it was."

If Marr was equally frustrated, it was because the band's debut album didn't represent their sound as well as some of the aborted takes with Tate had. Speaking to *Spin* in April 2012, he ultimately acquiesced, "We wanted to be a modern band and impress our friends who had good taste and I think we did that."

15

England Is Mine

The Top 30 and *Top of the Pops*

Stage Invaders

The Smiths' concert audiences grew considerably in the fall of 1983, in large part because of the ongoing interest of radio hosts John Peel and Kid Jensen. A gig at London's Venue on September 15, with the support of Rough Trade labelmates the Go-Betweens and Felt, marked the live debut of the new Morrissey/Marr compositions "Still Ill" and the forthcoming single "This Charming Man." A review of the show in the *NME* the following week described the band as Geoff Travis' "most commercial offering yet; deserving successors to Scritti [Politti] and [Aztec] Camera."

While Morrissey was disheartened to be opening for Gang of Four at the Lyceum Ballroom in London on September 25, an intimate headlining gig four nights later at the undersized Fernando's in Blackburn found the front man and his band in top form. For each concert high at this point—usually on London stages—there were lows, like insignificant and sparsely attended shows at the University of Birmingham (September 30) and the University of Bangor (October 14). The latter gig, in front of just a few dozen people, was cut short after just twenty minutes, with Morrissey taking his frustration out on a bouquet of daffodils. From there, he led Marr, Rourke, and Joyce off the stage.

By the time the Smiths reached the University of Sheffield on October 17, they had switched out "I Don't Owe You Anything" for another new number, "This Night Has Opened My Eyes." If fan turnout in tertiary cities was hit-and-miss at this early stage, attendees were frenzied when the group returned to London on the 21 was reassuring and a little chaotic. This show, at North East London Polytechnic, was packed. Fans in the front row found themselves crushed against the stage and, in some cases, injured, until the promoter took the microphone and asked everyone to retreat a few steps.

This concert also signified the first obvious attempts by Morrissey to change his lyrics around during gigs to suit his mood. A case in point was "Reel Around the Fountain," where he begged his suitor to "shag" him, as opposed to "slap" him on the patio. "Goodbye! Stay handsome," the singer told the crowd (according to a bootleg recording from this night) as the Manchester foursome left the stage.

Back in London a week later, after a pair of lackluster shows at Liverpool Polytechnic and Kingston Polytechnic, the Smiths experienced their first taste of fan pandemonium. The show in Mandela Hall at King's College started routinely enough, but as Morrissey continued to pull daffodils from a large box on the side of the stage and throw them into the audience, the crowd went wild. Despite noticeable mistakes, including a false start on "Pretty Girls Make Graves," the show was spectacular enough to prompt thirty or so disciples to invade the stage, with some of them trampling Marr's gear. Order was eventually restored, and the band ended the gig with an obligatory take on their regular encore, "Hand in Glove."

Warner Bros. Music

Through Geoff Travis, Morrissey and Marr were introduced to Peter Reichert, who was the managing director of Warner Bros. Music, the world-famous company's song-publishing arm. Because publishing was typically a good source of royalty income for recording artists, as it ensured payments from performances, airplay, and record sales, the band's label boss encouraged a deal with a company of this magnitude.

According to this proposed publishing deal, the principals of the Smiths would receive a respectable advance of around £80,000. This would mean that *The Smiths* would need to sell a conceivable 150,000 copies for the band to break even.

It helped that Reichert—after witnessing the band in London—believed Morrissey would be a star and felt that inking the Smiths made good business sense. He also liked the way the Smiths' rudimentary guitar sound flew in the face of the glossy pop bands of the day, like Duran Duran and Culture Club.

The deal was finalized sometime after the release of the group's first two singles, with initial pressings of "Hand in Glove" and "This Charming Man" credited to their own independent publishing outfit, Glad Hips Music. Although Travis had made the introductions, Morrissey kept him from attending any meetings with Warner Bros. Music out of concern that there might be a conflict of interest.

An advertisement for the Smiths' gig at the Electric Ballroom in Camden, London, on December 19, 1983. *Author's collection*

Smiths Business

If the Smiths' songwriting arrangement seemed potentially divisive, it was essentially no different than any of the business arrangements between Morrissey and Marr and their bandmates/employees, Rourke and Joyce. As the songwriters and decision-makers in the Smiths, they took the risk, they earned the credit, and, as such, it was understood that they received the bulk of the money.

Rourke and Joyce wouldn't be required, or expected—except with extremely rare exception—to labor over Smiths' records, or deal with Moss, Travis, promoters, publicists, or the media. In turn, Andy and Mike had no vote on band business—they were merely part of Johnny and Morrissey's vision.

During the recording of *The Smiths*, Morrissey pushed to get this business arrangement finalized by leaving the studio one night. Holed up at Rough Trade, he refused to head back to continue work on the project until matters concerning the group's split of royalty earnings were finalized.

"Johnny Marr came in and said, 'Morrissey wants me and him to get a higher percentage—or more money,'" Joyce would explain in the 2001 BBC documentary *The Rise and Fall of the Smiths*. "Johnny said, 'If you don't accept it, I'm going to leave the band.'"

"All me and Mike were trying to do was stop Johnny leaving the band," Rourke told the BBC. As a result, the Smiths' rhythm section each agreed to just 10 percent of the band's earnings. Johnny and Morrissey would split the remaining 80 percent of the group's royalties.

Performance pay was different from the 50/50 songwriting and 40/40/10/10 recording royalties. Each of the four members was purportedly paid equal amounts annually for their touring efforts and live work. The checks were to be paid by Smithdom Ltd., the aforementioned company that listed Morrissey and Marr as its directors.

In the years after the Smiths' demise, the lack of clarity over this supposed verbal agreement would result in legal actions against Morrissey and Marr by Joyce and Rourke.

"Charming" on *The Tube*

The Smiths made their debut television appearance on *The Tube* on Friday, November 4, 1983. Broadcast nationally on Channel 4, the pop music program featured a segment on Rough Trade Records' rising stars and included footage of the group lip-synching to "This Charming Man" from their Manchester rehearsal space.

In keeping with Morrissey's ongoing fascination with gladioli, the floor of the Portland Street warehouse was adorned with flowers, and the singer mimed the hit while clutching his own personal bouquet. With his dress shirt open to midway, the Smiths' vocalist exposed his bare chest and love beads, while the quiffed Marr strummed his Rickenbacker and Joyce and Rourke pretended to keep rhythmic time. Similar footage of the band miming "This Charming Man" in a room filled with flowers and dry ice was broadcast the following Monday on the BBC2 program *Riverside*.

Top 30

Geoff Travis had every intention of capitalizing on this television exposure, and in advance of the broadcasts had hired out the sales department of London Records to help get the single into the record stores on a national level. The aforementioned 7-inch and 12-inch singles, issued with different B-sides, were an obvious ploy to duplicate sales among the new Smiths disciples who craved all available tracks.

Scott Piering plugged the single to the powers that be at Radio 1 and the song became a chart hit. As a result, the Smiths were next tapped to appear on the biggest pop music program in the U.K., *Top of the Pops*.

"This Charming Man" landed in the Top 30, but while the band were pleased to have made a dent in the U.K. music market, Morrissey would eventually voice his disappointment in Rough Trade's ability to keep the shops adequately stocked to meet demand. He would not be satisfied until every conceivable Smiths fan could be reached.

The Top of the Pops

On November 24, 1983, the Smiths—with Johnny clutching his red Rickenbacker and Morrissey waving his trusty bouquet—made their first appearance on the legendary *Top of the Pops* television program. The Thursday evening appearance found the band sandwiched in between androgynous pop star Marilyn and the Thompson Twins.

At home in his bedroom, future Oasis songwriter/guitarist Noel Gallagher saw the appearance as an epiphany. "None of my mates liked them—they were more hooligan types," he remembered to *Uncut* in 2007. "They said, 'Fuckin' hell, did you see that poof on *Top of the Pops* with the bush in his back pocket?' But I thought it was life-changing."

Ironically, according to Morrissey, the band were billed in television listings of the *Sun* as "Dismiss."

Press On

With the release of "This Charming Man," the Smiths began to see a steady stream of media coverage. *International Musician* was first to plug the band in a two-page feature titled "Flower Power," penned by Adrian Deevoy, that found Morrissey describing the band as "pop music with brains." When asked about his vocal approach, the front man remarked, "I can't do *Bohemian Rhapsodies* and things like that, so there's no real point in trying."

By November, *Smash Hits* was running a full-page, full-color write-up on the group, describing the single as "excellent." And *Melody Maker* made the Smiths cover stars, running an Ian Pye feature called "Magnificent Obsessions" that touted them as "more than a group . . . they're a crusade dedicated to returning passion and optimism to our lives."

Meanwhile, Bill Black's article in *Sounds* tagged the Smiths as "real charmers" as Morrissey remarked how there is "nothing more repellant than the synthesizer." Elsewhere, Marr defended their simplistic image, from their clothes to their coifs. Although Johnny scoffed at bands in fashionable garb who had their "hair done by whatever hairdresser is in vogue," the irony was that they too had their own trendy stylist. Marr also asserted that they weren't revivalists, even though they were predominantly influenced by music from the 1960s.

No Gay Spokesperson

Record Mirror also lent support that month, focusing solely on Morrissey in its November 12 issue. In the piece, he opined that *Top of the Pops* was "there to be used . . . we just want to reach people." The article pointed out how the Smiths' singer was "non-macho," had received coverage in *Him*, and possessed a non-heterosexual attitude. Morrissey admitted that the gay connotations "would well be harmful when it comes to dealing with the press" but deflected them using careful words. "I simply can't get down to gender—I don't mind who listens. I wouldn't like to be thought of as a gay spokesman, though, because it's just not true."

A Sort of Homecoming

November 1983 was a fruitful month for the Smiths as they balanced radio, press, and television coverage with live shows. Energetic and uplifting gigs at Leicester Polytechnic on the 16th and Edge Hill College on the 18th had the band satiating audiences with three encores and building their setlist to fourteen original songs. Those gigs sandwiched an intimate, students-only event at London's Westfield College.

While formal touring initiatives were still a few months off, the foursome was playing in top form, as evidenced by their homecoming gig at the Hacienda on November 24. Although this show got off to a late start as a result of the band having to travel some 200 miles from that day's *Top of the Pops* appearance by train—Morrissey having refused to get in a hired helicopter—when the Smiths finally arrived in Manchester, the capacity crowd of nearly 2,000 fans gave them a gallant welcome.

The opening set by fellow Mancunians and future U.K. pop stars James had long since ended when the Smiths reached the venue on this spectacular night. Johnny would later exaggerate to an interviewer how the Smiths had to be carried through the streets while revealing how odd it was to be worshipped by some of the blokes he went to school with a few years earlier. In any case, it was the group's first true taste of fame.

Of course, many brought flowers for Morrissey, who joked, "Hello, you ugly devils," as Marr, Joyce, and Rourke took to their instruments and began to play "Handsome Devil." From there, they never looked back until they got to the final encore, the night's second performance of "Hand in Glove," delivering what was likely their most memorable—if not their finest—concert yet.

Derby Day

On December 6, the Smiths played a show at the Assembly Rooms in Derby. Tickets were free, with details of the show announced by John Peel on his radio show, which resulted in a rabid crowd of Smiths fans, most of whom had been introduced to the band through Radio 1. A film crew was dispatched to capture the event for *The Old Grey Whistle Test*, which aired the concert twice the following weekend.

Although the crowd was rowdy, the gig got off to a strong start with songs like "Handsome Devil," "Still Ill," and the often-requested "Reel Around the Fountain." Unfortunately, midway through "Miserable Lie," Morrissey was smacked in the eye by a flower, which prompted him to drop his microphone halfway through and exit the stage to tend to ensure he wasn't seriously injured. The show resumed, and when the Smiths performed "This Night Has Opened My Eyes," he added the line, "I will never see again."

One fan took to the stage to hug Morrissey, and others soon began infiltrating the band's space, dancing around them during "You've Got Everything Now" until it became impossible to continue. Once Hacienda security managed to clear the stage, the group returned for a closing rendition of "These Things Take Time." Curiously, when the show aired on television, the events of the evening were shifted, with the broadcast positioning the night's most chaotic moment at the end of the concert.

Electric

The Smiths left England for the first time as a band to perform in Dublin, on the campus of Trinity College, on December 9. Ten days later, the band took the stage at London's Electric Ballroom, where they introduced two new songs— "Barbarism Begins at Home" and "Back to the Old House."

It turns out Morrissey had been imbibing alcohol backstage ahead of the show, which led to a lengthy delivery of the former, as Mike Joyce remembered in April 1993, telling *Select*, "Mozzer had been knocking the red wine back and we got out there and it was about seventeen minutes long. Moz kept going into that middle bit—yodeling. Fuckin' on and on. Johnny kept coming over and looking at me, and every time he did it I thought, 'Thank God, he's going to stop it.' We were knackered."

In advance of the Electric Ballroom gig, *Time Out* championed the band in a piece for its December 8 issue titled "Song-Smiths." In it, writer Mick Wall marveled at how "the success of the Smiths is a sudden and unexpected phenomenon." He was not wrong.

Police Brutality

The Police—Sting, Steward Copeland, and Andy Summers—were easily the biggest rock act in the world in the fall of 1983, touring on the strength of their multimillion selling album *Synchronicity*. When the group with the biggest hit single of the year, "Every Breath You Take," plotted their extensive, sixteen-date arena tour through Scotland and England that December, the Smiths were asked if they might be interested in opening for the massive trio.

It was an opportunity that almost any other band at the level of the Smiths might surely jump at—but Morrissey and Marr refused the slot. Defending his decision to Andy Strikes in *Record Mirror* in February 1984, the singer confidently, if not arrogantly, explained how the Smiths "were more important than the Police will ever be."

The same month, Marr told Katie Neville of the *Face* that they snubbed the Police because, "It didn't make any artistic sense."

16

Prudence Never Pays

Handsome and Popular

All Trade Booking and Featherstone

With *The Smiths* complete, Morrissey, Marr, and Moss teamed with concert promoter Mike Hinc at All Trade Booking late in 1983 to finalize plans for the band's first official U.K. tour for early the following year. The seven-week run would begin at the University of Sheffield on January 31 and run until March 20 at the Tower Ballroom in Birmingham.

The band's live shows also began to focus more on ambiance with the hiring of lighting director John Featherstone—at Johnny's insistence, after the two hit it off instantly. Featherstone, who was just nineteen, had first officially worked with the band on their *Old Grey Whistle Test* special after working the lights on spec at the group's Leicester Polytechnic a month earlier.

Festive Fifty

At the end of '83, John Peel counted down a survey of his Radio 1 listeners' favorite songs. The year-end radio special, billed as his "Festive Fifty," saw the Smiths' "This Charming Man" land at #2, right behind the undisputed top U.K. single of 1983, New Order's "Blue Monday."

Morrissey/Marr tracks dominated the survey, with "Handsome Devil" (#33), "Hand in Glove" (#9), and "Reel Around the Fountain" (#6) also making appearances. While New Order also had three other songs in the chart, they also had a best-selling album—*Power, Corruption, and Lies*—out that year. The Smiths' debut was still unreleased.

New York Mix

In late 1983, after "This Charming Man" had peaked at #25 in the U.K. pop charts and then fallen off, Rough Trade elected to release a 12-inch pressing of the song. Reworked by U.S. DJ Francois Kevorkian, the "New York" mix of the song was released throughout Europe and then imported into America by Sire and serviced to DJs in an effort to draw attention to the label's latest signing.

Morrissey first learned of the remix when he stopped by the Rough Trade offices and saw boxes of it stacked high. When he confronted Travis, the singer

Phil McIntyre presents

The Smiths

+ The Telephone Boxes

LEICESTER de MONTFORT HALL
Sunday 18th March at 7.30pm

SHEFFIELD CITY HALL
Monday 19th March at 7.30pm

Tickets £3.50 available from the Box Office
Leicester 0533 54444, Sheffield 0742 735295/6

A gig advertisement for two shows at the tail end of the Smiths' first fully fledged U.K. tour in support of their eponymous 1984 debut album. *Author's collection*

was told that the danceable version was essential to keep the proper song alive. Geoff rationalized that guitar bands like Echo & the Bunnymen, U2, and new Sire labelmates Talking Heads had all been remixed for the clubs, with noticeable outcomes. But the Smiths were not pleased with the move, as Morrissey explained to Andy Strikes in *Record Mirror* in February '84. "It was entirely against our principles," the singer complained, before explaining that there was also talk of releasing an "Acton Version" of the track, which would have been named for an area of west London.

Moss Quits

In an effort to try to establish a foothold in the United States, the Smiths had been booked to play some East Coast dates after Christmas 1983, including a New Year's Eve show in New York City. However, this journey would be made without Joe Moss, who had withdrawn from his managerial role after the group's Electric Ballroom show.

According to Marr, arguments between Moss and Morrissey had escalated to the point of being unbearable. "Rather than let that friction cause problems between me and Morrissey, he took himself out of the picture," Marr told *Q* in February 2001. Joe had also recently become a father, and after spending the days leading up to Christmas at home with his infant daughter, he decided that he just couldn't leave. Traveling around the U.K. with Marr's increasingly busy band had become more than he could manage. After much deliberation, he informed Johnny he was quitting.

Joe believed it was a good time to bow out, as the Smiths were on the verge of worldwide success. Despite this, he continued to remain an ally to the band, and even drove them to the airport for their first overseas trip.

Moss's absence would be felt for years to come as Morrissey and Marr attempted to run the business aspects of the Smiths while writing songs, making records, and touring. While Johnny understood Joe's desire to step away from the role, the absence of a proper manager they could trust left him frustrated and overwhelmed. "After Joe, we had just one managerial disaster after another," Marr told *Musician* in September 1989.

Johnny and Angie Split

On the eve of the group's New York trip, Marr and his girlfriend Angela Brown broke up following a Christmas argument. Although the split was only temporary, after five years of daily companionship, Angie's absence from the band's sojourn to Manhattan left Marr in a fractured state. Instead of celebrating the group's ascent, he was at an all-time low, according to Smiths soundman Grant Showbiz, who had made the trek with the band. New Year's Eve without Angie was no celebration at all, as Johnny ran up sizable long-distance bills while they worked through their quarrel.

Danceteria

When the Smiths touched down at JFK airport on the afternoon of December 30, Danceteria promoter Ruth Polsky had a limousine pick them up. That same evening, Polsky invited the Smiths to her Manhattan apartment for dinner.

The next night, New Year's Eve, the Smiths took the stage at the world-famous multicultural music club just after midnight. The same night, an up-and-coming pop singer named Madonna, who had also just signed to Seymour Stein's Sire Records, performed her early singles "Burning Up" and "Holiday," among others.

Although the Smiths' exact setlist remains unknown, Johnny Marr would later recall that the group performed seven songs. At one point during the show, Morrissey was blinded by the venue's lighting and fell off the stage.

Clearly injured, the singer climbed back up on the platform and retreated to a backstage bathroom to assess his badly bruised right leg. While Johnny looked on with worry, Morrissey would later reveal in the pages of *Autobiography* just how outraged he felt that Rourke had simply stood there laughing at his injury. He was equally appalled when Travis ordered him to get back onstage.

Although Morrissey—who had supposedly over-indulged on wine during a dinner of Indian cuisine to ease his pre-show jitters—was unaware of it, the rest of the band and entourage had been doing cocaine backstage with pioneering hip-hop artist, DJ, and producer Lovebug Starski. Regardless, the next day, Travis was on the receiving end of an irate call from Morrissey's mother, who expressed her outrage over his failure to get her son suitable medical attention.

Marr's New Guitar and Andy's Heroin Slip

During their initial meeting in the U.K. the previous year, Seymour Stein had promised Johnny Marr that in exchange for agreeing to partner with Sire, he would buy him a guitar. Marr was duly gifted a Gibson 355 hollow-body guitar, bought at a store in Manhattan's music district, which he used during the trip to write the music for what would become "Heaven Knows I'm Miserable Now" in his hotel room.

Meanwhile, Rourke kept himself from boredom during their downtime in other ways. According to the recollections of Grant Showbiz in Tony Fletcher's book, he was tempted by Manhattan's easily acquired heroin.

Tour Woes

Alongside Morrissey's stage mishap, the Smiths' maiden ten-day United States voyage was hampered by other distresses. Upon being booked into the Algonquin Hotel—the preferred inn of Morrissey's dead heroes James Dean and Oscar Wilde—the singer found himself mortified by the accommodations. After witnessing an infestation of large cockroaches, the front man slept at the midtown hotel—which has long since been renovated—fully clothed.

Subsequent shows in the early days of January in New Jersey (where the Smiths rehearsed), Boston, and a planned return to Danceteria a week after the first all wound up being shelved when Mike Joyce purportedly came down with chicken pox. This cover story would be used to explain the cancelations for years until Morrissey revealed in his 2013 book that the drummer had contracted "Lebanese warts" (a.k.a. genital warts) after an "unlucky dalliance."

Either way, Andy wasn't the only unfortunate one. In a 1984 interview disc, Morrissey explained that certain members of their entourage had come down with the flu, prompting a sooner-than-expected return home.

If I Ruled the World

While the Smiths were en route back to England, the January 7 issue of *No. 1* was hitting the newsstands at home. In a one-page Q&A by writer Karen Swayne, Morrissey was behaving very much the celebrity as he offered up his opinions on technology, government, sex, and children. He snubbed kids as "very monotonous creatures," denounced common people as "powerless" against government, and spoke yet again of his desire to "cleanse the world of sexual stereotypes."

Freezing Morrissey Out

The New York trip nearly broke the Smiths, and upon their return to Manchester, the band's members went their separate ways.

Although Jon Moss was no longer the band's manager, he was still Marr's confidante, and Marr and Rourke wound up taking occupancy with him. Johnny was working things out with Angie but they were living apart, while Andy was trying to get clean from his recent heroin lapse and knew the temptation of drugs at home, where his brothers resided, was not an option.

Somehow, Johnny and Moss managed to keep Rourke's drug use from Joyce and Morrissey. The singer was naïve about drugs and kept an anti-drug profile in interviews, unaware of Andy's well-hidden problem. Meanwhile, Johnny kept hoping his friend would overcome his demons.

During the next several weeks of inactivity, Morrissey singer had minimal contact with his bandmates, which led him to believe he was being frozen out. He imagined that Moss was trying to stage a coup in order to resume management of the group and oust him, and even suggests in *Autobiography* that Joe "coerced" the others into formally "axing the singer."

If this was ever really the case, obligations including a BBC TV appearance and the launch of a six-week U.K. tour by month's end put plans for such a firing on ice.

Life in London

While the Smiths' guitarist, bassist, and drummer resumed life in Manchester, Morrissey had already pulled up stakes and moved to London. In January—in celebration of the band's honor of being named "Best New Act" in *NME*'s year-end reader's poll—he was photographed and interviewed in his new Kensington apartment.

Morrissey's home was subdued and not at all what one might expect from a pop star of the day. His living room featured a modest sofa and two chairs, a table with a typewriter and neatly stacked paper, and an abundance of books, including all of Oscar Wilde's works and several on James Dean. He also had three framed photographs of himself, but when a Dublin reporter visiting at the time asked him whether he thought he was handsome, he spouted back, "I'm ugly."

Morrissey's new residence was located in a posh area on Campden Hill Road called Hornton Court, and his neighbors included newly knighted *ITN News at Ten* television anchor Sir Alistair Burnet and actor Robert Powell, who had appeared in notable films like 1969's *The Italian Job* and the Who's 1975 movie *Tommy*. Geoff Travis had found Morrissey the flat, which had recently been vacated by Skids singer Richard Jobson.

London allowed Morrissey to remain close to Smiths business at Rough Trade and enjoy his celebrity by entertaining pop stars and actresses alike. Visitors of the day included the English Beat's Dave Wakeling—who was launching his new act General Public—and Elton John's manager, who came offering to represent him. Associates singer Billy MacKenzie and movie star Vanessa Redgrave also make social calls.

Morrissey insisted that being several hours away from his bandmates had no bearing on the group's relationship in a February *Record Mirror* interview. Marr was within easy reach by telephone, even if that meant racking up sizable long-distance bills. The upside, he added, was a tremendous uptick in magazine articles about the group.

The Smiths

THE NEW SINGLE

WHAT DIFFERENCE DOES IT MAKE?

b/w BACK TO THE OLD HOUSE
on 7" – RT 146
plus 12" with extra track THESE THINGS TAKE TIME
RTT 146

Rough
TRADE

An in-store poster promoting "What Difference Does It Make?," featuring the single's original cover star, Terrence Stamp. Soon after its release in January 1984, the song shot to #12 in the U.K. *Author's collection*

"What Difference" on 45

Upon its release on January 16, 1984, the Smiths' third single became their first significant chart appearance, reaching #12 in the U.K. For its sleeve, Morrissey had originally hoped to use an animated photograph of actor Terrence Stamp clutching a chloroform pad from the set of the 1965 movie *The Collector*. Geoff Travis, who was friends with 1960s pop singer Sandie Shaw—a pal of Stamp's—assumed that Stamp would sanction the release of the sleeve. But when Stamp refused to allow the Smiths the rights to use his image, much to the singer's frustration, Morrissey did a credible job of re-enacting the shot for the single's first pressing, notably substituting the actor's prop with a glass of milk.

With the song achieving immediate popularity, Stamp quickly acquiesced, and the single's cover emerged as originally planned for subsequent copies of "What Difference Does It Make?" As a result, the initial sleeve has become a collector's item.

Morrissey first suggested to reporter that his lyrics were designed to point out the insignificance of worrying over things like having great hair or perfect teeth. He has long since insisted that "What Difference Does It Make?" is one of his least favorite Smiths songs. There is speculation that the lyrics are about how the singer was once snubbed by a friend in whom he confided that he was gay, although this has never been confirmed. He did eventually tell the fan blog *Following the Mozziah* that the song was "musically interesting but lyrically it is very . . . Simon Le Bon," in reference to the well-known Duran Duran singer.

"I find the lyrics facile and mildly embarrassing," he explained. "Otherwise it's a majestic pop melody by Johnny and, ironically, had the lyrics indeed been penned by Simon Le Bon, I would probably cover it! As it is, I'd feel too ashamed."

It all goes a long way to explain why he pushed for "Pretty Girls Make Graves" to be the band's third 45, only to be vetoed by Travis and the Rough Trade staff. And rightly so, as the single holds its place as one of the band's finest musical moments, thanks in large part to Marr's undeniable guitar arrangement.

Television

The impressive chart performance of "What Difference Does It Make?" wasn't helped much by the BBC, which only played the song sparingly. Instead, exposure in the music papers and television appearances before and during their upcoming tour was to thank for the track's hit status.

The Smiths taped two separate and distinct performances of the song on the BBC's *Top of the Pops*. The first had Morrissey quite hilariously and memorably sporting a hearing aid for the group's lip-synched spot on January 26. The band then mimed it again on February 9. On February 6 and 10, the band played the song on the BBC North West program *Y.E.S.* and BBC2's *Oxford Road Show*, respectively. The former also broadcast a delivery of "This Night Has Opened My Eyes."

Television fit into the band's aspirations. Morrissey and Marr wanted to build an audience as large as they could. In a February interview with *ZigZag*, they revealed that were hoping to build a massive fan base. "We want to be on *Top of the Pops* whenever we can," Johnny told William Shaw, embracing what he called "the whole sell-out trip."

By the year's end, Morrissey would disclose to journalist Ian Pye that he actually loved the medium. "I find doing *Top of the Pops* great fun," he explained. "They always give us a semi-royal reception," and added, "I think the groups that criticize *Top of the Pops* are those that probably know they'll never get on there!"

No Videos

Despite the growing popularity of music videos and the emergence of MTV in the United States, Morrissey spoke emphatically against the promotional form in his first live television interview. Speaking at 7:30 in the morning with Paul Gambaccini for the nationally televised ITV news program *TV-AM* in early 1984, the Smiths' singer was seen sitting on the couch in a pair of faded Levi's, with a purple and gold-lamé striped blouse, as he explained his group's anti-video stance.

"I think it is pantomime, I think it's trivial," he asserted. "I really believe the record is the only prop that one should need." When anchor Henry Kelly suggested that the rise of music video was nothing more than an advertisement for a new song, the Smiths' front man opined how the medium was "dangerous" because it "detracts from what it's supposed to be."

Morrissey—who had had the opportunity to sit silently next to one of his father's heroes, George Best, in the studio's green room—went on to relay how people were seeing "the Smiths as being terribly real," unlike many modern groups that were hiding behind such "props."

False Start

Although Morrissey remained unaware, Rourke was still struggling with his heroin addiction when the Smiths climbed into their seat-less panel van for their first proper U.K. tour. In order to accommodate their growing crew, which included sound engineer Grant Showbiz, new tour manager Phil Cowie, and the occasional Rough Trade staffer, the communal mattress had been joined by several beanbag chairs and carpeted walls.

Cowie struggled with his leadership role. Without a proper manager, the band had become what Marr would describe to _Q_ in 2001 as a "rudderless ship." Showbiz did not care for Cowie and refused to take orders from him. When Phil asked Grant to help empty the group's equipment truck, he reminded Cowie he was not a roadie. Morrissey and Marr were forced to step in to try to settle such disputes.

Operational issues aside, the Smiths' first gig on the trek—at the University of Sheffield on January 31, 1984—was a success. The performance marked the live debut of two new songs, "Girl Afraid" and "Heaven Knows I'm Miserable Now," and the return of recently premiered numbers "Barbarism Begins at Home" and "Back to the Old House." When the latter was introduced by Morrissey—who had taken to stuffing a few of the flowers, now required as part of the group's tour rider, down his pants—he dedicated it to "all you doomed delicates" in the audience.

Two nights later, after a gig at North Staffordshire Polytechnic in Stoke-on-Trent, the group played a shortened show at Coventry's University of Warwick after Morrissey had come down with a sore throat. The illness became severe enough that six planned gigs were postponed to the back of the tour.

Rough Trade publicist Gill Smith would later explain that the singer's propensity for illness was due to his poor diet. Being vegetarian didn't mean eating healthy—Morrissey was living on crisps, chocolate, and croissants at the time.

Piering or Polsky?

By now, Rough Trade was dealing directly with Morrissey on business matters. During the unexpected downtime that February, the label's American-born press officer Scott Piering was tapped to handle the group's day-to-day affairs. Days later, in London, Ruth Polsky—the agent who had recently booked the group's New York show—announced to Travis that she was now managing the band, with Morrissey's endorsement.

Ruth had convinced Morrissey that he deserved to be treated like the star he was becoming. When she contended that the Smiths deserved to be staying in finer hotels, ought to be on a bigger record label, and above all else commanded a better wage per show, the front man easily agreed.

The only issue was that Polsky's pushy, spoiled New York party perspective prompted her to misunderstand Morrissey's guarded interest in her pitch to represent his band. She assumed he had hired him, which he hadn't, and when she told members of the music industry that she was handling the Smiths affairs, he was quite furious. As was Marr, who told *Sounds'* Hugh Felder that month, "One thing I wasn't expecting were the leeches diving in," referring to people like Polsky wanting to cash in on their popularity. "At the moment, everybody we meet wants to be our manager!"

Piering proposed to Johnny and Morrissey that he become their official manager as a means of making Polsky go away. But while her personality clashed with the Smiths, Ruth's points about getting Morrissey what he deserved stayed with Scott. He argued for Morrissey to travel by limousine to television appearances and get his own dressing room at gigs.

As much as they were pleased with Piering's efforts, the Smiths' principals agreed there was no need to make it official with him for the time being. And, as long as Scott was on Travis' payroll, they didn't need to pay him a commission.

Electrifying Shows

On February 12, the Smiths played at London's Lyceum. Morrissey was still feeling off. He introduced "Still Ill" by explaining, "Listen, I've been really ill lately and I'm still ill so I'm going to sing about it." Music scribe Mary Harron of the *Guardian* was not impressed. "I suspect [their] success has more to do with the weakness of the competition than with their own talents: if these are the standard bearers, then the future is limp indeed."

Folk-punk singer Billy Bragg—who had recently landed a #1 on the U.K. independent albums chart with *Life's a Riot with Spy vs. Spy* and first witnessed the band at the Electric Ballroom show—opened the show. In tribute to his new friends, he covered "Jeane," having been taken by the simplicity of Marr's riff.

Mid-month gigs at the University of East Anglia, the University of Nottingham, and the University of Leicester were well received, but by the time the Smiths reached venues like the Dance Hall at the University of Essex, their audiences were a mix of fans and curiosity-seekers. Members of the band also began to encounter spitting and thrown water and beer from audiences.

At other shows—like Bournemouth's Town Hall on February 21—there was a noticeable disinterest from the crowd, prompting Morrissey to lead the band off the stage after only thirty-five minutes. Eventually, the audience clamored for their return, and they reluctantly did so, with the Smiths' singer scolding fans for their initial indifference. "Listen, we're really confused, do you actually like us or not?" he asked. When they responded positively, Marr kicked off the introductory lick to "What Difference Does It Make?"

The next evening, at the University of Reading, Marr was drenched with water thrown from the front row. Johnny was nearly electrocuted and became understandably upset. He stopped playing for five minutes, and when he resumed the set he played the rest of the show with his back to the audience. He vowed to never play in Reading again—and the band never did.

Sold-out shows at the University of Bristol's Anson Rooms and Brighton Polytechnic on February 24 and 25, respectively, were reassuringly incendiary, as Morrissey, Marr, Rourke, and Joyce fed off the crowd's energy. At the second show, the singer introduced the group on the heels of "Hand in Glove" by saying, "Good evening, we're four *scooby* individuals called the Smiths." And with the band's debut album selling impressively, Simon Scott's *Melody Maker* review of the gig got it right when he suggested: "next stop—the world."

If early-March concerts at the University of Glasgow and the University of Dundee were frenzied, a March 5 show at Coaster's in Edinburgh almost never happened after the group's equipment truck arrived late, only turning up after they had located another P.A. and arranged to borrow equipment from show openers the Red Guitars. Smiths pandemonium had taken hold by the time of the Middlesbrough Town Hall gig on March 8. A few dozen fans had climbed on top of the band's van in an attempt to reach their second-floor dressing room after the show. For a time, the group was trapped. "It was like being in *A Hard Day's Night*," Johnny told *Q* in 2001.

A poster advertising the Smiths' non-album single "Heaven Knows I'm Miserable Now," which was released in May 1984 and became the band's very first U.K. Top 10 hit. The sleeve's star was Viv Nicholson, who rose to fame after winning over £152,000 in the 1961 U.K. football pools. *Author's collection*

Rumors of a tour-bus crash on March 9 before a show at the University of Lancaster gave fans unnecessary worry, while by March 12, the Smiths were booked into London's 3,000-capacity Hammersmith Palais. Here, special guest Sandie Shaw was invited onstage to perform her version of "I Don't Owe You Anything"—which would also serve as the B-side to her upcoming take on "Hand in Glove"—as Morrissey stood backstage.

The only issue was that, because Shaw was a practicing Buddhist, she had gone into hiding to calm herself before her appearance. It took several minutes to locate her for her turn at the microphone.

When he returned for his proper encore, Morrissey joked to fans, "I knew I'd get dethroned eventually." He then introduced "Reel Around the Fountain" by joking, "This song is called 'There's Always Something There to Remind Me.'" He was, of course, referencing the Burt Bacharach/Hal David song that Shaw had first made famous in 1964. Much to Marr's delight, Elvis Costello was on the guest list that night.

The next night, at Manchester's Free Trade Hall, Shaw performed "I Don't Owe You Anything" once again. For the band, this show was the highlight of the entire tour, giving them an awareness that they were on the way up. Just before they took the stage, Morrissey approached Marr and told him how, when he saw them at the very same venue, T. Rex had drawn considerably fewer people.

By the time the Smiths wrapped up the tour with a week of make-up dates at venues like the de Montfort Hall in Leicester and Birmingham's Tower Ballroom, the band were already looking beyond their debut. "Heaven Knows I'm Miserable Now"—which they had just tracked with John Porter at Hammersmith's Fallout Shelter—was being introduced as their forthcoming single.

Souvenir Film

On the second-to-last night of the tour, at Sheffield's City Hall on March 19, soundman Grant Showbiz shot footage of the band at soundcheck, during their time backstage, and onstage. The film was designed to be a souvenir for the group and their road crew and featured the Smiths playing nine full songs and an instrumental. According to fan site Passions Just like Mine, it also included footage of the Smiths performing "What Difference Does It Make?" on *Top of the Pops*, plus a clip of support band the Telephone Boxes. Scenes of Marr giving Morrissey a guitar lesson, and of the singer dancing onstage, were also included in the movie, which was shown at a February 1997 "Smiths Convention" held in Pasadena, California. In March 2001, it was webcast by the now defunct www. deo.com to commemorate the twenty-fifth anniversary of Rough Trade Records.

More TV

As the U.K. tour wound down, the Smiths' television opportunities continued with a March 16 appearance on Channel 4's *The Tube*, where they performed

"Hand in Glove," "Still Ill," and "Barbarism Begins at Home." The latter—which was still a year away from proper release—was a funk-inspired attempt at dance music, and an indication that the band had much more up their sleeves musically than Marr's chiming Rickenbacker.

A performance and interview of "What Difference Does I Make?" for Belgium's *Elektron Pop* program two days later found Johnny playing with an on-set skull as Morrissey fielded questions with subtitled answers. Then, on March 31, they were back on Channel 4 for a feature on *Ear Say* that included an early mix of the upcoming single "Heaven Knows I'm Miserable Now." The show also broadcast a live interview with Morrissey and Sandie Shaw, before she lip-synched her version of "Hand in Glove."

On April 7, Morrissey and Marr guested on the ITV children's show *Datarun*, fielding questions from the children in the audience and delivering an acoustic rendition of "This Charming Man." The appearance was accompanied by video shot during a soundcheck on March 13 in Manchester.

ZigZag Revelations

Around the release of the Smiths' first album, Morrissey spoke candidly to William Shaw about a number of issues in the February 1984 issue of *ZigZag*. He took aim at the "shallow creatures" that occupied the pop charts at the time and embraced his forthcoming wealth by declaring, "I'm having the money." He also shunned the Smiths' inaccurate categorization as "hippies," because of their fondness for flowers and their anti-synth stance, as "completely lazy journalism."

Not Surprised

Morrissey's confidence about the ascent of the Smiths was overflowing when he spoke to Allan Jones in *Melody Maker* that March. "I had absolute faith and absolute belief in everything we did and I really did expect what has happened to us to happen," he asserted, of the group's high-charting debut LP.

When people suggested the Smiths' rise to fame had come too quickly, the singer was quick to dismiss such notions. "I have to disagree. I feel as if I've waited a very long time for this," he told Jones, reminding readers that his band had reintroduced a "human element" to popular music.

Sandie's "Hand"

The Smiths' relationship with Sandie Shaw began in the summer of 1983, when Geoff Travis told her about his latest signing. Travis told Shaw that Morrissey and Marr were huge fans and that they had penned a song, "I Don't Owe You Anything," with her in mind. The 1960s pop singer had recently released a modestly received one-off album for Virgin called *Choose Life*—her first in more than a

Morrissey and Sandie Shaw together in London in April 1984 during promotional efforts for her single version of the Smiths' "Hand in Glove." The Morrissey/Marr original was her first U.K. Top 30 hit since "Monsieur Dupont" in February 1969.

decade—when Geoff presented Shaw with a demo of the song and a handwritten letter from Morrissey and Johnny explaining their fascination with her music.

The fawning note had them announcing themselves as incurable fans and offering their songwriting services. But Shaw was unsure about the offer because the Smiths had only just released "Hand in Glove." It wasn't until the year's end—after the group had established themselves on the pop landscape—that Sandie and her husband, music executive Nik Powell, came back to Travis, now interested in working with the Smiths.

Travis brought Morrissey to Shaw's Harley Street apartment, where she greeted him in her pajamas and offered him toast. Much to Morrissey's excitement, Shaw agreed to record the aforementioned "I Don't Owe You Anything," which would be backed with her version of "Hand in Glove."

Tracked in London at Matrix Studios, with accompaniment from Marr, Rourke, and Joyce—presumably during Morrissey's aforementioned illness—the planned A-side and B-sides were switched by the time it was released on April 9 via Rough Trade. Shaw also recorded a version of "Jeane," which was included on the 12-inch version of the single.

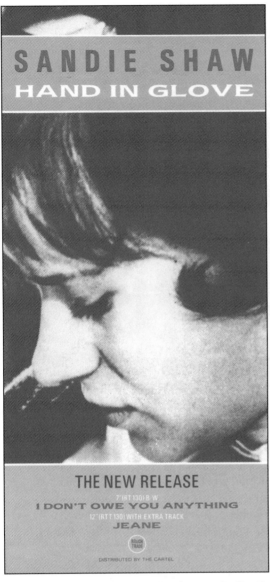

SANDIE SHAW

HAND IN GLOVE

THE NEW RELEASE

7" (RT 130) B/W
I DON'T OWE YOU ANYTHING
12" (RTT 130) WITH EXTRA TRACK
JEANE

ROUGH
TRADE

DISTRIBUTED BY THE CARTEL

A Rough Trade Records promotional poster for Sandie Shaw's version of "Hand in Glove." Shaw was backed by Marr, Rourke, and Joyce on the single, which also counted two Morrissey/Marr compositions as its B-sides. *Author's collection*

Shaw's rendition of "Hand in Glove" became a modest hit and her first chart entry since the 1960s, peaking at #27 in the U.K. pop singles survey. The song's popularity was bolstered by an appearance with the Smiths' instrumentalists on *Top of the Pops* on April 26 that found the thirty-six-year-old singer memorably falling to the floor and thrashing about. The band (sans Morrissey) appeared onstage barefoot in tribute to the singer, who had often performed without shoes in her heyday.

Shaw's Insults

In a May *Record Mirror* article arranged to publicize her new hit, Shaw was asked about her collaboration with the Smiths and revealed that at first she was turned off by their early demo. "It was with a fan letter and I really don't know why I listened to more than two bars of it—it was awful . . . really awful," she told writer Graham K. Although she was convinced to trust Morrissey after meeting him, she would later explain that she couldn't imagine him as a sex symbol. "I don't find him sexy at all!" she proclaimed.

Morrissey was insulted by these remarks and let his anger be known in an interview with the *Face* two months later. "I was never happy," he told Elissa van Poznack, "because she never said anything good about me."

If his experience of dealing with Shaw after the release of the single wasn't frustrating enough for Morrissey, he and Marr were tremendously upset to learn that Travis—without their permission—had allowed Shaw's version of "Hand in Glove" to be appended to Japanese pressings of *The Smiths*.

Over time, he would get over his anger about Shaw's remarks and remember the joy he felt when she covered "Hand in Glove." A little over a year later, in September 1985, he told the same publication's Eleanor Levy that hearing Sandie sing one of his songs for the first time was "the happiest day of my life."

Amanda Malone

Morrissey first befriended eighteen-year-old Amanda Malone during the Smiths' maiden voyage to New York City. Malone was Ruth Polsky's U.K.-born assistant who was living in the States with her gay, divorced father.

Although Morrissey was five years her senior, the pair became close during the Smiths' ten-day stay in America. Amanda was heavy set at the time but had dreams of becoming a singer, and Morrissey was fond of her voice. He invited her to return to the U.K. with the idea of making a record together.

That April, during a break between tours, Morrissey—inspired by the outcome of his work with Shaw—brought Malone into Power Plant Studios in Willesden to record her singing "This Charming Man" and the newly tracked Smiths number "Girl Afraid." Travis—who was producing the session—did not care for Malone or her voice. And while the remaining members of the Smiths were pleasant to Amanda, it became obvious that they did not like the outcome of the recording either. Plans to release a single were scotched.

Quando Quango

In April 1984, Hacienda DJ Mike Pickering and producer/New Order front man Bernard Sumner were collaborating on a dance music project called Quando Quango, which would also include A Certain Ratio's Simon Topping on percussion, among others. Remembering Marr had previously steered the funk band Freak Party, they invited him down to the studio to play on some tracks. The end result was the "Atom Rock"/"Triangle" 12-inch single, released on Factory Records that June. "It was just a spur-of-the-moment thing," Johnny told *Uncut* of the session, in April 1999. Of course, Marr and Sumner became fast friends, and would later collaborate in the post-Smiths duo Electronic.

Europe, Part One

The Smiths had been booked to perform at the fifth anniversary concert for Dutch music magazine *Vinyl* at Amsterdam's de Meervaart on April 21. The first concert of their first European tour, it was recorded for broadcast on the Netherlands' KRO station (Katholieke Radio Omroep) and included recordings of new material like "Girl Afraid" and "Barbarism Begins at Home" among the thirteen songs performed.

The next day, the band played the Breekend Festival in Bree, Belgium, opening for the Bollock Brothers, before heading to Zurich for a gig on April 24. The Rote Fabrik show would mark the band's only Swiss concert. Perhaps it was the language barrier or the Smiths' odd pairing with an obscure punk group, but these shows were unspectacular. It was Morrissey's opinion—and one shared by others in the band's camp—that certain European audiences just didn't seem to *get* them.

The same day, the Smiths were asked to back Sandie Shaw for her *Top of the Pops* appearance just two days later, on April 26. Although Morrissey wouldn't be seen on the *BBC* program, he had every intention of sharing in the achievement just the same, so the entire group flew home to London for the performance.

Germany Canceled

On the morning of April 27, the members of the Smiths and their entourage were picked up at their London hotel and taken to Heathrow Airport so that they could resume their European tour. But upon checking in for their flight, Morrissey announced he was unwilling to get on the plane. Despite Marr's best attempts to convince him otherwise, the singer appeared disconsolate, and he wasn't budging.

Five shows funded by Rough Trade's German arm were canceled. Morrissey's last-minute change in plans was costly, and it did not sit well with Travis, Hinc, or Piering, but Marr would ultimately support his partner's call. "I think we all just felt fucked," he told Fletcher, thinking back on the European market's perceived indifference. "I felt like, '[Morrissey's] expressing what we all feel.' We were trashed."

Morrissey vs. Mac

Morrissey appeared alongside Echo & the Bunnymen singer Ian McCulloch on the cover of the April 28 issue of *No. 1*. In a feature dubbed "The Rivals," both were named "the enigmas of rock."

For the piece, Morrissey was flown to the Bunnymen's hometown of Liverpool. Despite their being played up as adversaries as front men, spokesmen, and lyricists for the most popular cult bands in the U.K., their conversation—documented over tea on the verge of the Bunnymen releasing their landmark LP *Ocean Rain*—was extremely cordial.

While the Smiths would go on to surpass the Bunnymen in terms of global cult status, there was never any real competition between the groups as they largely appealed to the same audience of alternative music fans.

Europe, Part Two

After some time off the road—and with some convincing—the Smiths did go forward with a performance at Markthalle in Hamburg on May 4, which was tied to a television commitment. Upon their arrival, they were pleased to be in the company of exuberant fans who invaded the stage, much to Morrissey's delight.

The band's lone German gig of the shortened tour was a triumph, replete with three encores, that was filmed in its entirety for the German music program *Rockpalast*. The concert was also recorded for audio broadcast on the public radio network Norddeutscher Rundfunk 2 (North German Broadcasting).

On May 6, Marr, Joyce, and Rourke backed Sandie Shaw for a lip-synched performance of "Hand in Glove" on the German television show *Formel Eins*. Three days later, the Smiths proper took the stage at L'Eldorado in Paris for another TV obligation. The well-received, flower-laden show was filmed for the French program *Les Enfants du Rock*. The Smiths' performances of "Girl Afraid," "Still Ill," and "Barbarism Begins at Home" would later air on May 18 via the national Antenne 2 network.

Love of the Irish

After an eight-day rest, the Smiths embarked on a three-day run through Belfast in Northern Ireland and Dublin and Cork in the Republic of Ireland. The three successive gigs at Ulster Hall, the SFX Centre, and the Savoy, respectively, were played to enthusiastic audiences who had a strong appreciation for the Mancunian/Irish outfit.

Morrissey was sure to plug the band's looming single, "Heaven Knows I'm Miserable Now," at each of these shows, while the Dublin gig marked the return of "Jeane" to the live set after fifteen months. It went well enough that the group also performed it at the Savoy on May 20.

In advance of the shows, Morrissey was interviewed by the Irish music weekly *Hot Press*. He took the opportunity to pledge his allegiance to the country, which helped to bolster the Smiths' fan base there. "It's an immensely attractive place, obviously," he asserted. "Having Irish parents as everyone in the group has, we're all deeply imbedded here."

17

Caligula Would Have Blushed

A Top 10 Single, a Henke Problem, a Thatcher Thrashing, and More

"Heaven Knows"

When Marr spoke to *Sounds* in February 1984, he was emphatic that he had no desire to replicate *The Smiths*. The band's next studio album would defy expectations. If performances of "Barbarism Begins at Home" also suggested to fans that a change was afoot, the band's new single, "Heaven Knows I'm Miserable Now" (released on May 21), affirmed that Morrissey and Marr were due a major chart hit. It peaked at #10 on the U.K. singles survey in June after a lip-synched rendering on *Top of the Pops* on May 31.

Penned on January 2 on Marr's brand new Gibson ES-355, the melodic, mid-tempo "Heaven Knows I'm Miserable Now" was tracked at Island Records' Fallout Shelter Studios that March with producer John Porter. With the band working for the first time with Stephen Street, the facility's house engineer, the session for the single marked the first of several important collaborations between the two parties in the coming years.

Street was well aware of the group and excited to work with them after witnessing their performance of "This Charming Man" on *Top of the Pops* a few months earlier. The Smiths' principals were equally impressed, and remembered him when they needed an engineer for their second studio album in late '84.

As Morrissey's lyrics explain, the song's subject is miserable, forcing a smile at people he hates. Depressed whether with or without a job, he mentions Caligula and suggests that a woman's advances toward him would have made that debauched Roman Emperor—who had incestuous relationships with his sisters, among other depravities—blush. The title is a play on Sandie Shaw's failed single "Heaven Knows I'm Missing Him Now."

The sleeve art for the track features Viv Nicholson, who rose to notoriety in 1961 after she won a vast sum (£152,319) in the U.K. football pools. Nicholson burned through her money quickly on cars, parties, and expensive clothes. Morrissey had first proposed a cover photo of the English actor Albert Finney, but the star of 1970s films like *Gumshoe* and *Murder on the Orient Express* refused to approve its use.

The inner etching of the 7-inch pressing—which included the album track "Suffer Little Children" on the B-side—reads "Smiths Indeed" on the front with "Ill Forever" on the back. The 12-inch etching differs, reading "Smiths Presumably"/"Forever Ill."

The music for "Girl Afraid," also tracked with "Heaven Knows," was appended to the flip side of the 12-inch. That song was also written on January 2 by Marr in his Manhattan hotel room, and he spoke of them as companion pieces in a 2013 *NME* interview. The latter was conceived by Marr on a studio piano, before he transferred it to guitar. Johnny would claim he wrote the piece with a quick, New Orleans–style piano part in mind, before it became "a Kinks-style, real '60s erratic drum beat bop," in a February 1985 interview with *Guitarist.*

Moz

According to Morrissey, the success of "Heaven Knows I'm Miserable Now"— made his name synonymous with the word "miserable." After playing around

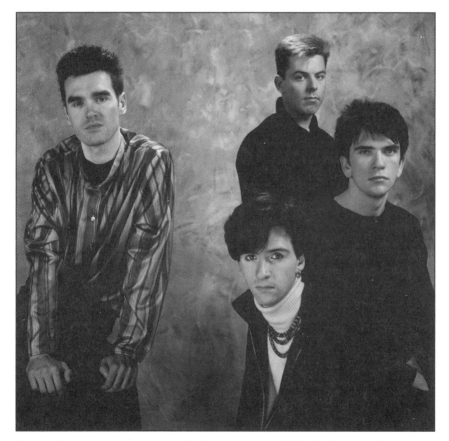

The Smiths photographed together in London in early 1984. *Chalkie Davies/Getty Images*

with the term and his singer's name, Marr came up with the phrase "misery mozzery" during the summer of '84. Johnny continued to toy with the words until he arrived at an abridged name for his songwriting partner: "Moz." Within a few short years, the name became synonymous with the Smiths' singer.

Depressed in Finland

Morrissey found himself deeply depressed and tearful during a horrific plane ride ahead of the Smiths' June 3 performance at the Provinssi Rock Festival in Seinajoki. It carried over into the band's hotel check-in and soundcheck. After the band and crew—which counted new tour manager Stuart James—gave Moz his much needed space by retreating into their novels, magazines, and Sony Walkmen, he got it together enough to pull off their Sunday afternoon performance.

In keeping with Morrissey's mood, it began to rain heavily as they took the stage. Despite the downpours, the group got off two new live debuts. The first, "Nowhere Fast," would eventually surface on their second album. The second new number, a succinct and sprightly tune called "William, It Was Really Nothing," was already being plugged to the crowd as the band's next single, even though it was more than two months away from release.

On the Road to Glastonbury

The Smiths' second U.K. trek of 1984 was scheduled between two substantial June festival appearances. The first, headlining London's free "Jobs for a Change" benefit at the Jubilee Gardens with support from Billy Bragg, was funded by the Labour Party–led Greater London Council. The June 10 event gave Morrissey an opportunity to stand in formal opposition to Margaret Thatcher while playing for 10,000 people—the bulk of whom were Smiths fans.

The band's summer headlining tour was a strong draw in Scotland, with energetic crowds propelling mid-June stops at Carlisle's Market Hall, Glasgow's Barrowlands, Caley Palace in Edinburgh, and Eden Court in Inverness into unforgettable shows. The Carlisle gig on the 12th required a mid-set restart of "William, It Was Really Nothing" after troublemakers up front began heckling and spitting, with Johnny scolding the crowd by saying, "If you spit on Morrissey, he's not going to sing to you." The audience took heed and sang along to "Heaven Knows I'm Miserable Now," calling the band back for three encores.

The Glasgow crowd was also full of spitters, prompting Marr to warn them, too, that the show would be canceled unless the behavior ceased, with Moz exiting the stage until things could be corrected. The hecklers were far outweighed by true fans, who chanted "Morrissey! Morrissey!" until he returned to lead a frenzied sing-along of their recent massive hit. By this point, the singer was bare-chested, having thrown his shirt into the crowd.

At Blackpool's Opera House on June 20, a section of the flooring collapsed, resulting in a few minor injuries to fans who fell through to the basement below. Despite this incident, however, the show went on after the affected area of the venue was cordoned off.

On June 23, the Smiths arrived for their scheduled performance at the legendary Glastonbury Festival—still considered a "hippie" gathering at the time, and nowhere near the massive, globally recognized event it has since become—where the quartet encountered fans and hecklers alike. They were given a strict set time, which allowed for just ten songs. Although the group's #2 chart success made them a massive draw, and would have earned them a headlining slot at the event, said accomplishment had come after the Smiths had agreed to play the festival.

"We'd always played to manic, devoted audiences who were more like supporters at a cup final," Marr told the *Guardian* of the event in 2010, admitting the Smiths were a little out of their element alongside aging bands like Weather Report, Joan Baez, and the Band. "We were very 'urban' compared to the other acts. Our songs were so fast that we got through our first four in about the time it took for the other bands to finish their intro."

Although the group's set was plagued with sound woes—the guitar and the vocals were both somehow coming through Rourke's bass amp—Marr felt things came together for their finale, "Hand in Glove." It was during this number that he also helped start a stage invasion by pulling up one fan, who next helped another, and so on. Before long, it felt like an official Smiths concert.

Morrissey's Image

In the days before he had a suitable clothing budget, Morrissey would tuck in his shirt collars because he found them unmanageable. By mid-'84, he was opening up about his public image and his desire to be seen as a cross between James Dean and Oscar Wilde.

With some money starting to trickle in, Morrissey spoke to *Undress* of how being a pop star meant that he was constantly being judged by his appearance—be it his hair or his wardrobe. "I would find it absolutely impossible to speak to somebody if they were wearing a duffle coat . . . or if they had a repugnant hairstyle," he half-joked.

Elsewhere in the article, he admitted to writer Iain Webb that he bought many of his unique stage shirts from the outsize ladies' clothing shop Evans. The singer paired these prized blouses with vintage Levi's Jeans, which he had purchased and cherished during his earlier treks to the United States. Underneath, he often went commando—without boxers or briefs. As for shoes, the Smiths' front man would round out his ensembles with a pricey pair of buckle-strapped slip-on loafers by designer Manuel.

Suicidal Fan Mail

Morrissey spoke openly against his chart peers, opining how other acts of the time were not good role models for the youth. Others were shallow; he was well-thought. Others wrote obscure and mysterious lyrics without clear messages; he spoke directly to fans with his simple but powerful messages.

Moz also proudly answered fan mail at this stage in his career, even though some of it worried him. Speaking to *Hot Press* that year, he acknowledged he received suicide letters but felt unsure of how to deal with them. Remarkably, though, Morrissey was trying to be there for his troubled disciples. He spoke to fans who approached him in the street whenever he could and actually listened to what they had to tell him. "I can't think of anyone more qualified," he told the Dublin weekly, of his attempt to help the Smiths' sad followers resolve their issues. "I've been through it and I understand it." He went on to reveal that he even admired those with the strength to go through with suicide, and expressed how he felt that those who took total control of their lives and bodies to end things were "quite honorable."

Catholicism Absurd

While Morrissey had long since dismissed himself as a practicing Catholic, his new level of fame prompted the media to ask for his thoughts on religion. He made no secret of his stern Catholic education and told one reporter of how he imagined Christ looking down on the severity of the Roman Catholic Church, which thrived on perpetual fear and guilt. In his assessment, it was all "quite absurd."

The Smiths' front man would surely have raised a few eyebrows in the '84 *Hot Press* cover story when he equated the church to a police state that had been designed in part to ensure that the working classes behaved. He also caused a stir by suggested that Pope John Paul II was a hypocrite for judging working-class women who had abortions for economic reasons, and opined that his actions were a means to keep the lower classes down.

Moz went on to criticize the Pope for "giving long, overblown, inflated lectures on nuclear weapons" before sitting down for tea with Margaret Thatcher. It wouldn't be long before the British prime minister herself would also be ripe for criticism by the outspoken pop star.

Media Hog

Between the pages of *Melody Maker*, *NME*, and *Smash Hits* at home, where the band were plugging their new single, and in U.S. publications like *Creem*, *Musician*, *Penthouse*, and *Rolling Stone*, which were publicizing the album's release via Sire, Morrissey was downright media-happy. "I would never shun an interview," he told *Jamming!* that May. If anything, Morrissey—who was by and large the group's spokesman—was too accommodating. At one point, an insider revealed to the *Face* how the Smiths' singer gave twenty-four interviews in a single day.

If it all helped "Heaven Knows I'm Miserable Now" chart well, and *The Smiths* sell a staggering 300,000 copies in the U.K. alone, the notion of Morrissey appearing on television shows like *Pop Quiz* and *Eight Days a Week* more than three decades after the fact sounds downright laughable. The overexposure left him fatigued and recognizing the need to start pacing himself.

All the same, others in the band were all too happy to let their mouthpiece have all the fun. In his first proper interview ever with *Record Mirror* in September 1984, Andy Rourke said, "Morrissey's so good at getting our views across that we don't need or want the exposure. . . .What he says is good, and he handles it very well."

Depth of the Smiths

In spite of his group's traditional rock lineup, Morrissey continued to use the press to convey his belief that the Smiths were something special. For Moz and Johnny, the band's music was gimmick-free and different from the "mundane and moronic" pop groups the former had spoken of in *Jamming!* It may have only been made using guitar, bass, and drums, but that was in part because they needed their releases to be accessible—although not necessarily commercial—while having a kind of depth rarely heard from the band's chart rivals.

The Smiths were never willfully obscure. Their insistence that their records be memorable injected a new attitude into the music world, which was still recovering from atrocities like Duran Duran's *Seven and the Ragged Tiger*. From the songs to the lyrics to the sleeves—which had and would continue to offer unique cover stars that probed thought and discourse among fans—the Manchester outfit established themselves as a unique pop entity while working within the confines of customary rock 'n' roll instrumentation.

Morrissey's Sexuality

The Smiths' singer's sexual proclivities remained a routine topic for journalists to discuss. With Morrissey having already proclaimed himself to be several years celibate—previously telling Allan Jones that he found the act of having sex "particularly unenjoyable"—writers became intrigued by the notion of that changing, especially because a star of his caliber would certainly have been able to reap the sexual benefits of fame, were he not completely sexless.

Although Morrissey strove to keep gender specifics out of his songs, his lyrics—notably on the first album—conveyed the idea that he might be obsessed with sex. All this made him a rare figure in the phallic and masturbatory world of rock. While he wasn't a traditional sex symbol, pictures of him with his blouse unbuttoned would still soon adorn the bedroom walls of teenage boys and girls alike.

If his open shirt and beads projected ambivalence, he was subtle about it in a way that others, like Soft Cell's Marc Almond, Bronksi Beat's Jimmy Somerville, and—in a more extreme sense—Culture Club's Boy George, hadn't been. Through image and song, Morrissey remained ambiguous without being flamboyant. In doing so, in spite of his occasionally suggestive lyrics, he was able

A Rough Trade publicity shot released to the U.K. press in late 1984. *Author's collection*

to keep the Smiths from being pegged a "gay" band, which he recognized could have alienated certain otherwise unaccepting record buyers.

Rolling Stone Controversy

Quite egregiously, *Rolling Stone*'s June 7, 1984, feature on the Smiths—which was supposed to introduce the foursome to the wide-open U.S. market—wound up cold-shouldering them as Sire's pressings of the LP were shipped. For the article, writer James Henke had flown to London to interview Morrissey and, upon delivering his one-page piece, announced in his opening sentence how the front man had admitted "that he's gay but adds that he's also celibate."

Morrissey was horrified at the magazine's presumption, which lacked a supporting quote. Although many of the singer's friends would later contend to Fletcher that they always knew he was gay—with some even suggesting that Moz might have actually been sexually active at the time of his professed celibacy—it was still the star's prerogative not to make it public.

He wrote to Henke with his objection over the piece's irresponsible assumption and took to the *Face* that July with his denial. Although *Rolling Stone* never issued a retraction, writer Kurt Loder helped make some amends with his glowing four-star review of *The Smiths*.

The following November, Morrissey told Ian Pye of his objections about Henke's feature. "That brought a lot of problems for me," he complained, denying ever having made such a statement. It's understood why the singer never took a legal recourse against the publication—making enemies with *Rolling Stone*, America's only major music magazine, was not a good idea for a band trying to crack the U.S. market in 1984. Besides, drawing the matter out in the American courts would surely end up publicizing the subject and "outing" him, if he was, in fact, homosexual.

Curiously, Morrissey—who also reacted to *Ear Say* TV personality Nicky Horne calling him the "Quentin Crisp of pop" with a scathing letter about the embarrassment it caused him—sidestepped the topic of these accusations altogether in his 2013 biography.

Press On

Further U.S. market coverage came that June from sources including *Musician*, the *New York Times*, and *Creem*. In the latter, speaking to Merle Ginsberg, Morrissey described the band as "artists" along the lines of the Velvet Underground, Patti Smith, and Television, declaring, "Our music is the music that's needed in England now—and even more so in America."

Morrissey revealed a desire for success in the States, but it would need to be on his terms. The Smiths, as he told *Musican* writer Roy Trakin, would not go "door-to-door . . . I want it the easy way." But the band's unwillingness to tour the United States in support of the album didn't help them garner any significant sales for Sire, or any significant airplay outside of college radio.

Anti-Videos

The lack of a music video with which to promote the record was also detrimental to the success of *The Smiths* in North America, where MTV had become an instrumental medium for breaking untraditional, international acts without touring. Morrissey was adamantly against the proven promotional form, insisting it tainted the music, which should speak for itself.

"I believe [videos] reflect one's disbelief in the work and himself," he told Trakin. Moz held firm on his position for some time, decreeing late in '84 that the Smiths would never, ever make a music video.

Blasting Margaret

Although Morrissey was devastated by the way *Rolling Stone* had depicted him, the article would also cause a successive controversy because of his lashing out at Margaret Thatcher in it for her history of "violence and oppression and horror." Moz continued his tirade by suggesting she could be destroyed, and told Henke, "I just pray there is a Sirhan Sirhan somewhere." Sirhan, of course, was convicted of the 1968 assassination of U.S. senator Robert F. Kennedy.

Later in the year, in a *Melody Maker* cover piece, Morrissey would speak out against the British prime minister again in the wake of an IRA terrorist bombing of Brighton's Grand Hotel, which occurred during the yearly Conservative Party Conference on October 12 and resulted in five deaths. "The sorrow of the bombing is that Thatcher escaped unscathed," he said, the following month. "I think that, for once, the IRA were accurate in selecting their targets."

Rourke, Morrissey, Joyce, and Marr appearing on *The Tube* on March 16, 1984, where they performed "Hand in Glove," "Still Ill," and the then-new and still-unreleased song, "Barbarism Begins at Home." *Rex USA*

More Moors

The singer's criticism of Thatcher prompted the conservative newspaper the *Sun* to again criticize the Smiths for "Suffer Little Children." That summer, it ran a story about how upset a sibling of victim John Kilbride became after hearing the song (the B-side of "Heaven Knows I'm Miserable Now") on a pub jukebox.

The newspaper next tracked down Ann West, the mother of Moors victim Lesley Ann Downey, who was said to be equally disgusted by the track. In an article titled "MOORS MUM RAPS MURDER SONG," she insisted that Morrissey "must be as sick as the killers." Not long after that, Morrissey and West became acquainted, and he made it clear to her that the Smiths' song was not designed to glamourize the case but to condemn it. Morrissey invited her to his London flat and he agreed that, if asked about Myra Hindley's upcoming parole, he would do everything in his power to prevent it. (Hindley would eventually die in prison, on November 15, 2002, after contracting bronchial pneumonia.)

Morrissey the Critic

Throughout 1984, Morrissey's ascension to stardom coupled with his penchant for outrageous remarks, and his past history as a music journalist made him an ideal choice for record reviews. During the year, he provided guest commentary on new singles in the pages of *Record Mirror*, *Melody Maker*, and *Smash Hits*—usually with downright hilarious results.

In the February 4 issue of *Record Mirror*, Moz branded Sade's "Your Love Is King" as "dull," Genesis' "Illegal Alien" as "murderously dull," and revealed he was unimpressed with Style Council's "My Ever Changing Moods." As for Ultravox's latest, "One Small Day," he contended, "This might not be the worst record in the universe, but it's certainly in the running."

Later in the year, Morrissey praised the Go-Betweens' song "Part Company" and championed the Woodentops' "Plenty" in the August 4 issue of *Melody Maker*. He listed the latter as his choice for "Single of the Week," but the same could not be said of Howard Jones' "Like to Get to Know You Well," of which he said, "One can listen to it for hours and hear nothing." Elsewhere, former glam star Suzi Quatro was thrashed as "worthless," with the Smiths' singer answering the title of her latest, "I Go Wild," by snidely quipping, "At your age? I sincerely doubt it."

Two months later, on October 24, Moz was in the pages of *Star Hits*, giving his approval of the Psychedelic Furs' "Heartbeat," Prefab Sprout's "When Love Breaks Down," Lloyd Cole's "Rattlesnakes," and "Keep on Keepin' On," by the Smiths' former tour-mates the Redskins. While those records were solid, his praise of Duran Duran's dreadful "The Wild Boys" as "a truly good Duran single" was way off base. So was his view that Alphaville's now beloved "Forever Young" "should have been drowned at birth," and that Cyndi Lauper's enduring pop ballad "All Through the Night"—penned by cherished American songwriter Jules Shear—was "grossly unmusical."

18

Good Times for a Change

"William"

With the chart success of "Heaven Knows I'm Miserable Now," Marr knew he needed an ace follow-up single and set about writing some new material over the course of a four-day period in June 1984. Johnny and Angie had gotten back together that spring and moved to a flat at Nevern Square in London's Earls Court. It was here that he came up with the music for three new songs, which he crafted on his four-track Portastudio that month. Morrissey would soon pen the lyrics for and title the tunes "William, It Was Really Nothing," "Please, Please, Please Let Me Get What I Want," and "How Soon Is Now?"

With the fully complete, fast, short, and upbeat "William" planned as the A-side, the group entered Jam Studios in North London in July for a three-day weekend session with producer John Porter that would prove extremely fruitful. The band cut the first number in just a few hours before moving along to the less developed "Please, Please, Please." Marr wrote the latter—which he envisioned as the new single's B-side—in 6/8 waltz time to differ from its buoyant precursor. He tracked his musical parts for the song using only a Gibson acoustic guitar and a mandolin.

In a June 2004 interview with the *Guardian*, he explained how it was inspired by a song his parents used to play when he was a child, Del Shannon's somber "The Answer to Everything." "I tried to capture the essence of that tune; its spookiness and sense of yearning."

Tracking "How Soon Is Now?"

"How Soon Is Now?"—which would soon become the group's signature anthem—was Marr's attempt to change things up again. "I decided to write a long, swampy one with a groove," he explained in the 2014 book *Mad World: An Oral History of the New Wave Artists and Songs That Defined the 1980s*, while revealing his tendency at the time to write songs in threes.

As a result of the band's efficiency in the recording studio, they had almost two full days of studio time remaining when Porter asked Johnny what other songs he had. Marr's guitar was tuned to F-sharp when he delivered two memorable, confidently executed riffs. If one of them was—in John's estimation—a little too similar to "William," the other had a sinister Bo Diddley–derived groove that everyone in the room responded to immediately.

"We started digging it," Porter told www.soundonsound.com in September 2012. "I said, 'Just play the groove thing for fucking ages and then go into that other "William bit"—the 'B' section—but do it two octaves down at the same tempo as the groove.'"

With engineer Mark Wallis in tow, the producer programmed a percussion loop on a Linn Drum machine and brought in Rourke and Joyce—who were now sharing an apartment in the London suburb of Willesden—to track their parts to it. After instructing them to try to hold the groove down, Porter took the best parts of their two takes and wove them together.

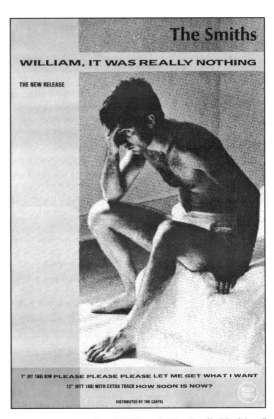

The track's legendary tremolo guitar effect followed, with Porter and Marr using a Drawmer "noise gate" programmed into the drum machine, which they triggered with a cowbell. Utilizing three Fender Twin amplifiers and, later, a Leslie cabinet, they adjusted the tremolo speeds to capture the wavering tones. From there, John laid harmonics atop some slide-guitar licks he tracked and sampled them, plus some additional guitar parts of Johnny's, for use on the track.

That afternoon, Porter put a tape of the music in Morrissey's mail slot on his way home to sleep. The next day, Moz showed up at the site—which once housed Decca Studios—with his notebook of lyrics. He sang his part twice, with John using his second take on the finished version of the song. Unlike most Smiths numbers tracked to this point, the title was not extracted from the lyrics.

A poster announcing "William, It Was Really Nothing," the band's second non-LP single of 1984. It features a cropped version of the image from the record sleeve—which was originally featured in an early-1980s advertisement for stereo speakers—and shows a shirtless man in tennis shorts. *Author's collection*

Upon completion of the song, Morrissey and his bandmates knew it was brilliant. The following day, the singer and spokesman took a taxi to Rough Trade's offices to play it for Travis. When he first heard it, Geoff dismissed the song as insignificant, even though Scott Piering, who was also present, thought it was tremendous.

As the Smiths' front man relayed in *Mad World*, "[Geoff] said, 'What is Johnny doing? That's just noise!'" As a result, Travis agreed it would be the bonus track on the 12-inch for "William, It Was Really Nothing," but the label had little else planned for the tune at the time.

In fact, as excited as the band and their producer were about "How Soon Is Now?," the seven-minute-long song troubled Travis enough that he prevented the Smiths from working with Porter for some time after that session. "I got fired because they said I was changing the sound of the Smiths too much," the producer told www.soundonsound.com, explaining how he was trying to broaden their sound in the hope that they might appeal to U.S. audiences.

Of course, John had the last laugh when Travis changed his mind, releasing "How Soon is Now?" as its own proper A-side in early 1985. At the same time, he also watched as the song marked the group's first dent in the U.S. market.

"William" on 45

"William, It Was Really Nothing" was purportedly written about one of Morrissey's friends, Associates singer Billy Mackenzie. It depicts a love triangle between an engaged couple and the groom's homosexual paramour. The song's lyrics find the subject—presumably Morrissey—pleading with his lover to reconsider wedding a selfish "fat girl."

Morrissey claimed he wrote the song after observing that nearly all pop songs about marriage up that point had always been written for the female voice and from the female standpoint. "I thought it was about time that there was a male voice speaking directly to another male, saying that marriage was a waste of time," he explained, in the 1985 book *The Smiths in Quotes*. Elsewhere, he would suggest that some of the song's lyrics were inspired by *Billy Liar*, the 1959 Keith Waterhouse novel of a working-class British teenager who was aspiring to become a successful comedy writer.

Like "Heaven Knows I'm Miserable Now," the stand-alone single was not included on a proper Smiths studio album, although it would later feature on several compilation discs. It was released on August 24, 1984, and peaked at #17 on the U.K. singles survey. Its original artwork was lifted from an early-1980s advertisement for A.D.S. audio speakers, depicting a man in tennis shorts and nothing else sitting on a bed next to a stereo speaker. Legal issues required the Smiths to change the artwork for future pressings. The replacement cover featured a provocative still of the actress Billie Whitelaw sitting up in bed, extracted, with permission, from the 1967 film *Charlie Bubbles*.

The A-side label for the U.K. 7-inch pressing of "William, It Was Really Nothing."
The single was released on August 24,
1984, and peaked at #17 on the U.K.
singles chart. *Author's collection*

THE SMITHS

ROUGH
TRADE

(℗)5661

RT 166

A SIDE
45 RPM
TIME: 2.10

©1984
Warner Bros.
Music

**WILLIAM,
IT WAS REALLY NOTHING**
(Morrissey and Marr)
Produced by JOHN PORTER
Made in the UK

In tandem with the
single's release, the Smiths
mimed the song on *Top of
the Pops.* During the performance, which aired on
August 30, 1984, Morrissey—
who sang without a micro-
phone as a prop—tore open his
shirt to show viewers that he had
written "MARRY ME" on his chest.
At the end of the set, the show cut
back to the show's co-hosts, one of whom
had lifted his own shirt to deliver the bare-
chested message, "WE LOVE THE SMITHS."

Unfortunately, the love that the BBC's radio division had shown the band
the year before was all but absent when it came time to play "William." Morrissey
blamed programmers for the alluring track's commercial stall. "They couldn't
wait to get rid of it," he told Ian Pye that November. "It shows how many friends
we have on the jolly old radio stations. I don't think they trust us."

Meanwhile, Moz took umbrage with Sire, which had opted against releasing
the group's two recent U.K. hit singles in the U.S. He described this to Pye as
an "absolute insult" and a "terrible situation," considering their debut had
performed reasonably well with minimal label support.

Common Thread

Marr handled a good portion of the promotional duties for the "William" single,
sitting down with *Smash Hits, ZigZag,* and *No. 1.* In his profile for the latter, titled
"Johnny Too Bad," Nick Adams depicted the extroverted rock-and-roller Johnny
as the virtual opposite of the reclusive Morrissey. Within the article, however,
Marr relayed that in spite of their differences, they were kept glued together by
their similar backgrounds and senses of humor.

"We're all very different; we should hate each other," he explained to Adams,
but he insisted that their mutual experiences in Manchester in the 1970s and
shared associations had kept them aligned. "Morrissey and I know each other
intuitively—we've developed together," he continued. "His game is words, mine
is music. He feels about his literary influences like I feel about [the Rolling
Stones'] Brian Jones' guitar playing."

The Smiths' other members were equally loyal to the cause around this time. Joyce was supportive of Morrissey's lyrics, telling writers Graham K. Smith and Dylan Jones in September how they were "just incredible, so powerful, and always right." Rourke asserted to the same journalists that the Smiths were "the best band in the world—there's nobody better."

Snide Remarks

The decision for Johnny to handle some of these publicity duties may have come in the wake of Morrissey's acrimonious remarks to the *Face* the month before. When questioned about other modern Smiths—including the Cure's Robert and the Fall's Mark E.—Moz went inexplicably on the offensive, taking aim at them both. While some applauded his nasty remarks, others felt he came off badly after accusing the Fall's brainchild, a fellow Mancunian, of scorning him and saying mean and fallacious things about him. He then called Robert Smith a "whingebag" and proudly asserted, "I've never liked the Cure."

Gay Voice

For a time, after his sympathy with gay culture blew up on him, Morrissey was understandably distrustful of the press. "If you have sympathy, you are immediately a transsexual," Morrissey grumbled to the *Face*, explaining how—after skirting over the topic—he was made out to be a "great voice of the gay movement."

When asked by *Record Mirror* the same month if the lyrics to "William" might be construed as being "overtly gay," Marr fielded the question perfectly, offering his complete support to his songwriting partner without ever disclosing Morrissey's sexual persuasion. "One of the reasons our records are timeless is because the lyrics are so good," Johnny explained. "And whatever gay overtones are there I endorse 100 percent."

Pop Shows

Morrissey was also busy plugging his records on television in the U.K. in 1984, appearing on *Pop Quiz* and *Eight Days a Week*, which featured pop stars answering trivia questions about past and present chart hits and talking about new material, respectively.

Eight Days a Week placed him in the company of Wham! singer George Michael and British DJ Tony Blackburn to promote "Heaven Knows I'm Miserable Now" that spring. As part of the panel discussion, he was asked his opinion of Everything but the Girl's new album *Eden*, which he liked, his thoughts on the U.S. film *Breakdance*, which he called "repellant," and his memories of Joy Division, whose live shows he said he saw "by accident."

Although he would soon call the experience of being on television "unbearable," he wound up back on the tube later in the year. For Morrissey's autumn-1984 appearance on the BBC game show *Pop Quiz*, he was teamed with singers Alvin Stardust and Kim Wilde and fielded questions about Billy Fury and Echo & the Bunnymen. The opposing team was made up of Thin Lizzy's Phil Lynott, a member of Kajagoogoo, and Simple Minds' Derek Forbes.

When asked about it later, he regretted putting himself in front of the television cameras. "I just thought, 'Oh no! I shouldn't be here,'" he told Russell Young, before admitting that he had only made the appearance because he had nothing else to do that day.

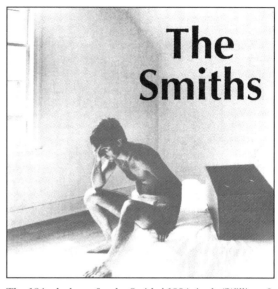

The 12-inch sleeve for the Smiths' 1984 single "William, It Was Really Nothing." Unlike its companion promotional poster, the single's actual artwork includes the large stereo speaker that originally featured in a magazine ad for the A.D.S. brand. *Author's collection*

Wales

The Smiths embarked on a three-day run of live dates in late September 1984, touching down in Gloucester on September 24 before moving on to Wales for a pair of gigs in Cardiff and Swansea. The shows were initially planned as a quick warm-up for an imminent North American tour that had been booked for October but was scotched at the last minute after Morrissey and Marr elected to work on their second studio LP instead.

Quite dramatically, the Smiths took the stage to the sound of "March of the Capulets," from Prokofiev's *Romeo & Juliet*, at Gloucester's Leisure Centre, with the intro music becoming omnipresent at all future shows by the band. The group's live set incorporated an all-new unrecorded number called "Rusholme Ruffians" plus "How Soon Is Now?" and "Please, Please, Please Let Me Get What I Want," which had never been played live before.

Because the original recording relied so heavily on the studio, with two simultaneous guitar parts, Marr was initially worried about how he might reproduce "How Soon Is Now?" live. Recognizing its importance in the band's evolution, he found a way to make it work by conventionally tuning his bottom four strings while tuning the E string a third above the B string and running it through a digital delay. "I was really panicking before the gigs, but it turned out okay," Johnny told *Guitarist* in February 1985, acknowledging that while it sounded different in concert, it was still as powerful and atmospheric as the recorded version.

Two nights later, at the Mayfair in Swansea, Morrissey dared his audience at the outset of "How Soon Is Now?" by saying, "If anybody really understands this song, come and see me later." Elsewhere, on "You've Got Everything Now," he sang of how he never had a job, "because I'm too fey!" Before an encore of "Please, Please, Please," he expressed his gratitude to the Smiths apostles who had taken to traveling to see the band. "We know who you are and we love you," he told the cheering crowd.

Hatful of Hollow

In spite of the fact that *The Smiths* had been a strong seller in the U.K. and other territories throughout 1984, Morrissey was displeased with the album's sound—which he would describe as a "blunted thud" in *Autobiography*—and approached Travis with the idea of Rough Trade releasing a compilation album as a stop-gap between the debut and the foursome's next studio set, which it was planning for 1985.

Sensing another hit, Geoff went along with the idea for the record, which would be titled *Hatful of Hollow* and would aim to give proper release to their heartfelt early sessions. Set for a November 12 release in the U.K., it consisted of the Smiths' two recent singles and their B-sides, plus most of the group's 1983 BBC Radio 1 recordings, which Morrissey and Marr had long argued were a better representation of their true sound.

Bookended by "William, It Was Really Nothing" and "Please, Please, Please, Let Me Get What I Want," and with "How Soon Is Now?" surfacing midway through the sequence, the sixteen-track album culled three tracks from the John Peel session of May 31 ("Handsome Devil," "Reel Around the Fountain," and "What Difference Does It Make?") and two from the David Jensen session on July 4 ("These Things Take Time" and "You've Got Everything Now").

Hatful was also bolstered by "Accept Yourself," which the band had recorded for Jensen on September 5, 1983, and the four numbers they cut on September 21 for Peel ("This Charming Man," "Back to the Old House," "Still Ill," and "This Night Has Opened My Eyes"). The disc was rounded out by the original single version of "Hand in Glove" plus the non-LP 45 "Heaven Knows I'm Miserable Now" and its B-side, "Girl Afraid."

A Decroix Sleeve

The sleeve for the *Hatful of Hollow* album utilized a photograph of Fabrice Colette taken by Gilles Decroix that had featured in a special July 1983 issue of the French national newspaper *Liberation* dedicated to Jean Cocteau, the author, poet, artist, filmmaker, and national hero.

An article about Colette's devotion to Cocteau included Decroix's image of the then-unknown Frenchman sporting a tattoo of a drawing by his idol that had been marked on his left shoulder a month before the picture was taken. For the sleeve, which was overseen by Morrissey, the black-and-white picture was placed over a light-blue background, with the band's name and the LP title bordering the top and bottom of the photo.

Inside the gatefold sleeve—marked "Pay no more than £3.99"—fans found a photo of the band in the studio. Rourke clutches his bass, presumably tracking a part, as Marr, Morrissey (wearing spectacles), and Joyce (smoking a cigarette and wearing tennis shorts) look on inquisitively.

The Legacy of *Hatful*

Upon its release in late 1984, *Hatful of Hollow* became a huge success in the U.K., where it peaked at #7 on the charts and earned a platinum certification, spurred by Christmas sales. It stayed on the U.K. album survey for a remarkable forty-six-week run and sold over 25,000 copies in the U.S. as an import, where the group's cult status rose without any touring.

Issued at budget price to ensure sales from fans who already owned the group's previous releases, Morrissey explained its existence in an official Rough Trade press release by stating, "As far as we're concerned, those were the sessions that got us so excited in the first place and apparently it was how a lot of other people discovered us also."

The response to the record was overwhelmingly positive. "These charming Smiths are vivid and in their prime," Adrian Thrills wrote in the November 17 issue of the *NME*. *Smash Hits* called the album "the best place for any interested people to start exploring the wonderful and frightening world of Morrissey," rating it eight out of a possible ten. Elsewhere, *Sounds'* Bill Black championed it as "the perfect stop gap/document depending on your predilection for the Smiths," and *Jamming!* proclaimed it a "perfect way to map the fluctuations of the Smiths so far, contrasting the sweeping grace of the early sessions with the later recorded works."

The record has held up well through the years. In 2000, *Q* magazine placed it at #44 in its survey of the "100 Greatest British Albums Ever," while *Pitchfork's* Douglas Wolk rated it ten out of ten in 2011. A decade earlier, www.allmusic.com had given it a perfect five-star rating.

Marr looked back on *Hatful* in a February 2008 essay for *Uncut* in which he revealed his surprise at the compilation's immediate popularity. "It definitely captured that time when we were in between phases and somewhat embryonic," he wrote, explaining how it reflected the Smiths' girl-group influence and was far more complex than he initially thought. "It's definitive, but quite what it's defining is mysterious. And that's a good thing."

Hatful of Ireland

Upon the release of *Hatful of Hollow* in November '84, the Smiths embarked on additional live dates in Ireland. The success of the new record lured fervent fans to the Savoy in Waterford and a pair of shows at the SFX in Dublin, plus gigs in Cork and Donegal. It was at these shows that the band unveiled

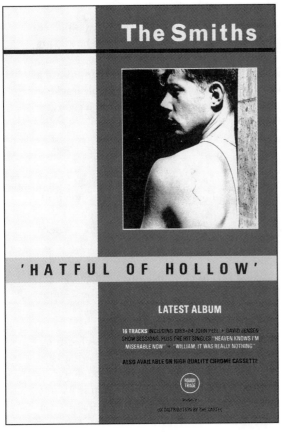

The Smiths

'HATFUL OF HOLLOW'

LATEST ALBUM

16 TRACKS INCLUDING 1983–84 JOHN PEEL + DAVID JENSEN
SHOW SESSIONS, PLUS THE HIT SINGLES "HEAVEN KNOWS I'M
MISERABLE NOW" • "WILLIAM, IT WAS REALLY NOTHING"

ALSO AVAILABLE ON HIGH QUALITY CHROME CASSETTE

ROUGH
TRADE

ROUGH76
UK DISTRIBUTION BY THE CARTEL

An in-store poster designed to help market *Hatful of Hollow*, the Smiths' highly cherished 1984 compilation of early non-album singles and radio sessions. *Author's collection*

three new Morrissey/Marr compositions—"What She Said," "Nowhere Fast," and "I Want the One I Can't Have"—that they had been readying for their next studio album.

Fan enthusiasm hit a fever pitch in Waterford on November 11, where two rows of chairs were demolished after rabid audience members stood on them. Although Morrissey introduced "I Want the One I Can't Have" as the group's next single on both nights in Dublin, those plans would change. The crowd participation at these shows was so loud, meanwhile, that it left Morrissey moved to tears, as he later told journalist Russell Young, by the "tremendous, overblown emotion" that he felt.

For the most part, the short tour of Ireland was a massive success, although the Smiths' concert at the Leisure Centre in Letterkenny, Donegal, on November 20 was the exception. The 1,000-capacity venue was less than half-full, and a good portion of those in attendance were curious onlookers. When Moz left the stage, shouting, "We'll never forget you," he was obviously joking.

Ten days later, the Smiths returned to France for a special filmed concert at the Parc Des Expositions in the south of Paris on December 1. Shot in both black-and-white and color and later broadcast on French television, the gig focused on recent material like "How Soon Is Now?" plus new, unreleased songs like "Rusholme Ruffians," while curiously forgoing "Please, Please, Please."

Back to Manchester

While publicizing *Hatful*, Morrissey revealed that he had recently moved back to Manchester, where he had bought a home in an affluent part of the city for his mother and him that was a far cry from Whalley Range. "It's this nice, neat little house," he told the *Melody Maker*. "It's just a pleasure."

Returning to Manchester a hero had some disadvantages, however. Morrissey would joke to the paper that while there were some local fans that might want to smother him with affection, there were just as many who would like to disembowel him. While he hadn't felt things had gotten to the point where he needed a bodyguard, he spoke that November of being increasingly nervous about going out in public.

Bigmouth

Morrissey used his *Hatful* publicity campaign as a means to get a number of things off his chest. He disliked Frankie Goes to Hollywood, who had recently topped the charts in the U.K. with "Relax" and "Two Tribes," and accused the band's Holly Johnson and Paul Rutherford of being puppets for producers Paul Morley and Trevor Horn. "The degree of success they've had is slippery and dangerous," he scoffed to Ian Pye, comparing them to disposable pop stars like Adam Ant and Gary Numan.

Elsewhere, he called pop acts like Culture Club and Scritti Politti "meaningless." He was also adamant about steering clear of supporting charitable events such as Who guitarist Pete Townshend's anti-heroin concerts, which took place that fall, and an animal-rights initiative steered by former Kajagoogoo singer Limahl. For Morrissey, the idea of working with the latter would be "artistically and aesthetically wrong."

Morrissey went on to reveal to Pye that he was thinking of involving himself in local government because he was disturbed by the way Manchester was being run and overdeveloped. "It's so ugly now," he said of his hometown, before opining that local politics should not be left to "other slobs."

When asked about his relationship with Billy MacKenzie, Morrissey described the Associates singer as unpredictable. Elsewhere, he spoke of his friendship with the budding pop star Lloyd Cole, who had recently charted with hits like "Forest Fire" and "Are You Ready to Be Heartbroken?" with his band the Commotions.

Morrissey—A Bored Star

If 1984 had started terribly, with Morrissey's fall from the Danceteria stage, it ended quite spectacularly. It was the year that Morrissey became not only a star in the music press but also a household name throughout England from his television exposure as the Smiths reached mainstream acceptance and sold large and unexpected quantities of records.

The achievements of this "most thrilling year" weren't lost on the singer, who proudly revealed to *Jamming!* in December that he and Marr had few regrets. According to Moz, his bond with Johnny remained unbreakable—he called it "impenetrable"—while he spoke of being closer than ever to Rourke and Joyce.

If stardom meant needing to dodge paparazzi while he bought socks (as Morrissey claimed in the interview) and consoling Smiths apostles in public and

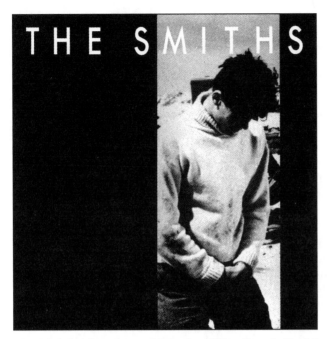

by fan mail, it also meant that between creating, performing, and promotional duties, his schedule was overflowing. He made sure he avoided succumbing to the chemical and sexual excesses of fame as a means of coping with the pressure. He adhered to his own strict set of personal rules to avoid such temptations, fearing they would keep him from concentrating on his lyric writing and negatively impact his creativity. After performing, he would return to his hotel alone to stay focused and well-rested.

The sleeve for the commercial single of "How Soon Is Now?," which was reissued by the Smiths' record label against Morrissey's wishes, and in spite of market saturation. The track had initially appeared as the 12-inch B-side to "William, It Was Really Nothing," and was also included on the band's recent hits compilation *Hatful of Hollow. Author's collection*

"It's easy to get further and further away from the council estate," he told Russell Young, acknowledging how quickly he could forget the somber existence of his first quarter-century if he allowed the lures of stardom to take hold. Ironically, he was already becoming bored with the chores that accompanied the fame he once dreamt of—specifically the headache-inducing monotony of interviews required to publicize each new single and album.

"How Soon" on 45

The Smiths received the honor of topping John Peel's 1984 "Festive Fifty" with "How Soon Is Now?" as the BBC host's national listenership voted the 12-inch B-side the best song of the year. This prompted Rough Trade to consider shelving immediate plans for a lead single from the group's forthcoming album in favor of reissuing the tremolo-happy number as an A-side in its own right.

Morrissey was against the idea, figuring the track had already run its course. He pushed to release a new single called "Shakespeare's Sister" instead. Travis promised that, as long as he could release the "How Soon" as an A-side first, he would allow the new song (which wasn't even on the forthcoming album) to become a single a few months down the line.

In the U.S., Sire had already announced its intentions to issue the single domestically in the spring after it picked up steam in alternative dance clubs on import. Seymour Stein and his staff also spoke with Travis about appending the song to the North American version of the Smiths' next album release.

Back home in the U.K., the single was released on January 28, 1985, and the Smiths promoted it with a Valentine's Day lip-synched performance on *Top of the Pops*. Yet the record's chances of cracking the Top 20 were thwarted because nearly all of the group's British fans already owned the song. Following its appearance on both the "William" 12-inch and its parent album, *Hatful of Hollow*, "How Soon Is Now?" was already at saturation point with the group's audience. Its B-sides, the melancholy "Well I Wonder" and the 12-inch bonus instrumental "Oscillate Wildly," just weren't enough of an incentive for fans to rush out and buy a third copy of the exact same song. So, regardless of how amazing the song was—and still is—it only peaked at #24 in the U.K. pop charts.

The U.K. single artwork comprised an image of the actor Sean Barrett, taken from the 1958 film *Dunkirk*. Barrett was actually praying in the picture, but because it looked as if he was holding his crotch, Sire Records elected to release a yellow-sleeved 7-inch single with large blue type instead.

The Legacy of "How Soon Is Now?"

"How Soon Is Now?"—which clocks in at nearly seven minutes—ranked #4 in the *NME*'s year-end poll. In the U.S., the *Village Voice* listed it at #17 in its "Pazz and Jop" list of the year's best singles.

Over time, the song has grown legs, especially in the U.S., where alternative radio stations like Boston's WFNX ranked it the #1 song of the decade in 1989. Then, in 1999, the now defunct WLIR-FM in New York—perhaps the first commercial U.S. station in the country to ever play the Smiths in 1984—named it the #2 song of all time in its Top 300 survey (behind Alphaville's "Forever Young").

San Francisco's Live 105 placed the song at #2 in its 2006 "Top 500 Countdown" (behind Nirvana's "Smells Like Teen Spirit"), while Cincinnati's legendary WOXY placed it at #1 in that year's Top 500, followed by other revolutionary songs like Joy Division's "Love Will Tear Us Apart" and the Sex Pistols' "Anarchy in the U.K." In 2010, listeners to New York's WRXP placed it at #3 in a countdown of the 1,019 songs of all time, behind Pearl Jam's "Black" and the Verve's "Bittersweet Symphony."

When asked about the song, which has clearly endured as one of the best of the rock era, by Smiths biographer Johnny Rogan, Sire Records head Seymour Stein called it "the 'Stairway to Heaven' of the eighties."

19

Cemented Minds

Meat Is Murder

Porter Out

In support of their upcoming single, "William, It Was Really Nothing," the Smiths re-teamed with John Porter for a third John Peel session on August 1, 1984. When the results of this studio work aired eight days later on BBC Radio 1, they offered a glimpse at what the band's future might sound like. In addition to an alternate take on the A-side and its lengthy and experimental bonus B-side, "How Soon Is Now?," the Peel session included renditions of "Nowhere Fast" and "Rusholme Ruffians," two tracks planned for the group's upcoming album.

This would be the last time that the Smiths would work with John Porter for some time, however, despite of the producer's efforts to hold on to his high-profile job. Morrissey didn't relate to Porter—who was a decade his senior—the way that Marr did. John tried to become friends with the singer, even inviting him to his home one night for a lavish vegetarian dinner cooked by his wife, Linda. The singer never showed up, however, making it clear that he had little if any interest in sustaining a working relationship.

Although Marr would later reveal that he would have been content to continue on with Porter, Morrissey convinced Johnny, still only nineteen, that they should produce the band's next proper studio album—which they would title *Meat Is Murder*—by themselves. For this, they would seek the help of twenty-four-year-old engineer Stephen Street, who they first hired to work on "Heaven Knows I'm Miserable Now."

Amazon

In October 1984, Street traveled north from London to take occupancy in a Manchester hotel. From there, he would commute with the Smiths each day in an old, large white Mercedes sedan to Amazon Studios. Located in the Liverpool suburb of Kirby, the facility had famously accommodated Echo & the Bunnymen while they tracked their 1983 hit album *Porcupine*. It was hardly extravagant, and the Smiths could certainly have afforded something more lavish by this point, but Amazon served its purpose.

The group worked ten-hour days for several weeks, wrapping up each night by 8 p.m., at Morrissey's insistence. In *Autobiography*, he writes of how, without Porter there to constrict the sessions, he and the rest of the band felt a sense of relief.

Street paid attention to Morrissey's needs in a way that Porter never did, focusing closely on the volume and production of the vocal tracks, which were usually finished in just three takes. In the event that one take didn't stand out, Stephen would pick the best parts from what he had to present Morrissey in a way he appreciated.

Of course, the instrumental tracks came first, with Marr and Street overseeing the arrangements, which allowed for Joyce to play his drums "rock-steady" and "with horse-race pace," as Moz writes in his book. As for Rourke, his "brilliance flourished" out from under Porter's "schoolmasterly ear," while Johnny— after rolling up his sleeves and digging into the making of the record—thrived at the helm.

Marr had the band track roughs one after the other to assess what they had to work with. These recordings were forceful, angry, and full of life. They knew they were on the right path. "The whole idea was to control it totally," Morrissey told a *Melody Maker* fanzine panel in March 1985. "Without a producer things were better. We saw things clearer."

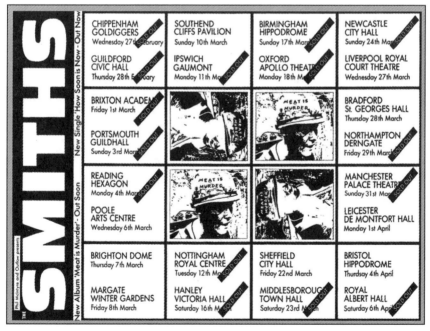

An ad promoting the Smiths' extensive 1985 U.K. tour that ran in several music weeklies early in the year, ahead of the release of the group's new album, *Meat Is Murder.*
Author's collection

When the album was finished—after overdubs were added at Ridge Farm in Surrey in November, and the album was mixed by Street at Island Records' Fallout Shelter studio at year's end—the production was credited to the Smiths.

Meat Is Murder

From the outset, Morrissey proposed naming the album after the song "Meat Is Murder," although to begin with, Marr worried that he might not have a full album's worth of music to match the seriousness of such a title. Calling the record *Meat Is Murder* was controversial, and the album's overall themes of violence and anger were unexpected for the Smiths. But having dealt largely with messages of love, sex, and heartache on their previous releases, Morrissey now felt it was his responsibility to set his strong opinions—from cruelty to animals to brutality in his Catholic upbringing to the threat of nuclear war—to music.

"I think violence is quite attractively necessary in some extremes," he told the *NME* in December 1984, while announcing the album title to the world. He spoke specifically of the U.K. organization Campaign for Nuclear Disarmament and explained that violence on its behalf was justified when "communication via peaceful methods are laughed at and treated with absolute violence by the government."

To do so, he began writing less about himself in the abstract and acknowledged the change. *Meat Is Murder* marked the first time he would write songs in the third person, as a spectator, or, as he told the music weekly, "the sympathetic vicar."

The ultimate goal was to make a thought-provoking album that would define the Smiths as a band and set them apart from the insipid pop dominating the charts while continuing to grow their audience. In alignment with the record's release, Moz spoke to *Melody Maker* about the importance of breaking certain rules. "We haven't become sloppy and we haven't become cushioned and we haven't become fat and lazy," he assured his fans, while thanking them for their support.

"If you try and do something with a grain of intellect, you have to answer for it every single day of your life," he continued, justifying the Smiths' position on the album. Although he acknowledged it was an irksome part of the music industry, he was up to the task.

"The Headmaster Ritual"

Johnny Marr says he wrote this song on his acoustic guitar using an open-D tuning with a capo at the second fret, akin to something that folk singer Joni Mitchell might do. "The actual progression is like what she would have done had she been an MC5 fan or a punk rocker," he told *Guitar Player* in 1990.

Marr claims the actual composition marked the longest period of time he had ever worked on a song. He first introduced it to Morrissey when they were

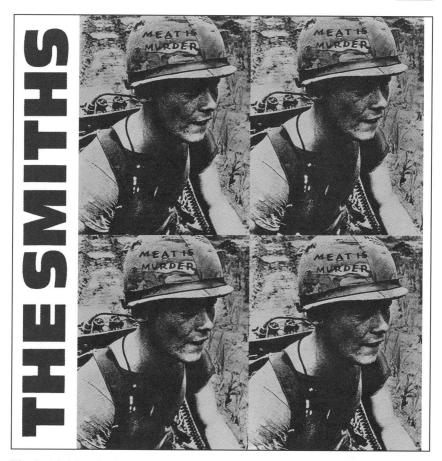

The Smiths' iconic sleeve for *Meat Is Murder* utilized a 1967 photograph of Marine Corporal Michael Winn that was chosen by Morrissey. Shot during the Vietnam War, the image was extracted from Emile de Antonio's 1968 documentary film *In the Year of the Pig*. *Author's collection*

recording with producer Troy Tate in the summer of 1983 and finally finished it a year later—while he was living in Earls Court—after he took the bridge and chorus parts from another song.

The guitar parts for "The Headmaster Ritual" were heavily overdubbed, with the main double-tracked Rickenbacker riff accompanied by two tracks of Martin D-28. An Epiphone Coronet strung with the high-strings of a 12-string set was used on the end of the song.

The album's opening salvo—a college-radio favorite in the U.S., and a single release in Holland—was a scathing look at a childhood rife with physical and mental abuse in Manchester's Catholic schools. Morrissey used the song to protest the corporal punishment of children and—when asked about it—argued that as long as there was an absolute lack of sensitivity were life was concerned, there would always be war.

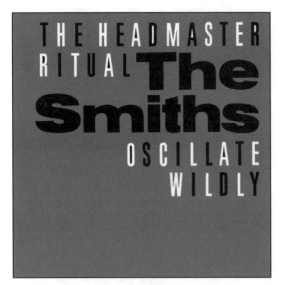

A rare 7-inch single released in a paper sleeve in early 1985 by Megadisc, which distributed Rough Trade products in Holland. *Author's collection*

"Rusholme Ruffians"

This superbly sung song, built from a rockabilly foundation, stemmed from thoughts of Morrissey's childhood summers visiting the Manchester fairgrounds and the unsavory types it attracted and chronicles a murder, a meaningless encounter between strangers, and a pair of smitten teenagers testing the waters of love for the first time. Originally clocking in at just under seven minutes when it was written in mid-1984 and initially attempted with Porter that July at Jam Studios in London, it was revised and shortened at Amazon. The end result has Rourke's bass front and center with Morrissey's vocals, standing out against the shuffling of Marr's acoustic guitar and Joyce's rat-a-tat drumming.

"I Want the One I Can't Have"

Morrissey paired the uplifting music penned by Marr for this song with couplets about an impoverished newlywed couple, revealing that the line about acquiring a double bed came from the idea that when newlyweds first live together, their top priority was obtaining this essential piece of furniture. "It was like the prized exhibit," he told the *NME* ahead of the record's release, noting that owning appliances—even a functional heater—was always considered less essential.

Morrissey was, of course, speaking firsthand about the impoverished family members he had witnessed taking up a threadbare existence after marriage. He found it disappointing that their wedding day was the lone big event in their adult lives.

"What She Said"

This memorable number took shape when Johnny introduced it to Andy and Mike during soundchecks on the Smiths' September 1984 tour of Wales, with Morrissey adding his vocal part during rehearsals for the album. The lyrics depict an unhappy woman who kills time reading and droning on about the books she reads to anyone who will listen. The dejected character Moz presents in the song is a real agony aunt who acknowledges that she smokes in the hope that her despicable habit might expedite her death.

"That Joke Isn't Funny Anymore"

This song was purportedly written about some of the U.K. music scribes who had criticized Morrissey for his unhappy lyrics—or, as he told *Melody Maker* in March 1985, those who were "trying to drag me down and prove that I was a complete fake." But the song actually goes deeper than that by alluding to a sexual encounter "on cold leather seats." A 1998 article in *Uncut* suggested that the song's inspiration came from a dalliance the singer had with a certain unnamed music writer at the time it was penned.

An emotive ballad in waltz-time, "That Joke Isn't Funny Anymore" was released as a single in the U.K. on July 1, 1985. Curiously, it followed the non-album A-side "Shakespeare's Sister" by a few months. And although it was heralded by critics at the time of its release, it wound up being one of the group's lowest-charting numbers, stalling at #49.

The song's failure wasn't helped by the fact that the single lacked any new tracks to draw in its loyal fans. So, with sales waning, Morrissey and Marr pulled out of a scheduled performance of the track on *Wogan*, the popular BBC TV show hosted by the enduring broadcaster Terry Wogan.

Perhaps, the Smiths—who were incredibly prolific—decided against continuing to promote the track because they were anxious to get to work on their third studio album. In any case, "That Joke" has held up well in the decades since its emergence. It is widely considered among fans to be one of Morrissey's finest-ever vocal turns.

For his part, Marr described it to *Uncut* in February 2008 as one of his favorite Smiths songs. He also revealed to the magazine that its musical arrangement simply arrived before him, with minimal effort. "It was one of those lovely times when the feeling just falls down on you from the ceiling somewhere and it almost plays itself," he explained. "It gives an almost esoteric feeling."

The front of the cowboy-themed EP *Headmaster Ritual*, released in the Dutch market, features a unique black-and-white image selected by Morrissey and taken from the 1965 movie *The Uncle*. In addition to the A-side, the EP includes four live tracks recorded live at the Oxford Apollo in March 1985. *Author's collection*

"Nowhere Fast"

On the Smiths' first musical condemnation of the Royal Family, Morrissey famously sings of his desire to drop his trousers before Queen Elizabeth II. To emphasize his dislike of the monarchy, he proudly spoke out against Her Royal Highness and her brood in interviews. Discussing the song with writer Danny Kelly in July 1985, he called the Royals very existence "fairy story nonsense." It wouldn't be the last time he would express his distrust of the Queen for spending thousands of pounds on lavish dresses at a time when there were still U.K. citizens living in squalor with no money for food.

As chronicled elsewhere, Moz had first revealed to audiences in the fall of 1984 that the Smiths' then-new number "Nowhere Fast" would be issued as the follow-up to "William, It Was Really Nothing." As we now know, this idea was squashed. Perhaps this was Marr's doing, as the guitarist had made it no secret that he was displeased with the finished product. In an interview with *Melody Maker* dated August 2, 1985—only six months after the release of *Meat Is Murder*—he expressed the opinion that, although he was pleased with the record overall, this particular version of the song "could have been done better."

Speaking to the *Guardian* in September 2013, nearly three decades later, Marr explained that at the time the album had been written, he was looking back on forms of American music that had been disremembered, citing Eddie Cochran, Elvis Presley, and Bo Diddley. "'Nowhere Fast' has that rockabilly rhythm, and 'Shakespeare's Sister' was written entirely from that rhythm; some idea of a fucked-up Johnny Cash on drugs. It sounds half like that."

"Well I Wonder"

The genesis of "Well I Wonder" dates to a home demo Marr cut in late 1983, which was then reattempted while still an instrumental during the London sessions with Porter at Jam Studios the following July. It became the flip side to the Rough Trade pressing of the "How Soon Is Now?" single, with Marr praising the song to *Record Collector* in November 1992 by saying, "It's one of those things that a modern group could try and emulate but never get the spirit of. It's so simple."

Johnny began finalizing the instrumental upon moving back to Manchester in the autumn of 1984. The move home was intentional, in order for him to get the proper atmosphere for the tracks. The Smiths anticipated that the song would be popular with their fans, because, as Marr told *Uncut* in '08, "It had that real sense of yearning."

"Barbarism Begins at Home"

With its funky bassline, this track harkened back to the kind of music that Rourke and Marr had first attempted before the Smiths. Paying homage to James Brown and underground white funk acts like the Pop Group and James

Chance, the song—which was issued as a single in Germany and Italy—had been in the group's live set for nearly a year by the time they cut it at Amazon.

Of course, the lyrics dealt with the abuse many children grew up with, which for Morrissey was the precursor to war. As he explained to *Melody Maker* upon the release of the album in March 1985, "From the time you get hit when you're a child, violence is the only answer. Conversation is pointless."

The distinctive artwork for Sire's double-45 single of "How Soon Is Now?" and "Shakespeare's Sister." The U.S. release also includes "The Headmaster Ritual" on the flip side. *Author's collection*

"Meat Is Murder"

The album's daring title track—Morrissey's bold statement about the disturbingly vague treatment of animals—was designed to be jarring. It was his contention that most humans turned a blind eye to the horrific manner in which meat arrived on their dinner plates, and he wanted to highlight that.

For his part, Marr—who concocted an alarming soundscape of guitars, butcher's saws, and simulated animal cries—wasn't caught off guard by the direction of the song. He revealed to *Spin* in 2012 that some of the earlier songs they did for the album were "actually more radical." In fact, Morrissey's stance on eating animals was enough to convert Marr to vegetarianism during the making of the album. Through the years, Johnny found himself gratified over and over again by the fact that fans followed suit after hearing the album's closing number. "Who says pop music can't change lives?" he asked *Spin* in hindsight.

Meat Cover

For the album's unforgettable front cover, Morrissey selected a 1967 photograph of Marine Corporal Michael Winn, shot during the Vietnam War and used in the following year's Emile de Antonio documentary, *In the Year of the Pig*. The band altered the original wording on Winn's helmet from "Make War Not Love" to the album's title.

Speaking to a reporter in March 1985, Morrissey explained that the *Meat Is Murder* cover was designed to make protest groups rethink their easygoing approach to issues like animal rights, the meat industry, and nuclear weapons. As he told a scribe for the fanzine *Debris* in 1985, "It seems to me now that when you try to change things in a peaceable manner, you're actually wasting your time and you're laughed out of court. The only way we can get rid of such things is by really giving people a taste of their own medicine."

Release and Reception

Released on February 11, 1985—less than a month after "How Soon Is Now?"—the Smiths' second studio LP became the band's first and only #1 album. It shipped gold from the factory, achieving sales of 100,000 on its first day in the shops and knocking Bruce Springsteen's *Born in the U.S.A.* from the top perch. Despite this achievement, the album fell out of the U.K. album charts in just thirteen weeks.

Hilariously, Morrissey would later relay a story in *Autobiography* about how Geoff Travis acknowledged the Smiths' massive chart accomplishment by bringing him a gift. Expressing his gratitude to the band for finally giving the label its first #1 record, he handed the singer a bag of biscuits with the price tag still on it. The treats cost Travis a mere £2.75.

Meat Is Murder was massively popular among the band's fan base, which helped to propel the record up the charts even though it received little advertising by Rough Trade. Morrissey asked for television commercials; instead, the label kept things on the cheap, maximizing publicity interest by landing cover stories in the music papers and magazines, plus exposure in traditional newspapers.

In keeping with the album's politics, Morrissey—somewhat controversially—appeared on the cover of the U.K. pop bible *Smash Hits* clutching a kitten. Inside, he endorsed the reactionary tactics of the Animal Liberation Front, who had recently claimed to have poisoned candy bars throughout the U.K. as part of a well-orchestrated hoax.

As expected, there were a number of opportunities to support the album on television, including performances on *Oxford Road Show*, for which the band lip-synched "The Headmaster Ritual" and "Shakespeare's Sister," and *The Old Grey Whistle Test*. The band also appeared on Granada Reports, which was hosted by television presenter and Factory Records partner Tony Wilson, where they were interviewed during rehearsals for their upcoming tour.

Reviews for the album—the first by a Manchester band since the Hollies' 1968 *Greatest Hits* to reach the top spot—were overwhelmingly strong. In a lead review for *Sounds* titled "Steak Your Claim," Bill Black gave the album four and a half stars, writing, "*Meat Is Murder* is something for Smiths consumers to sink their teeth into." For *NME*'s Paul Du Noyer, "Lyrically, these nine new tracks display the bard of Whalley Range at his most direct," while *Melody Maker*'s Ian Pye concluded, "Their music is way beyond the trivial novelty we've come to know as pop."

Despite these accolades, there were still some dissenters. Washed-up rocker Noddy Holder from Slade expressed his disdain for the band in a national radio interview that spring, while Cockney Rebel's Steve Harley told the *Daily Mail* that he, too, loathed the group. And by August of '85, Morrissey was speaking out about his disappointment with the album's performance. "Its lifespan was embarrassingly short," he told *Record*, acknowledging that with the amount of media attention it received, it should have performed much better.

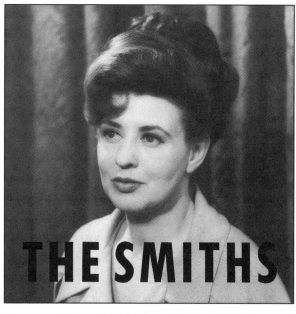

The cover of the Smiths' 1985 non-LP A-side "Shakespeare's Sister." Released on March 18, the song was a commercial disappointment, stalling at #26 in the U.K. *Author's collection*

The Legacy of *Meat Is Murder*

As the BBC acknowledged in 2007, there was no other British group making music quite like the Smiths' in 1985. Four years earlier, the album had ranked at #296 on a list of the "500 Greatest Albums of All Time" in *Rolling Stone*.

In 2003, singer/songwriter Joe Pernice wrote a book specifically about the album, and named after it, for the 33 1/3 series by Continuum, describing it as "an album that was so raw, so vivid and so melodic that you could cling to it like a lifeboat in a storm. And in 2011, *Pitchfork* looked back on the record and rated it a respectable 8.1 out of 10.

Johnny Marr would concede that the band had been less concerned about singles during the construction of this album than while making its predecessor and the non-LP sides that charted in '84, and the notion that the disc was written to be a complete presentation might explain why its lone U.K. single sold poorly compared to other recent Smiths 45s. It also supports Sire's insistence that "How Soon is Now?" be appended to the LP for U.S. audiences in order to give it a marketing hook.

"Shakespeare's Sister"

As promised by Travis, the succinct "Shakespeare's Sister"—with its galloping rockabilly presentation—was released as a non-album A-side single on March

18, 1985. Recorded in early 1985, at the same session that produced "Oscillate Wildly," the song was backed by the *Meat Is Murder* number "What She Said" and the alluring non-LP 12-inch bonus offering "Stretch Out and Wait."

The song's title referenced Virginia Woolf's feminist essay *A Room of One's Own*, which Morrissey had studied as a teen. It suggests that if William Shakespeare had had a sister of equal intelligence, her gender would have suppressed her genius. Writer Simon Goddard claims in his 2009 tome *Mozipedia* that the track also pulls inspiration from Billy Fury's "Don't Jump" and the Elizabeth Smart novella *By Grand Central Station I Sat Down and Wept*.

Looking back on the song—which clocks in at just over two minutes—in a 2007 *Guardian* article, writer Jon Savage marveled at "what a very odd song it is," calling it "a suicide drama set to a demented rock 'n' roll rhythm." Just the same, it peaked at #26 in the pop charts, helped by a performance on *Oxford Road Show*. American music writer Jack Rabid claimed in a www.allmusic.com review that it evoked "the tragic Romeo and Juliet quality of so much teenage romance."

The single's cover star was Pat Phoenix, who starred on Morrissey's long-standing favorite U.K. television drama, *Coronation Street*, as Elsie Tanner. Moz sat down for an interview with the actress for an article that ran in the May 1985 issue of music publication *Blitz*.

In August, Morrissey would tell the writer Eleanor Levy that "Shakespeare's Sister" was "the song of my life—I put everything into that song and I wanted it more than anything else to be a huge success." While that wasn't to be, Marr also loved the track—specifically its rhythm pattern—and justified its release as a single. He even suggested to the *Melody Maker* that summer that if Joyce and Rourke had been around to back Elvis Presley, he would have been an even bigger star.

The track's engineer, Stephen Street, felt the song was a little hasty. Or, as he told Tony Fletcher, "I don't think the song was up to the standard required to be a single for the Smiths." As time would assert, the bonus track on the 12-inch, "Stretch Out and Wait," would have been a far more deserving A-side. With its beautiful, swaying arrangement, the ballad—replete with lyrics about giving in to one's sexual urges—had no right to be relegated to "bonus track" obscurity.

Blacklisted

Morrissey could blame the failure of "Shakespeare's Sister" on himself to some extent. He suggested to Danny Kelly that the Smiths had become blacklisted from daytime radio play on BBC Radio 1 because of remarks he had made against the BPI in its role as organizer of the BRIT Awards. "With our status, ['Shakespeare's Sister'] should have automatically had a high profile," he argued. "The sinner must be punished."

Lashing Out at Travis

Morrissey also criticized Rough Trade's lack of interest in the "Shakespeare's Sister" 45, claiming to Kelly that the label "had no faith in it whatsoever" in the song, and that its lack of marketing and promotion caused the single's failure.

The Smiths' bard had already taken aim at the label's owner, Geoff Travis, in *Time Out* that March, telling Simon Garfield of his objections to the company that he once longed to be a part of. "We were really their last vestige of hope," he insisted. "I'm convinced that if the Smiths hadn't occurred, then Rough Trade would have just disappeared."

While the label's principals couldn't deny that the band had resuscitated Rough Trade with a massive influx of cash, they just didn't support "Shakespeare's Sister." Discussing the reason why it didn't make the U.K. Top 10 with Smiths biographer Fletcher, Richard Boon snorted, "There's a very simple answer to that. It's not a very good record."

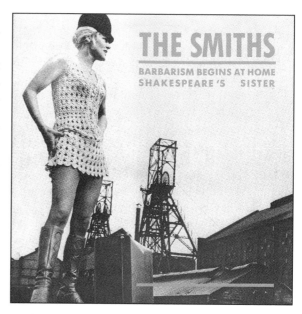

"Barbarism Begins at Home" was—at seven minutes long—a curious choice for an A-side. This Germany-only pressing paired it with the non-album B-sides "Shakespeare's Sister" and the ballad "Stretch Out and Wait," while the sleeve was the second release in a year to feature Viv Nicholson. This picture was chosen by Morrissey from Nicholson's 1977 book *Spend Spend Spend. 991.com*

When asked about the label's lack of support for the track in 1992, Marr echoed Morrissey's sentiments. "It was a disappointment for me," he told *Record Collector*. "As a 7-inch single at the time, it was quite inventive. There was something about that riff that I always wanted to do. I just flipped recording it. I really loved doing it."

Bad Aid

While publicizing the group's new releases, Moz took umbrage with the recent charity single "Do They Know It's Christmas?" by Band Aid, the all-star chart-topping 45 featuring U.K. stars like Duran Duran, Culture Club, Paul Young, Bananarama, and U2's Bono. And when Boomtown Rats front man Bob Geldof—who oversaw the single with Ultravox singer Midge Ure—condemned Morrissey on national radio for his criticisms of Band Aid, the Smiths' singer earned more publicity for calling Geldof a "nauseating character."

"One can have great concern for the people of Ethiopia," Morrissey sniped to *Time Out*, "but it's another thing to inflict daily torture on the people of England." It was this outspokenness that he felt contributed to the music industry's detesting him and denying the phenomenon of the Smiths. "I think it's because we have this grain of intellect, and when you as a band are trying to lay down the rules you're actually spoiling things for so many middle-aged mediocrities who control the whole sphere of popular music."

Morrissey went on to describe "Do They Know It's Christmas?" as "tuneless" and hit out at the Royal Family yet again in the process, suggesting that if they partnered with prime minister Margaret Thatcher they could solve the Ethiopian problem in under ten seconds.

Too Many Enemies

Those remarks came on the heels of Morrissey's *Smash Hits* cover a month prior, in which he had promised to stop criticizing others—including fellow vegetarians like Kajagoogoo singer Limahl. It was not that he wanted to hit the ski slopes with the members of Spandau Ballet or attend parties with the members of Duran Duran, but Moz had a hard time living up to the promise that he would try not to drag people down.

Speaking of his vegetarianism, he told writer Tom Hibbert that his daily diet included staples like bread and yogurt. And although he had lived a meat-free existence for most of his life, before he gave it up as a boy, he admitted having what he called a "moderate bacon fetish."

Painfully Shy

Moz may have been outspoken with reporters, but according to Johnny, he was still a hopeless introvert in real life. The guitarist spoke of their "brotherly" relationship to Nick Kent that May, revealing that he was Morrissey's "greatest fan" and that "he's so open, so romantic and sensitive to other people's emotions."

With that said, Marr went on to talk about Morrissey's sexual "confusion" while suggesting that his unusual front man (who himself told a different reporter he liked to spend his Friday evenings doing laundry) would probably relish a perfect bedroom opportunity. Johnny went on to convey that Morrissey would probably be better equipped to handle his anger if he had "a good humping."

U.K. Roadwork

With *Meat Is Murder* riding high in the U.K. charts, the Smiths embarked on a five-week tour, beginning at Golddiggers in Chippenham on February 27. In addition to holdovers from recent tours, new songs in the live set included "Shakespeare's Sister," "Stretch Out and Wait," "The Headmaster Ritual," "That Joke Isn't Funny Anymore," and the album's title track.

If early stops on the tour at concert halls in Guildford, Reading, and Portsmouth were routine, the group's March 1 show at London's Brixton Academy was chaotic, with fights between audience members and teenage girls passing out with daffodils in their arms. The Smiths' rising celebrity meant the implementation of barriers at venues like the Arts Centre in Poole, which

Morrissey felt obliged to apologize for. "This is to protect you from Moz," he told the crowd on March 6. When audiences weren't as enthusiastic as he expected, such as the Winter Gardens crowd in Margate on March 8, Morrissey poked fun. Returning for an encore, he joked, "We don't want to force this on you. I know it's very painful."

"The Headmaster Ritual" was rewritten on the fly for "Birmingham schools" at the band's show at the Hippodrome on March 17, but the band's performance—or, presum-

ROYAL ALBERT HALL
GENERAL MANAGER: D· CAMERON McNICOL
THE FACE OF THIS DOCUMENT HAS A COLOURED BACKGROUND
SATURDAY 6TH APRIL 1985
AT 1930.DOORS OPEN AT 1845.
OUTLAW & PHIL MCINTYRE
PRESENT
THE SMITHS
PLUS SUPPORT
ADMIT TO:-
GRAND TIER BOX
ENTER BY DOOR 9
PRICE (INC. VAT)   BOX   SEAT
608 0450 X   £6.00   40   4
THE BACK OF THIS DOCUMENT CONTAINS AN ARTIFICIAL WATERMARK
TO BE RETAINED   See Reverse

A ticket stub from the Smiths' performance at London's Royal Albert Hall, which marked the conclusion of the U.K. leg of the *Meat Is Murder* tour. Dead or Alive singer Pete Burns joined the band onstage during the show. *Author's collection*

ably, Andy's—did not sit well with Johnny, who kicked his bass drum in frustration at the end of the night. The next evening's gig, at Oxford's Apollo, fared much better, and was recorded for radio broadcast on Janice Long's BBC program.

By the end of the month, radio's failure to acknowledge "Shakespeare's Sister" had Morrissey venting to the crowd about programmers and Rough Trade staff alike during stops in Middlesbrough and Bradford. "This is our new single which all your favorite DJs will not play," he complained at the former, while at the latter he carped, "This is our new single which thanks to Rough Trade promotion has leapt in at #29 this week."

Fans remained frenzied anyway, clamoring to get close to Moz as three rows of chairs collapsed during a March 24 gig at City Hall in Newcastle upon Tyne. Feeding on this energy, the singer gleefully threw his shirt into the audience and watched two of his disciples fight over it.

The Smiths' triumphant show at London's Royal Albert Hall concluded the tour with an unexpected appearance by Morrissey's old friend Pete Burns—the androgynous singer for Dead or Alive who would become best known for that year's #1 "You Spin Me Round"—during "Barbarism Begins at Home." Later, Moz dedicated "Meat Is Murder" to "everybody who stopped at the hamburger stand outside—we're watching you."

Remembering the tour's culmination at the prestigious venue, Morrissey copped to being in a bad mood that night after microphone woes. "[The fans] just want you to get out there and be Bugs Bunny," he complained to the *NME* in June 1985.

Tim Booth of James, the tour's support act, had begun to notice how fame made Morrissey a prisoner in his hotel room on the road. Booth cherished the conversations they had shared on a trek through Ireland the year before, but such interactions were becoming less and less likely now that Moz had begun to travel with his own security.

Although Morrissey conceded to Danny Kelly that the tour had been victorious, he acknowledged that while some shows were "quite religious," others were difficult, mentioning how, at one unnamed stop, hecklers threw sausages at him, causing him to leave the stage in horror. Summing up the journey, he concluded, "It was long, very, very long and very exhausting."

20

I Want to Be Loved

Touring Europe and Conquering America

"How Soon" in the U.S.

The Smiths' North American presence was mostly nonexistent at the outset of 1985, and the fact that Morrissey and Marr continued to resist making a suitable music video to promote their new album didn't help matters. Responding to continued pressure from Sire Records, Rough Trade proposed a compromise—a clip comprised of live footage. The U.S label was projecting that *Meat Is Murder*—anchored by the bonus track "Hatful of Hollow"—might sell 250,000 copies or more—provided the band would tour North America, agree to the video, and participate in a press campaign.

In tandem with the stateside release of the record, Sire spliced together a video for the song without the band's approval, interspersing footage of a blond model with snippets of collapsing buildings and grainy footage of the group onstage by Grant Showbiz. Morrissey was not pleased. He would tell *Creem* magazine that spring that the "foul video" was "degrading" and "quite disastrous."

The companion single featured the group's name in blue block letters against the double A-side track names "How Soon Is Now?" and "Shakespeare's Sister" when it was released that April. It also included a version of "The Headmaster Ritual" to tie into the album. It was yet another marketing catastrophe, according to Morrissey, who badmouthed Sire to *Creem* for its selection of an "abhorrent" sleeve, before griping that "How Soon Is Now?" was unlisted on the album art and overlooked in the lyric sheet. Sire had also goofed, in his estimation, in leaving "That Joke Isn't Funny Anymore" off cassette pressings of the album, and he blamed these failures for the fact that it stalled at #110 on the *Billboard* 200. It fared better to the north, reaching #40 in the Canadian chart.

Perfect Fit for Modern Rock

If these North American chart performances sounded like failures to Morrissey, the alternative-music market was still very much untested in early 1985. And yet, before the Smiths had even announced their U.S. summer tour, there was already anticipation for the group, who appealed to fans of established modern-rock acts like the Ramones, U2, the Clash, Elvis Costello, and R.E.M.

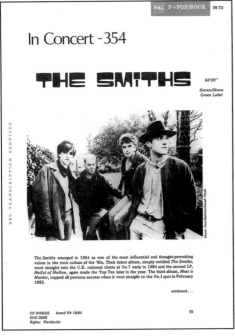

The jacket and promotional insert for the Smiths'
1985 appearance on the BBC's *In Concert*. The
special program was broadcast that May. *Author's
collection.*

Adventurous radio stations like New
York's WLIR-FM, Boston's WFNX, L.A.'s
KROQ-FM, WHTG-FM in New Jersey,
and 91X in San Diego had recently
gotten a foothold by playing the aforementioned bands, plus up-and-comers
like Echo & the Bunnymen, New Order,
the Cure, and Depeche Mode. Like the
college radio outlets that quickly lifted
"How Soon Is Now?" to the top of the
CMJ retail charts, U.S. modern-rock
stations embraced the Smiths' first big
anthem when it arrived in early 1985.
As with these other groups—which
were either signed to or distributed by
arms of Warner Bros.—the Smiths did
actually benefit from being on a major
record label, which had recently established its own alternative marketing
department to bolster acts of their ilk
on both coasts.

If the heartland lacked the same
kind of radio support for the band,
the song's music video made up for
it. Directed by Paula Grief, it included
footage shot by Grant Showbiz that Sire
had somehow acquired without the
group's authorization. With this supposedly unsanctioned clip—which had
been commissioned by Steven Baker,
the Smiths' contact at Warner Bros.,
with the blessing of the label's creative-
services head Jeff Ayeroff—the group
began to receive liberal airplay on MTV
that spring, driving sales of the album
in unexpected markets.

U.S. Tour Plans and *People*

With the band developing an ever-
strengthening grip on the North
American market, acting manager Scott Piering (who essentially handled all of
the things that Morrissey didn't want to deal with) and U.K. booking agent Mike
Hinc worked with the U.S.-based Frontier Booking International (a.k.a. F.B.I.) to

set a tour routing and get venue confirmations. With the help of the U.S. agency—which was owned by Ian Copeland, brother of Police drummer Stewart—a tour plan was established and live dates were announced for June 1985.

The problem was that the band were still not certain how they wanted to handle the equipment-moving aspects of touring. Piering recommended letting local promoters hire the P.A. system and lights for each show, but the Smiths and their road crew were partial to renting the necessary equipment and trucking it from stop to stop. The latter was far more expensive, but when Piering pressed the singer to make a decision, he claims Moz hemmed and hawed for weeks, placing the tour in jeopardy, despite the fact that tickets were already on sale in markets like Los Angeles, Chicago, Detroit, Toronto, and Boston.

Meanwhile, Morrissey had left Fred Hauptfuhrer, a writer from *People*, stranded in Manchester's Brittania Hotel in early May because he wasn't in the mood to talk. The interview with the mainstream American entertainment magazine—which had a readership of nearly 30 million at the time—was eventually rescheduled by Rough Trade's publicist Pat Bellis, and Hauptfuhrer's two-page story was timed to run at the onset of the tour.

Detour to Italy and Spain

In May 1985, as the Smiths continued to gain traction in the U.S. ahead of their North American tour, the band stopped off in Italy and Spain to fulfill a few promotional obligations in Rome, Barcelona, and Madrid.

Rome

In mid-May, as the Smiths continued to gain traction in the U.S., the group flew from Heathrow to Rome for a concert at the large tent venue Tendastrisce and a one-off performance on the Italian television equal to *Top of the Pops*. When they arrived, on May 14, they were met by representatives of Virgin Records, which distributed Rough Trade's releases in the country.

Unfortunately, the Smiths' relationship with Virgin Italy soured almost instantly, as the band opposed the old-world, heavily tiled hotel accommodations that the label had booked. Morrissey immediately insisted on a different arrangement, and the Smiths found rooms at the airport Sheraton on short notice.

Although the Smiths were playing on rented instruments in Italy, that night's gig was a remarkable success. While the band played most of the same songs that had made the U.K. dates memorable, they sidestepped the lengthy "Barbarism" and opted to play "This Charming Man" and "You've Got Everything Now" instead. To Morrissey's surprise, the audience cheered heavily and sang along with most of the songs.

The following day, things went awry when the Smiths arrived at the television studio to discover they would be playing against a backdrop of kites and replicas of decaying pillars. After rehearsing for the show, Morrissey worried the performance would make the group look ridiculous. He told representatives from Virgin that he wasn't going to be humiliated and walked out on the show.

Marr—still only twenty-one and living the rock-star life, partying much of the time with Joyce and Rourke—supported Morrissey and followed him out of the door, much to the rage and embarrassment of the Virgin publicists present. Soon after, Travis' lucrative licensing agreement with the label was disbanded. But by this point, the Smiths' co-founders were no longer concerned about whether their actions might damage their relationship with Rough Trade.

Barcelona and Madrid

The following day, the band arrived in Barcelona, where they had been booked to play a club show at Studio 54 that was to be filmed for Spanish television. Although Morrissey worried for a while that the audience couldn't understand him, he was pleased when he asked the crowd if they spoke English and they unanimously replied "yes."

Seven songs from this nightclub set ("Hand in Glove," "Handsome Devil," "Barbarism Begins at Home," "Heaven Knows I'm Miserable Now," "Rusholme Ruffians," "The Headmaster Ritual," and "Miserable Lie") would eventually air as a one-hour TV special titled *Arsenal*. The program also featured studio material and interviews with Morrissey and Johnny.

Two nights later, the Smiths were back in front of TV cameras when they were filmed in front of a large audience at Madrid's Paseo de Camoens. The well-attended free gig had been financed by the city's town hall to celebrate the Saint Isidro holiday and was shot for the television show *Edad de Oro*.

At one point in the night, Morrissey criticized the Spanish audience members' heritage. "We have seen your national sport . . . and it's not very kind," he said, making reference to the brutality of bullfighting, before introducing "Meat Is Murder." That uncomfortable moment aside, the vibe of the Madrid show was overwhelmingly festive, with Moz clearly in a good mood as he danced during encores like "Barbarism" and "This Charming Man."

Grower Hired, Piering, and Rough Trade Fired

Just prior to leaving London for Rome that week, Morrissey and Marr made their frustrations with Rough Trade over "Shakespeare's Sister" known by hiring an attorney named Alexis Grower. Grower, who worked for the law firm Seifert Sedley Williams, fired off a letter to acting manager Scott Piering on May 16, advising him that the agreement they had originally signed with Rough Trade on May 1, 1983, was being terminated. The Smiths were planning to leave the label, Grower explained, adding that letters to this effect had also been sent to Travis' London offices and telexed to Sire in New York.

Grower's letter also advised the parties that the Smiths would be working directly with Ian Copeland and F.B.I. to line up merchandising for the American tour. Furthermore, an outside accountant of their choosing—and not Hector Lizardi, as Piering had recommended—would be hired to keep track of all U.S. earnings during the trek.

While Scott Piering figured he was being relieved of his unofficial managerial duties with the Smiths—despite the fact the letter didn't come right out and say it—he wanted to hear it from Moz and Johnny firsthand. He flew down to Madrid to try to arrange a meeting with them, but the band and tour manager Stuart James avoided him. Mike Hinc, who had since become a strong ally of Morrissey's, and was in Madrid to run interference, was charged with breaking the news to Scott. Ironically, Piering then returned to his main role as the Smiths' promotions man (for the time being) at Rough Trade.

San Sebastian Fracas

On May 19, with the impact of the letter still being felt among the Smiths' business associates, the band traveled onward to San Sebastian, where they were scheduled to play a Sunday-night concert. However, when the group arrived, the venue had delivered the wrong equipment.

Although a soundcheck was attempted, the band realized they weren't able to proceed with the show and went back to their hotel rooms until they could return to England. Meanwhile, the promoters—realizing how much money they were losing—directed all press inquiries and angry fans to the hotel where tour manager James—who had only come on board a few months earlier—was on the receiving end of abuse from those looking for answers.

The police turned up, too, but instead of calming the situation, they considered arresting the crew. Fortunately, someone in the camp knew to contact the British consulate, and early the next morning, the Smiths flew to Heathrow from Bilbao.

When James announced to Hinc—who had returned to London a day earlier—that he was resigning due to stress later that day, he was advised that Morrissey had already sacked him. A few days later, he was rehired—with a pay increase—for the U.S. tour.

Travis Holds Firm

Back in London, Geoff Travis mulled over Grower's letter. After a little initial worry, he decided to pay it no mind. He knew that Johnny and Morrissey had no basis to terminate their agreement with Rough Trade, which called for an initial three-year, three-album term.

In spite of their massive success, the Smiths were wrong to believe *Hatful of Hollow* could satisfy their contract, as it wasn't "previously unrecorded material." This meant that Rough Trade was still due one more album, and it had options for two additional records over as many years. And with the Smiths—happy or not—clearly his flagship band, Travis would never agree to let them leave until he was legally obligated.

Morrissey continued to hit out at the label, telling reporters that it was clear Rough Trade had grown bored of the group. He also made it known that healthy major-label proposals had been made to the Smiths. This was essentially his way of soliciting additional and hopefully extravagant offers.

U.S. Tour

On the eve of the Smiths' North American dates, Morrissey revealed to the *NME* his wish to travel to Indiana to visit James Dean's grave. But with a tight tour routing in place, the closest he would get would be Chicago's Aragon Ballroom.

The Smiths' U.S. tour—for which they were accompanied by Billy Bragg, who stepped in when usual openers James backed out—got underway on June 7. Ahead of Bragg's acclaimed one-man-band delivery of favorites like "A New England," "The Saturday Boy," and "St. Swithin's Day," audiences in each market were treated to performances by local drag queens.

If such entertainment was unorthodox, enthusiastic crowds embraced the Smiths at the Aragon and the next night at the Royal Oak Theater in Detroit. On the road with the band for the first time was their brand new manager, Matthew Sztumpf, who had been hired after successfully managing U.K. ska-pop band Madness.

Upon his arrival in the Windy City, Morrissey was quick to point out his problems with Sire's approach to "How Soon Is Now?" After sharing these sentiments with a *Creem* reporter, he and the Smiths moved on to Toronto for an encouraging show at the Kingswood Theatre, where he encouraged fans to have a good time despite the venue security. "Don't be frightened," he told the sold-out audience. "They're just big marshmallows really." Late in the set, he dedicated "Meat Is Murder" to "all you chubby little sausages—you know who you are."

Two days later, the band played Washington D.C.'s Warner Theater, and that too went extremely well. The band were in good spirits, with Moz joking that the first encore, "Heaven Knows I'm Miserable Now," was for "sexy security staff."

On June 16, the Smiths conquered Boston's Opera House with a memorable show that saw the unexpected return of "Jeane" and included multiple encores.

A ticket stub from the Smiths concert at Toronto's Kingswood Music Theatre on June 9, 1985. *Author's collection*

That paved the way for a pair of sold-out shows at Manhattan's Beacon Theater on June 17 and 18, with fans rushing the stage at both, embracing Morrissey and draping him in flowers. To keep things interesting for any loyalists returning to Manhattan the second night, the Smiths inverted most of their live set. Backstage, they

A ticket from the Smiths' June 27, 1985, concert at the Hollywood Palladium in Los Angeles. *Author's collection*

were thrilled to learn that Andy Warhol was in the house.

After several travel days, the Smiths took the stage at the H. J. Kaiser Auditorium in Oakland, California, on June 21. Unfortunately for Bay Area fans, the show was plagued with sound problems—specifically feedback originating from Morrissey's microphone.

The group's San Diego show on June 25 at the State University Open Air Theater went much better. The band found that by launching the shows with "Meat," and by making "How Soon is Now?" the main-set finale, just before the encores, the night flowed much better. At one point, after being on the receiving end of an object thrown from the crowd during "Stretch Out and Wait," Morrissey left the stage, only returning after Marr, Rourke, and Joyce had started "Heaven Knows I'm Miserable Now" without him.

The two Palladium Theater gigs in Los Angeles on June 27–28 were high-energy affairs, although the first show had a short hiccup when a guitar pedal of Marr's went inexplicably missing. The second was re-sequenced to avoid being redundant, with the band delivering a much-appreciated performance of "Reel Around the Fountain" and a fiery take on "Hand in Glove."

The U.S. tour finale got underway at Irvine Meadows Amphitheater in Laguna Hills on June 29. Aside from a few technical glitches during "Nowhere Fast," the show brought a celebratory ending to proceedings, bolstered by three encores, including a powerful rendition of "Miserable Lie" and the band's lengthiest version of "Barbarism Begins at Home" to date, complete with a wild stage invasion by fans. Clocking in at just over fifteen minutes, it didn't only signify the last song of the tour—it was also the last time the Smiths would ever play the song live.

Stein Declined

Morrissey's outrage over Sire's improper handling of the Smiths' U.S. tour—including the lack of a publicist for the campaign, and the absence of a television commercial to promote the band on MTV—prompted him to have Stuart James call Seymour Stein and inform him he was off the guest list for the Beacon gigs. The Smiths didn't want the president of their American label sharing in their success because they felt that he had undermined their triumphs.

Much to the singer's chagrin, Stein—who had put the bulk of his resources at the time into promoting Madonna's second album, *Like a Virgin*—was in the house for the band's 16,000-capacity Irvine Meadows gig. Backstage before the gig, Seymour marveled at the ticket sales. During the show, Moz made his frustration with the company known to the sell-out crowd. "I would like to thank those who made all of this possible . . . the Smiths," he snipped. Although Seymour had been trying to right some of the wrongs with Morrissey by taking him to dinner at the Ivy in L.A. a night earlier, and introducing him there to the legendary Paul Simon, another Warner Bros. act, the front man's remarks made clear that he was still irritated.

For all the stage invasions and rabid applause from adoring crowds, Sire afforded the group few extravagances in June 1985. Save for a Concorde flight into New York, the band traveled in coach. There were no photo shoots, no *MTV News* camera crews, and no Top 40 radio play, despite the fact that the tour of select markets was an overwhelming success.

Although the band had minor write-ups in *Rolling Stone* and *Spin* that year, the U.S. press coverage barely acknowledged what Morrissey, Marr, Rourke, and Joyce had accomplished on the road. Only *Creem* came close to giving them their due by calling the Smiths "England's Brightest Hope."

Marr would eventually concede that the Smiths were a difficult group for an American record label to try to break at the time. "We couldn't understand why we weren't bigger," he told *Musician* in 1989. "We'd just blame the whole country. We thought we could bring back the singles ethic and we were coming up against this monstrous machine."

Back on home turf, Morrissey summed up the tour to Eleanor Levy in the August 3 issue of *Record Mirror* as an overwhelmingly positive experience. "We didn't expect any fanatical fervor or uncontrollable hysteria," he told her of the American music-buying public. "I was rendered speechless . . . they turned out to be rational, incredibly sensitive, poetic human beings."

Marr Marries

As the Smiths' tour shifted to the West Coast, Johnny and Angie Brown were married, after a lengthy courtship, at a civil ceremony in San Francisco. Fittingly, Marr's oldest friend, Andy Rourke, was a witness at the June 20 nuptials, while Morrissey was charged with looking after the rings. The milestone was celebrated that evening with a party thrown by the Smiths crew at the Westin Miyako Hotel in Japantown.

Looking back on the event nearly thirty years later, Johnny clearly still cherished the relationship. "I know I'm very lucky," he told the *Arts Desk* writer Nick Hasted. "It is the most, and always will be the most important relationship in my life."

"That Joke"

In order to breathe new life into the Smiths' second album, a live version of "Meat Is Murder" was briefly in consideration as the title track of a proposed concert EP. Rough Trade even made test pressings of the prospective 7-inch and 12-inch release during the late spring of 1985. But because the song's subject matter risked alienating carnivores—and its general arrangement lacked the kind of appeal that would make it chart-worthy—the group rethought the idea.

The 12-inch single sleeve for "That Joke Isn't Funny Anymore," the second U.K. single extracted from *Meat Is Murder*.

Instead, Morrissey and Marr opted to release an edited version of "That Joke Isn't Funny Anymore" as a proper single, even as they recognized that the track might be too somber for the airwaves. The 7-inch single would be augmented with a live flip side of "Meat Is Murder" that had been recorded during the group's March 18 Oxford Apollo gig. In addition, the three other live tracks ("Nowhere Fast," "Stretch Out and Wait," and "Shakespeare's Sister") from the same show that had initially been planned for inclusion on the abandoned live EP would instead appear on the 12-inch.

From the start, Geoff Travis claimed to be against the idea of releasing "That Joke" as a single, knowing full well that when it failed—which he was sure it would—Moz would turn around and blame him. When it barely cracked the Top 30 on the good graces of devoted fans, "That Joke" became their second botched single in a row. And, as suspected, Travis would take his lumps from Morrissey as a result.

EMI

While the Smiths' figurehead continued his private condemnation of Rough Trade (after taking aim at Travis in the music papers earlier in the year), Johnny Marr went on record about the band's plans in August 1985. In his first solo cover for *Melody Maker*, he informed readers that, despite fan concerns that the band might jump to a major, the next collection of Smiths songs would be released through the independent label. The band and their attorney had come to accept they would be staying put for one last album.

This didn't stop EMI Records' managing director David Munns from pursuing the Smiths after reading of Morrissey's unhappiness with Travis' company in the U.K. weeklies. Munn knew what the importance of signing an established band like the Smiths would mean to a label like his from a credibility standpoint. After all, EMI was still feeling the fallout of having famously signed the Sex Pistols in 1976, only to let them go and later be ridiculed by the band in the song "EMI" from *Never Mind the Bollocks*.

Munns wanted Morrissey and Marr on his label, and he began calling Alexis Grower every few weeks to explain his desire to sign the band to EMI. Because Rough Trade was holding the Smiths to their agreement, Grower had to say no for the time being, but Munns made sure the attorney let Morrissey know that EMI was extremely interested in signing the band, and that he wasn't giving up.

The lure of EMI—which had the Beatles, the Beach Boys, Queen, Kate Bush, David Bowie, Duran Duran, and Pink Floyd on its roster at one point or another—had to appeal to Moz's ego. It also had to intrigue him from a standpoint of worldwide reach, considering he was complaining to *Record Mirror* of being broke that August. "It's especially hurtful when you meet so many in the industry who don't quite have your status but are laughably rich," he carped.

21

It Sounds Like a Wonderful Thing

All About The Queen Is Dead

Marr Speaks

When Johnny Marr opened up the doors to his new home in the leafy Manchester suburb of Bowdon that July for the *Melody Maker* cover that would run a few weeks later, it was one of the first real opportunities for fans to get an in-depth look at the Smiths' guitarist. In the Barney Hoskyns piece, titled "Strumming for the Smiths," Johnny proudly announced the September release of the band's upcoming single, "The Boy with the Thorn in His Side," as he shared his opinion on a number of topics.

For one, he wanted to make it perfectly clear that the Smiths were in no way revisionists. For too long they had been lumped in with the groups of the 1960s, but in Marr's eyes, they were a proud '80s band—part of what he called a "very honorable" generation. Johnny also spoke of the recent Live Aid charity concerts. While he found the cause admirable, he supported Morrissey's previous remarks that the Band Aid single "stank." He also objected to the way former Roxy Music vocalist Bryan Ferry used the event for personal gain by plugging his solo album *Boys & Girls* without playing any older material.

Johnny—who had also recently produced the single "August Avenue" for up-and-coming major-label act Impossible Dreamers—also confessed that he was disappointed in his hero, Keith Richards, for being unable to successfully play Bob Dylan's "Blowin' in the Wind" on acoustic guitar. It was Marr's belief that heroin had finally taken its toll on the Rolling Stones' guitarist.

"The Thorn"

Tracked in July with Stephen Street, "The Boy with the Thorn in His Side" saw official release via Rough Trade on September 16, 1985. If it wasn't the massive hit single the Smiths deserved, the track's alluring melody and stellar guitar presentation—credited to producers Morrissey/Marr—performed respectably, peaking at #23 in the U.K. and resulting in an invitation to once again appear on *Top of the Pops* on October 10.

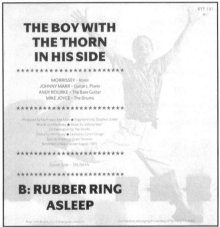

The front and back covers of "The Boy with the Thorn in His Side," featuring cover star Truman Capote. *Author's collection*

Johnny Marr wrote the song along with several others that would be heard on the group's third studio album while on tour with the Smiths in the U.K. earlier in the year, pulling together the arrangement with Rourke and Joyce over a couple of soundchecks. Originally intended as a demo for the group's third studio album, "The Boy" was recorded at the 8-track Drone Studios in Manchester, where the Smiths had made their initial EMI demos a few years before. The group liked the end result so much that they elected to use it as their next single, only stopping to add some overdubs when they converted it to twenty-four tracks at RAK Studios in London in early August while cutting the B-sides, "Rubber Ring" and "Asleep."

When asked by actress Margi Clarke about the song's meaning during an appearance on *The Tube*, Morrissey explained that the thorn of which he sang was the music industry, and the idea behind the song was to show people from the past who never believed in him or his music that he had persevered.

The single preceded its parent album, *The Queen Is Dead*, by nine months and boasted a yellow sleeve featuring a memorable photo taken by Cecil Beaton in 1949 of a young Truman Capote leaping through the air. On the eve of its release, Morrissey seemed to be only half-joking to the *Hit*'s Paul Du Noyer when he dramatically threatened, "If this single isn't a hit, I'm going to pack up my tent and rucksack and go into the Welsh mountains, and you won't see me again."

"The Boy" Video

With this song, the Smiths finally relented and produced their first ever band-sanctioned music video. On the strength of the June tour of North America, Sire wanted to release the single in the U.S., but without a parent album to tie it to, they needed a video for MTV exposure. The clip depicted an old man—presumably an aging Morrissey—thumbing through his back catalog of singles and albums and looking back on his heyday in the band. The other group members are then shown through a glass partition, performing "The Boy with the Thorn in his Side" in a recording studio.

When all was said and done, Marr said he wished they hadn't succumbed to label pressure. While the band had agreed to the video, he told Tony Fletcher, "They still managed to make us look like twats."

"Rubber Ring" and "Asleep"

For the flip side of 12-inch pressing of "The Boy with the Thorn in His Side," the Smiths crafted two separate songs—the first a mid-tempo shuffle and the second a haunting piano ballad—and fused them together through the use of a voice sample that Goddard would refer to as "a spectacular combination" in *Songs That Saved Your Life.* "You are sleeping, you do not want to believe," the part repeats, as it gives way to the sound of a frigid wind.

If "Rubber Ring" was, as some have suggested, Morrissey's way of reminding his loner fans—as they came out of their shells to dance and sing and finally live—to think of him "kindly," the track's abrupt ending floats into the suicidal thoughts that permeate "Asleep."

The mournful piano number never actually uses the word "death" but has Morrissey singing deep from within about his feelings on despair and loneliness. "There is a better world," he croons, of what awaits on the other side, as Marr delivers the somber and determined piano tones before concluding the track with a snippet of "Auld Lang Syne" during the fadeout. "Asleep" alone would comprise the B-side of the single's 7-inch pressing.

In 1986, after a pair of obsessed Smiths fans committed suicide, Morrissey spoke to his despondent followers through Martin Aston in the Dutch magazine *Oor.* He explained that while his hopelessness had never resulted in him following through with the act, he understood how deep depression could drive someone to take their own life. "The despair you feel is true and it's common," he told them. "Not enormously common, but common."

Tour of Scotland

A short, seven-date tour of Scotland—overlooked on the band's U.K. tour the previous March—got underway in September, with fellow Mancunians Easterhouse as the support. These shows have long been considered by those closest to the band to be some of the greatest in the history of the Smiths.

On September 22, the tour got started at the Magnum Leisure Centre in Irvine, where the group unveiled their new hit, "The Boy with the Thorn in His Side." Two other new songs featured prominently in the set for the tour: "Bigmouth Strikes Again" and "Frankly, Mr. Shankly," both of which had been tracked a month earlier at RAK Studios. And, to keep things interesting, the Smiths covered James' song "What's the World?," while Morrissey incorporated the first verse of Elvis Presley's 1961 U.K. #1 hit "(Marie's the Name) His Latest Flame" into "Rusholme Ruffians."

Multiple encores were common, as were fan chants of "Johnny Marr, Johnny Marr" and—at Edinburgh's Playhouse on September 24—a frightening stage invasion that took several security men to pull fans away from Morrissey. Although he needed their help, the shirtless singer was hardly appreciative, taunting them as "macho men."

The next night's show at Barrowlands in Glasgow has been named by everyone from Geoff Travis to Grant Showbiz to Marr as possibly the best gig the Smiths ever played. Taped for broadcast on Glasgow's Radio Clyde, it had a magnetic Morrissey leading the charge while Johnny, Andy, and Mike fired on all cylinders.

Energy was high throughout, even though the crowd had to be disappointed with Marr's decision to pull "How Soon Is Now?" from the live set, displeased with how it had been sounding live with only one guitar. Curiously, "The Headmaster Ritual" was also dropped from the set before this gig. And unlike the former song, which would resurface on the band's final tour, the Smiths would never perform the opening missive from Meat Is Murder again.

While the group's show at Dundee's Caird Hall went well, the Smiths' journey far north to the Shetland Isles was quite a spectacle. Their surreal show at the Clickimin Centre in Lerwick on September 28 drew spectators of all varieties—from punks and metal-heads to curious middle-agers and true fans—to an area unused to getting a lot of national acts. Some heckling was attempted, but seeing as punters had been spitting on Morrissey for several years, he was unfazed by the crowd's predictable antics. So while he took the high road as the group worked through their setlist, Moz got his shots in when he could, such as when he dedicated "Stretch Out and Wait" to the "macho heavy-metal fans" of Lerwick.

The Capital Theatre in Aberdeen on September 30 marked a return to normalcy, with a positive vibe prompting the unexpected return of "Jeane" to the set, where it would be played by the band—who incorporated a snippet of the Beatles' "Day Tripper" into the song—for the very last time. Morrissey and Johnny each took turns being saluted by the audience, which chanted their names with glee.

On the final night of the Scottish tour, at Eden Court in Inverness on October 1, the Smiths played "Asleep" for the first and only time in concert. A piano on the side of the stage presented Johnny and Morrissey with the opportunity to perform the song, and while they had soundchecked it—along with other new material like "The Queen Is Dead," "There Is a Light That Never Goes Out," and future B-side "Unloveable"—the crew was unable to move the instrument during the show, so for "Asleep" Marr could not be seen, only heard by the crowd.

Before the Smiths' final encore, Johnny told the audience that the current tour of Scotland had been "really, really good" and that the band was in an extremely positive frame of mind. The reaction of the many exuberant fans in attendance—some of whom had torn Morrissey's shirt to shreds—showed that they concurred.

Perry Boys

The tour openers, Easterhouse, were steered by Morrissey's childhood neighbor Ivor Perry, with whom he bonded over literature, and also featured Ivor's brother Andy. They were a politically driven act. The Perrys were members of the Revolutionary Communist Party and keen on the idea of changing the world.

While their revolution didn't happen, the group's debut album, *Contenders*, earned some acclaim when it was released in the United States in 1986 through a deal arranged by Travis between Rough Trade and Columbia Records. If some thought the album drew too heavily on Marr's guitar sound, it does feature some great roaring anthems like "Whistling in the Dark" and "Out on Your Own" that are worth seeking out.

Margaret on the Guillotine

When work first got underway in earnest on the Smiths' third studio album, the record had a provisional title that was decidedly anti-Thatcher and matched Morrissey's public objections to Great Britain's existing administration. Andy Rourke would later reveal to the *Daily Beast* in 2013 that the title *Margaret on the Guillotine* stemmed from a song of the same name that was in the running for the album. Of course, by the time all was said and done, the name of the record would shift to its final monarchy-condemning handle.

The band's efficient efforts at RAK that August were such that they went far beyond their original plan, which was simply to record some B-sides. Work on another song, "Bigmouth Strikes Again," was nearly complete, and Marr was in a great headspace while writing his musical portion of the new material, revealing to *Melody Maker* during the summer that these songs would change the public's perception of the Smiths. He announced he was drawing on blues influences like Elmore James and John Lee Hooker, while again looking to early Elvis arrangements, and promised to uphold his melodic and pop sensibilities.

Johnny and Morrissey revisited their earliest writing approaches that August, writing a number of new songs face-to-face one evening in a planned working session at Marr's house in Bowdon that resulted in material including "I Know It's Over" and "Frankly, Mr. Shankly." Bonding that night as they had at the outset of their band, their friendship grew stronger. Moz even encouraged Marr—who now had the money to buy pretty much anything he wanted—to backtrack and buy all of the cherished singles he had traded or lost along the way while in his pursuit of a music career. Together, they purportedly drove from Manchester to Brighton in Marr's car just to buy a copy of the 1973 Chicory Tip 45 "Good Grief Christina."

At the time—on Geoff Travis' suggestion—the Smiths had approached the famed Beatles producer George Martin to oversee the record. Martin declined. From there, Morrissey and Marr met with 1970s producer Tony Visconti—the man behind classics from T. Rex and David Bowie—over tea, but he too rejected their advances.

These refusals, coupled with the success of *Meat Is Murder*, prompted Morrissey and Marr to rethink the idea of working with a weighty producer. Instead, they decided to take ownership of the sessions, continuing on with Stephen Street alongside them in an unofficial co-production capacity. (He is officially listed as the album's engineer.)

Each of the members of the Smiths responded appreciatively to the attention Street paid them. Equal focus was given to the drums, the bass, the vocals, and all of Johnny's musical parts. This special treatment went a long way with Morrissey, but for Street—who was as much a fan as a collaborator—the singer was special. The engineer truly believed that Moz was brilliant, and as such he did everything he could to keep his client happy.

Street was deeply pleased with how the RAK sessions had started at RAK, with the Smiths moving on from "Bigmouth" to "Some Girls Are Bigger Than Others." Sensing that Johnny was equally happy, and believing he had become integral to the shape of the Smiths' sound, Stephen asked Marr for a royalty point for his efforts.

Johnny discussed Street's proposal with Morrissey, and the partners agreed that it made sense to give Stephen a royalty of one single percentage point on the album, which would soon take on the new and final title *The Queen Is Dead*. Street felt rewarded and honored, and with a new level of commitment, he—like Johnny and Morrissey—was invigorated, and keen to ensure that the record would be the best it could be.

Jacob Studios

Not long after the Smiths wrapped their tour of Scotland, the group convened at Jacob Studios, which was located inside a Georgian mansion in Farnham, Surrey. "I Know It's Over" was the first song they attempted.

Although this was an exciting time to be in the Smiths, Marr quickly became obsessed with the outcome of the project and wound up distancing himself from his usual accomplices, Andy and Mike. Johnny was left to write the music and arrange and tweak the material. When he wasn't obsessing over the tracks, he was summoning Morrissey to the studio from his new apartment at 66 Cadogan Square, one of the most expensive residential areas in London. It was common for the guitarist and the vocalist to see each other coming and going: Moz usually recorded with Street in the daytime hours, while Marr typically slept on site after working all night.

"It polarized my life," said Marr, speaking about the challenges of making the album with *Record Collector* in 1992. "I knew we were working on something really good. There was a feeling in the studio that we were at an important point in our career."

Rough Trade Woes

Not long after *The Queen Is Dead* had been perfected, Rough Trade became concerned that the Smiths were holding on to the album. The label wanted the master tapes and was granted an injunction that was served directly to Morrissey at his home on Cadogan Square just five days before Christmas.

The writ advised the Smiths that they were required to hand over the masters, and that the album would not be released until a court hearing could determine whether or not *Hatful of Hollow* might stand as a contractual album. A few months later, it would be Marr, not Morrissey, in attendance at the court hearing, where Geoff Travis' attorneys emerged victorious, upholding the Smiths' contractual requirement to deliver one last studio album to Rough Trade. As a concession, Rough Trade agreed to shorten the contract—which had called for five albums in total—by one.

If the dispute was in part about money, Morrissey's new and lavishly decorated apartment on Sloane Street in the heart of Chelsea was an assurance that he had plenty. After all, the profit-sharing between the band and Rough Trade was far more generous than most label/artist agreements. The wrangling was more about being free of Travis' control, and his perceived operational mistakes.

Marr—who still felt the chafe of Travis' attorneys—also wanted out. Late one night, he and crewmember Phil Powell even drove the 200 miles south to Jacob Studios from Manchester in an attempt to repossess the master tapes. When they arrived early the next day, however, the facility manager told Marr that because the masters hadn't been fully paid for, he had no intention of letting them out of his sight.

From then on, it was Morrissey—who had previously stayed clear of the courtroom—who handled all dealings with Travis and the label's publicity and promotional obligations. Geoff had been stunned by the album he had been absorbing—but not sharing with the rest of the world—for several months. He wrote to Morrissey to express just how brilliant he believed the project was.

With no further reason to delay it, both parties agreed for the record's Rough Trade release date to be set for Monday, June 16, 1986. A U.S. launch would follow via Sire on the Tuesday of the following week. "Bigmouth Strikes Again" was quickly announced as the album's next single. Released on May 19, it came eight months behind its predecessor, "The Boy with the Thorn in His Side."

God Save *The* Queen?

According to Morrissey, during the legal wrangling leading up the release of the album, Johnny Marr had come to him, unsure about the controversial title. In his 2013 autobiography, the singer relays how his musical partner's parents were upset about the implications of naming their record *The Queen Is Dead*.

Marr evidently petitioned Moz to reconsider the title, suggesting *Bigmouth Strikes Again*. Morrissey remained adamant about the name and advised Johnny to have faith in his decision, as the title was a strong reflection of the material. Upon its release, the title would be deemed a perfect match to what would become known as one of the finest British rock albums ever recorded.

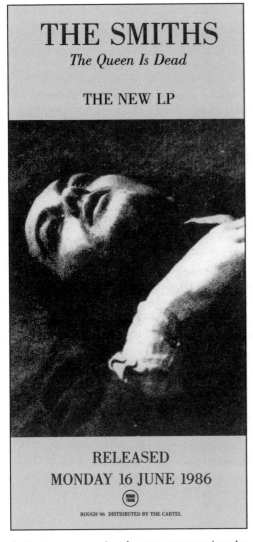

THE SMITHS
The Queen Is Dead

THE NEW LP

RELEASED
MONDAY 16 JUNE 1986

ROUGH 96 DISTRIBUTED BY THE CARTEL

An in-store promotional poster announcing the U.K. release of the Smiths' third album. *The Queen Is Dead* was released by Rough Trade on June 19, 1986. The following week, on Tuesday, June 25, the album was released via Sire Records in North America. *Author's collection*

"Sweetness"

Released a month ahead of the album, "Bigmouth" had been penned by Johnny Marr with the hope that he might craft a guitar riff as memorable and lasting as Keith Richards' on the Rolling Stones' epic 1968 single "Jumping Jack Flash." He later told *Guitar Player* that he wanted to write "something that was a rush all the way through."

The lyrics reflect Morrissey's sense of humor, as he compares himself to French martyr Joan of Arc with a melting hearing aid, throwing out barbs to the demanding and ruthless media—telling one reporter how he would like to smash every tooth in his/her head—before coyly retracting them and claiming he was only joking. At the time he penned the lyrics, he had long been seen performing wearing a hearing aid in support of a hearing-impaired fan. When asked about it in September 1987, he told a *Melody Maker* writer, "I would call that a parody, if it sounded less like self-celebration, which it definitely wasn't. It was just a really funny song."

Although Morrissey believed the reflective "There Is a Light That Never Goes Out" was a stronger track, Marr pushed for "Bigmouth" to be the lead single from the album, believing the upbeat, playful number was the best candidate to set the tone for the LP. The single—featuring a cover picture of James Dean taken by Nelva Jean Thomas against a purple border—reached #26 in the U.K. charts in June 1986.

The song's superb flip side, "Unloveable," was certainly strong enough to earn a slot on the Smiths' third studio album, but because there were already several somber tunes in the running, it was relegated to B-side status. This memorable number also features some of Morrissey's most confessional lines, as he admits that he appears "strange" because, in fact, he is.

Ferry and Pratt

The 12-inch bonus track included on the "Bigmouth Strikes Again" single was an instrumental called "Money Changes Everything." It was a blues-influenced number Marr had written late in sessions for *The Queen Is Dead* that Morrissey disliked so much that he refused to collaborate with him on the song.

With time in the studio remaining after re-tracking "Frankly, Mr. Shankly" with John Porter, but without the presence of Rourke and Joyce, Johnny played the bass part on the recording himself. The drums were provided by a machine that Porter had programmed.

If Morrissey saw little worth in the song, vocalist Bryan Ferry thought it was aces. Ferry was at work on the follow-up to his 1985 solo album *Boys and Girls* when he learned about the instrumental from Porter. The one-time Roxy Music front man reworked the track, writing a vocal part and renaming it "The Right Stuff."

In the spring of 1986, Ferry invited Marr to play on it, overdubbing his part in the studio at Chalk Farm. Johnny had badmouthed Bryan to *Melody Maker* a year earlier by suggesting he had used Live Aid to re-start his solo career, so was surprised by the offer, but he went for it with the support of the rest of the band.

During the session, Johnny befriended Ferry's bass player, Guy Pratt, a Londoner who had also played with acts like Icehouse and Robert Palmer. They started hanging out together, while Pratt's girlfriend, Caroline Stirling, hit it off with Marr's wife.

Electric Landlady

Johnny and Angie had recently moved back to London, having found Bowdon and his celebrity status in Manchester restrictive. The Marrs now occupied Kirsty MacColl's vacant flat off of Holland Park Road. In fact, Johnny took to calling her his "Electric Landlady," which would eventually become the name of her 1991 album. That record would feature a collaboration between them in the form of the minor hit "Walking Down Madison."

Living back in London helped Marr nurture friendships with people like Pratt and Stirling plus MacColl and producer Steve Lillywhite, who in turn introduced him to Rolling Stones guitarist Ron Wood, having produced the Stones' recent studio album *Dirty Work*. On occasion, the guitarists came together to hang out and jam.

The Queen Is Dead

The Queen Is Dead was finished by December 1985. Looking back on it nearly thirty years later, Morrissey credited Johnny's "soaring attitude" for the album's amazing outcome. "Johnny [was] the full vigor of his greatness," Moz writes, in *Autobiography*. "He [was] a deluge of ideas and motion."

THE SMITHS
The Queen Is Dead

The vinyl album cover for the U.K. pressing of *The Queen Is Dead*, replete with a sticker informing buyers that the record contains the Smiths' two most recent singles. *Author's collection*

This was most evident in the record's lead-off title track, a mind-blowing number that reinvented the Smiths by resetting the bar of what they could do sonically.

"The Queen Is Dead"

Based on a song Marr had started writing in his teens, the album's opening missive and title track was one of the last numbers recorded for it. Opening with a sound clip of Cicely Courneidge singing the World War I–era standard "Take Me Back to Dear Old Blighty" from the 1962 Bryan Forbes film *The L-shaped Room*, it quickly gives way to Mike Joyce's rolling tom-tom assault and Johnny's wah-wah guitar proclamation that the band is about to shred any preconceived notions of the Smiths.

The song's title—like its parent album—was taken from Hubert Selby's 1964 novel, *Last Exit to Brooklyn*, which was extremely controversial at the time for its depictions of drug use, rape, homosexuality, and domestic abuse. The lyrics feature commoners thinking twice about royalty and religion as they succumb to drugs and alcohol as a means to numb themselves about their meager means under Thatcherism.

"The Queen Is Dead" was the most brutal criticism of the British monarchy in song the Sex Pistols' 1977 single "God Save the Queen." In it, Morrissey calls out both Queen Elizabeth (referring to her as her very "lowness" while imagining her with her head in a sling) and Prince Charles (pondering whether he might like to appear on the cover of the *Daily Mail* tabloid in his mother's bridal veil.)

That June, Morrissey would relay his belief to the *NME* that the monarchy's very existence in 1986 was "a hideous joke." Cleverly—and knowing full well that "queen" was a euphemism for a homosexual—he would relay to reporters in interviews about the album that there was a safety net in the title, which was that the old queen could, in fact, be him.

Marr would later reveal that the music for this track materialized from a thirteen-minute jam session in which he was trying to evoke a vibe akin to guitarist James Williamson's guitar playing on Iggy & the Stooges' 1973 classic *Raw Power*. Fellow Motor City rockers the MC5 were also a point of influence. "Conceptually, I was trying to do that Detroit thing," he told the *NME* in June 2011. "But if you're lucky, that stuff comes out sounding like yourself anyway."

In 1989, Marr explained to writer Dave Haslam how the band felt when they listened back to the track, replete with its squealing feedback: "It made the hair on the back of our necks stand up."

"Frankly, Mr. Shankly"

This thumping toe-tapper is a thinly veiled attack on Rough Trade boss Geoff Travis and was penned by Morrissey and Marr at Johnny's Bowdon home in the late summer of 1985. Johnny would later reveal that the pair had tried (but failed) to recreate the structure and feel of Sandie Shaw's Chris Andrew–penned track "Yesterday Man" for it. Marr hoped to get Linda McCartney of Wings to play piano on the song and invited her to do so by postcard, but she declined.

In the song, Moz advises Mr. Shankly (a.k.a. Travis) about how he wants to leave the label and suggests that in doing so he might wind up in the hands of a more capable record company and become a historically important figure in pop music. Years later, Travis would admit that he found the song amusing, and would also provide clarity about his "bloody awful poetry" by conceding that he once sent the Smiths star some of his original prose. Morrissey's groan for Geoff to "give us your money" at the end of the song was his hilarious and unforgettable parting shot.

A first attempt at the song featuring a trumpeter was scotched, while a subsequent finished version that was earmarked for the album was ruined when a technical glitch on the tape was discovered by Street as he went to mix it from its digital source. With no time to waste and with Street already working to get the rest of the tracks prepped for mastering, Marr turned to John Porter to help recreate it at Wessex Studios in London.

"I Know It's Over"

Also written in Bowdon, with Johnny strumming his acoustic guitar while Morrissey sang into a tape recorder placed on his knee, "I Know It's Over" is a haunting ballad about a dying elderly man looking back on his lonely and uneventful existence with regret.

As the first song tracked when the Smiths shifted over to Jacob's Studio, it was recorded at teatime one dark, wet afternoon. It would fittingly soon earn the distinction of rivaling "Asleep" as the group's bleakest moment on wax. Yet for all of its sadness, the song's presentation was a triumph in Marr's eyes. In a 1992 interview, he would describe watching Morrissey cut this stirring, melancholy vocal as one of the highlights of his life. "It was that good, that strong," Johnny told *Record Collector*. "It was just brilliant."

"Never Had No One Ever"

The origins of this track date back to December 1984, when Johnny Marr recorded a song he had written based on the Stooges' "I Need Somebody." When he and Morrissey completed it in August 1985, the lilting mid-tempo song became a testament to the loneliness and insecurity Morrissey felt on the streets of Manchester.

The fact that he had lived in the city his entire life but still felt uncomfortable was a source of "constant confusion," as he told Melody Maker in September 1986. "I never really felt, 'This is my patch. This is my home. I know these people. I can do what I like, because this is mine.' It never was. I could never walk easily."

"Cemetry Gates"

Johnny Marr wasn't so sure that the guitar line that drove this track was enough to build a song around, but when Moz heard it, he insisted that they develop it. As a result, "Cemetry Gates"—spelled incorrectly on purpose—was a late-minute addition to the track list of *The Queen Is Dead*.

The song became the forum for Morrissey to reply to critics who had previously dinged him for reciting texts by authors like Shelagh Delaney and Elizabeth Smart. Taking matters a step further, Morrissey sided with Oscar Wilde, who had once been accused of plagiarism. (The Smiths' bard would also use the Wilde quote "Talent borrows, genius steals" on the run-out groove of the 12-inch single for "Bigmouth Strikes Again.")

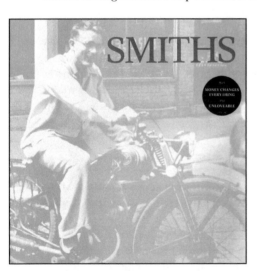

The cover of the 1986 Rough Trade 12-inch release of "Bigmouth Strikes Again." The sleeve's star is the actor James Dean, in a photo taken by Nelva Jean Thomas. The lead single from *The Queen Is Dead*, it was issued on May 19 and peaked at #26 in the U.K. *Author's collection*

"Bigmouth Strikes Again"

In addition to the facts already revealed about "Bigmouth," there's a funny anecdote about this track (and the album as a whole) involving Kirsty MacColl. The late U.K. pop singer—who was on the charts at the time the Smiths were working on *The Queen Is Dead* with a cover of Billy Bragg's "A New England"—was brought in to cut a backing vocal for this song and a few others. When she arrived at RAK Studios that summer, she came fully stocked with alcohol, clutching a plastic shopping bag of assorted canned beers presumably brought from home. She quickly informed Morrissey that if they were going to sing together, they should have a good time.

Although a friendship was formed, and Kirsty would again work with the Smiths, her vocals for the single were shelved when Morrissey began experimenting with effects on his voice. The pitch-shifting, female-sounding backing vocals heard on "Bigmouth" were instead recorded with a harmonizer that Stephen Street had set up.

Morrissey was incredibly amused by his shrill vocal parts and, at one point, fell to the floor in hysterics at the Chipmunks-like sounds he had created. His backing vocals would be credited on the album to the clever alias "Ann Coates," a play on the Ancoats area in northeast Manchester.

To promote the song, the Smiths appeared on BBC2's *Old Grey Whistle Test* on May 20, 1986, playing this and another new number called "Vicar in a Tutu." The performance marked the band's first public appearance with second guitarist Craig Gannon.

"The Boy with the Thorn in His Side"

While this song has already been chronicled in detail above, it's worth noting here that there is a difference between the original single version and the album version. Strings can only be heard during the coda of the track released in September 1985, but on the album version there are synthesized strings throughout. Additionally, Morrissey would cite "The Boy with the Thorn in His Side" as his all-time favorite Smiths song when questioned in 2003.

"Vicar in a Tutu"

This last-minute addition to the album supplanted the pensive ballad "Unlovable" with a playful, rockabilly gallop that pokes fun at religion. Morrissey even cites Manchester's Holy Name Church in the song and criticizes its good servants for always ensuring that the donation baskets were overflowing. He also sings of the church's unusual vicar sliding down the bannister to land in front of the worshippers. In all, it was another humorous victory for Morrissey that—like "Bigmouth"—lent some welcome levity to the record.

"There Is a Light That Never Goes Out"

Johnny Marr once explained that this song—another written in that one-night flurry of creativity in Bowdon—lifted musical elements from the Rolling Stones' version of Marvin Gaye's "Hitch Hike" and the Velvet Underground's "There She Goes Again." It makes sense, then, that Morrissey's lyrics take inspiration from "Lonely Planet Boy" by the New York Dolls.

Morrissey's lyrics, which would earn comparisons with the narrative of James Dean's 1955 film *Rebel Without a Cause*, form what is perhaps the Smiths' finest love song. It finds the singer riding in his paramour's car, begging them not to drop him at home. He is, in fact, so infatuated with his companion that he goes on to reveal that if a "double-decker bus" were to crash into their car at that very moment, it would be a "heavenly" way to pass on.

Moz and others in the Smiths camp would eventually push for the song to be the lead single from the record, but at one point prior to that he had actually suggested to Johnny that it be left off *The Queen Is Dead.* Like "The Boy with the Thorn in His Side," this enduring song also features a synthesized string arrangement. While Moz relayed to Johnny his preference for getting a true string section to play on the album, a desire to stay on budget led him to support the alternate approach.

According to Johnny, the song took only a half-hour to arrange and another ten minutes to record, before he put it aside and later overdubbed strings, flute, and some extra guitar parts. The results were magical. "The Smiths were all in love with the sound we were making," Marr wrote in the *NME* in 2007. "We loved it as much as anyone else but we were lucky enough to be the ones playing it."

Speaking to the same publication four years later, on the twenty-fifth anniversary of the album's release, he added, "Someone told me that if you listen with the volume really, really up you can hear me shout 'That was amazing' right at the end."

Johnny would also explain to *Select* in 1993 that, while he didn't think the song was single-worthy at the time, he did believe it was the best song he had ever heard. Twenty years later, in *Autobiography*, Morrissey would acknowledge that it became "greatly loved as one of the most powerful components of the Smiths canon." The song was finally released as a single in 1992, when it was used by WEA to promote the band's . . . *Best II.*

Mojo would later place the track at #25 on its list of the "100 Greatest Songs of All Time," while VH2 placed it atop its "Top 500 Indie Songs" survey.

"Some Girls Are Bigger Than Others"

Johnny Marr first sent a demo of the music for "Some Girls Are Bigger Than Others" to Morrissey by mail in mid-1985, with the singer then adding his lyrics and melody sometime after that. When he presented the title and words for the song, Marr was caught off guard by the seemingly sexist and downright frivolous lyrics his partner wanted to pair with what was an otherwise beautiful song.

"Who would expect *that?*" Johnny asked the *NME* in 2011. And, for a long time, Marr believed the lyrics did a disservice to his composition.

Twenty-five years earlier, Moz had justified his lyrics by explaining to the same publication that the song was actually about the way he had left womanhood unexplored for most of his life to that point. "I'm realizing things about women that I never realized before," he clarified. "[It's] just taking it down to the basic absurdity of recognizing the contours to one's body."

With the opening line derived from the 1964 film *Carry On Cleo*, in which Anthony (Sid James) opens a crate of ale while making his observation known to

Cleopatra (Amanda Barrie), the song's absurdly merry words were yet another opportunity for the Smiths to offset the stark outlook of the album's title track. In doing so, Morrissey gave the record a perfect balance of moods.

Musically, "Some Girls Are Bigger Than Others" is one of Marr's finest arrangements. But rather than leave it intact from start to finish, Stephen Street suggested they include a false fadeout near the beginning of the song, designed to give the impression of a door closing and reopening. The ending was also edited by Street, who extracted a little more than a minute of the tune's original outro, leaving the song to fade out and come back up before dipping back down at its conclusion. In doing so, he helped deliver one of the Smiths most distinctive musical moments yet.

Delon

The cover of *The Queen Is Dead* was designed by Morrissey, and portrays an image of French actor Alain Delon from the 1964 film *L'insoumis*. Set against a dark green-grey photograph of the film star, the band's logo and the album's title appear in bright pink lettering. Morrissey would later reveal that he had previously approached British actors Sir Alan Bates and Albert Finney, plus Manchester United football hero George Best, with sleeve ideas, but had been refused by them all.

The LP pressing had a gatefold sleeve—even in North America—signifying to the world that the Smiths were a prestigious rock act. Inside the gatefold, the lyrics were printed on one side with a large picture of the group on the other. The interior photograph of the band, which would later become widely used, was taken by a fan named Stephen Wright in front of the decaying Salford Lads Club, showing Morrissey, Marr, Rourke, and Joyce stood in the cold, damp afternoon against iron gates. Wright was surprised to get the prestigious gig after submitting to Smithdom a selection of pictures of the group that he taken during an earlier live show.

Commercial Reception

If the U.K.'s daily tabloids expressed their displeasure with the Smiths for their criticism of the Queen and leftist political stance—*the Daily Mail* used the headline "SICK MORRISSEY" in objection to the record's disrespectful title—it was only because the Smiths still held such a strong cultural grip on U.K. record buyers. The album didn't top the charts as its predecessor had, though, but instead debuted at #2 in the U.K., behind Genesis' chart-topping mainstream rock offering *Invisible Touch*.

This was nonetheless an impressive showing, considering the Smiths had received absolutely no daytime airplay on Radio 1 and the leading commercial station, Capital Radio. There was no music video, either, at a time when to release one would have grown the group's audience exponentially.

And "Bigmouth Strikes Again" wasn't a significant-enough hit to warrant an invitation to *Top of the Pops*.

As an artistic achievement—which nearly everyone who heard it agreed it was—*The Queen Is Dead* had the kind of lasting power its predecessors lacked. As such, it remained on the U.K. album survey for twenty-two weeks and earned a platinum certification from the British Phonographic Industry for sales over 300,000, substantially outselling its gold-certified chart-topping predecessor.

In North America, where the band had announced a summer tour in 1986, the album peaked at #28 on the Canadian album chart and reached #70 on the *Billboard* 200.

Positive Reviews

The critical response to *The Queen Is Dead* was astonishingly positive. In *Melody Maker*, Nick Kent wrote, "Here, in the marrow of this extraordinary music, something precious and innately honorable flourishes." Across the pond, *Rolling Stone* gave the record a rare five stars, as reviewer Mark Coleman pointed out the humor in Morrissey's lyrics and insisted, "Like it or not, this guy's going to be around for a while."

Only Ireland's *Hot Press* had anything negative to offer, in a piece titled "The Crown Slips." "Their third album goes far towards proving that Morrissey is but an astutely publicity-conscious and individual minor talent," wrote Bill Graham. "Over exposed and over extended by the demands made on him."

Legacy

In 2013, *NME* named *The Queen Is Dead* "the greatest album of all time," ahead of the Beatles' *Revolver*, David Bowie's *Hunky Dory*, and landmark records by the Strokes, the Velvet Underground, Pulp, the Stone Roses, Pixies, Oasis, Nirvana, and Patti Smith. Elsewhere, *Pitchfork* rated the Smiths' third album a perfect ten out of ten, having previously ranked it as the sixth best album of the 1980s.

Gavin Edwards of *Rolling Stone* also reflected on the Smiths' recorded achievement while celebrating its twenty-fifth anniversary, calling it "one of the funniest rock albums ever" and again scoring it a perfect five stars, just as the same magazine had in 1986. Edwards went on to suggest that while the disc may have displeased the Queen, "she was the only one."

Looking Back

Johnny Marr acknowledged to *Spin* writer David Marchese in 2012 that around the time he got to work on *The Queen Is Dead*, he knew that the Smiths were held in high regard. His goal was to try to do his own thing, although he was frightened and humbled. He remembered standing in his kitchen in 1985, thinking to himself, "'Holy shit. You're gonna have to dig deep now.'" As for the outcome, he added, "That was just a very fruitful time for me and Morrissey."

Although it is widely regarded as their best album, Marr confessed at this juncture that it still was not his favorite Smiths album. Nor would it be Morrissey's. That album was yet to come.

22

Do You Think You Can Help Me?

Rourke Fired, Gannon Hired

Red Wedge

In early 1986, with *The Queen Is Dead* completed but the legal dispute with Rough Trade still ongoing, the Smiths aligned with their former tour-mate and friend Billy Bragg for a show in support of the new British political movement known as Red Wedge. Bragg banded together with an assortment of liberal musicians—including Style Council, the Communards, Jerry Dammers of the Specials, Lloyd Cole, Madness, and Prefab Sprout—who opposed Thatcherism, and eventually aligned with the Labour Party, which represents the U.K.'s working class.

Initially, when the Red Wedge tour rolled into Manchester on January 25, it was just Johnny and Andy playing with Bragg, accompanying the singer on his song "A Lover Sings," the Smiths' "Back to the Old House," and a rendering of the Rolling Stones' "The Last Time" to the delight of attendees. A similar performance took place in Birmingham, which prompted Marr to telephone Mike and Morrissey to see if they would want to play as a band in Newcastle.

The band came together at Newcastle's City Hall to perform a short, unannounced set using Style Council's gear. And if Morrissey would later admit that he felt that Labour Party leader Neil Kinnock was the lesser of two evils, he was happy to lead the Smiths through a fiery four songs at this one-off show on January 31. When the band walked onstage, the place went bonkers. As Marr explained to Fletcher, "We just tore the roof off the place."

Launching the set with an impassioned rendition of "Shakespeare's Sister," the band played vibrant takes on "I Want the One I Can't Have" and "The Boy with the Thorn in His Side." Moz introduced the finale, "Bigmouth Strikes Again," as the Smiths' new single, even though it was still four and a half months from release.

From Manchester to Ireland

On February 8, the Smiths appeared alongside New Order and the Fall for a benefit show at Liverpool's Royal Court called "From Manchester with Love." The sold-out concert had been organized to support popular Liverpudlian

Labour Party City Councillor Derek Hatton, and, at Morrissey's insistence, his group headlined to a wildly devoted audience.

The show marked the live debuts of *The Queen Is Dead* tracks "Cemetry Gates," "Vicar in a Tutu" and "There Is a Light That Never Goes Out." The encores included a protracted rendition of "Meat Is Murder" and an unexpected finale of "Stretch Out and Wait."

Ahead of the Liverpool gig, the Smiths had originally planned to perform a three-date run of shows in Ireland and Northern Ireland, beginning on February 3, but these were postponed by one week after Marr turned up ill to board the tour bus at Morrissey's mother's Manchester home on February 1. After collapsing, Johnny was being treated by Betty in an upstairs guest room, where he was sick on one of her favorite comforters. He eventually found the stamina to board the bus so that the band and crew could depart on their journey to Dublin. But upon their arrival in Ireland, the guitarist needed to be transported by ambulance to a local hospital, where he was treated for exhaustion. He was overworked, dehydrated, and improperly nourished.

A week later, in Dublin, Marr was on the mend but Andy Rourke seemed out of it as the Smiths played their first full-length show of the year. Joined by one of Morrissey's favorite groups, the June Brides, the band played before 2,000-plus fans at National Stadium on February 10, rendering a set that mixed older material like "Miserable Lie" and "Still Ill" with their recent, playful medley of "(Marie's the Name) His Latest Flame" and "Rusholme Ruffians." Introducing "There Is a Light," Morrissey told the rabid audience that it was their new single, suggesting that they still weren't definite about using "Bigmouth" as their new album's lead track.

The next night, at Dundalk's Fairways Hotel, the set list closely mirrored the Dublin show, with the exception of "Hand in Glove," which was delivered as the encore after some time out of the group's concert repertoire. Then, at Whitla Hall at Belfast's Queens University on February 12, the band played it again, only for Morrissey's voice to

This ticket stub is a remnant of the Smiths' short 1986 tour of Ireland, although it is unclear which of the three shows it represents. Although the band had already recorded *The Queen Is Dead*, which was held up by a legal dispute with Rough Trade, the stub shows the artwork for *Meat Is Murder*. The band played these dates with support from London indie band the June Brides. *Passionsjustlikemine.com.*

give out during the encore. Not that the Smiths needed to worry, for the loud sing-along of adoring fans during the encore would almost always compensate. The loud shrieks from stage-invading loyalists were a much-needed reinforcement during the legal delay between albums.

Smoking Heroin

Johnny Marr wasn't the only one feeling unwell in the Smiths organization in the early days of 1986. Andy Rourke had been smoking heroin for some time, but his drug use didn't come to Morrissey's attention until the band appeared in Dublin that February. The bassist had very much hoped to kick his addiction and had attempted to go cold turkey while the band worked in Surrey the previous fall. As is typical, he experienced withdrawals, including sleep deprivation and nausea, suffering in silence as the band worked at Jacob Studio.

Because his studio efforts were spot on, Stephen Street, like Morrissey, had no way of knowing that Andy was a drug addict—let alone one trying to detox on his own. When the symptoms of withdrawal got too much to take, Andy would fly home to Manchester from Heathrow on a shuttle plane to "get well." Once home, he could discretely cop a few hundred pounds worth of heroin, get back on the plane, and head back down to London before he was gone from the studio too long.

In the New Year, Marr sought to distract his oldest friend from his drug problem by taking him along with him to play the Red Wedge. Meanwhile, Mike Joyce was also worried about Rourke's well being, but the drummer was unsure of how to deal with the situation. When Rourke's health continued to decline, Joyce looked the other way.

By this point, certain members of the Smiths camp—notably Grant Showbiz—had also grown aware of Andy's drug problem, but there was a very discrete "don't ask, don't tell" environment among those who knew, especially when Morrissey was around. For a long time, the singer was still very much in the dark about Rourke's problem, while others enabled him by accepting it and/or turning a blind eye. But that would change very soon.

Andy Fired

Rourke had kept his heroin addiction hidden from Morrissey for several years, with Johnny and Mike helping keep his cover. This secret was abetted by his dislike of needles, since smoking the drug left no obvious marks. Decades later, he would describe himself as Houdini-like in his ability to hide the problem from Moz for so long.

Ironically, just months earlier, the front man had spoken out about his disapproval of drugs in the media, specifically to *Time Out*. As far as the world knew, the Smiths were drug free.

When the quartet embarked on a short Irish tour that February, Rourke worried how he might manage his needs outside of England. He knew better than to try and smuggle heroin into Ireland—if he was caught, he'd shame the band's name and likely go to prison. Instead, he compensated by bringing a large quantity of valium and sleeping pills that he obtained from his doctor to help fight any symptoms of withdrawal. Unfortunately, the side effects of those prescription medications, which he also abused, made him feel completely wasted much of the time.

While the rest of the band and crew knew Andy was off his game at National Stadium—clearly blowing performances of "Cemetry Gates" (by using the wrong bass) and "What She Said"—critics, fans, and even the group's own tour manager, Stuart James, were none the wiser. As Rourke fumbled through the songs and appeared wobbly, James figured the bassist had probably smoked a fat joint with Johnny and Mike—as they were prone to do—before the show.

Of course, this was not the case, and when the band came offstage, Morrissey and Marr unleashed on Rourke. In doing so, Moz was finally made aware of Andy's heroin struggles. While the remaining shows went off without incident, the bassist was fired after the Belfast show, shortly after the band returned to Manchester.

Rourke, who had just bought a new house in Altrincham, discovered he had been sacked when he found an envelope with a postcard inside it—which he presumed was from Morrissey—left under his car's windshield wiper outside of the home. As the bassist later explained to multiple sources, it read, "Andy, you have left the Smiths. Good luck and good bye."

Morrissey would deny ever writing the note, releasing a statement to the fan site True to You in 2009 that explained "no such postcard was ever written by me, and no dismissal postcard was ever placed on Andy's car with my knowledge or consent." He went on to explain that he was "irked that such an alleged deed has gone down in the fairy tale footnotes of the Smiths lore."

Regardless, Rourke—who later insisted the actual postcard was still in his ex-wife's possession—was heartbroken when he went to Marr's house after absorbing the news. He cried in Johnny's arms. But while Marr loved his friend, his music career was everything to him, and no one—not even Andy—was going to jeopardize it.

Marr explained to Johnny Rogan in 1992 that he had allowed the bassist to continue to use heroin while he remained in the Smiths because he thought Rourke would eventually be able to stop. He also wanted to shield Morrissey from having to deal with the issue. "It was better that he didn't get involved," the guitarist told *Record Collector* in 1992. "I took care of Andy. And that's how our relationship worked."

Or, as Rourke explained to the *Daily Beast* in October 2013, "Morrissey was kept in the dark because Johnny thought it would freak him out."

Busted

Marr and Morrissey weren't exactly in agreement about Andy's sacking. Johnny thought it was a little extreme, and that the door should be left open for his return under certain conditions. Even though Moz cared about Rourke, he had no time for drug users.

Morrissey and Marr agreed that Rourke needed to get clean once and for all and hoped his firing would be the wake-up call he needed. Johnny, for one, couldn't take the idea of his lifelong friend killing himself with heroin. Yet any hope of him undoing his discharge was damaged by the fact that Rourke—whose world was unraveling—continued to use it.

Just two weeks after he was canned, the bassist went to his dealer's place in Oldham to score some smack. Unfortunately for him, the local cops had the dealer under heavy surveillance, and when Andy went in to buy his drugs, a dozen or more police officers came storming in. Alongside the dealer, Andy was arrested.

News of Rourke's bust for heroin possession made that evening's *Granada Reports*. It was the fear of hard jail time—plus the shame he felt about what he had done—that finally compelled him to get clean.

Enter Craig Gannon

After the tour of Ireland, Johnny Marr realized that the complexities of the group's new album presented challenges for the band to perform the material as a quartet. Some of the new songs—and older ones like "How Soon Is Now?"— had elaborate guitar parts. With a fifth member in the band, these numbers would be easier to replicate live.

Thinking about a way to execute this, Marr called on his old friend Simon Wolstencroft to see if he knew of any players that might be a good fit. At the time, "Funky" Si had been playing in the touring version of the Colourfield—the group fronted by former Specials and Fun Boy Three singer Terry Hall—with a young guitarist named Craig Gannon. Marr instantly recognized Gannon's name and remembered him from his guitar work with Aztec Camera a few years earlier. He asked Wolstencroft to let Gannon know that he wanted to meet him as soon as possible to discuss an opportunity.

Gannon hailed from nearby Salford and was just nineteen at the time. Born on July 30, 1966, he had graduated from piano to guitar when he was twelve. He was initially influenced by the Beatles catalog, as well as various soul and disco singles like Billy Paul's "Me and Mrs. Jones" (1972) and Odyssey's "Native New Yorker" (1977), plus albums like the Electric Light Orchestra's landmark 1977 LP *Out of the Blue* and the *Saturday Night Fever* soundtrack. Gannon soon discovered punk and began to play this style of music with friends by the late 1970s.

After playing in local bands and taking cues from the Clash, Stranglers, and Buzzcocks, Gannon got up the nerve to answer a classified ad in *Melody Maker* that would change his life. Just sixteen and fresh out of school in 1983, he auditioned for a spot in Aztec Camera, the Scottish band fronted by Roddy Frame. Craig, who was already a massive fan of the band and their Postcard Records labelmates Orange Juice, was the last one to arrive for tryouts due to a

A rare promotional picture of the Smiths with short-lived member Craig Gannon, as serviced to the U.S. media during the band's August 1986 tour of the United States. *Author's collection*

train delay en route to London from Salford. Despite his lack of punctuality, he had the look and the ability that Frame wanted. He was hired.

Gannon traveled home to Manchester with Aztec Camera for his first professional assignment—playing alongside Frame on a radio session and staying with the band for a year, during its global tour in support of *High Land, Hard Rain*, and the singles "Oblivious" and "Walk out to Winter." On the road at the time, Gannon played with Aztec Camera on their North American amphitheater tour supporting Elvis Costello & the Attractions.

The next year, Gannon joined another Scottish outfit, the Bluebells. This short-lived but wildly successfully quintet, fronted by Robert Hodgens, released one hit album, *Sisters*, in 1984 that produced two U.K. Top 10 singles, "I'm Falling" (#11) and "Young at Heart" (#8).

Craig left the Bluebells in 1985 and had just wrapped a tour with the Colourfield when he was invited to Johnny's home on Marlborough Road to meet and hang out. He wasn't terribly familiar with the Smiths but he had a remarkable resume for a musician his age. It seemed as if Marr already had his mind made up when the conversation turned to the bassist vacancy in the band. The only issue was that Craig played guitar.

During this meeting, in which Marr played some new demos and jammed on guitar with Gannon, Johnny also explained that they would probably be looking to add a second guitarist, but if Craig wanted to play the bass, he could join on the spot. As they parted company, Craig explained that, although they had really hit it off and he would love the opportunity to play with the Smith, he had no real desire to join on the four-stringed instrument.

Days later, despite turning down Marr's first offer, Gannon was summoned to join Johnny, Mike Joyce, and their driver, Phil Powell, for a trip down to Morrissey's Chelsea apartment to introduce the singer to their potential new second guitarist. Afterward, Johnny told Craig he was in the band—without a formal audition. As Gannon would tell later *Mojo* in May 2011, Marr explained to him, "Moz likes you, we all like you, you're as much a Smith as me, Mike, or Morrissey." He was given the group's back catalog on vinyl and a copy of the completed but still-unreleased third album, *The Queen Is Dead*, to study.

Rourke Rehired

Not long after Andy's drug arrest and commitment to get clean, Johnny and Morrissey agreed to have him return to the band. Rourke didn't actually go to rehab—he just exercised his willpower to kick heroin. This served him well only for the short term, but it did mean that he would be invited back into the fold that spring.

By the time the news finally broke in the April 19 *Melody Maker* that Rourke had been relieved of his duties following the Smiths' February tour of Ireland and was being replaced by Gannon, Andy was already back in the band. Morrissey explained Rourke's return to writer Max Bell in the issue of *No. 1* dated June 28, 1986.

"He was ill and it seriously invaded the Smiths, it infested our place," Moz said. "He rejoined because his leaving seemed more wrong than his staying. It was too easy to turn like a pack and say, 'You're useless! Get Out!'"

In truth, Rourke's bass playing was integral to the band's sound and not easily replaced. And if his distinctive performances on the band's records were exemplary, his unobtrusive and compliant presence added an important dynamic. Still, he was totally grateful to be home again after two months in limbo. Looking back on these events in 2013, he told the *Daily Beast*, "I totally understand why I got thrown out, and I was incredibly lucky to be given the chance to come back."

Rehearsing as a Five-Piece

The band came together as a quintet in April to rehearse in the basement of Mike Joyce's Altrincham home. Gannon was understandably nervous. He wasn't yet twenty, he was still somewhat shy and introverted, and he was the newcomer in the Smiths!

Thankfully, things came together quickly and easily, much to the delight of Marr. "In the first rehearsal, they did everything they could to make me comfortable," Craig later told music website *Ear Candy*.

"Everyone made me feel like I was the new official fifth member of the Smiths," he later told *Mojo* scribe Martin Aston. "It seemed to work straight away without us spending ages making it work."

23

I Left the North Again

John Hughes, "Panic," and the Road

Pretty in Pink

The success of John Hughes' mid-1980s teen movies *Sixteen Candles* and *The Breakfast Club* helped introduce alternative music to North American teens who may not have had such an opportunity otherwise. U.K. band Simple Minds scored a U.S. chart-topper with "Don't You (Forget About Me)" in the spring of 1985 following its use in the latter film, starring Molly Ringwald, while Hughes' next movie, *Pretty in Pink*, which took its name from the 1981 Psychedelic Furs song, afforded the Smiths' "Please Please, Please, Let Me Get What I Want" its first North American release.

The song's appearance in the film that spring allowed for the group's inclusion on a massively popular soundtrack album that also featured music from Orchestral Manoeuvres in the Dark, INXS, New Order, and Echo & the Bunnymen. Then, in the summer of 1986, a cover of the same Smiths song by U.K. trio the Dream Academy would be heard on the soundtrack to Hughes' next film, *Ferris Bueller's Day Off*. In September 2013, *Rolling Stone* ranked the accompanying album at #11 on its list of the best movie soundtrack albums of all time.

Sztumpf Dumped

Morrissey and Marr flew to Los Angeles in the spring of 1986 to meet with Sire Records executives about the U.S. touring and marketing plans for *The Queen Is Dead*. The Smiths' then-manager, Matthew Sztumpf made the trip to help finalize the tour arrangements, while Rough Trade publicist Pat Bellis scheduled long-lead interviews with music publications like *Spin* and *Creem*.

Sztumpf called on his well-connected friend, Ken Friedman, who represented the U.S. interests of Simple Minds and UB40, among others, to see if he might be interested in helping to grow Smithdom in North America. Friedman was well aware of the Smiths' commercial potential, and intrigued by their dynamic, their rabid fan base, and Morrissey's ability to manipulate the media.

Friedman and Marr met first and got along splendidly, especially after Ken relayed his confidence that the Smiths would be stars in America. His ambition left a mark on Johnny, who then introduced Ken to Morrissey. Together, they

SMITHS
PANIC

THE NEW RELEASE   MONDAY 21st JULY

7" (RT 193) B/W
VICAR IN A TUTU

12" (RTT 193) WITH EXTRA TRACK
THE DRAIZE TRAIN

DISTRIBUTED BY THE CARTEL

A promotional poster for the non-album A-side "Panic," which was released in the U.K. on July 21, 1986. *Author's collection*

visited bookstores in San Francisco, where Friedman was based, and where he got his start working for rock promoter and executive Bill Graham. Friedman was hired to work with the Smiths.

If Sztumpf was happy to handle the European end of things, it wouldn't be for long, for Morrissey fired him upon their return to Manchester. The singer hadn't told Johnny he was planning to let Sztumpf go, however, and when he showed up at Marr's door looking for an explanation, the guitarist was caught off-guard and perplexed by his partner's actions.

"Panic"

In April 1986, John Porter was working on Billy Bragg's forthcoming album *Talking with the Taxman About Poetry* when he called on Marr to come down and play on the session. These efforts could later be heard on Bragg's rendition of the Left Banke's "Walk Away Renee," while the studio collaboration with Porter prompted Marr to again push Morrissey to go again go with him for their next single session.

"Panic," which extended the Smiths' unorthodox tradition of releasing a non-album A-side, was a chiming guitar song written by Marr in homage to the classic 1972 T. Rex number "Metal Guru." Its lyrics were purportedly influenced by the Chernobyl nuclear disaster, news of which broke on April 26, 1986.

According to Smiths lore, Morrissey and Marr had been writing together at Bowdon at the time they first learned of the tragedy from zany BBC DJ Steve Wright, who came away from the somber news by introducing Wham!'s single "I'm Your Man." They were disgusted by the inappropriateness of the broadcast. "I remember actually saying, 'What the fuck does this got to do with people's lives?'" Marr told Simon Goddard in 2003, recalling how, having heard of the devastation, they were then expected to shimmy around the room to Wham! only seconds later.

On a broader scale, "Panic" was perceived as a commentary on the tepid state of pop music in 1986, which music writer Nick Kent later touted as a decree for "rock terrorism." In support of the song, the band even commissioned a

T-shirt with a picture of Steve Wright along-side Morrissey's slogan, "Hang the DJ!"

The Smiths tracked the song on May 5, a week after they first learned of the disaster, at Livingston Studios in London. With the song clocking in at just 2:20, producer John Porter supposedly felt that it was too short, so he copied the band's first take and appended it to the end to increase the total length. Upon hearing the expanded version, however, Morrissey and Marr insisted he revert to the original.

With Marr's and Gannon's guitar parts layered together alongside Joyce's clopping drums and Rourke's thumping bass, the recording finds Morrissey singing of chaos erupting in Dundee, Carlisle, Humberside, Leeds, Birmingham, and beyond. Midway through the song, Moz puts the blame on pop music, imploring fans to torch a disco and—accompanied by a chorus of schoolchildren—to "hang the DJ." Ironically, "Panic" became one of the Smiths' biggest radio hits, peaking at #11 in the U.K. and #7 in Ireland upon its release that July 21. The singer was thrilled that it received daytime airplay alongside the other pop records it condemned.

The single's sleeve featured an image of Richard Bradford, the actor who played the lead in the 1967 British TV show *Man in a Suitcase*. It was backed with the album track "Vicar in a Tutu" and "The Draize Train," another instrumental penned by Marr that Morrissey refused to write words for because he didn't believe the music was good enough.

A promotional poster for "Panic," featuring Morrissey's handwritten lyrics to the song. *Author's collection*

During these same sessions, the Smiths also attempted to record the urgent and explosive rocker "Sweet and Tender Hooligan," but they weren't happy with the outcome. The song would eventually be recorded during a Peel Session broadcast on December 2, 1986, and subsequently included on the 1987 U.S. compilation *Louder Than Bombs*.

Eurotube

Ahead of "Panic," and hot on the heels of *The Queen Is Dead*, the Smiths appeared on Channel 4's *Eurotube* on July 5, where they performed live versions of "There Is a Light That Never Goes Out" and their forthcoming non-album single.

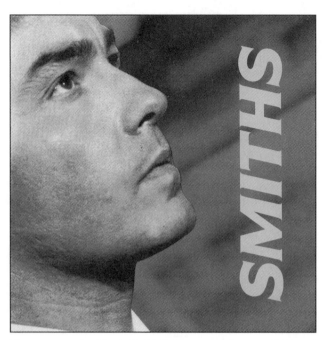

The cover art for "Panic," which features an image of Richard Bradford, the star of the 1967 British television series *Man in a Suitcase*. The song was one of the group's most successful singles, reaching #11 in the U.K. in the summer of 1986. *Author's collection*

This version of the then-unreleased "Panic" boasts a longer drum introduction, while Morrissey had a young boy join him onstage to sing the high-pitched backing vocals— a child actor dressed in a schoolboy shorts and blazer as a miniature version of the singer, replicating Moz's onstage look with a hearing aid and a bush hanging out of his back pocket.

Derek Jarman

That same month, avant-garde filmmaker Derek Jarman delivered a thirteen-minute film called *The Queen Is Dead*. Utilizing the title track of the Smiths' third album, plus "Panic" and "There Is a Light That Never Goes Out," the mini-movie balances full color footage of urban blight in and around Manchester with a mixture of dark, sinister, and, above all else, thought-provoking imagery.

With the Smiths unable to perform "Panic" on television due to their looming U.S. tour, Rough Trade would extract it from Jarman's film for use as the single's official music video and service it to *Top of the Pops*. Later in the year, Sire Records would snip "There Is a Light That Never Goes Out" from the project and lend it to MTV for play on the Sunday night alternative-music program *120 Minutes*.

Allegations of Racism

Some critics that summer would unfairly suggest that "Panic" was racist because it lashed out at the "disco" and the "DJ." Speaking to *Melody Maker*'s Frank Owen by phone from a hotel room in Cleveland, Morrissey decried the writer's suggestion that he was leading a "black pop conspiracy." Owen had pressed Morrissey after Scritti Politti's Green Gartside had publicly accused the song—and the Smiths themselves—of being racist in the press.

Of course, Morrissey's denials weren't helped by his claims in the same article that reggae was "the most racist music in the entire world." Nor were his suggestions that modern R&B performers like Diana Ross, Stevie Wonder, and Janet Jackson didn't "say anything whatsoever." His insistence that "Third Finger, Left Hand" by Motown's Martha Reeves & the Vandellas was his favorite song of all time came too late to save him.

When the article came out, Morrissey was appalled and worried at how he was being perceived. While the singer and his loyalists suggested he had been quoted out of context—even threatening to sue *Melody Maker* by suggesting Owen had fabricated the remarks—the writer had his tapes, which he gave to the publication's lawyers.

Even Marr got defensive, later telling the *NME* in 1987 that he would happily "kick the living shit" out of Owen if he ran into him, such was his disgust at the slant of the article, while contesting that disco music did not always equate to black music. The guitarist went on to remind the world that New Order, for example, weren't black but still made some of the most recognizable dance music in the world.

Meanwhile, before the interview even took place, the Smiths had agreed to headline an anti-apartheid benefit slated for November 14 at London's Royal Albert Hall and promising an opening set by the Fall.

Dear Old Blighty

A few weeks before leaving for their North American tour in August 1986, the band played a handful of warm-up shows in Scotland and Northern England. The quintet took the stage at Barrowlands in Glasgow on July 16, playing the bulk of *The Queen Is Dead* while also launching the shows with "Panic" and including two other new songs, "Ask" and "Is It Really So Strange?"

The next night, at the Mayfair in Newcastle upon Tyne, troublemakers tried to ruin the experience for fans and the band. People in the crowd—some of whom may have been upset with Morrissey's anti-Royal stance—threw pint glasses of beer and urine at the stage, goaded the band, and spat at the singer, who replied, "Thank you for all of your phlegm—we didn't really want it." As would be the case for the remaining U.K. shows of this run, the crowd was treated to the full audio recording of "Dear Old Blighty" before the Smiths returned to the stage for their encore.

Back home in Manchester on July 19, the Smiths participated in the "Festival of the 10th Summer," a gig at G-Mex organized by Factory's Tony Wilson and designed to celebrate ten years of punk music in the city. The Smiths co-headlined the concert with New Order on a bill that also counted A Certain Ratio, the Fall, the Virgin Prunes, Pete Shelley, and others. As with the previous show, the band's final encore was the re-activated "Hand in Glove." The set was recorded for Piccadilly Radio and aired the following year, on the day of the 1987 FA Cup Final.

The final night of these warm-up shows took place at the University of Salford, not far from Gannon's childhood home. The gig would later be listed by *Q* magazine as one of the hundred best concerts ever. From the outset of

"Panic," the show was pure pandemonium; part of the stage collapsed and the show had to be halted until it could be made safe. Johnny happily introduced Gannon as a local boy and was met with resounding cheers. During "The Queen Is Dead," Morrissey set down a sign that held the album's title/slogan in block letters, removed his sweat-drenched "Hang the DJ!" T-shirt, and threw it into the crowd. He duplicated this act again during an encore of "Rusholme Ruffians," sacrificing another shirt for the sake of the two rabid fans who tore his clothing in half.

His Master's Voice

Morrissey met with EMI's David Munns for tea one Sunday at a hotel in Oxfordshire, following an initial telephone conversation, and it was at this meeting that the Smiths' front man made it known that he intended to sign with the massive, world-renowned record company.

Both Morrissey and Marr had already talked over EMI's offer of a four-album deal with a mid-six-figure advance per record and found it agreeable. On paper, Munns was offering a lower royalty rate than Rough Trade, but it was still significantly higher than the industry average, reflecting the fact that the Smiths had become one of the most important bands in England by the summer of 1986.

Were they to in fact sign with EMI, the Smiths would no longer be subject to the kind of payment delays and operational issues that they faced when Rough Trade had money woes. The group's royalties could be counted on as agreed, as EMI was a proven and publicly traded company with no cash flow concerns.

Munns paired Morrissey and Marr with Nick Gatfield, an A&R executive who had previously played saxophone in Dexys Midnight Runners. As the courtship continued, Johnny and Morrissey were excited by the notion of signing to EMI on prestige alone—it was, after all, the home of the Beatles.

In an effort to lure Morrissey and sign the Smiths, Munns sent him details of all of EMI's assorted imprints. Morrissey chose HMV, which stood for "His Master's Voice" and was best known for its 1950s and 1960s heyday. Originally featuring the image of a dog named "Nipper" listening to a nineteenth-century cylinder phonograph that originated from an 1899 painting by Francis Barraud, the HMV POP label was home to the first U.K. single by Elvis Presley.

When all was said and done in late July 1986, the Smithdom partners signed the new agreement while waiting to board a Canada-bound plane at Heathrow Airport. From there, Alexis Grower send it off to Munns. Weeks later, Travis got an in-person affirmation from the Smiths that the band had jumped to EMI for their next record.

There was one snag, however. Morrissey and Marr had never renegotiated the terms of their agreement with Sire when they settled their label issues with Rough Trade. This meant they still owed their North American label one more album. Therefore, EMI would be obliged to license the Smiths fourth studio album to Seymour Stein's company.

"Ask"

In June 1986, the Smiths entered London's Jam Studios with John Porter to track "Ask," an upbeat pop song that found Morrissey singing of writing poems to a bucktooth girl in Luxembourg, featuring backing vocals by Kirsty MacColl, who had previously found her singing left off of "Panic." The tune's uplifting nature made it an ideal A-side contender.

One version of events suggests that the bare bones of the song—specifically its chord sequence—originated from something Craig Gannon came up with when he Johnny were playing guitar together one day in May with the tape rolling. Marr would later dispute this notion in Johnny Rogan's book *Morrissey and Marr: The Severed Alliance* and insist that he had already come up with the sequence when he introduced it to the second guitarist. And when it was eventually released, on October 20, the non-LP single was credited to Morrissey/Marr.

Featuring the distinctive dueling strumming of Marr and Gannon—who played Martin acoustic guitars—"Ask" actually had five guitar parts throughout that gave way to the sound of seagulls before picking up again. At Morrissey's request, and without Porter's knowledge, the recording was mixed by MacColl's husband, producer Steve Lillywhite, best known at the time for his work with U2, Peter Gabriel, Simple Minds, and Big Country. Lillywhite finished it off at his home studio in the London Borough of Ealing.

The 7-inch single was backed with *The Queen Is Dead* track "Cemetry Gates," while the 12-inch appended the bonus track "Golden Lights." It would reach #14 in the U.K. singles chart that month, and would also receive a limited U.S. release through Sire the following month. The sleeve featured a picture of U.K. television actress Yootha Joyce, star of the ITV series *Man About the House* (1973–76) and *George & Mildred* (1976).

"Golden Lights" was a song from Morrissey's childhood by female pop star Twinkle (a.k.a. Lynn Annette Ripley) that had reached #21 in the U.K. 1965. At the time, Moz identified with the song, which the then-seventeen-year-old had written about her disillusionment with the music business. Marr and Gannon played acoustic guitars and mandolin on the recording, which excluded Rourke and Joyce. Porter played bass on the track and programmed a Linn Drum to provide its beat. MacColl also lent her distinctive voice to the song, providing a memorable harmony part. Stephen Street mixed this number, too, adding a flange effect to Morrissey's voice and burying the guitars' bossa-nova vibe. The Smiths were generally displeased when they heard the results, having entrusted Street to finalize the mix without their ultimate approval.

During the Jam sessions that June, the Smiths also tracked a version of "Is It Really So Strange," but they weren't happy with the outcome. The version heard on the 1987 compilation *Louder Than Bombs* was tracked during the band's December 1986 John Peel Session.

Tabloid Trouble

The Smiths' popularity made them good fodder for headlines, even fabricated ones, as music and mainstream news tabloids in the U.K. utilized the group's good name to engineer stories that would help sell newspapers. In the weeks after *The Queen Is Dead* rose to the upper regions of the album charts, headlines like "MORRISSEY: ROYAL LOW" and "MORRISSEY APOLOGIZES" would appear without any credibility. Rough Trade's press office was delighted, believing that any exposure—true or not—would correlate with sales. Of course, Morrissey never said he was sorry for his position on the royals.

Elsewhere that summer, the *Daily Mail*—the publication name-checked in "The Queen Is Dead"—ran a story under the headline "SICK MORRISSEY." In it, the tabloid claimed that the singer had publicly endorsed a bisexual lifestyle, when of course he had done nothing of the sort. Nor had he answered his front door in a tutu, as *NME* writer Ian Pye had joked in a profile to plug the album.

The previously mentioned bothersome Frank Owen *Melody Maker* feature would even suggest that Morrissey spent his youth hanging around Manchester's public toilets, looking to pick up gay men. When Morrissey cried defamation to Rough Trade, the label gave him little support, suggesting he accept the libelous claim because it had appeared in a cover story—a sign that the band's profile was getting bigger.

C86

In the summer of 1986, the *NME* released a promotional cassette featuring a number of independent guitar bands titled *C86*. The compilation was compiled by writers like Roy Carr, Neil Taylor, and Adrian Thrills, and featured a number of bands that drew on the guitar-driven sound of the Smiths.

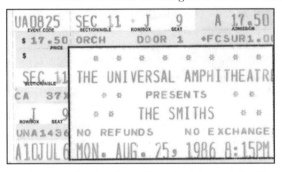

If they weren't directly influenced by the Morrissey/Marr catalog, groups like the Soup Dragons, the Mighty Lemon Drops, the Close Lobsters, the Pastels, Primal Scream, and the Wedding Present certainly shared similarities with them. The Smiths had clearly paved the way for these bands, and fans of the Manchester giants would find themselves drawn to many these outfits as they carved out their own existences in the coming years with varying degrees of success.

A ticket stub for the first of two back-to-back Smiths concerts held at the Universal Amphitheatre in Los Angeles on August 25 and 26, 1986. The chaotic audience response at the first show prompted officials to bring in a heavier police presence the second night to help control the crowd. *Author's collection*

Pratt on Standby

In the weeks before the Smiths' U.S. tour, which was slated to kick off in Ontario on July 30, the band camp became increasingly concerned that Andy Rourke's work visa might be denied because of his recent heroin arrest. Marr had a substitution solution in his new friend Guy Pratt, who began attending the

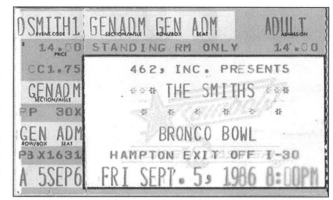

A souvenir ticket from the Smiths' Bronco Bowl performance, which took place on September 5, 1986, in Houston. *Author's collection*

tour rehearsals, which were held at a lavish farmhouse in West Sussex, not far from Gatwick Airport.

Pratt was a quick study of Andy's bass parts, but he still needed to become accustomed to playing them with Johnny, Mike, and Craig. Of course, Guy knew that his being hired for the American tour was contingent on Andy being unavailable, which seemed more and more likely. Then, after the last rehearsal in the fourth week of July, Rourke's U.S. work visa was granted. Andy—who had already accepted his fate—was stunned to learn that he could in fact join the trek.

1986 North American Tour

When the Smiths returned to North America in the final days of July 1986 for a six-week tour, the five-piece band were booked into substantial venues that were, in the case of their three planned southern California shows, bigger than the majority of venues they were playing in England. More remarkable was that *The Queen Is Dead* was by no means a blockbuster. It was a steady seller that sold phenomenally well in some markets, like Los Angeles, Boston, and New York, giving it enough inertia to peak at #70 in the *Billboard* 200.

Santa Monica–born lesbian folk singer Phranc had been tapped by Morrissey to open the shows. Born Susan Gottlieb, she was signed to Rhino Records at the time and was touring in support of her acoustic album *Folksinger*, which featured the song "Everywhere I Go (I Hear the Go-Go's)" and a cover of Bob Dylan's 1964 composition "The Lonesome Death of Hattie Carroll." She also opened for alternative-rock acts Hüsker Dü, the Violent Femmes, and Billy Bragg around this time, and eventually signed to Island Records in 1989. At the time, the androgynous performer touted herself as "The All-American Jewish Lesbian Folksinger."

London to Montreal

The Smiths' biggest U.S. chart achievement occurred during the week the band arrived in Toronto to launch their North American tour at Centennial Hall in London, Ontario. Upon arrival, Morrissey was thrilled to make the acquaintance of actress Eartha Kitt in the airport, not least because she had evidently once slept with his hero, James Dean.

For a few days leading up to this July 30 concert, the Smiths retreated into the Centennial, rehearsing and hanging out in the venue while ensuring that the band and crew were in sync. But the lack of a band manager and the inexperience of hastily hired tour manager Sophie Ridley meant that Marr had to step up. He insisted on last-minute tour support from Sire and threatened to cancel the tour if he didn't get it. He also handled an array of equipment troubles and even had to figure out how to get the crew paid.

Once all of this was sorted, the Centennial Hall gig and the show the next night at the Kingswood Music Theatre were triumphs, even if the latter—an outdoor event—was marred by rain. Morrissey blamed the Queen for the weather and criticized Sire for refusing to release their new single, "Panic." The singer's repeated onstage condemnations of the label for holding up the song's stateside release only made him want to play it more. The band opened many dates on the tour with the song and played it every night. After enough fan inquiries, Sire elected to put it out right around the time the tour wrapped that September.

When one of the fans brazen enough to invade the Kingswood stage tore the T-shirt off of Morrissey's torso, he remained bare-chested. That was until another fan gave him another one to wear—a Smiths souvenir shirt from the 1985 North American summer dates that read "I'd like to drop my trousers to the Queen."

For his part, Gannon did his best to fit in and keep up with the band. This included celebrating his twentieth birthday by drinking twenty shots of cognac under the guidance of Marr, Rourke, and Joyce. He woke up the next afternoon ready to play the Toronto gig, where he subtly complimented Johnny's playing. For his part, Gannon felt like a good fit and was more and more amazed by Morrissey's stage presence with each successive show.

These gigs and those that followed—including the band's final Canadian shows at the Capital Congress Center in Ottawa on August 2, and at the Centre Sportif de L'université de Montréal the

KBCO WELCOMES

ED.SEPT. 3.1986/7:30PM

U EVENTS CENTER THEATER

THE SMITHS

PRODUCED BY

CU PROG. COUN. & IMAGE

SEC	ROW	SEAT	ADMISSION
15	25	04	$ 11.00 TAX INCLUDED

A surviving ticket stub from the Smiths' concert in Denver, Colorado, on September 3, 1986. *Author's collection* next night—marked the reappearance of "How Soon Is Now?," which hadn't been played live for more than a year. Of course, the Smiths would never get away with leaving it out of their American sets, as it had remained their most enduring song in this part of the world.

The Montreal show was plagued by pushing from attendees inside the venue, hoping to get closer to the band, and the crush resulted in some down in front being hospitalized with injuries. Frenzied Smiths fans stormed the stage, including three excited young men who wound up knocking Morrissey to the ground— where he stayed, curled up in the fetal position, until venue security cleared the area. Later, during the "Hand in Glove" finale, a female fan stood next to Moz onstage, putting her arm around his waist and caressing him as he crooned.

Northeast and the Midwest

The group's first U.S. concert of 1986 took place at the 15,000-capacity Great Woods Performing Arts Center in the suburbs of Boston on August 5. In an effort to minimize stage-rushing at the end of the show, the group decided to try launching their concerts with "How Soon Is Now?" but found it altered the momentum of the performance, so the song was moved back to the end of the set list at the following night's Pier 84 show in Manhattan, which was attended by luminaries including Mick Jagger,

THE SMITHS
ASK
THE NEW RELEASE MONDAY 20TH OCTOBER

7" (RT 194) B/W *CEMETRY GATES*

12" (RTT 194) WITH EXTRA TRACK *GOLDEN LIGHTS*

DISTRIBUTED BY THE CARTEL

A poster advertising the release on October 20, 1986, of a new, non-album Smiths single, "Ask." The Morrissey-designed artwork features a picture of the British television actress Yootha Joyce. The song would peak at #14 on the U.K. pop chart. *Author's collection*

likely on the recommendation of Marr's friends Ron Wood and Steve Lillywhite.

With "There Is a Light That Never Goes Out" picking up steam with fans and radio play on stations like WLIR in New York and WHFS in Washington, D.C., the Smiths used it to open shows in those markets and beyond. While these gigs were memorable for fans, the show at George Washington University on August 8 was marred when, during the final encore of "Bigmouth Strikes Again," Morrissey leaned over to shake hands with members of the front row and one of them nearly pulled him off the stage. Marr and the band kept playing the song

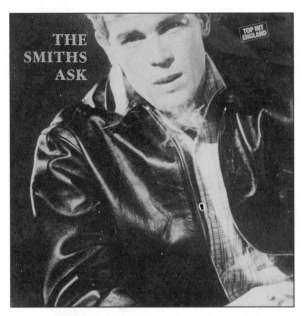

THE
SMITHS
ASK

A German pressing of "Ask," featuring a picture of the actor Colin Campbell taken from the 1963 movie *The Leather Boys*. *Author's collection*

as an instrumental while Moz was freed by security, only to head for his tour bus.

There was a similar occurrence on August 11 at the Music Hall in Cleveland, when Morrissey tried to reach out to fans in the front row during the finale. Reaching over the barrier in front of the orchestra pit, he lost his balance and fell into it. Screaming concertgoers climbed over their side of the barrier to touch Moz and venue security had to pull him free from the crowd not once but twice as he made his way back up to the stage.

Stage invasions also occurred at the Fulton Theatre in Pittsburgh—where the show had to be stopped to clear the area—and the Aragon Ballroom in Chicago, where rows of seats were smashed as fans rushed to the front. Throughout it all, Morrissey kept his sense of humor, joking in Detroit that they had written "Stretch Out and Wait" in the hope that it would be made famous by Whitney Houston. In the Windy City, he told the crowd that the B-side (which was still unreleased in the States) had been heavily inspired by Ozzy Osbourne.

California

A six-day, mid-month break followed to allow for the band's crew and equipment to travel west, while the group had some rest and relaxation. Morrissey went to visit his family in Colorado for a few days, while the rest held court at Le Parc Suites in Los Angeles. Girlfriends and wives were invited along, as well as friends like Guy Pratt and his girlfriend. Producer John Porter came over from London for several days, too, and Mike Hinc flew over to assist the group and crew in the wake of the Smiths' issues with Sophie Ridley.

Live work resumed at the Arlington Theater in Santa Barbara, California, on August 22. The 2,000-capacity venue allowed for what was perhaps the most intimate show of the trek. It served as a needed warm-up for the next night's gig at Berkeley's Greek Theatre, a wild evening that ranks as Gannon's favorite of the tour in terms of excitement. This despite the fact that Morrissey kept his onstage banter to a minimum.

August 25 and 26 marked sold-out Universal Amphitheater shows that were bolstered by an enormous local-radio presence on KROQ in Los Angeles. Here, hysterical fans rushed onstage, and the overall audience reaction was crazy. Morrissey would later marvel that the police presence on the first night was insufficient to control the crowd. He claimed that the army was brought in to assist them on the second night.

These gigs were a celebration, and Morrissey was in a playful mood. Introducing "How Soon Is Now?" during the first show, he teased, "This next song was written by one of our most talented songwriters—Madonna." Later on, he teased fans by telling them that if security tried to stop them getting to him, they should kiss them on the lips.

Stage-climbing continued the next night as the group introduced "Reel Around the Fountain" for the first time in a year. It was as much an event for the band as it was for the crowd, as the Smiths' front man said, "We're enjoying you immensely." Later, he thanked all the folks who came to both L.A. shows, "which was obviously every one of you!"

If the roaring crowd at the August 28 show at Irvine Meadows in Laguna Hills wasn't charged-up enough, Morrissey encouraged the audience to erupt as the show hit its apex. Ridiculing the security guards, he altered the lyrics to "The Queen Is Dead" to "Life is very long, when you're a bouncer," and informed the crowd that the stage was theirs for the taking, because the security was outnumbered.

Late in the concert, Moz and Marr were both stunned at how the crowd was being treated down in front. Johnny called the security guards "Neanderthals" and "fucking idiots" from the stage before the band began the second encore, "I Know It's Over." Midway through, Morrissey halted the song to shout at a bouncer. "Jesus Christ!" he can be heard yelling, in a recording of the gig. "Don't be so stupid! Leave him alone, you stupid idiot!"

Coke and the Concorde

A positive, mostly uneventful show at San Diego's Open Air Theater on August 29 was followed by a lackluster gig in Boulder on September 3 that left the band feeling unfulfilled. By this point, it seemed as if the extensive touring was catching up with the Smiths, and the audience was picking up on it. Fan enthusiasm seemed low, and the group appeared to be going through the motions. In frustration, Marr complained out loud. "This is like a library," he sniped, at the quiet Events Center audience.

It's no secret that the band's heavy partying was starting to take its toll. As documented in books by Rogan and Fletcher, and by Marr's own subsequent admission, he and some of the others had begun to include cocaine in their regular regimen, alongside copious amounts of Remy Martin. It was rare for Rourke, Joyce, and Gannon not to keep their hotel bars open into the late hours. On a few rare occasions, even Morrissey found himself over-served, clutching a cigarette in a hotel bar.

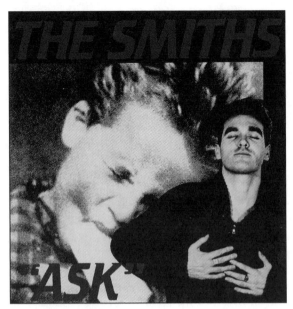

The front and back covers of the Australian pressing of "Ask," released in early 1987 and featuring alternate artwork. Morrissey alone was features on the single sleeve, marking the first time he or any other member of the band appeared on a Smiths release. *Author's collection*

By now, some friction had developed between Craig—who was trying to drink like one of the lads—and Johnny. Marr later attributed this to some hotel-room damage caused by the fifth Smith, although Johnny assured Tony Fletcher it was hardly a "sacking offense." Just the same, Gannon began to keep a lower profile, occasionally traveling on the crew's bus in order to allow for a cooling-off between the guitarists.

The Smiths were low on energy by the time they reached Texas for smaller-capacity concerts in Houston and Dallas on September 5 and 6, respectively. Multiple accounts suggest that, by this point, Morrissey had become fatigued and tired of the road, and Johnny had to coax him onstage. Meanwhile, Johnny continued to use cocaine whenever the opportunity presented itself, as was the case backstage at their show at New Orleans' McAlister Auditorium two days later, where he and the promoter supposedly shared a small white mound of the powder.

"When there's too much alcohol and drugs around, things get very melodramatic," Marr explained to Fletcher, remembering how everyone in the band seemed upset. Without a suitable manager in place to keep the quintet on course by telling them to curtail their drinking, eat better, stop using so much coke, and get some sleep, everything fell apart.

The next gig, at the Bayfront Center in St. Petersburg on September 10, wound up being the Smiths' last ever U.S. show. While it was the most exuberant audience reception they had received since they performed in Orange County two weeks before, the Smiths still had four more shows to play, and the group was fried. The final, lasting memory of the trek was of the fan who clung on to Morrissey's leg and refused to let go until security could pry her free.

The next morning, when Marr was either unwilling or unable to get out of bed, Johnny's wife had the good sense to try to put a stop to things. Angie summoned Andy, but Rourke had trouble motivating him—he, after all, was downing a large bottle of Remy Martin himself each day. Angie convinced Johnny to tell Morrissey that he could no longer continue the tour, and the singer was in no position to talk him out of it.

On September 11, the Smiths canceled their sold-out shows in Miami, Atlanta, and Nashville, plus a high-profile finale scheduled for New York's Radio City Music Hall. But the band's final day in Florida would not be without incident. As Marr and Morrissey worked through the impact of canceling the tour, Andy Rourke decided to take a swim in the ocean, where he was stung by a stingray that very nearly killed him.

With the pain from the stinger stuck in his foot running up through his body, Rourke came upon Mike Hinc, who quickly took him to a nearby hospital. Because of a delay caused by confusion over medical insurance, the tetanus shot that he required was delayed by ninety minutes.

With a Smithdom credit card in hand, Angie Marr arranged to fly the band home while the needs of Andy's foot were met. A Concorde flight to London from Miami would be their last overseas plane trip as the Smiths. Decades later, Marr would express regret that he hadn't been able to stick it out and play the remaining dates of the trek.

Spin

While the Smiths' tour was on the wane, U.S. music monthly *Spin* ran a sizable article on the band, with a full-page picture of Morrissey, in its September issue. Unfortunately, the publication—which was still only a year and a half old—still hadn't decided whether it wanted to be a mainstream rock or modern rock presence on America's newsstands. And so the cover went to Ozzy Osbourne.

The very next month, the band's biggest college-radio and alternative-music rivals at the time, R.E.M., landed on the cover of the same magazine's "Back to School" issue. Although the bands were playing similarly sized venues that

An open-shirted Morrissey, joined by a young boy mimicking his moves, appears with his bandmates on *Eurotube* on July 5, 1986, to perform their new non-album single "Panic" and *The Queen Is Dead* extract "There Is a Light That Never Goes Out." *Rex USA* summer and catered to the same audience, the latter group had a slightly stronger foothold in the U.S., where they had just released their fourth album, *Life's Rich Pageant.*

EMI News Breaks

The same week that the Smiths returned to England, news reached the music papers that they were definitely leaving Rough Trade for EMI. Although Geoff Travis had already shared the news with his key staff, chief publicist Pat Bellis pretended to be surprised when asked for comment.

EMI celebrated the announcement, proclaiming, in a press release, "The contracts have been signed." Later, as relations grew increasingly strained between the band and the label, Geoff Travis would accuse the Smiths of "excessive greed."

While Rough Trade was still due one more studio album, Sire expected two studio discs under its agreement with the band. And, six months after the Smiths signed their agreement with EMI, the band had only received one advance payment. To make matters worse, all of that went to pay the Smiths' legal bills to Alexis Grower, whom Morrissey had since fired.

Nightmarish Finances

With the Smiths lacking a proper manager, there was no one in the group's corner, remembering to collect on the money due to them. According to Warner Bros. Music's managing director at the time, Peter Reichert, the company was holding a quarter of a million pounds that belonged to Morrissey and Marr, but no one ever asked for it.

Acting on behalf of the band, Ken Friedman—who had begun working with the Smiths on their 1986 U.S. tour—had the group's publishing advances increased. He also hired U2's accountant, Oz Kilkenny, to look after the band's earnings, bills, and investments.

With pressure from Mike Joyce's father to give his son a better deal, Friedman sought advice from U2 manager Paul McGuinness, who suggested that each member get an equal share. But while Friedman suspected Johnny would have supported the idea, he knew Morrissey never would. Instead, Ken suggested that Rourke and Joyce be paid at least ten percent of all Smiths earnings—which Marr fully supported. But Moz squashed the suggestion, and it was never brought up again.

24

Alabaster
Crashes Down

Gannon Goes, Marr Flips

"You Just Haven't Earned It Yet, Baby"

In the early days of October, ahead of a planned U.K. tour to support "Ask," the Smiths entered Mayfair Studios for sessions that were split between John Porter and Stephen Street. It was at this facility in Primrose Hill that they first attempted "You Just Haven't Earned It Yet, Baby." Astoundingly, the song was finalized and recorded in just twenty-four hours, after Morrissey took home a cassette of the music following a writing session. "We'd decided, very unexpectedly for us, impulsively, to do an A-side," Johnny told the *Guardian* in September 2013. "The next morning, all the words were written. We were pretty prolific."

The song's unforgettable pop arrangement was strengthened by Marr and Gannon's jangling guitars and Rourke and Joyce's solid, rhythmic stomp. Of course, it was Morrissey's refrain—formulated around a statement made by Geoff Travis—and convincing delivery that made the song into a single-worthy number. The song even made it to the white-label test-pressing stage before Rough Trade yanked it from release as an A-side. Once Travis realized it was about him, he was adamantly against putting it out.

"He thought it was a personal letter addressed to him," Morrissey told the *NME* in February 1988. And he wasn't wrong.

"Half a Person" and "London"

The next two tracks of the Mayfair session were realized with Street, who earned his first co-producer credit on a Smiths recording. The first, "Half a Person," was written by Morrissey and Marr, who locked themselves away and wrote it in the time it took Johnny to play it.

A lilting keeper of a song that was finished in the studio's stairway, it offers a mostly first-person account of a shy sixteen-year-old who moves to London hoping to find his way in the world. The mid-tempo number would ultimately become the B-side of another new tune, "Shoplifters of the World Unite," which was released the following January.

A companion song, "London," was about the city where Morrissey and Johnny both maintained residences. This explosive, feedback-laden, punk-inspired tune dated to the previous summer, and had even been played during a soundcheck in London, Ontario. It would first appear as the bonus track on the "Shoplifters" 12-inch and—like "Half a Person"—later surface on the *Louder Than Bombs* compilation.

You Can Break My Face

A month after the Smiths' aborted U.S. dates, the group hit the road in their homeland to continue promotion of *The Queen Is Dead* and their new chart hit, "Ask." The quintet rocked the Sands Center in Carlisle on October 13, opening with "Panic" and introducing the newly tracked "London" to the set list. Morrissey was in rare form, purportedly returning to the stage for a second encore by shouting, "Okay, cocksuckers!" before ripping into "Still Ill."

As with nearly all shows on this tour leg, fans swarmed the stage, but security kept it manageable as Moz and Johnny interacted with their eager audience.

Two shows later, at Wolverhampton's Civic Hall, the energy between the crowd and the band was magical as the audience sang along to recent singles and classics alike. During "Panic," Morrissey swung a noose around to emphasize his "Hang the DJ!" slogan, while fans rushed the stage to hug their beloved pop star. When they played still-unreleased songs like "London" and "Is It Really So Strange?," fans looked on respectfully.

Things went awry at the Leisure Centre in Newport, Wales, on October 19, however, when Morrissey held out his hands during "The Boy with the Thorn in His Side" and was pulled down to the floor by overexcited fans. After security got the singer back on his feet, it was clear he had been hurt, so he was taken backstage. When he didn't immediately return, the rest of the band performed an instrumental, "The Draize Train."

When it became clear that he wasn't coming back, Grant Showbiz came onstage to inform the crowd—which by now had begun chanting "Morrissey, Morrissey"—that the show would need to be canceled. Showbiz was hit in the face with a bottle. A riot broke out and the hall was vandalized after the show was abandoned midway through, with a half-dozen fans arrested. A day later, the *Sun* had the audacity to claim that Moz had actually been injured by a group of Monarchists objecting to the Smiths' performance of "The Queen Is Dead."

Two nights later, Morrissey was back in top form for the group's gig at Nottingham's Royal Concert Hall. The crowd's fervor for favorites like "There Is a Light That Never Goes Out" and "What She Said" was appreciated by Morrissey, who took the stage for an encore of "How Soon Is Now?" sporting a James Dean T-shirt, which he threw into the crowd before changing into a "Hang the DJ" shirt, which he also tossed into the crowd during "Still Ill." During "Bigmouth," the singer pulled fans up onstage while Marr and Gannon performed a mock guitar duel.

By the time of the group's October 24 concert at London's Brixton Academy, however, the Smiths seemed fatigued. Marr's guitar work was uncharacteristically sloppy, and Morrissey's energy seemed low, but they recuperated for a London Palladium gig two nights later, which was widely praised by the media, and is since considered to be a high point within the band, especially Gannon, who would count it as his favorite from his tenure with the group. There were no stage invasions at the Palladium gig, which was attended by one of the Smiths' heroes, Iggy Pop. In fact, the audience had been expected to sit through the "performance," but fans stood from the opening notes onward, and there was nothing the venue's employees could do. The show was filmed in part for the French television show *Les Enfants Du Rock.*

The Smiths' October 27 show at Preston's Guildhall was over in just one song after Morrissey received a head injury. The show had begun with "The Queen Is Dead," during which Johnny assisted Mike Joyce with the song's drumming introduction. As he began his guitar part, he threw his drumstick into the audience—not counting on having it tossed back at the band. But an audience member did in fact throw a drumstick back onstage, hitting Morrissey on the head. Understandably, the singer dropped the microphone after being struck and left the stage. The injury required that he be hospitalized, and the show was canceled. Afterward, thankfully, there was no crowd violence, only disappointed fans.

Back home in Manchester, at the Free Trade Hall on October 30, the band were greeted with a "Welcome Home" banner and an increased security presence to help avert any further injury to their front man. At one point, before "What She Said," Mike Joyce teased the crowd by playing the introduction to local favorite "Reel Around the Fountain." The concert was Craig Gannon's final performance with the band and marked the conclusion of what would be the band's last-ever tour.

A ticket stub from the Smiths' concert at the National Ballroom in Kilburn from October 23, 1986. This show was part of a short, two-week U.K. tour in continued support of *The Queen Is Dead* and the group's latest non-LP single, "Ask." *Author's collection*

And Then There Were Four

Guitarist Craig Gannon had no way of knowing his days in the Smiths were numbered when he tracked three new songs with the band a month earlier. After all,

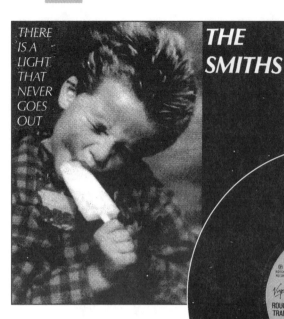

The unique "sour popsicle" sleeve for the single "There Is a Light That Never Goes Out" was released in France in early 1987. Also shown is the A-side of the vinyl 45. *Passionsjustlikemine.com*

he played ably and effectively with the band on those Mayfair recordings, and on the Smiths' ensuing tour. But Marr let it slip to Stephen Street that a change was coming on their final day at Mayfair. Street had been praising Gannon's work ethic and his attention to detail in the studio to Johnny while they were packing up equipment, only for Marr to inform him that Craig wouldn't be around much longer.

On tour, Gannon began to feel like an outsider. He no longer felt like he was a good fit in the group, which made sense because they had already decided to sack him. And, based on the vibes on the road, the only one who was unaware was Craig.

Following the last gig at Manchester Free Trade Hall, communication dried up between Gannon and the others. In a 2011 interview with *Mojo*, Craig recalled that he learned he had been let go by word-of-mouth, via Ivor Perry of Easterhouse, a mutual friend of his and Johnny's. "My mate said, 'Give Johnny a ring. I don't think you're in the band anymore,' which was a strange way to hear it. But I put it behind me."

Gannon accepted his fate but was left with no way to contact Johnny—who had changed his phone number—to figure out how to collect his pay for his touring and recording efforts. Not to mention that some of his equipment was still at Marr's house. With no proper management channels to go through, either, Craig had been locked out.

Not long after Gannon was relieved of his duties, Marr explained his decision to revert to a quartet by admitting he had grown complacent as a musician with Craig there to augment his playing so well. Johnny would acknowledge to Tony Fletcher that, at the time, he wasn't in a position to see what a tough spot Gannon had been in. Despite everything, he managed to perform "great" and "appropriately" through it all. "What was he going to do, sit down in between me and Morrissey and say, 'I think you should do things differently?'"

The following spring, with his compensation still unresolved, Gannon took formal steps to get what he felt he was rightly due. "As I wasn't paid for my work in the Smiths, which included live fees, wages, various recordings, and video/TV appearances, I had no option but to take it further," Gannon wrote by email in September 2014. Asked about Morrissey's suggestion in *Autobiography* that his claims were "whimsical frolic," Gannon responded by saying, "Contrary to what Morrissey has said, the matter went nowhere near a court and no judges were involved. The Smiths offered me a figure out of court, which I accepted. All I wanted was to be paid for my work in the Smiths and what I'd been promised. Nothing more, nothing less."

Surprisingly, Morrissey would use his 2013 book to denigrate Gannon by writing how "nothing useful vibrates in Craig's upper storey." Of course, if this were actually true, one has to wonder why Moz would rehire Gannon in 1989 to play guitar with him on two of his most successful and enduring singles, "The Last of the Famous International Playboys" and "Interesting Drug."

Marr Contemplates Quitting

During the October tour, Marr continued to struggle on the road with drugs and alcohol, which caused him to feel exhausted and, in turn, depressed. He was also frustrated with the aggression exhibited by fans that had led to his singer getting injured and several shows being scotched. He also felt anxious about breaking the news to Gannon that he was reverting the Smiths back to a quartet.

Marr would reveal in Tony Fletcher's book that he had considered leaving the band, at the end of this tour. Between the drama and the hindrances, there was a final solution: he could end the Smiths. While that wasn't something he was ready to do just yet, he knew that it would be a real option when he was eventually ready to jump ship. Having this in the back of his mind made things bearable—for a while.

Johnny Flips

About a week and a half into November 1986, Johnny Marr had been out socializing in Manchester with Smiths drummer Mike Joyce and his girlfriend when he got behind the wheel after imbibing wine and tequila and very nearly killed himself on his way home. It was rare for Johnny to be driving at the time, and he didn't even have a license. (At this point, he was usually chauffeured by either Angie or Smiths staffer Phil Powell.)

After dropping Joyce at his place nearby on Springfield Road, Marr headed home in the pouring rain. When he came to a fork in the road, the cassette of home demos he had been listening to turned over and a new song started. So, instead of taking the path that led to his house, which he was only about 500 feet away, he took a longer route home and gunned the accelerator as he listened to the track. He quickly lost control in the slippery conditions and the car went into a stone wall at a bend in the road, flipping over on its side as it bounced back into the middle of the street before coming to an upright halt.

"I couldn't believe that I was still alive," Johnny told Rogan in 1992. Stunned, and experiencing an adrenaline rush, he crawled from the wreckage and ran toward his house. He summoned Powell and Angie—who had not been with him—and they helped him to clear the destroyed vehicle from the middle of the road. The authorities were contacted and—because it would have been illegal for Johnny to drive—it was explained to them that his wife had been behind the wheel.

Johnny wound up with only minimal injuries, and was released from the hospital after a few hours, wearing a neck brace and ordered to rest. For several days, while he recuperated, he was understandably stiff. The day after the crash, he was interviewed by a local policeman who happened to be a massive Smiths fan. As luck would have it, Johnny was let go without being charged. He felt lucky to be alive, and the experience became the wake-up call that the hard-partying guitarist needed. "It absolutely reset me in such a fabulous way," he told Fletcher.

All the same, the accident forced the last-minute cancelation of the Royal Albert Hall benefit. When fans complained to the letters section of the U.K. music papers about the Smiths withdrawing, Marr became furious. "That was the first time I can remember feeling a separation between what the fans were believing and the truth," he told *Record Collector*. "It taught me a lesson."

"Shoplifters"

Marr was still wearing his neck brace when the Smiths went into Trident Studios in London in the third week of November 1986 to record a new song, "Shoplifters of the World Unite." The track, penned by Johnny and Morrissey earlier that month, was produced solely by Johnny, as Stephen Street was not available on such short notice to participate in the session.

The song—which would supplant another planned A-side, "You Just Haven't Earned It Yet, Baby," as the next Smiths single—was mixed by Alan Moulder, who would go on to become one of the best-known producers in modern rock, thanks to his work with Arctic Monkeys, the Jesus & Mary Chain, Ride, My Bloody Valentine, the Killers, Nine Inch Nails, Smashing Pumpkins, Interpol, and Foo Fighters. The song was tracked in Trident's tiny "Jingle Room" and not in the facility's larger studio—where acts like David Bowie, the Beatles, and Lou Reed had once worked—and the lack of space meant that Joyce's drum parts had to be recorded in the reception area after the staff had gone for the day.

Musically, the song has been compared to the 1972 T. Rex classic "Children of the Revolution," although Marr would claim that the solo, for which he used false harmonics, was in fact informed by Nils Lofgren's playing. "[It] is a steel player's technique," he told *Guitar Magazine* in January 1997. "You touch the strings with a right-hand finger an octave higher than where you're fretting, and then pluck the string with your thumb."

The title alluded to either the communist slogan "Workers of the world, unite!" or the 1966 David & Jonathan single "Lovers of the World Unite," while Morrissey also made reference to the Rickie Lee Jones song "The Last Chance Texaco," expounding on her line, "He tried living in a world and in a shell."

The track was heightened by Morrissey's remarkable vocal. He would tell reporter Shaun Duggan in 1987 that the track represented "spiritual shoplifting, cultural shoplifting, taking things and using them to your own advantage." In a subsequent 1996 interview with *RTE Guide*, he would assert that it remained one of his all-time favorite songs. The following year, speaking to KROQ-FM in Los Angeles, he called it a "very, very witty single and a great moment for the Smiths in England. I think it was probably the best days of our career."

"Shoplifters" was released as a non-album A-side single on January 26, 1987, and climbed to #12 the next month, where it remained for two weeks, becoming one of the Smiths' better-charting hits. The cover featured a photograph of Elvis Presley taken by James R. Reid.

In support of the song, the Smiths were asked to perform on the U.K. music show *The Tube* under the condition that Morrissey make a public statement clarifying the song's true meaning. In order to secure the slot, Rough Trade's promotional staff pressured him to tell the world that the song was not actually about stealing, even though, in actuality, it was.

Moz yielded but was hardly repaid for his trouble. When the Smiths appeared on the show, host Paula Yates introduced him as "some prat." She was forced by her bosses to apologize the following week.

25

Boot the Grime of This World in the Crotch, Dear

A Final Performance, "Sheila," and a Pair of Compilations

Final Concert

Although there was no way that they could know it at the time, the four remaining members of the Smiths performed their final full-length concert as a band at London's Brixton Academy on December 12, 1986.

With Marr fully recovered from his automobile accident, the group made good on their promise to headline the aforementioned anti-apartheid show, which had originally been planned to take place at the Royal Albert Hall. It was the Smiths' second performance at the Brixton Academy in under two months, but this one-off show proved to be a far more thrilling experience for not only the concertgoers but also the band, who felt reinvigorated and—without the exhaustion of touring—in a much happier state. Marr, Rourke, Morrissey, and Joyce were seen smiling and even laughing together during "Still Ill."

High spirits aside, the show was significant as it marked the band's first (and only) concert performances of tracks like "Some Girls Are Bigger Than Others" and "Shoplifters of the World Unite." It also featured a revival of "This Night Has Opened My Eyes," which hadn't been played onstage in two years.

A dozen or so fans made it to the stage during the encores before the band played their last-ever live song, "Hand in Glove." Bringing it back to the start with their first proper single, the band's performance was spot on. Morrissey sang the song's final line, bidding adieu to the crowd by crooning, "I'll probably never see you again." Of course, there was no way he could know at the time just how apropos the line would be.

Peel Sessions

Twenty-eight months after the Smiths' third Peel Session, the group entered Maida Vale Studio #4 on December 2, 1986, with producer John Porter to track four new songs—"Is It Really So Strange," "London," "Half a Person," and "Sweet and Tender Hooligan"—for the BBC radio host. The first and the fourth would become the definitive, officially released versions of the songs in question. The recordings would debut on Peel's show on December 17, 1986.

"Sheila Take a Bow"

On December 13, immediately after the Brixton Academy gig, the Smiths had planned to enter Solid Bond Studios in London's Marble Arch to track "Sheila Take a Bow." Working with producer John Porter in the facility owned by Paul Weller of the Jam and Style Council, the group worked through the musical arrangement of the song, the bones of which dated back to a February 1986 soundcheck.

Morrissey—possibly drained after the effort he had put into the show the night before—called in sick for the session, which would have been permissible had he not invited Sandie Shaw to sing backing vocals on the track. When Shaw arrived at the studio, Marr was stuck making excuses for Morrissey's inexplicable absence.

A few weeks later, just after the New Year, the entire band reconvened with Porter, this time at Matrix Studios, where they had first tracked *The Smiths*. But the overall outcome was not to Johnny or Morrissey's liking as Shaw's backing vocals didn't quite fit. Neither did the inclusion of an emulated sitar part. Yet other elements of the recording—including an uncredited guitar part played by Porter—were retained and extracted for use when the song was reattempted days later, with Stephen Street.

It was at Good Earth Studios, the London recording compound owned by veteran Bowie producer Tony Visconti, that the roaring guitar number finally came to life. Street and Marr even incorporated an audio snippet of a brass marching band from the 1954 movie *Hobson's Choice* in the introduction, having scrapped the sitar idea. Unfortunately, the single signified the very end of the group's studio efforts with Porter.

Hilariously, Shaw would later describe "Sheila" to writer Simon Goddard as "a horrid song." But when the single—the group's

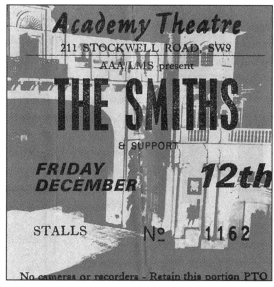

A surviving ticket from the Smiths' last-ever concert at London's Brixton Academy on December 12, 1986. *Author's collection*

fourth non-LP 45 in ten months—was eventually released on April 13, 1987, it shot to #10 in the U.K., becoming the Smiths' highest-charting hit. The cover art featured a picture of the actress Candy Darling, a transgender woman affiliated with Andy Warhol and featured in the 1971 movie *Women in Revolt.*

The U.K. 7-inch single was backed with the aforementioned Peel Session recording of "Is It Really So Strange?," while the 12-inch added another Maida Vale number, the fiery "Sweet and Tender Hooligan." Johnny Marr had written the music for both of these tracks in early 1986, with Morrissey adding his lyrics sometime later. The former was first attempted during the "Ask" sessions, while a slower take on the latter was tried out during the "Panic" sessions at London's Livingston Studios, before the Peel Session versions were settled on as the definitive takes.

San Remo Festival

In January 1987, Ken Friedman shifted his operations from San Francisco to London and somehow convinced Morrissey and Marr to officially retain him as the Smiths' manager. If the American wasn't entirely sure what he had gotten himself into, specifically with the band's singer, he would find out backstage at Italy's San Remo Festival on February 7.

Appearing on a revolving stage with an array of U.K. acts like Pet Shop Boys, Spandau Ballet, Paul Young, and Style Council, the band mimed a five-song

The iconic sleeve for the Smiths' single "Shoplifters of the World Unite," featuring a photograph of Elvis Presley. The track rose to #12 on the U.K. singles chart after its release on January 26, 1987. *Author's collection*

set that included "Shoplifters," "There Is a Light That Never Goes Out," "The Boy with the Thorn in His Side," "Panic," and "Ask." But there was a snafu with the sound playback, and the glitch required that the Smiths return to the stage to repeat their performance.

This wouldn't have been a big deal except that, backstage, Morrissey was refusing to duplicate his efforts. That was until Friedman talked some sense into him, explaining what the ramifications of his uncooperativeness might be. In doing so, Ken coaxed Morrissey out of his tantrum and convinced him to complete the mission.

Friedman also encouraged Morrissey to force himself to be more outgoing, the result being that he and the others in the Smiths seemed to be happy to mix it up with the other acts on the bill. Moz was even seen having a conversation with the actress Patsy Kensit. Later, he and Bob Geldof buried the hatchet, with Friedman's urging, after the Band Aid and Live Aid organizer stopped by the Smiths' trailer for a visit. And finally, while in Italy, Marr, Joyce, and Rourke even hit a disco with members of Spandau Ballet.

The World Won't Listen

Released on February 23, 1987, *The World Won't Listen* was a compilation of the Smiths' non-album singles and B-sides released between 1985 and 1987. Issued by Rough Trade outside of North America, the album also recycled the fan favorite "There Is a Light That Never Goes Out"—which was only issued as a promotional single—and "Bigmouth Strikes Again" from *The Queen Is Dead*. It also included the aborted "You Just Haven't Earned It Yet, Baby" and the just-dropped single "Shoplifters of the World Unite," plus its flip sides. Curiously, the version of "Stretch Out and Wait" had a different vocal than original, and the recent "Ask" flip side "Golden

A highly collectible promotional-only release of "Shoplifters of the World Unite," serviced to college and alternative radio in early 1987 by Sire Records. *Author's collection*

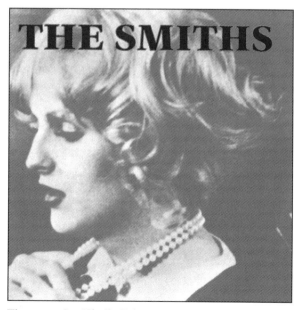

The cover for "Sheila Take a Bow" features a still of the transgender actress Candy Darling, an associate of Andy Warhol's, taken from the 1971 movie *Women in Revolt*. *Author's collection*

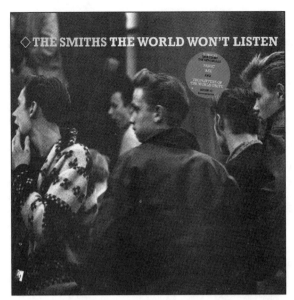

The vinyl LP sleeve for *The World Won't Listen*, released in February 1987, which proved popular among European fans of the band who were thankful to have all of the group's non-album 45 sides from 1985 and 1986 on one album. *Author's collection*

Lights" was left off the original pressings altogether, but was added as a CD bonus track in 1992.

The title of the record was said to represent Morrissey's dissatisfaction with mainstream radio programmers and music consumers, who in his eyes hadn't given the band the attention he felt they deserved. Upon its release, *The World Won't Listen* was well received by European fans, who were thankful to have all of these 45 sides on one album. If critics deemed the album unnecessary, the public clearly disagreed, propelling the disc to #2 on the U.K. album survey during its fifteen-week chart run.

The LP cover art—designed by Morrissey—utilizes a picture of a 1950s fairground scene, while the CD and cassette versions use a photo by Jürgen Vollmer, taken from the book *Rock 'N' Roll Times: The Style and Spirit of the Early Beatles and Their First Fans.*

To promote the "Shoplifters" single and the compilation album's imminent European release, the Smiths booked a run of television appearances, beginning on February 1 with a lip-synched performance of the single on the Italian television program *Festival Primavera*, which was broadcast on Italia 1. Six days later, another television appearance by the quartet aired on RAI as part of special on the San Remo Festival. It featured performances of five lip-synched numbers ("There Is a Light That Never Goes Out," "The Boy with the Thorn in His Side," "Panic," "Ask," and "Shoplifters of the World Unite").

Meanwhile, a mimed performance of "Shoplifters" aired on BBC 1's *Top of the Pops* on February 5. Finally, a live performance of the same song was broadcast on *Megamix* in Ireland on February 13.

Louder Than Bombs

Six weeks later, on March 30, 1987, Sire released its own compilation—a double album of every Smiths song that had not been released on a U.S. LP. Spanning the group's entire recording career from 1983 to early 1987, it was more than your typical odds 'n' sods compilation. The disc offered the single version of

"Hand in Glove" and every indispensable non-album 45, plus material from the 1984 non-U.S. stopgap album *Hatful of Hollow*.

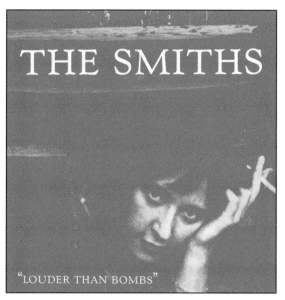

THE SMITHS

Cracking the cellophane on the album, fans were treated to the six newest Smiths sides first, beginning with "Is It Really So Strange?" The song was still two weeks from release in the U.K. as the B-side to the "Sheila Take a Bow" single, giving North American fans the unusual treat of owning a Smiths track ahead of those in the group's native land.

Clocking in at nearly seventy-three minutes, the album's twenty-four songs eliminated the need for record buyers to track down every imported rarity. The package featured a gatefold sleeve, lyrics to the material, and an orange sleeve designed by Morrissey, while the cover fea-

"LOUDER THAN BOMBS"

The cover of *Louder Than Bombs*, a Sire Records double-album compilation released on March 30, 1987. The album featured all of the material covered by Rough Trade–only releases *Hatful of Hollow* and *The World Won't Listen*, which had previously been unavailable in the U.S. *Author's collection*

tured a photo of Salford-born playwright Shelagh Delaney that had originally been featured in the *Saturday Evening Post*. The picture was taken when Delaney was just nineteen, shortly after the premiere of her acclaimed play *A Taste of Honey*. (Delaney, of course, had long been one of Morrissey's literary heroes, and the inspiration for some of his early lyrics, including "This Night Has Opened My Eyes," which could be heard on the fourth side of the record.)

Morrissey extracted the title *Louder Than Bombs* from poet Elizabeth Smart's 1945 novel of prose, *By Grand Central Station I Sat Down and Wept*. Her literary work had already influenced elements of songs included on *Louder Than Bombs*, like "London" and "Shakespeare's Sister."

Designed to supplant *The World Won't Listen* and *Hatful of Hollow* in one fell swoop, the project rendered the former superfluous by besting it with the inclusion of the new "Sheila" single and other B-side tracks that were exclusive to the album. Among these were "Golden Lights," versions of "These Things Take Time" and "Back to the Old House" from the single "What Difference Does It Make?" and the original take of "Stretch Out and Wait."

It didn't take long for U.S. pressings of *Louder Than Bombs* to find their way into record shops in the U.K.—at an inflated price. Recognizing an opportunity, in the wake of continuing interest in the popular import, Rough Trade began pressing up copies for the U.K. that May. Smiths fans who had already bought *The World Won't Listen* griped, and, as a result, Geoff Travis and his staff marketed the double LP at a single-album price. It became a modest success, reaching #38 on the British album survey.

In the U.S., the album performed very well on college radio, topping the CMJ chart that spring. In 1990, the album was certified gold by the RIAA, for sales in excess of 500,000, and the collection even ranked among *Rolling Stone*'s "Top 500 Greatest Albums of All Time in 2003," coming in at #365.

26

A Rush and a Push

Strangeways, Here We Come

Untentionally or not, the Smiths began work on the first song for their fourth studio album in January 1987, using the remaining studio time they had at Good Earth after finishing up "Sheila Take a Bow" to attempt a reggae song called "Girlfriend in a Coma." Displeased with the outcome, Marr took a different approach to the song when the foursome started work in earnest on the album that March at Wool Hall Studios in Beckington, on the outskirts of Bath. Here, the band took a second pass at "Girlfriend in a Coma" with the always-helpful and increasingly skilled Stephen Street. The track became the catalyst for the rest of the album, and would serve as its lead single.

These sessions, for what would become known as *Strangeways, Here We Come*, were distinct in that they marked the first time since the formation of the group that Morrissey and Marr wrote and arranged the songs in the studio. The approach was much different from past records, and the lack of preparation lent itself to artful, experimental songs like "Death of a Disco Dancer" and "A Rush and a Push and the Land Is Ours."

While the partners were no longer writing together in the same room, neither Smiths principal seemed to feel any pressure in the studio, as the sessions were drawn out for weeks. Although the sessions were made more protracted by experimentation and Marr's determination to move away from his patented Rickenbacker sound, the tracking also benefited from the fact that all four members of the band were now quite experienced in the recording studio. These efficiencies also compensated for the fact that the guitarist and the singer seemed unprepared by their usual standards. As Street would explain to Johnny Rogan, they started with no more than "a couple of half-baked ideas." Halfway through the making of the album, Morrissey felt stressed because he didn't have enough lyrics for the record. According to the producer, Moz then retreated to Manchester with the backing tracks for about four days to get himself sorted.

Strangeways, Here We Come

As Mike Joyce would later relay to biographer Tony Fletcher, of all the Smiths' recording projects, the Wall Hall sessions that spring had the "best atmosphere" of any Smiths project to date. It was a sentiment Morrissey would agree with in 2013, when he called the album's creation "the most joyful and relaxed" of their career, while championing Marr, Rourke, and Joyce's expert musicianship.

A picture of the Smiths in one of their last photo sessions. It was taken by Andre Csillag in March 1987 during a break from recording sessions for *Strangeways Here We Come*, which became the group's final studio album. *Rex USA*

After tracking two or three songs a day, Johnny, Mike, and Andy would listen back to their recorded accomplishments at night, sharing cases of beer and other libations from the Wool Hall wine cellar. Although Morrissey was usually absent from such shenanigans—he continued to keep to the daytime studio schedule he had established on the group's earlier albums—Marr, Rourke, and Joyce would jam together as they grew more and more intoxicated. After working hard for ten-to-twelve hours on songs for their upcoming album, it wasn't uncommon for them to joyfully play songs from the soundtrack of the fake heavy-metal documentary *This Is Spinal Tap*. With the overdubs complete, the boys—including Street—would party all night long and play numbers like "Hell Hole," "Big Bottom," and "Sex Farm."

Despite the fact that the sessions were positive, the camaraderie between Morrissey and Marr seemed to have run its course. "I've got loads of photos and loads of video footage of us making the album," Marr told Johnny Rogan. "You can see us talking and having a laugh. But toward the end of the band, when we weren't doing the music, we weren't able to be comfortable with each other anymore."

"A Rush and a Push and the Land Is Ours"

The song that starts the Smiths' fourth studio LP was crafted in the studio by Johnny Marr and Morrissey and—aside from the 1985 B-side "Asleep"—it is the only Smiths song to forgo the guitar altogether for a buoyant piano part. The track's other musical elements include synthesized flutes and marimbas, as well as a syncopated piano line created with an Emulator synthesizer.

While the lyrics are essentially about the strains and pains of heartache and falling in love against your better judgment, Morrissey borrowed the song's title from the writing of Oscar Wilde's mother, Jane. Lady Wilde, who wrote about the Potato Famine in the Irish newspaper the *Nation* in the 1840s, under the pen name "Speranza," would cause quite a controversy in her day, using the publication to encourage an armed revolution in Ireland.

"I Started Something I Couldn't Finish"

This rocking number stemmed from a jam Marr first attempted with Rourke and Joyce during the January sessions at Good Earth that January. By the time it was finished, Marr had drawn heavily on the Emulator for drum parts and horn sounds. Special effects were added, as well as a humorous spoken-word snippet of Morrissey, caught during the addition of his vocals, in which he can be heard asking Stephen Street if he'll need to put down a second take.

Work on this song wasn't entirely jovial, however. According to Fletcher's biography, when Street delivered the rough mix of the track to the cottage next door to Wool Hall, where Morrissey was lodging, the singer told the producer to tell Johnny that he didn't like it. When Street came back into the studio to deliver the message to Marr, the overworked musician was not pleased. "Fuck him," he snapped. "He can think of something, then."

Morrissey must have changed his mind, though, because the song would eventually become a single in the U.K. Released on November 2, 1987, appended by the 1983 Troy Tate production of "Pretty Girls Make Graves" and a live version of "Some Girls Are Bigger Than Others." It peaked at #23.

The single's sleeve features a still of the actress Avril Angers from the 1966 film *The Family Way*. The run-out etching of the A-side of the single reads, "Murder at the Wool Hall (X) Starring Sheridan Whiteside." The name refers to one of Morrissey's pseudonyms, and was lifted from the 1939 play *The Man who Came to Dinner*. The B-side etching inverts the lyrics to "Asleep" and reads, "You are believing, you do not want to sleep."

"Death of a Disco Dancer"

Drawing on the Beatles' "Dear Prudence," Marr structured "Death of a Disco Dancer" around a repetitive chord sequence. After Morrissey added his vocals to the tune's traditional song structure, it evolved into a soaring, experimental rock 'n' roll jam. Later, the singer would overdub his first-ever musical contribution— a piano part he conjured up while banging on an aging Red Lion piano that sat in the vocal room at Wool Hall.

"It was the first time the group played it together, and we just switched the tape on and didn't take it terribly seriously," he told *Sounds* in June 1988. "We

```
┌─────────────────────────────────────────────────┐
│ Tape: METAL    (Use normal or 120 μs Eq.)        │
│       PARTICLE                    ☐☐[DOLBY HX PRO]®│
├─────────────────────────────────────────────────┤
│                  THE SMITHS                       │
│        Side 1                  Side 2             │
│ *A Rush And A Push And   *Last Night I Dreamt     │
│   The Land Is Ours         That Somebody Loved    │
│ *I Started Something I       Me                   │
│   Couldn't Finish        *Unhappy Birthday        │
│ *Death Of A Disco Dancer *Paint A Vulgar          │
│ *Girlfriend In A Coma       Picture               │
│ *Stop Me If You Think    *Death At One's Elbow    │
│   You've Heard This One  *I Won't Share You       │
│   Before                                          │
│ WARNER BROS. RECORDS         WB-25649             │
└─────────────────────────────────────────────────┘
```

An advance cassette of *Strangeways, Here We Come*, produced by Sire/Warner Bros. for promotional purposes. *Author's collection*

kept the tape because it had some unnamable appeal."

In fact, when Marr later asked the singer if he minded him taking a stab at it to make it better, Morrissey had told him, "Yes." So it was left as is. Stephen Street would eventually edit the song down to keep it from running too long. The producer/engineer extracted a full minute from the song, using the same "snipping" practice he had first implemented on "Some Girls Are Bigger Than Others."

"Girlfriend in a Coma"

Marr and Morrissey were fans of the 1970 Bob & Marcia reggae song "Young, Gifted, and Black," and used it as the impetus for what would become *Strangeways'* first single. They first tested it in the studio in rock-steady style in late 1986, shortly after writing it, before putting it aside for the time being. When the band revisited it in Wool Hall, they gave it more of a playful, country-tinged thump, and—at just two minutes and two seconds—a more succinct presentation.

The lyrics concern a man with conflicted feelings of worry and inattentiveness over the dire condition of his girlfriend. But because Morrissey's sexuality to this day has never been made completely clear, some who believe he is homosexual have suggested the song is sarcastic. Another possibility is that the song may represent the failing health of a platonic or non-sexual girlfriend, or possibly even a feminine boyfriend the singer is referring to as his girlfriend.

"Girlfriend in a Coma" would eventually be selected as the album's first single—against Johnny Marr's wishes. Upon its release on August 10, 1987, the tune was banned by BBC Radio 1 but still managed to peak at #13 in the U.K. Its sleeve was the second Smiths release that year to feature playwright Shelagh Delaney, this time in the form of a photograph culled from the 1961 edition of *A Taste of Honey*.

In May 2006, Morrissey himself questioned whether the track was truly single-worthy, telling the *Independent*, "You're not really supposed to like those songs. They're very depressing and not supposed to be played on radio."

In support of the song's parent album, Morrissey alone collaborated with director Tim Broad on a music video, which was shot after Johnny Marr had left the band. The clip features Moz singing the song in color atop black-and-white footage extracted from the 1964 British movie *The Leather Boys*.

In its 12-inch form, "Girlfriend in a Coma" is significant in that it includes the non-LP B-sides "Work Is a Four-Letter Word" and "I Keep Mine Hidden." The former is a cover of the Cilla Black track that Marr famously disliked, while the latter was Morrissey's unsuccessful attempt to make amends with Johnny.

"Stop Me If You Think You've Heard This One Before"

A chiming guitar-pop song that endures to this day as one of the most immediate in the Smiths' canon, the lyrics to "Stop Me" were penned by Morrissey about an unfaithful drunk who lied to his significant other in order to justify his long absences. During work on the track, Morrissey was questioned by Stephen Street, who was concerned about his erroneous grammar in the line "who said I lied because I never." But the song's intentionally incorrect language was widely overlooked, especially when plans for a U.K. single were thwarted by the BBC. The almighty radio network objected to the insensitivity of Morrissey's lyrics about "a shy, bald Buddhist" planning "a mass murder" and banned the track from daytime radio play in the wake of the Hungerford Massacre of August 19, 1987, in which a twenty-seven-year-old gunman named Michael Ryan killed sixteen people in Berkshire. Although Morrissey's line was clearly unrelated to the tragedy, it was a case of bad timing.

In the U.S., Australia, Germany, and other markets, "Stop Me" was released as a commercial single. It was also used as the soundtrack for a music video featuring Morrissey and a large group of Smiths fans riding bicycles throughout Manchester. One notable landmark shown in the clip is the Salford Lads Club in Manchester's Ordsall section, which the Smiths had previously used in the inner album art for *The Queen Is Dead*.

The single's sleeve utilizes a photo still of the actor Murray Head from the 1966 motion picture *The Family Way*. Head, who was also a musician, would become best known for his 1984 novelty-pop smash "One Night in Bangkok."

"Last Night I Dreamt That Somebody Loved Me"

Marr developed the chord structure for this song following the Smiths' Carlisle gig in October 1986; the introductory piano part came from elsewhere, but he ultimately elected to splice it in as the song's beginning. The crowd noise that opens the track originated during the 1984–85 miner's strike and was lifted from a BBC sound effects record.

Going into the making of the record, Morrissey and Marr had a goal of writing at least one enduring ballad. As well as featuring sound effects and other samples, the song also includes an orchestral part crafted by Johnny using an Emulator synthesizer. According to reports, he worked on the arrangement for almost two full weeks before Morrissey was brought in to cut his soul-baring vocal. In the meantime, Morrissey had been given a cassette featuring a rough version of the tune. He went away with it and came back

THE SMITHS
"STRANGEWAYS, HERE WE COME"

The cover art for the Smiths' final studio album, *Strangeways, Here We Come*, features a blurry picture of the actor Richard Davalos, who co-starred with James Dean in *East of Eden*. Released on September 28, 1987, the LP debuted at #2 on the U.K. chart. *Author's collection*

with his heart-wrenching prose.

Edited for release as a single—with the crowd noise extracted—on December 7, 1987, "Last Night" became the group's final release, save for subsequent reissues. Featuring a picture of early-1960s U.K. singer Billy Fury, the single—which was backed with Peel Session takes on "Rusholme Ruffians," "Nowhere Fast," and "William, It Was Really Nothing" in its 12-inch version—stalled at #30 in the British charts.

In the December 1993 issue of *Select*, Johnny Marr revealed that Morrissey had recently told him that this was his favorite Smiths song. A year earlier, British rock legend David Bowie had also named it his favorite Smiths track, telling *Q*, "I still rate Morrissey as one of the best lyricists in Britain."

"Unhappy Birthday"

Hilariously maudlin, this contemplative but lighthearted song is perhaps the greatest moment on *Strangeways*, outshining "Girlfriend in a Coma." Musically, the track is brilliant in every sense, with Marr writing and arranging one of his finest. Lyric-wise, Morrissey's ill will toward someone he once cared deeply about but now clearly holds in contempt are downright sinister. Of course, the singer only sounds half-serious when he threatens to kill the subject's dog, and, later, himself.

"Paint a Vulgar Picture"

A tale of greedy record company executives repackaging a dead star, it made good sense that Rough Trade's Geoff Travis assumed this was Morrissey's final dig at him, but in fact Moz would explain to the *NME* in February 1988 that it was a comment on the music industry as a whole. "It was about practically anybody who's died and left behind that frenetic, fanatical legacy which sends people scrambling," he explained, citing several artists who had gone too soon, like Marc Bolan and Billy Fury.

Johnny Marr would later joke about getting the ambience just right when it came to recording his guitar part at Wool Hall. He kidded to *Guitar Magazine* in January 1997 about lighting a few candles and making everyone exit the studio while he did his overdubs. His true goal, he would explain, was cutting the best possible part. "I always thought that if you played a guitar solo," he reasoned, "it should be something people could whistle."

"Death at One's Elbow"

This two-minute shot of rollicking rockabilly evokes the spirit of "Shakespeare's Sister"—while besting it. Throughout its urgent presentation, Morrissey can be heard warding off death as his bandmates play like they are having the time of their lives. "Death at One's Elbow" is significant in that it marks Johnny Marr's first attempt at studio vocals. In 2013, Morrissey would describe his former musical partner's singing as a "tremulous quaver." It's a fair assessment, as Johnny is virtually—and no doubt purposely—inaudible on the tune.

"I Won't Share You"

A hauntingly sung torch song, "I Won't Share You" is offset by several funny lines, each brilliantly delivered by Morrissey, such as when he asks, "Has the Perrier gone straight to my head?"

For the track, Marr located a lyre dating from 1777 that had no sound hole. Its strings were evidently made of horsehair, but when Marr picked it up, the effect was "mesmerizing," as Moz explains in *Autobiography*. "It is a fascinating moment when Johnny's inner ear leads the way to somewhere unknown—somewhere mistrusted by all until the final depth of thought strikes. The technical term is *bling*."

Her Majesty's Prison

Morrissey came up with the title *Strangeways, Here We Come* by adapting a line from the 1959 Keith Waterhouse novel *Billy Liar*. In it, the author writes, "Borstal, here we come," making reference to a youth detention center in the United Kingdom.

Strangeways is a name familiar to Manchester residents as the high-security prison that first opened in 1868. It was closed for renovations in April 1990 after a riot by inmates over living conditions led to major damage to the structure. It reopened in 1994, as Her Majesty's Prison, Manchester, but many still refer to the facility by its original name.

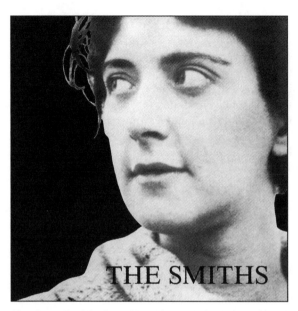

The sleeve for "Girlfriend in a Coma," which was released on August 10, 1987, in the U.K. In spite of being banned by the BBC, the song reached #13 in the British singles survey. *Author's collection*

At first, Marr was reportedly unhappy with the title, which Morrissey apparently decided on after Johnny had estranged himself from the group. The guitarist now claims to like it. From Morrissey's perspective, as he told *Melody Maker*'s Gary LeBoff in September 1987, the name of the record was inspired by the uncertain state of the band that summer. "The way things are going, I wouldn't be surprised if I was in prison twelve months from now," he explained, relating how the title reflected just how odd and crazy things had gotten. "Really it's me throwing both arms up to the skies and yelling, 'Whatever! Next?'"

Davalos

Although Morrissey originally chose a still of Harvey Keitel from the 1967 Martin Scorcese film *Who's That Knocking at My Door* for the cover of *Strangeways, Here We Come*, the actor refused the Smiths the right to use the image. Instead, Moz picked an image of actor Richard Davalos, who was James Dean's co-star in the 1955 classic *East of Eden* and later became an acquaintance of the singer's.

Morrissey had first met Davalos—who also starred in the 1967 prison drama *Cool Hand Luke*—backstage in Los Angeles in 1986, and for a time wore a silver ring that the retired actor had given him. According to *Autobiography*, Davalos was a true fan of the band who even sent Morrissey a number of letters after their meeting.

Commercial Reception

The week after its release, on September 28, *Strangeways, Here We Come* rose—like its predecessor—to only #2 on the album survey, much to Morrissey's irritation. Despite the group's status, Rough Trade made excuses and cited the massive major-label marketing budget behind its chart rival, the pop compilation *Hits 6*, which included Whitney Houston, George Michael, Terence Trent D'Arby, Starship, Whitesnake, Fleetwood Mac, and Club Nouveau.

Stateside that autumn, the record climbed to # 55 on the *Billboard* 200, thanks to a culmination of college and commercial-alternative radio support. The regular airing of Tim Broad's music videos for "Girlfriend" and "Stop Me" on MTV's *120 Minutes* also helped the Smiths achieve their highest American chart debut. On September 19, 1990, the disc earned a gold certification from the RIAA.

Reception and Legacy

In December 1987, critic David Browne heralded the album in the wake of the band's demise. Citing "Stop Me" in *Rolling Stone,* he wrote, "Marr and the Rourke-Joyce rhythm section whip up a frenzied brew that amply compensates for Morrissey's tale of rituals of self-punishment following a failed love affair. Marr's piercing solo at the end of the song not only is one of the record's emotional highlights—it also proves it's best the band split up rather than attempt to replace him."

Although the value and importance of *Strangeways* is still upheld by Smiths disciples, it is not held in the same regard as *The Queen Is Dead,* which is considered by most to be the group's masterpiece. Marr addressed this topic in the December '93 issue of *Select,* saying, "[It] suffers because it was our last record, so people think there were arguments and horrors in making it, but there weren't. Morrissey and I both think it's possibly our best album." Nearly two decades later, in April 2012, Marr's opinion of the album remained firm. "The whole thing just has a spirit to it that I love," he told *Spin's* David Marchese.

Moz was confident of this as early as September 1987, when he told Gary LeBoff, on the eve of the album's release, "*Strangeways* perfects every lyrical and musical notion the Smiths have ever had. It isn't dramatically, obsessively different in any way, and I'm quite glad it isn't, because I've been happy with the structure we've had until now. It's far and away the best record we've ever made."

In March 2012, *Slant Magazine* placed it at #69 on its list of the "Best Albums of the 1980s," but remained undecided as to where it ranked among the group's succinct studio catalog. "Whether or not *Strangeways, Here We Come* ended the Smiths' brief career with their best album has been the subject of considerable debate for nearly a quarter century, but it definitely stands as the band's most lush, richest work."

27

If You Think Peace Is a Common Goal . . .

The Smiths Fall Apart

No Show, No Call

With *Louder Than Bombs* performing well on U.S. alternative radio and music buyers taking note, MTV clamored for a proper Smiths video to play on its Sunday night music show *120 Minutes*. The marketing executives at Sire/Warner Bros. also hoped to push for regular daytime rotation on the network, which had recognized the importance of the group after the success of *The Queen Is Dead*.

Label executives forged a plan to give the band the kind of stateside exposure they had always wanted and deserved but never received. Of course, this was all contingent on the group cooperating with Sire Records to make a proper music video. But now, with a nearly completed studio album on deck, Morrissey and Marr were committed to the clip and seemed excited by the potential for exposure.

Sire flew director Tamra Davis, a veteran of successful clips for Depeche Mode and New Order, to England that month to make a video. After getting to know the group and encouraging the band's creative input, Davis spent time alone with Moz, who shared an idea to mix new footage of the band performing "Sheila Take a Bow" at Wool Hall—where they had been working on their fourth LP—with footage from old Hollywood movies.

A soundstage was booked in Battersea, South London, and a full film crew and catering team was hired. Johnny, Andy, and Mike arrived on time, as planned, ready to work. But Morrissey—who was typically late—failed to show up or even call to explain his absence.

The clock was ticking, costing the group thousands. Worried that Morrissey might be hurt or in danger, the band went to his home on Cadogan Square with Davis and recently hired manager Ken Friedman, and—after determining he was inside—tried to get him to come to the door. They pleaded to him from the outside, explaining that his absence was costing them not only buckets of money but also their reputation, but he never answered the door.

Marr was outraged. It wasn't the first time his partner had pulled a stunt like this, but Johnny had resolved the he could no longer accept this kind of oddball behavior without good reason. He was so angered and upset by Morrissey's lack of courtesy to his bandmates, their business, and the future of the Smiths organization, that he told Friedman he was done with the group. He had had enough of Morrissey's drama and was walking away from the band.

The next morning, after going out and getting drunk with Tamra, Ken, Andy, and Mike at the Portobello Hotel with the members of New Order, who were in London for a gig at Brixton Academy, Johnny rethought his decision to quit. He wasn't quite ready to walk away from the Smiths—he loved what they had created, and still cherished playing with Andy and Mike—but Morrissey was wearing him down.

The Tube

To promote "Sheila Take a Bow," the Smiths performed the song on the British television show *The Tube* on April 10, just a few days after Morrissey had abandoned the "Sheila" video shoot. Despite his anger with the singer, Marr came together with the band to play the new single, plus "Shoplifters of the World Unite." This would mark the group's final public appearance.

That same week, Marr demanded a meeting with Morrissey at his home on Cadogan Square, during which they spoke about the state of the band. Morrissey explained his failure to turn up at the video shoot was his way of telling Marr he was unhappy with Friedman and wanted him gone. But the idea of returning to handling the day-to-day business of the group felt like too much for Marr to bear. He was no longer interested in that role and trusted Ken to keep things moving forward on an even keel. Someone else could handle the record labels, the booking agents, the lawyers, and the offers. Simply put, as the band had become more and more popular globally, Johnny no longer wanted to be the one responsible for dealing with the things Morrissey refused to handle. He was tired of being—or at least trying to be—the voice of reason in their partnership.

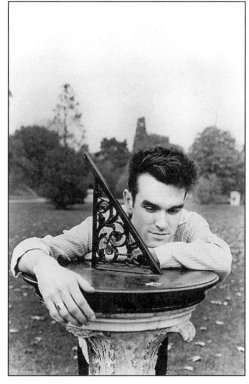

A publicity photo of Morrissey serviced to media in the fall of 1987, after Johnny Marr quit the band and the Smiths were dissolved. *Author's collection*

Johnny declined to discharge Friedman, and Morrissey refused to move ahead with Friedman in place. As had been the case with Joe Moss and John Porter before him, he had never liked any outside influences on Marr. They were deadlocked. Friedman, meanwhile, had gone on vacation to Thailand and Napal, and wasn't present to help a group in crisis mode.

Marr Walks Away

Ahead of the "Sheila" performance, Marr proposed to Morrissey that they dissolve their business partnership. And by becoming separate entities, he suggested, they could carry on creatively together while meeting their own individual management and legal needs. However, Morrissey was unable to immediately consider such a drastic change, and the discussion was tabled. In the meantime, the singer began to consider the notion that Marr was looking for a way out.

Days later, Johnny called a band meeting on neutral ground. The members of the Smiths gathered at Geale's, a seafood restaurant in Notting Hill, where Marr announced that he had been asked to play on Talking Heads' upcoming album, which was being recorded in Paris with producer Steve Lillywhite. Meanwhile, "The Right Stuff," his co-writing effort with Bryan Ferry, was being released as the first single from Ferry's new solo album, *Bête Noire*, and Marr had been asked to help promote the album by making live appearances with the singer and appear in the video for the song.

Marr informed Rourke, Joyce, and Morrissey that he wanted to take some time away from the Smiths to participate in these outside activities. On top of that, he said, he was exhausted; he needed a break from the group and wanted to go away for a couple of weeks. "I thought, if ever there was a time for us to take a break, this was it. I felt I shouldn't write for a bit; I should just get away, try to rethink this," he told *Musician* in 1989. Marr felt stifled stylistically, creatively, and even politically.

This idea did not sit well with Morrissey, whose own insecurity made him think that Johnny was being disloyal. Unable to accept Marr's request, the rest of the Smiths took from the meeting that this was Johnny's way of leaving the band. After all, his request for an unplanned "hiatus" came a time when they were anticipating a very busy year as they geared up for the release of their fourth LP. Although there was no immediate tour on the horizon, offers were being considered.

Instead of considering that Marr was suggesting something that would encourage not only his own reinvention but also the band's, the rest of the Smiths interpreted this as his exit. As time went on—and as insinuations that Johnny had been disloyal got back to him from insiders—communication between Morrissey and Marr stopped.

Final Session

That fateful meeting in a London fish-and-chips restaurant was followed by a two-week cooling off period, during which Morrissey and Marr were incommunicado. Johnny had gone to Paris to record overdubs with the Talking Heads, as planned. Morrissey, however, had insisted before the end of their restaurant summit that Johnny return to the studio with the group to cut some B-sides for the "Girlfriend in a Coma" single.

Although Johnny initially resisted Morrissey's request for them to come together for one final session, he recognized there wasn't any leftover material from the album sessions to round out the release. Eventually, he relented, and the band gathered the third week of May 1987 at the Cathouse, the Streatham home studio of Fred Hood, with Grant Showbiz serving as producer. Things were very tense, and the group's principals barely uttered a word to each other as they completed two new tracks, left two other instrumentals unfinished, and took a couple of failed stabs at Elvis Presley's "A Fool Such as I."

"It was total madness," Joyce told Rogan, remembering how he felt the sessions were a mistake the minute he walked into the studio. "Everybody was losing it. . . . It was a strange atmosphere. I didn't feel there was any need for us to be there." At one point, Showbiz—who had been with the band for years and rarely witnessed them arguing in the studio—was stunned to find Johnny and an intoxicated Morrissey fighting with each other over a song.

Joyce went on to explain that he would have been fine with Marr's request for an extended holiday. "If he'd said six months, it wouldn't have bothered me."

Despite the miserable environment, the Smiths did manage to complete several recordings, even though Marr hated the notion of recording the Cilla Black number "Work Is a Four-Letter Word." "That was the last straw," he told *Record Collector* in 1992. "I didn't form a group to perform Cilla Black songs."

A look at the lyrics suggests that Morrissey might have been trying to use the song to subtly express remorse for the behavior that had led to their recent standoff. However, the song's message that love and loyalty can help overcome tough times and difficult tasks was ignored by Johnny, who had gone beyond listening.

And while the final Morrissey/Marr original, "I Keep Mine Hidden," was tracked under joyless conditions on May 19, 1987, Moz would look back on the song itself in a 1990 interview with the *Face* as a high point in the band's career. "When I play the Smiths—which I do a lot—that song is always the first I play. And it's the one that makes me feel the happiest."

Perhaps it's because the song was an apology. As Showbiz told *Uncut* in 1998, "[It] was basically Morrissey saying, 'I'm sorry, Johnny. I'm a complete fuck-up but please forgive me.' With lots of specific references. It was a very direct song."

May Day

Despite the troubles, the recording session at Hood's studio wasn't without the occasional pleasantry. But if anyone on the inside of the Smiths camp was holding on to hope that Marr would just go off on a holiday and rejoin the band after a few weeks, they would soon be very disappointed.

The 7-inch U.S. promotional single of "Stop Me If You Think You've Heard This One Before," released to radio in October 1987. *Author's collection*

On May 22, 1987, at the Cathouse, during their very last day together as the Smiths, Marr walked up to Rourke and asked him quietly and confidentially if he knew things were about to end. Andy nodded his head in acknowledgment, and Marr took this as a sign of approval. Morrissey, who had already cut his vocals for the new recordings and was that day celebrating his twenty-eighth birthday, was not in attendance.

On the final day of May, the Morrissey/Marr partnership was officially severed with the filing of the relevant legal documents. Morrissey may not have understood all of Marr's reasons for leaving, but he had given Johnny the freedom he wanted.

Los Angeles

With the paperwork severing their partnership already in motion, Marr left for a holiday in Los Angeles, with a quick stopover in New York City. "L.A. was the only place I knew there'd be sunshine," he told Rogan in 1992. "So off I went."

On May 24, Johnny appeared on WLIR, the New York radio station that "Dared to be Different," to promote *Louder Than Bombs*. From there, he and Angie traveled on to L.A., as planned, where on May 28 Johnny served as a guest DJ on KROQ-FM. When an announcer asked him on air about Morrissey's whereabouts, he gave no indication that anything was wrong.

"I haven't seen him for a whole week," Marr told the listeners, following Friedman's advice to hold off announcing the split. "I really miss him." It didn't sound like a lie, but it probably was. Ironically, Morrissey had also left London for a holiday in Los Angeles around this time.

"Smiths to Split?"

On August 1, 1987, an *NME* cover story appeared with the headline "Smiths to Split?" At the time, Marr believed Morrissey had gone to *NME* editor Danny Kelly to leak the news that the guitarist was quitting due to "personal reasons."

The story, which originated from an "unnamed insider," wasn't entirely incorrect. The article's blunt suggestion that Johnny had grown tired of Moz "acting the self-centered star" and that the singer disliked Marr's social circle were pretty close to the truth. When Kelly called Mike Joyce at home to ask to talk to him about the split, the drummer's wife told him "he doesn't want to talk about that," giving Kelly the journalistic green light to pursue the story.

The reality was that Johnny and Morrissey had reached an impasse, following the breakdown in communication over band business, and Morrissey's lack of musical flexibility was frustrating to Marr. Feeling the need to give his version of events, Johnny phoned the publication to clarify that he had, in fact, left the Smiths because he was growing bored with what the band was becoming. He wanted to broaden his musical scope, he said, but Morrissey was resisting. In making this statement, in an August 8 *NME* cover story titled "Why I Quit," he had officially confirmed his exit.

"Toward the end of the Smiths, I realized that the records I was listening to with my friends were more exciting that the records I was listening to with the group," Marr told Dave Haslam in June 1989. "Sometimes it came down to Sly Stone versus Herman's Hermits. And I knew which side I was on."

While Morrissey suggests in his autobiography that Factory's Tony Wilson was somehow behind the *NME* story, it would appear that the leak actually came from Haslam. Haslam, who had been a Hacienda DJ and friend of Marr's in addition to one of the publication's Manchester stringers, had let it slip to Kelly that Johnny had stopped working with the Smiths. Of course, the editor took the scoop and ran with it.

THE SMITHS
"LAST NIGHT I DREAMT THAT SOMEBODY LOVED ME"

THE LAST SINGLE   AVAILABLE ON 7" (RT 200) AND 12" (RTT 200)
DISTRIBUTED BY THE CARTEL

This poster for the Smiths' final 45, "Last Night I Dreamt That Somebody Loved Me"—billed as "The Last Single"—features a picture of the singer Billy Fury. The single was released on December 7 and stalled at #30 on the U.K. chart. *Author's collection*

Not long after the split, Morrissey would argue that Johnny left because he was no longer satisfied with standing in his shadow. In Moz's opinion, his former partner wanted to make a name for himself. Being the guitarist in the Smiths wasn't enough for him anymore. He wanted to be recognized as Johnny Marr.

Nearly two and a half decades later, Marr was still upset about the tone of the *NME* story and Morrissey's subsequent remarks. "It really pissed me off to be talked to like I was about to be treacherous," he told Fletcher. Morrissey, meanwhile, was still mourning what he felt was the premature death of an amazing band. "The Smiths were almost like a painting," he told Len Brown in 1988. "Every month you'd add a little bit here and a little bit there . . . but it wasn't quite complete and it was whipped away."

Three years later, Morrissey told *Select*'s Mark Kemp that he felt "a complete sense of hopelessness about the demise of the Smiths," while suggesting that the group had "evolved too quickly." He also finally recognized the need for a strong managerial presence, acknowledging that they'd failed in part because they lacked a "guiding light."

"Girlfriend" Drops

Morrissey selected "Girlfriend in a Coma" as the first single from the band's new album—against Marr's wishes. The song would premiere on BBC radio the same day that Johnny's *NME* cover explaining his exit emerged. Officially released two days later, on August 10, 1987, the tune would become a steady seller, peaking at #13 in the U.K.

Johnny's Replacement

Just as Marr was speaking out about the reasons he split from the Smiths for the August 8 issue of *NME*, Rough Trade issued a statement on the guitarist's departure. "The Smiths announce that Johnny Marr has left the group," the statement read. "However they would like to confirm that other guitarists are being considered to replace him."

Of course, Marr was irreplaceable, but that didn't stop Morrissey considering his next move with the brand he had helped personify. First, he locked in Joyce and Rourke, who as the Smiths' underpaid rhythm section had become best friends when Andy and Johnny started growing apart. Despite having been at odds with Morrissey in recent years, Geoff Travis also aligned himself with the singer, offering to get Aztec Camera's Roddy Frame to join the band. The only problem was that Frame had no desire to leave his own band to become Morrissey's sideman.

At this point, Moz had decided to hold off touring in order to get a guitarist lined up and assess the situation with the band. He also wanted to record B-sides for the subsequent *Strangeways* singles he had planned. Ivor Perry—who ironically had left his brother's politically driven band Easterhouse to form a new group, the Cradle, with none other than Craig Gannnon—was asked to audition. Rough Trade's Jo Slee made contact with Ivor on behalf of Moz, and a meeting was set at the singer's London home.

Morrissey was adamant about keeping the Smiths going, but Perry—who had known the singer for years—told him it wouldn't work. Ivor knew Johnny was matchless and felt he would have to be a lunatic to try to fill the slot. Still, he went along with Morrissey's request for him to play on some B-sides, including an early version of what became "Bengali in Platforms," and was promised that he would be paid extremely well.

Perry was curious about how the band might sound with him on guitar and turned up for a session at the Power Plant in London with some songs he had written since he quitting his previous group a year earlier. Stephen Street was brought in to produce, agreeing to do so in spite of concerns that Marr might consider this an unforgivable act.

Marr considered the idea of Morrissey, Mike, and Andy continuing on without him to be a real act of treason. He was deeply hurt. "To be replaced so quickly by your friends, before you've even had a chance to change your mind, was the end of it."

Not that Johnny had any intention of letting Morrissey use the group's name. In any case, Perry was not a good fit for the group. "The new songs sounded okay but it was clutching at straws," Mike Joyce told *Mojo* in 1997. "The real beauty of the Smiths was gone."

In typical Moz fashion, he delegated the chore of breaking the news to Joyce and took off back to Manchester after one day of work. Ivor was never paid for his studio efforts with the remaining Smiths. Meanwhile, Morrissey had been thrilled to discover that the 1987 *Collins English Dictionary* listed the Smiths with the definition, "A Manchester pop group." He tore it out and sent it to Marr, but there was no reply.

A few weeks after the session at the Power Plant, on Friday, September 4, 1987, Mike Joyce released a statement announcing he had "fulfilled his role" in the band. It really was the end. A few days later, Morrissey announced the end of the Smiths. Three weeks after that, *Strangeways, Here We Come* was officially released.

Depressed but Ready

In the fall of 1987, Morrissey felt alone and unhappy, and uncertain about his future. Speaking to the *Observer* in 2002, he said, "[Johnny] knows that at the end, I was in a very, very depressed state—and that possibly the fact that he broke up the Smiths could have killed me."

Out of concern, Johnny sent Grant Showbiz down to London to check on Morrissey, unwilling at the time to do so himself. Of course, Morrissey's situation was his own doing, and the fact that he had tried to go forward without Marr was something Johnny couldn't forgive too soon.

John Featherstone, who had been crashing at Marr's home in Bowdon, had continued to pray for Morrissey to come to the door and make an apology and express regret. Moz never came. Instead, he called Johnny on the phone and asked him if he would be up for one final farewell concert at the Royal Albert Hall. Marr passed on the offer.

Early the following year, while plugging his first solo album, *Viva Hate*, Morrissey put out a message to Johnny in the *NME*. "I would be totally in favor of a reunion," he explained to Len Brown in February 1988. "As soon as anybody wants to come back to the fold and make records, I will be there!"

Of course, much as Moz and his supportive fans hoped it might happen, Marr never showed up.

Wolverhampton

On December 22, 1988, Morrissey resumed performing after a two-year break from the stage. His concert at the Wolverhampton Civic Hall was also an unofficial farewell to the Smiths. That night, the singer was backed by Andy Rourke and Mike Joyce, with "Fifth Smith" Craig Gannon assuming lead guitar duties. Admission was free to anyone wearing a Smiths or Morrissey T-shirt, and the turnout was so large that thousands were turned away. Inside the venue, the show interspersed Smiths songs from 1987 that had never been performed live with recent and in some cases still-unreleased solo material.

The band played Smiths tracks "Stop Me If You Think You've Heard This One Before," "Death at One's Elbow," and "Sweet and Tender Hooligan" alongside Morrissey's recent solo chart hit "Suedehead." Future Morrissey singles "The Last of the Famous International Playboys" and "Interesting Drug"—which he had just recorded with Rourke, Joyce, Gannon, and Stephen Street at Wool Hall, and would release in 1989—were also played, as was "Sister I'm a Poet," the B-side to "Everyday Is Like Sunday."

Looking back on the event, Morrissey remembered feeling a little wobbly about being back onstage, and in fact would not do so again as a solo artist until April 1991. When asked by *Record Mirror* in September 1989 how it felt to have Rourke, Joyce, and Gannon behind him, he explained it was "very tearful," but that there was "a radiant feeling onstage."

Unfortunately, the show would mark Morrissey's last musical involvement with any of his former bandmates. Three months later, in March 1989, Joyce and Rourke started legal action against Morrissey and Marr, contending that they were equal partners in the Smiths and as such were entitled to 25 percent of all profits the group earned outside of songwriting and publishing.

I'll Probably Never See You Again

At one point in 1993, after seven years of silence, Morrissey decided to write Marr a letter—and, to his surprise, Johnny wrote him back a week later. A week after that, the former partners came together for a quiet meeting at Betty Dwyer's home.

Then, with Marr behind the wheel of his white Mercedes, they drove off toward Saddleworth Moor and talked. Johnny explained why he had left—to make his life sane—and the end result was that the two didn't just re-establish contact. They parted as friends.

28

Life Is Very Long

After the End

Morrissey

Not long after the Smiths ended, Morrissey launched a solo career that has endured for over a quarter of a century. If he was uncertain about the direction of his career in the months that followed Marr's exit and the group's ensuing dissolution, Moz soon overcame his anxiety and stepped up to forge a hugely successful, if not occasionally controversial, livelihood without his former partner.

Viva Hate and Bona Drag

In October 1987, Morrissey overcame his sadness about the Smiths' demise by teaming up with Stephen Street at Wool Hall studios to begin work on new material. In addition to serving as the project's producer, Street helped co-write the record—which would be Morrissey's first solo album—and played bass on it. Guitarist and pianist Vini Reilly of the Durutti Column was also recruited, at the suggestion of Geoff Travis, while Street's friend Andrew Paresi, whom he had met while mixing a single for his previous band, A Pair of Blue Eyes, played drums.

Morrissey titled the album *Viva Hate*. It was released on March 14, 1988, and was his first album under his global EMI deal, although he remained on Sire in the U.S. Preceded by the single "Suedehead" (U.K. #5), his first solo album entered the U.K. charts at the top spot and spawned a subsequent hit, "Everyday Is Like Sunday" (U.K. #9).

When asked that February if the album had been impacted by the breakup of the Smiths, Morrissey told the *NME* it wasn't, explaining that it would be the "next expected thing to do . . . I don't really want to do that . . . there are no bitter references to the past." As for the title, he said, "Love [is] very difficult to find. Hate makes the world go round."

Despite the album's incredible popularity, Morrissey was still unwilling to tour and wouldn't resume roadwork until the spring of 1991. Around that time, he acknowledged in an interview that—with the exception of a few key songs like the aforementioned singles and the track "Hairdresser on Fire," *Viva Hate* wasn't very good, and in no way rivaled the greatness of *Strangeways*, either lyrically or musically.

Morrissey released three new singles in 1989. "The Last of the Famous International Playboys" (#6) and "Interesting Drug" (#9) were recorded with ex-Smiths Andy Rourke, Mike Joyce, and Craig Gannon, plus producer Stephen Street, and were both Top 10 successes in the U.K., in February and April, respectively. His next song, "Ouija Board, Ouija Board," was recorded without any former Smiths, and when it was released that November, it barely made the Top 20, halting at #18.

The A-sides kept coming in 1990, with April's "November Spawned a Monster" (#12) and October's "Piccadilly Palare" (#18) marking Andy Rourke's final work with Moz in the lead up to *Bona Drag*. Released on October 15 that year, the album compiled all of his non-album singles and B-sides and peaked at #9 in the U.K. and #59 in the U.S.

Kill Uncle, Your Arsenal, and Vauxhall and I

After writing "November Spawned a Monster" with Clive Langer, Morrissey recruited the producer and his partner Alan Winstanley— who together had been veterans of strong records by Madness, Elvis Costello, Lloyd Cole & the Commotions, Hothouse Flowers, and They Might Be Giants—to oversee his next album, 1991's *Kill Uncle*. It debuted at #8 in the U.K. and reached #52 in the States.

For the album, Morrissey teamed with Fairground Attraction's Mark E. Nevin, who had had a worldwide smash with "Perfect" (U.K. #1) in the spring of 1988. The record yielded two singles, "Our Frank" and "Sing Your Life," both of which bubbled under the U.K. Top 20. Two non-album singles followed that year, the rockabilly driven "Pregnant for the Last Time" and the poppier "My Love Life," which featured harmony vocals from Chrissie Hynde. Both also just scraped into the Top 30.

This publicity photo of Morrissey—shot by Eamonn J. McCabe—accompanied promotional copies of his solo debut, *Viva Hate*, when it was serviced to the media in early 1988. *Author's collection*

Morrissey was back in 1992 with *Your Arsenal*, which was produced by one-time David Bowie guitarist Mick Ronson. Featuring new guitarists Alain Whyte and Boz Boorer, the disc peaked at U.K. #4 and U.S. #21 and earned a Grammy nomination for "Best Alternative Album." Ronson's influence gave the record a harder guitar sound that resonated with U.S. audiences. It included the singles "We Hate It When Our Friends Become Successful" (U.K. #17) and "You're the One for Me, Fatty" (U.K. #19).

Morrissey's next album, *Vauxhall and I*, emerged in March 1994. It was produced by Steve Lillywhite and was his second solo album—and first for six years—to peak at #1 in the British chart. *Vauxhall and I* also gave Morrissey his best ever U.S. album-chart placement, climbing to #18. The album's lead track, "The More You Ignore Me, the Closer I Get," hit #8 in the U.K. and # 46 in the States, where it topped the *Billboard* Modern Rock chart. A one-off duet with Siouxsie Sioux called "Interlude" appeared in August '94, with the non-LP single "Boxers" hitting shelves the following January.

Southpaw Grammar, Maladjusted, Recording Hiatus, and Latino Following

Morrissey again worked with Lillywhite on *Southpaw Grammar* (U.K. #4), his first album for RCA Victor. It was released in August 1995, and included the singles "Dagenham Dave" (U.K. #26) and "The Boy Racer" (#36).

Two years later, Moz released *Maladjusted* via Island Records (U.K. #8). Neither of its singles, "Roy's Keen" and "Satan Rejected My Soul," made the U.K. Top 30.

After his RCA deal ended in 1998, Morrissey went six years without releasing any new material. But he continued to tour, playing dates the following year at Coachella, and in Mexico and South America, where his music had become tremendously popular.

Latino fans identified with Morrissey, who was raised from Irish roots in England, brought up Catholic, and had an appreciation of sports like soccer and boxing. Explaining the appeal of the singer among Latinos, which by 2014 had ballooned, Los Angeles–based Morrissey impersonator Jose Maldonado told the *NME*, "It's kinda the same experience for a kid growing up with Mexican parents in L.A. That experience of not quite belonging somewhere that Morrissey sings about like no one else can—that's a very common feeling among the Latino people here."

A subsequent world tour in 2002 took Moz to the United States, Europe, Australia, and Japan. A documentary, *The Importance of Being Morrissey*, was filmed for the U.K.'s Channel 4 during the tour and aired the following year. The same year, Morrissey signed to Sanctuary Records, which resuscitated its obsolete reggae imprint Attack Records to release new material by the singer.

A Quarry Comeback

Morrissey's first album in seven years was *You Are the Quarry*, which had strong debuts in the U.K. (#2) and the U.S. (#11) after its release on May 17, 2004.

Produced by Jerry Finn—a veteran of albums by California punk bands like Blink 182, Bad Religion, Rancid, and Green Day—the album had a strong guitar presence that propelled its first single, "Irish Blood, English Heart," to #3 in the U.K. The successful world tour that followed included a concert at the Manchester Arena on the singer's forty-fifth birthday that was filmed and released on DVD in 2005 as *Who Put the M in Manchester?*

Tony Visconti—a veteran of classic records by David Bowie and T. Rex—came on board for *Ringleader of the Tormentors*, which was marked by the addition of guitarist Jesse Tobias, a Los Angeles–based musician who had previously played with Alanis Morissette and, very briefly, as a member of the Red Hot Chili Peppers. Recorded in Rome, it debuted at #1 in the U.K. and reached #27 in the U.S. in May of 2006.

In the first half of the following year, Morrissey toured the world, performing his biggest hits. Although he played 106 shows, eleven were canceled—including a six-night stand at London's Roundhouse.

In December 2007, Morrissey aligned with Decca Records and recorded a new song, "That's How People Grow Up," at Houston's Sunrise Sound Studio with Jerry Finn. The track reached #14 when it was released as a single in February 2008 to promote his *Greatest Hits* album, which contained all of his solo tracks to have reached the Top 15 in the U.K. and was designed to introduce new fans to his older material. His ninth studio album, *Years of Refusal*, was set for a September release, but when Finn—who was producing the project—died of a heart attack brought on by a cerebral hemorrhage, the project was delayed until February 2009.

Led by the single "I'm Throwing My Arms Around Paris" (U.K. #21), *Years of Refusal* debuted at U.K. #3 and U.S. #11. The disc was heralded by *Pitchfork* as Morrissey's "most venomous, score-settling album," and included an unusual collaboration with rock guitarist Jeff Beck, who lent his guitar playing to the track "Black Crowd." The year 2009 was marked by continued roadwork for Moz, who played in Russia for the first time. He played further dates later in the year in support of *Swords*, a collection of B-sides originally issued between 2004 and 2009 that was released in October. On October 24, 2009, during the second show of the tour, Morrissey collapsed onstage with breathing problems after a performance of the Smiths' "This Charming Man" at the Oasis Centre in Swindon. He resumed the tour after being released from the hospital the next day.

"Humasexuality" and *Autobiography*

Morrissey's toured the U.K. extensively in June of 2011, following the release of the EMI compilation *Very Best of Morrissey* the previous April. Dates at the Glastonbury Festival, a headlining spot at the Hop Farm Festival, and a run of European gigs followed. During the next two years, he toured North America, Europe, Greece, Turkey, and Israel. Although he was forced to cancel some of his North American dates after being diagnosed with a bleeding ulcer, he had the

The front cover of Morrissey's 1989 single "Interesting Drug." The song was recorded with former Smiths members Andy Rourke, Mike Joyce, and Craig Gannon. *Author's collection*

thrill of sharing the stage with his teenage hero Patti Smith when she opened his show at the Staples Center in L.A.

In June 2013, Morrissey hit the road again for shows in Mexico, Brazil, Argentina, Peru, and Chile in June 2013. Two months later, a film of the singer's March 2 Hollywood High School concert premiered in cinemas under the title *25Live*. A DVD followed of the gig, which celebrated Morrissey's first quarter-century as a solo artist, but a planned tour through South America that autumn was canceled due to a lack of funding.

Autobiography, Morrissey's memoir, was released on October 17, 2013, through Penguin Books' "Penguin Classic" imprint—at the author's insistence. Completed in 2011 but delayed by disputes over its content, the book received mixed reviews. The *Independent* criticized Moz's "droning narcissism," while the *Telegraph* heralded the book with a five-star review, naming it "the best-written musical autobiography since Bob Dylan's *Chronicles*." Although the London *Sunday Times*' A. A. Gill felt that "Morrissey is plainly the most ornery, cantankerous, entitled, whining, self-martyred human being who ever drew breath," fan interest was high. The book sold 35,000 copies in its first week and debuted at #1 in the U.K. book charts, setting a record for a music biography.

Meanwhile, U.S. fans griped that the title was unavailable domestically. The book was quickly licensed to G. P. Putnam's Sons and rush-released on December 3 in time to maximize Christmas sales, but not before one of the main revelations in the tome—that Morrissey had been in a two-year homosexual relationship with photographer Jake Owen Walters—had been excised, according to a report in the *Independent*. The U.K. newspaper also revealed that Moz had removed his name from a story about a night out he and Walters had with Chrissie Hynde in the 1990s. A photograph of Walters as a youngster was also removed from the Putnam pressing.

"It is not specifically noted that Morrissey and Walters were lovers in either edition, but the singer makes it clear the pair were involved, each holding a great fondness for the other," the *Independent* reported. In the U.K. pressing of the book, the singer explained how he and Walters met at a dinner in

London's Notting Hill and soon "fell together in deep collusion . . . and ate up each minute of the day."

Of course, Morrissey had always been cagey about his private life, and he had long contended he was celibate. Following *Autobiography*'s initial publication, he continued to be vague about the issue. "In technical fact, I am humasexual," he told his fan site, *True to You*. "Unfortunately, I am *not* homosexual . . . I am attracted to *humans*. But, of course . . . *not many*."

During the week of the U.S. release of his book, Morrissey seemed keen to change the subject. He issued an unexpected digital single of Lou Reed's "Satellite of Love" in tribute to the Velvet Underground founder and New York rock legend, who had passed away six weeks earlier at just seventy-one. Recorded in Las Vegas in 2011, the cover shot to the top the *Billboard* Hot Singles Sales chart after it was given a physical release the following month.

"No words to express the sadness at the death of Lou Reed," Morrissey told True to You, upon hearing the news on October 27. "He had been there all my life. He will always be pressed to my heart. Thank God for those, like Lou, who move within their own laws, otherwise imagine how dull the world would be. I knew the Lou of recent years and he was always full of good heart. His music will outlive time itself."

World Peace Pulled

In January 2014, Morrissey announced plans to record a new album in Paris as part of a two-record deal with Capitol Music's recently revived Harvest Records imprint. The album, *World Peace Is None of Your Business*, was produced by Joe Chicarelli (Spoon, the Strokes) and received a strong response from fans. After its July 15 release, the album entered the U.K. charts at #2 and debuted on the *Billboard* 200 at #14.

But 2014 wouldn't be without controversy for the singer. Ahead of the record's release, Morrissey hit the road in North America in May, but was hospitalized in Boston with a cold or virus and announced he was scrapping the rest of his scheduled dates. He later blamed the cancelations on the tour's opening act, singer Kristeen Young, who had supposedly fallen ill when the tour was in Miami, days earlier. True to You reported that Young had "a horrendous cold," which she had passed on to Morrissey. In a statement, Moz contended that Young "was asked to step down from the immediate upcoming shows, but instead she decided to leave the tour entirely."

In a Facebook post after the news broke, Young denied Morrissey's claim and insisted she was never contagious but had been treated for an allergy attack, from which she had quickly recovered, in Miami. Regardless, Young announced, she had been kicked off the tour.

"This is really too much and bizarre," wrote the singer/songwriter, who had once been Morrissey's protégé, and was handpicked by him in 2006 as an unknown to open his shows. It wasn't the first time they had had a strange falling out. In

2007, Morrissey had fired her as his opening act after she made profane comments about his sexual ability while audience members were chanting headliner's name. "Morrissey gives good head," she told the crowd, "I mean, err, cunnilingus . . ."

Young later claimed her comments were "metaphorical" and "overstated to make an artistic point." Writing on MySpace, she added, "The 'offending' statement, in particular, was in no way a literal statement. . . . I love Morrissey with all of my heart, soul, body, spirit, to the core of my existence and always will." In a subsequent *Village Voice* profile, in January 2013, she called the incident "traumatic" and declined to talk about it.

In early August 2014, three weeks after the release of *World Peace Is None of Your Business*, and despite a successful launch for the album, Capitol Music/Harvest Records surprised the music world by ending its contract with Morrissey. It appears that label head Steve Barnett dropped Morrissey after the singer criticized the label in a True to You post for failing to fund a music video for the album's title track.

The album was quickly yanked from physical record retailers and digital platforms like iTunes and Amazon, plus streaming sites like Spotify. Then, on August 20, 2014, Moz released a statement announcing *his* version of events. He stated that he had never actually signed a contract with the label, contending that he retained full ownership of the disc, and asserted, "Technically, [Harvest] have no right to sell it."

Johnny Marr

Johnny's August 1987 *NME* cover story explaining why he left the Smiths made it clear to interested parties that, hot on the heels of his collaboration with Talking Heads, he was available for work. The fact that he offered valuable skill and name recognition throughout the globe resulted in a number of offers. One of the first to come through was an opportunity to meet and play with a legendary Beatle.

Jamming with Macca

In August 1987, Marr fielded a phone call from Paul McCartney's manager, asking him if he had any desire to jam with the rock legend, who was gearing up to make an album of covers of early, influential rock 'n' roll numbers for release in Russia. After Johnny confirmed that he could play classics like "Lawdy Miss Clawdy" and "Twenty Flight Rock," plus Fab Four staples like "Get Back" and "I Saw Her Standing There," the offer was made. An anxious Johnny learned a long list of songs on guitar and went to jam for seven hours with Macca, drummer Henry Spinetti (a veteran of albums by Eric Clapton, Bob Dylan, and Pete Townshend), and another guitarist.

"It was one of the best days of my life, and one of the most disastrous," Marr told *Musician* in September 1989. Wracked with nerves, he played badly, even freezing a few times out of fear. While nothing materialized from the session for Johnny—McCartney ended up making the album, *Choba B CCCP*, with Mick Green on guitar—he came away from the day with an incredible and unforgettable story he imagined he might someday share with his grandchildren.

Session Man

Johnny's work on the aforementioned Talking Heads album, *Naked*, included the guitar parts on the record's first single, "Nothing but Flowers," which Steve Lillywhite and David Byrne recorded without Marr knowing tape was rolling. Another contribution, "Cool Water," was Marr's favorite on the session. It took shape after Byrne encouraged him to play a drone on an oddly tuned semi-acoustic 12-string Gibson 335 guitar.

Marr liked the idea of doing high-profile session work because he didn't want the responsibility that came with being in the Smiths. Having already established himself as a songwriter, he realized that his work with bands like Talking Heads allowed him to develop his guitar playing.

In addition to his primary musical efforts of this era, which are outlined below, Marr was an active session musician into the 1990s, co-writing and playing on Kirsty MacColl's 1991 single "Walking Down Madison," before playing on sessions with Pet Shop Boys, Black Grape, Oasis, and even Beck. And, in 1992, Marr and his early guitar mentor Billy Duffy tracked a recording of Ennio Morricone's "The Good, the Bad, and the Ugly" for the *NME* compilation *Ruby Trax*.

The Pretenders

Marr received an offer to join Chrissie Hynde's band, the Pretenders, in 1987, via U2's manager Paul McGuinness. Guitarist Robbie McIntosh had left the band two weeks before they were due to join U2's *Joshua Tree* tour of North America as the support act.

Marr, of course, was a massive fan of original Pretenders guitarist James Honeyman-Scott and felt honored to play with the band, even if it meant learning thirty of their songs in a short time. Walking out onstage to play "Kid" with Hynde was like a dream come true for Johnny, who used to warm up regularly to Honeyman-Scott's solo on that track.

Spending time with Hynde on tour was quite therapeutic for Marr. She had already survived the drug-related deaths of guitarist Honeyman-Scott and original Pretenders bassist Pete Farndon within a ten-month span between June 1982 and April 1983. Her insights about persevering in rock 'n' roll helped Marr cope with the fallout at the end of the Smiths.

Still, Marr's tenure in the band was extremely short. He left the Pretenders in early 1988 after playing on the one-off single "Windows of the World"/"1969," which was produced by U.K. guitar-pop icon Nick Lowe. Although he had been honored by the opportunity to play with Hynde and had established an important bond with her, he realized he wasn't the right fit for the band. Still, before his exit, Johnny and Chrissie wrote about six songs together, including "When Will I See You," which was eventually released on the group's 1990 studio album *Packed!*

The The

While he was in the studio with the Pretenders, Marr simultaneously joined The The, the already-established band led by his old friend Matt Johnson. Recognizing that Johnny wanted to venture away from the Rickenbacker style he had become known for, Johnson encouraged his old friend to try different things.

Johnson's band had already recorded a number of modern-rock favorites, including 1983's "This Is the Day" and 1986's "Infected," but Johnny's assistance earned the band its most successful single yet, when "The Beat(en) Generation" peaked at #18 in the U.K. in 1989. The song's parent album, *Mind Bomb*, also marked The The's first Top 5 achievement (U.K. #4). And with former Nick Lowe bassist James Eller, ex-ABC drummer David Palmer, and keyboardist D.C. Collard rounding out the group, The The toured the world into 1990.

Dusk followed in 1993, outperforming its predecessor by peaking at #2 in the U.K. on the strength of its first single, "Dogs of Lust." But after the band's *Lonely Planet* tour, Marr left to focus on his own project, Electronic. Still, *Dusk* ranks as his favorite of the two The The records he participated in. "It's one of the few records I've made that I can detach from and just enjoy as a listener," he told *Uncut* in February 2008. "We knew we were a great band and we'd had validation from the audience. . . . Matt was really adamant that I played as much harmonica as I could, because he really loved my playing."

Electronic

Alongside his work with The The, Johnny kept busy with his friend Bernard Sumner, the singer and guitarist in New Order. The two friends had first formed a creative alliance back in 1983, when Marr played guitar on a Quando Quango session that Sumner was producing, before coming together in the studio in the autumn of 1988 to make modern dance music as Electronic.

The project originated as a Sumner solo album after his primary bandmates conveyed they weren't interested in adding synth programming to New Order's sound. But as work progressed in the studio, Bernard realized he preferred working with a collaborator. He sought out Marr to see if he wanted to have some fun by joining forces in making a disco record.

Johnny's love of dance music was no secret to anyone who knew him and he had been up on current dancefloor styles, including house music, hip hop, and R&B. Together, Sumner and Marr crafted their first track, a white-label Factory Records 12-inch called "Lucky Bag" that was credited only to Electronic.

At some point in 1989, Pet Shop Boys singer Neil Tennant had become aware of the duo's efforts through an album-sleeve artist named Mark Farrow and asked about a possible collaboration. The end result was "Getting Away with It," the group's first proper single, which featured percussion by David Palmer and a string arrangement by Anne Dudley from the Art of Noise.

This heavenly slice of synth-pop—which features shared vocals by Sumner and Tennant—wound up selling an impressive 250,000 copies after its release on December 4, 1989. Then, in the spring of 1990, the song cracked the U.S. Top 40, peaking at #38. That August, Electronic—including Tennant—hit the road supporting Depeche Mode on select dates of its massive *Violator* tour, including back-to-back sell-out shows at Dodger Stadium.

An eponymous album followed, supported by the U.K. Top 10 single "Get the Message." *Electronic* was widely heralded and sold more than a million copies globally. Another single, "Disappointed," was tracked with Tennant and released in June 1992, peaking at #6 in the U.K.

Sumner resumed work with New Order in 1993 and Marr returned to The The, but by late 1994 the pair had begun working with Kraftwerk's Karl Bartos on a second album. *Raise the Pressure* was released in July 1996, spawning the singles "Forbidden City" (UK # 14) and "For You" (U.K. #14).

In 1998, Electronic tracked their final studio effort, *Twisted Tenderness*, as a four-piece band with Doves bassist Jimi Goodwin and Black Grape's drummer Ged Lynch. The album included one chart hit, "Vivid," which peaked in the U.K. Top 20 at #17. Marr and Sumner have remained good friends and occasional collaborators, including playing together with Doves at the "Manchester v. Cancer" charity concert in 2006.

The Healers

Johnny Marr + the Healers—consisting of Marr on guitar and vocals, drummer Zak Starkey (son of the Beatles' Ringo Starr), and ex-Kula Shaker bassist Alonza Beavan—came together in 2000 to record their one and only album, *Boomslang*. Released in the U.K. on Reincarnate Music and in the U.S. via Artistdirect/iMusic on February 3, 2003, the album was preceded by the 2001 single "The Last Ride." A second single, "Down on the Corner," was released alongside the album.

Finally out in front after being egged on by everyone from Hynde to Sumner to Johnson to front his own band, Marr's goal was to craft a thick-sounding, psychedelic rock album. Named for the venomous, tree-dwelling tropical snake, *Boomslang* received mixed reviews.

A second Healers record had initially been planned for release in April 2005, but it never materialized. Zak Starkey kept busy playing with the Who and Oasis, while Bevan reunited with front man Crispin Mills in Kula Shaker.

Modest Mouse

Although Marr had expressed interest in doing another Healers record, he was tapped to join Modest Mouse after the success of the group's 2004 breakthrough hit "Float On" and its parent album, *Good News for People Who Love Bad News.* Isaac Brock first brought Marr in as producer and co-songwriter in 2006 to help him with the songs that would eventually become the following year's U.S. #1 album *We Were Dead Before the Ship Even Sank.* Johnny ended up relocating to Portland, Oregon, where Brock was based, and became a full-time member of Modest Mouse.

The band hit the road in 2006 and toured extensively behind the album—which produced the singles "Dashboard," "Missed the Boat," and "Little Motel"—throughout 2007. The following year, Modest Mouse were the opening act on R.E.M.'s U.S. summer tour. Johnny would join the headline band during encores of "Fall on Me" each night, and occasionally during "Man on the Moon," at the insistence of his old friend, R.E.M. guitarist Peter Buck.

The Cribs

Marr left Modest Mouse after he became involved with the Cribs, a popular indie-rock band from Wakefield, England, consisting of twins Gary and Ryan Jarman (bass/vocals and guitar/vocals, respectively) and their drummer brother Ross. In January 2008, Johnny participated in songwriting efforts with the group after meeting them during a 2007 gig in Portland.

Marr joined the Cribs on tour and became an official member of the band. He was even introduced to audiences each night as "Johnny Jarman." Their initial plan to do an EP together led to a full album, *Ignore the Ignorant.* The band's fourth LP, it was released on September 7, 2009, having been recorded in Los Angeles the previous March with producer Nick Launay (the Church, INXS, PiL, Yeah Yeah Yeahs). The album debuted at #8, ahead of all but two of the thirteen Beatles albums that had been reissued in the U.K. that week.

After a year and a half of extensive touring, Marr played his last shows with the band at the Reading and Leeds festivals in August 2010. Johnny's departure—which was made official in April 2011—was amicable and planned, as he had plans to work on his own studio album. He did however join the Cribs onstage for a special Christmas show at Leeds Academy on December 19, 2013.

Solo Work

Johnny Marr's debut solo album, *The Messenger,* was released on February 25, 2013, via Warner Bros. in the U.K. and Sire Records in the U.S. the next day. A single, "Upstarts," preceded the album by a week. A second single, "New Town Velocity," was also extracted from the record, which was produced and largely performed solely by Marr—save for the bass work of a collaborator known only as Doviak—and earned positive reviews.

A second solo album, *Playland,* was released on Warner Bros. on October 6, 2014. The first single from the disc was titled "Easy Money," and first emerged on August 15. Recorded in London, hot on the heels of Marr's tour in support of

The Messenger with Doviak and other touring musicians, the album was inspired by *Homo Ludens*, a 1938 book by Dutch cultural theorist Johan Huizinga, which considers the notion of play as a forerunner and basic element of cultural development.

Looking back on the album's evolution in a press statement, Johnny said, "When *The Messenger* came out, I kept on writing. I liked that the band had a momentum going on tour and a connection with the audience, and I thought that the energy would be good to capture on the new record."

Marrguar

In 2012, after five years of development and design, the Fender Musical Instruments Corporation introduced the Johnny Marr signature Jaguar guitar, known to fans as the "Marrguar." Based on Marr's modified 1965 Jaguar, which has a body and neck based on a 1954 Stratocaster, the instrument retailed for $1,749 in the U.S. It was priced comparably to Fender's other American-made instruments and has been well received since its release.

Johnny has been partial to Fenders ever since he borrowed John Porter's in 1983 to track "This Charming Man." He often used a Jazzmaster during his tenure in Modest Mouse, and he regularly uses Fender amplifiers.

Gibson guitars have also played a significant role in his career. He acquired his cardinal-red Les Paul in 1984 and used it throughout his days in the Smiths and during his tenure with The The. In the '90s, Marr gave a vintage sunburst Les Paul that had previously belonged to Pete Townshend to Oasis' Noel Gallagher. When the guitar was destroyed by Gallagher, who smashed it over the head of a fan in a fit of rage, Marr generously gave him the black Les Paul he had used while making *The Queen Is Dead*.

While playing with the Healers, Johnny preferred to use his cherry-red Gibson SG. He also owns a cherry-red ES-355, famously purchased for him by Sire's Seymour Stein. He used it prominently while he was in the Smiths, although he regularly played a 12-string sunburst model on *Strangeways, Here We Come*.

Of course, throughout his career, Marr has most often been identified by his jangly Rickenbacker 330, which can be heard on early Smiths records. He also owns a Rickenbacker 12-string "360" that, like the sunburst Les Paul, once belonged to the Who's Pete Townshend.

Ten More Marr Accomplishments

1. In April 2001, Marr performed as part of the charitable collective 7 Worlds Collide, a super group organized by Crowded House front man Neil Finn that also featured Pearl Jam's Eddie Vedder, Ed O'Brien and Phil Selway of Radiohead, Sebastian Steinberg of Soul Coughing, and singer/songwriter Lisa Germano. A live album billed to Neil Finn & Friends included a version of "There Is a Light That Never Goes Out."

2. Johnny played guitar on the 2002 Oasis album *Heathen Chemistry*. His guitar work can be heard on the songs "(Probably) All in the Mind" and "Better Man." He also provided backing vocals on the latter, and played slide guitar on the track "Born on a Different Cloud."

3. In 2007, Marr was appointed as a visiting music professor at the University of Salford. He delivered his inaugural lecture in November of the following year and participated in workshops and master classes with students enrolled in the school's popular music and recording program.

4. While on tour with Modest Mouse in 2008, Marr visited the Los Angeles home studio of former Red Hot Chili Peppers guitarist John Frusciante, where he recorded guitar parts for the songs "Enough of Me" and "Central," which can be heard on Frusciante's acclaimed 2009 disc *The Empyrean*.

5. In 2007, Marr played guitar on the song "Even a Child" from Crowded House's album *Time on Earth*. Johnny's daughter Sonny provides backing vocals on the song.

6. In December 2008 and January 2009, Marr participated in a second group of Neil Finn & Friends concerts with veterans of the first event, members of Wilco, and singer KT Tunstall. These shows were recorded and released as *The Sun Came Out* the following August. All proceeds were donated to Oxfam, the international human-rights and poverty-solutions confederation.

7. Marr played 12-string guitar on the soundtrack to the 2010 science-fiction film *Inception*. The box-office smash was written and directed by Christopher Nolan and starred Leonardo DiCaprio.

8. Johnny's work in film continued when he recorded music for the 2014 blockbuster movie *The Amazing Spider-Man 2*.

9. In July 2012, Marr was given an honorary doctorate from the University of Salford for his contribution to popular music and the guidance he offered to students in his workshops and classes.

10. Alongside the likes of Nile Rodgers, Flea of the Red Hot Chili Peppers, Ronnie Spector, and Mark Knopfler, Johnny played on Bryan Ferry's 2014 album *Avonmore*.

Rourke and Joyce

After the demise of the Smiths, Andy Rourke and Mike Joyce were picked up by Sinéad O'Connor for her 1988 tour in support of *The Lion and the Cobra*. Rourke also appeared on her subsequent album and commercial break-through, 1990's *I Do Not Want What I Haven't Got*, playing bass and acoustic guitar on the sessions.

Nineteen eighty-eight also marked the rhythm section's short-lived involve-ment with the Adult Net, a band fronted by Brix Smith of the Fall, which also included Craig Gannon. Along with Gannon, both played on Morrissey's sessions for "Last of the Famous International Playboys" and "Interesting Drug" the following year.

After a number of years where they didn't collaborate, Rourke and Joyce joined forces with Stone Roses guitarist Aziz Ibrahim in 1998 for touring and recording. Three years later, they formed Specter, a band fronted by Manchester singer/guitarist Jason Specter.

Rourke and Joyce also teamed up with former Oasis guitarist Paul "Bonehead" Arthurs, Ibrahim, and ex-Happy Mondays backing vocalist Rowetta Idah in the hopes of launching a group known as Moondog One. When that project fell apart, Andy and Mike played in another Manchester band called Jeep.

When Salford singer/poet Vinny Peculiar came calling in 2005, the Smiths' rhythm section helped him track the single "Two Fat Lovers." Two years later, they teamed up for *Inside the Smiths*, a heartfelt documentary DVD release that chronicled their time with the band and included participation from Gannon, New Order bassist Peter Hook, and Buzzcocks front man Pete Shelley.

Joyce

In addition to his efforts alongside Andy Rourke, Mike Joyce worked in the studio with Suede in 1990, toured and recorded with the Buzzcocks in 1990 and '91, and toured with both Julian Cope and Public Image Ltd. in 1992. He also played with Pete Wylie, formerly of the Mighty Wah!, from 1996 to 1998.

Mike also served as a radio DJ, hosting *Alternative Therapy* on Manchester's Revolution 96.2 FM—a station overseen by former Inspiral Carpets keyboardist turned Music Director Clint Boon—from 2006. When the station changed format in 2008, he moved the show to Manchester Radio Online and Tin Can Media. He has since hosted *The Coalition Independent Chart Show* and *Stop. Look. Listen.* on East Village Radio, which streams out of New York. Joyce has also served as a guest host on BBC 6 Music, and has also thrived as a club DJ.

Rourke

On his own, Andy Rourke co-wrote the music for "Yes, I Am Blind," "Girl Least Likely To," and "Get off the Stage," which were released as Morrissey B-sides in 1989 and 1990. As a session musician, Rourke has played bass on albums by the Pretenders (1994's *Last of the Independents*), Badly Drawn Boy, and former Stone Roses front man Ian Brown (2007's *The World Is Yours*). Alongside other acclaimed, Manchester-based bassists Peter Hook (New Order and Joy Division) and Mani (the Stone Roses and Primal Scream), he formed the group Freebass in 2007 and played on the 2010 album *It's a Beautiful Life*.

Rourke had been a Saturday-evening host on Manchester's indie and alternative radio station XFM 97.7 in the late 2000s but has since relocated to New York, where he—like Joyce—has become a regular on East Village Radio. Rourke has since formed a DJ and audio-production team based in Brooklyn and known as Jetlag with Olé Koretsky. The duo have played at venues in New York City and remixed artists for the dancefloor.

Rourke was integral in organizing an annual series of benefit concerts known as "Manchester v Cancer." Proceeds from the all-star shows at the MEN Arena aided cancer research at the city's Christie Hospital, Europe's largest research and treatment facility.

After discovering that his manager's sister and father had both been diagnosed with cancer, Rourke set a goal of raising £1 million from the first concert on January 28, 2006, which featured sets by Nine Black Alps, Badly Drawn Boy, Doves, New Order (performing the songs of Joy Division), and Johnny Marr, who played "There Is a Light That Never Goes Out" and solo tracks with his band the Healers. At the end of the set, Rourke joined Marr to perform "How Soon Is Now?" It was their first public performance together in eighteen years. They played together again that night alongside the night's other performers in a finale of Happy Mondays' "Wrote for Luck" led by the group's one-time front man, Shaun Ryder.

A second show, on March 30, 2007, was headlined by Noel Gallagher and featured performances by the Charlatans, Paul Weller, Echo & the Bunnymen, and Ian Brown of the Stone Roses. By now, Rourke's charity had been renamed Versus Cancer to help broaden its identity beyond Manchester.

On February 23, 2008, another concert was organized and included new bands like the Fratellis and Athlete plus established acts like the Farm, Inspiral Carpets, Fun Lovin' Criminals, and Happy Mondays. During the encore—which included all-star versions of "Please, Please, Please, Let Me Get What I Want," Joy Division's "Love Will Tear Us Apart," and John Lennon's "Instant Karma!"—an image of Factory's Tony Wilson appeared on the arena's screens. Wilson had quickly succumbed to liver cancer in the preceding year. For these finale numbers, Rourke joined Badly Drawn Boy, Hook, Ibrahim, Monaco's David Potts, and Weller's drummer Steve White.

The fourth and final Versus Cancer event occurred on December 12, 2009, and featured performances by Snow Patrol, members of James, Happy Mondays, and Peter Hook with the BBC Philharmonic Orchestra.

Legal Dispute

From the outset of the Smiths, Morrissey and Marr each took 40 percent of the band's recording and performance earnings, leaving just a 10 percent share for Rourke and Joyce. Although the four members had originally agreed to equal shares, a verbal agreement was made circa 1983 to enforce the 40/40/10/10 split.

In March 1989, Andy and Mike sought legal counsel, arguing that they had been underpaid for their work in the Smiths because they were equal partners who deserved a 25 percent share of all profits aside from Morrissey and Johnny's songwriting and publishing. Because of mounting personal debt, Rourke accepted an early settlement offer of a lump-sum payout of £83,000 and 10 percent of future royalties, while also forsaking any further claims. Speaking about how the money was distributed during his time in the band, he told the *Daily Beast* in

October 2013, "We'd do a three-month tour, but it's not like at the end of the tour, [Morrissey would] go, 'Hey, here's your massive check.' It never happened."

At the time, Joyce was in a slightly better financial state and continued his suit, which eventually made it to the Chancery Division's High Court of Justice in December 1996. He argued that he was an equal partner in the Smiths and entitled to his quarter share. The drummer's barrister, Nigel Davis, complained that Joyce hadn't discovered he was only getting 10 percent of the profits until after the band broke up. This claim challenged Morrissey and Marr's contention that Joyce and Rourke understood and agreed to the business arrangement.

It's important to note that, at the time, Joyce was receiving Income Support because all of his royalties had been stopped until the case could be heard and decided. "I had no money coming in," he told *Q Classic* in March 2006, "I sold my car, my bike, video camera . . . there was nothing much left to sell."

Marr's lawyer, Robert Englehart, contended that, thirteen years after the 40/40/10/10 profit split came into being, it wasn't possible to pinpoint when the verbal agreement actually took effect. He did, however, point out that Morrissey and Marr always operated from the position that they would take 40 percent each.

After seven days of proceedings, during which time Rourke, Marr, and Morrissey were all summonsed, Judge John Weeks ruled in favor of Joyce, ordering that he receive nearly £1 million in back-payments and 25 percent going forward. Weeks called the former Smiths front man "devious, truculent, and unreliable"; in *Autobiography*, Morrissey gripes, "Weeks tore into me with a thunder reserved for rapists and murderers."

In a cover story for *Melody Maker* dated August 9, 1997, Morrissey recounted, "The judge was horrendous, and all the scrawly, sniveling little extremely physically ugly people involved, who viewed me as some kind of anarchic, and semi-glamorous if you don't mind me saying, free spirit." He launched an appeal, which proved unsuccessful. Joyce's victory prompted Rourke to consider his own legal options, but because he had renounced all further claims in 1989, he did not move forward.

Things flared up again when Joyce began an eBay auction in November 2005 of the Smiths rarity "Fast One," after premiering part of it on Marc Riley's BBC 6 Music radio show. The instrumental track—an early incarnation of "I Want the One I Can't Have"—dated to July 1984 and was produced by John Porter. Mike explained he was in need of money and was selling rare band recordings to the highest bidder on the auction service.

Morrissey released a statement through True to You on November 30, 2005, citing the lawsuit settlement and claiming that "at the very least, prior permission should be sought" from the other members of the Smiths. Taking this to be a legal threat, Joyce canceled the auction.

In his True to You posting, Morrissey also argued against Joyce's claims of poverty, suggesting his former bandmate was "extremely wealthy" and outlining the details of the original ruling against him. Moz and Johnny had each paid the drummer £215,000 in 1997, he revealed, before Marr made a final back-payment of £260,000 in 2001. Morrissey had failed to make a final payment in 2001 because he had been overseas and had never received the paperwork.

Joyce eventually obtained a default judgment against Morrissey, and, in doing so, evidently revised his outstanding claim to £688,000. He next received orders to place a lien on Morrissey's U.K. income and assets. Moz contended that, in summary, the drummer had cost him more than £1.5 million in recovered royalties and legal fees.

If there was ever any chance of the band reuniting, it seemed to end with that settlement. As Moz told reporter Jennifer Nine, eight months after the original 1996 ruling, "The Smiths were a beautiful thing and Johnny left it, and Mike has destroyed it."

Reunion Speculation

"I don't know a single person who wants a Smiths reunion!" Morrissey insisted to *Billboard* in February 2014, echoing his repeated position that the group will never reunite.

Eight years earlier, he revealed to music website www.gigwise.com that he had declined a $5 million offer to reunite the Smiths for one performance at the Coachella Valley Music and Arts Festival. "I would rather eat my own testicles than reform the Smiths, and that's saying something for a vegetarian," he said. A few months later, a report on the same website had Morrissey saying, "We are not friends, we don't see each other. Why on earth would we be on a stage together?"

All the same, offers for the band to play again made headlines in August 2007 when reports claimed Morrissey had received a $75 million offer from promoters to reunite only with Johnny Marr. Moz claimed to have declined the proposed fifty-date world tour, which would be billed as the Smiths. The story was later described as a hoax. So was an October 2008 story in the *Sun*, citing "sources close to the band," that claimed the Smiths would play Coachella in 2009. Marr's manager dismissed the report as "rubbish."

That's not to say that Marr has never considered a potential reunion. In October 2007, he answered questions from BBC Radio 5 Live about future Smiths performances by saying "stranger things have happened so, you know, who knows?" before adding, "Maybe we will in ten or fifteen years' time when we all need to for whatever reasons, but right now Morrissey is doing his thing and I'm doing mine, so that's the answer really."

In June 2009, Johnny confirmed there had been official offers while visiting XFM in London. "I think we were offered fifty million dollars for three . . . possibly five shows," he said. Money wouldn't be the impetus for any reunion, though, he added. The reasons were "really abstract."

29

At the Record Company Meeting . . .

Reissues

Post Breakup Releases

There have been a number of authorized releases since the conclusion of the Smiths in 1987, including a live album, a series of greatest-hits packages, a sundry compilation, and a pair of boxed sets. Although the band had only recorded four proper albums and released nearly all of their surplus material while active, these releases have, nonetheless, been strong earners.

Stop Me

The Smiths retrospective *Stop Me* was issued on January 21, 1988, by the band's Japanese record label, RCA Victor, and presents three of their final singles ("Stop Me If You Think You've Heard This One Before," "Girlfriend in a Coma," and "Sheila Take a Bow") in reverse order, alongside their respective B-sides. It overlooks the single "Last Night I Dreamt That Somebody Loved Me," which was issued in the U.K. the previous month, and replicates the Murray Head–starring sleeve for the U.K.-only single "I Started Something I Couldn't Finish," which had supplanted the controversial "Stop Me."

Rank

Released on September 5, 1988, *Rank* was the Smiths' only official live album, recorded on October 23, 1986, at the National Ballroom in Kilburn, London, with fifth Smith Craig Gannon in the lineup. That night's twenty-one-song set was condensed to fourteen tracks on the record.

Issued via Rough Trade in Britain and Europe and Sire in the U.S., the album, which fulfilled a contractual obligation, debuted at #2 in the U.K. and made #77 on the *Billboard* 200. The concert recording had originally aired on BBC Radio 1.

Consisting largely of material from the *Queen Is Dead* era, the disc also includes new and emerging material from the time like "London," "Ask," and "Is It Really

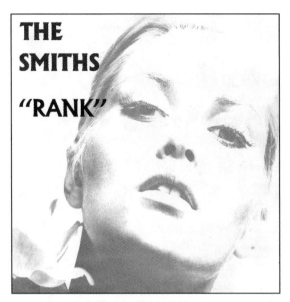

The cover art for the Smiths' live LP *Rank* features an image of the model Alexandra Bastedo taken from photographer John D. Green's 1967 book *Birds of Britain*. Upon its release, on September 5, 1988, the album debuted at #2 in the U.K. chart. *Author's collection*

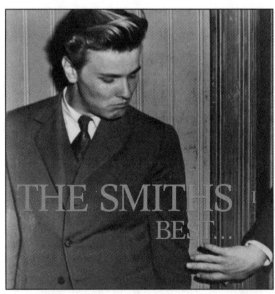

The CD artwork from the North American pressing of the Smiths' 1992 *Best . . . I* compilation, for which Morrissey again utilized a vintage image of actor and friend Richard Davalos. *Author's collection*

So Strange?" It was produced by Smiths soundman Grant Showbiz. Describing the album to blogger Julie Hamill, Showbiz said that *Rank* "defines what they sounded like live. I think of it as one of the great live albums with no additional overdubs."

Johnny Rogan would later write that Morrissey initially wanted to call the album *The Smiths in Heat*, but when Rough Trade protested, he went with *Rank*, which was Cockney rhyming slang for "wank." (According to www.urbandictionary.com, the term stems from filmmaker J. Arthur Rank's movie introductions, prior to the start of his productions, which depicted a muscular man in a toga banging a gong.)

The cover features an image of Alexandra Bastedo originally used in photographer John D. Green's 1967 book *Birds of Britain*. The interior photo of Morrissey having his shirt torn off onstage during the "Festival of the Tenth Summer" concert was shot by Ian Tilton.

NME would list *Rank* as the twenty-second best album of 1988. "It captures the Smiths during their most creative period, playing their music with speed, passion, and ferocity—three qualities the band possessed that were so often overlooked," the music weekly wrote, in its year-end double issue. "For those of you seeking a reformation it will only make matters worse and it's a recording of rare raw talent."

Best . . . I

With the sale of the Smiths' back catalog to WEA, now known as Warner Music, in 1989, after Rough Trade went bankrupt, highlights from the group's singles and albums were repackaged and reissued in 1992 on a pair of compilations. The first was issued on August 17 under the title *Best . . . I* in the U.K., where it debuted at #1, asserting the defunct band's continued popularity. In the U.S., where the album was released on September 29 by Sire, the collection stalled at #139.

Although critics argued that the compilation seemed to have been sequenced at random, the project's success in Britain was bolstered by the massive success of "This Charming Man," which was reissued alongside it and peaked at #8—the group's highest-ever singles chart placement. An edited version of "How Soon Is Now?" was also released and made it to #16 in the U.K.

The U.K. and Euro-pean versions of the disc utilize one half of a 1960s photograph of a biker couple sitting at a table taken by actor Dennis Hopper, but only the woman is shown. The stateside edition of *Best . . . I* was designed by Morrissey, and uses a still of *East of Eden* star Richard Davalos, who had also adorned the cover of *Strangeways, Here We Come*. The hand of James Dean can be seen in the picture.

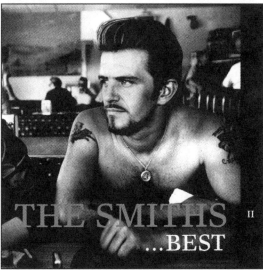

. . . Best II

. . . *Best II* was released on November 2, 1992, in the U.K., where it peaked at #29. A U.S.

The U.K. covers for the Smiths' 1992 *Best . . . I* and *. . . Best II* compilations differ from their U.S. counterparts. The sleeves use two halves of a photograph of a biker couple taken by the actor Dennis Hopper in the 1960s. *991.com*

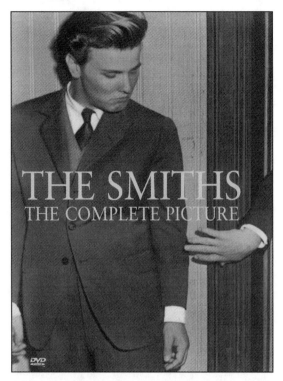

A full-color image of the actor Richard Davalos, which appeared first on the VHS version of *The Complete Picture* and later on this DVD reissue. *991.com*

release followed on December 8, but the album failed to reach the *Billboard* 200.

"There Is a Light That Never Goes Out" was released as the album's first single to precede the album, finally getting its due as an A-side, but only peaked at #25. The U.K. and European sleeve features the other half of Hopper's 1960s photograph of a biker couple, this time showing the man. In the U.S., another photo of Davalos was used instead.

Singles

The Smiths' A-sides were packaged together for this single-disc release, which dropped on February 20, 1995, in the U.K., where it quickly rose to #5. *Singles*—the group's seventh compilation overall—was issued in the U.S. three months later, but failed to chart.

"Ask" was released as a single in the U.K. but stalled at #62. In the U.S., Sire issued a CD single of rarities led by "Sweet and Tender Hooligan"—which wasn't even issued on a single—to promote *Singles*. Despite including non-album numbers "I Keep Mine Hidden," "Work Is a Four-Letter Word," and a September 25, 1985, recording of James' "What's the World?," the set did not chart. The "Hooligan" sleeve was designed by Morrissey and utilized a still of boxer Cornelius Carr, who had appeared in the video for his solo single "Boxers" earlier that year.

The *Singles* cover had been designed by Morrissey years earlier for another potential Smiths release but left unused. It features singer/actress Diana Dors, in a still from the 1956 movie *Yield to the Night*.

The Very Best of the Smiths

Designed to replace *Singles* when it went out of print in the U.K., Europe, and Australia, *The Very Best of the Smiths* was issued without consent or input from the group and expanded to include extra material. It was released by WEA outside of the U.S. and Canada on June 4, 2001, and peaked at #30 in the U.K.

Critics saw the project as a redundant and greedy act by WEA, and in response to its release, Morrissey and Johnny Marr asked fans to ignore the record. Although the material had been digitally re-mastered, Marr complained about the sound. Morrissey, meanwhile, scoffed at the artwork, despite the fact that the sleeve starred one of his favorite actors, Charles Hawtrey, the *Carry On* star for whom Moz had once written an obituary. U.K. music magazine *Mojo* picked up on this, too, sniping that WEA's efforts amounted to an "adman's approxi-mation of a Smiths cover."

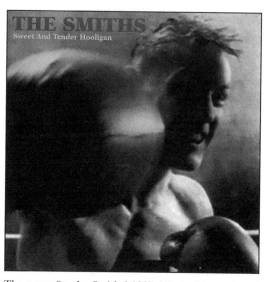

The cover for the Smiths' 1995 CD single pressing of "Sweet and Tender Hooligan," which was released in tandem with the compilation *Singles*. For the sleeve, Morrissey selected a photo of the boxer Cornelius Carr. *Author's collection*

The Sound of the Smiths

Yet another Smiths compilation surfaced on November 10, 2008, released in single- and double-disc editions. Marr helped master the release and Morrissey was involved in coming up with the title, which was changed at the last minute from *Hang the DJ: The Very Best of the Smiths*. The album reached #21 in the U.K. but stalled at #98 on the *Billboard* 200.

In addition to a slower version of "You Just Haven't Earned It Yet, Baby," which was re-mastered because Marr felt the original was too fast, the deluxe edition of the project appends rarities like "Jeane," "Handsome Devil (Live at the Hacienda, Manchester February 2, 1983)," "This Charming Man (New York Vocal)," "Wonderful Woman," "Meat Is Murder (Live at Oxford

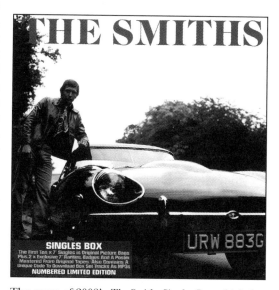

The cover of 2008's *The Smiths Singles Box*, which fea-tures American-born actor Joel Fabiani, who starred in the 1969 U.K. television series Department S. *991.com*

Apollo March 18, 1985)," "Pretty Girls Make Graves (Troy Tate Demo)," and "What's the World? (Live at the Barrowlands, Glasgow, September 25, 1985)."

The Smiths Singles Box

Issued by Rhino Records in the U.K. on December 8, 2008, this boxed set collects twelve 7-inch vinyl singles, beginning with 1983's "Hand in Glove" and ending with 1986's "Bigmouth Strikes Again." It overlooks all of the group's singles issued between July 1986 and December 1987.

The boxed set's cover star is American actor Joel Fabiani, who starred in the British television series *Department S.*, which aired in 1969 and 1970 on ATV in the U.K. Morrissey selected the picture.

Complete

The Smiths' boxed set *Complete*—released on September 26, 2011, via Rhino—consists of the standard versions of their four proper studio albums, the live album *Rank*, and the three compilations issued during the band's existence. It is spread over eight CDs or LPs, with a deluxe version of the project including both LP and CD formats, plus twenty-five 7-inch singles and a DVD of visual material.

The standard version of project does overlook the studio version of "The Draize Train," plus "This Charming Man" flip sides "Jeane" and "Wonderful Woman." Each record was re-mastered by engineer Frank Arkwright and Johnny Marr at London's Metropolis Studios.

30

So I Checked All the Registered Historical Facts

The Legacy of the Smiths

The influence of the Smiths on popular music is immeasurable, and was first heard in the sound of C86 bands like Primal Scream, the Mighty Lemon Drops, the Close Lobsters, the Wedding Present, and the Pastels. From there, it blossomed into the hits of Britpop heroes like Oasis, Suede, the Verve, Pulp, and Blur. The latter, for example, would later claim that they formed after seeing the Smiths on *The South Bank Show* in 1987.

Driven by Johnny Marr's guitar playing—which influenced everyone from the Stone Roses' John Squire to Noel Gallagher and the Libertines' Pete Doherty—the Manchester quartet has been described by the BBC as the band "that inspired deeper devotion than any British group since the Beatles."

Smiths author Simon Goddard called them "the only truly vital voice of the '80s" in a 2007 *Q* article, adding, "As the first indie outsiders to achieve mainstream success on their own terms, they elevated rocks standard four-piece formula to new heights of magic and poetry."

An artful, eccentric, clever, and *handsome* pop star, Morrissey may have been the most important presence in modern music during the heyday of the Smiths. Be it Radiohead's Thom Yorke, the late Jeff Buckley, Nada Surf, Death Cab for Cutie, or Pete Yorn, Morrissey's influence on the artists who developed in the wake of the Smiths was matchless.

The Decemberists' Colin Meloy went so far as to record an EP of Morrissey songs in 2005, while the Killers' Brandon Flowers has repeatedly spoken of the singer's influence and his love of the Smiths. All of this explains why Morrissey was called "one of the most influential figures in the history of British pop" by the BBC. And the iconic front man was named "one of the greatest singers of all time" in a 2010 *Rolling Stone* poll, which heralded him for "redefining British rock" and cited his lyrics and his unconventional vocal style.

When the Smiths were named the most inspiring band of all time by *NME*, outplacing the Beatles in 2002, it left the band's drummer, Mike Joyce, stunned. "It's an accolade that speaks for itself," he told Martin Hall in October 2008.

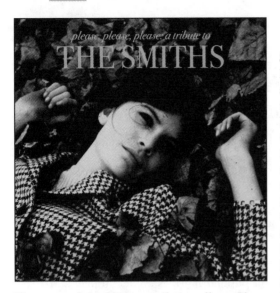

The cover of the 2011 compilation album *Please, Please: A Tribute to the Smiths*, which features modern interpretations of Morrissey/Marr classics by singer/ songwriter Greg Laswell, pop band Sixpence None the Richer, indie veterans the Wedding Present, Built to Spill's Doug Martsch, and former Belly front woman Tanya Donelly. *American Laundromat*

From defunct British pop group Shakespeare's Sister to indie rock act Pretty Girls Make Graves, the band's song titles have been repurposed, too, in homage. In the literary world, they have spawned novels like Douglas Coupland's *Girlfriend in a Coma* and Mark Spitz's *How Soon Is Never?* And the band's music has gone beyond the modern-rock genre, with punk, hard rock, and metal groups like Quicksand ("How Soon Is Now?"), Coheed & Cambria ("A Rush and a Push"), the Business ("Panic"), At the Drive-In ("This Night Has Opened My Eyes") lovingly covering the band. Of course, Radiohead's rendition of "The Headmaster Ritual," Nada Surf's "There Is a Light," Arcade Fire's "London," and Jeff Buckley's "I Know It's Over" make more immediate sense, but such tributes speak to the widespread appeal and legacy of the Smiths.

As Morrissey told *Select* back in July 1991, "It was a special musical relationship. And those are few and far between. The Smiths had the best of Johnny and me. Those were definitely the days." Or, as Marr told *Spin*'s David Marchese in April 2012, "Right up through making *Strangeways*, being in the Smiths was loads of fun. It was magical. I'm so proud of what we did. I'm happy to be looking back on it all."

Selected Bibliography

Books

Brown, Len. *Meetings with Morrissey*. London: Omnibus, 2008.

Carman, Richard. *Johnny Marr: The Smiths and the Art of Gunslinging*. Shropshire, U.K.: Independent Music Press, 2006.

Fletcher, Tony. *A Light That Never Goes Out: The Enduring Saga of the Smiths*. New York: Crown Archetype, 2012.

Goddard, Simon. *Mozipedia: The Encyclopedia of Morrissey and the Smiths*. New York: Plume, 2010.

Goddard, Simon. *Songs That Saved Your Life: The Art of the Smiths, 1982-1987*. London: Titan Books, 2013.

Majewski, Lori and Bernstein, Jonathon. *Mad World: An Oral History of New Wave Artists and Songs That Defined the 1980s*. New York: Harry N. Abrams, 2014.

Morrissey. *Autobiography*. New York: Putnam, 2013.

Morrissey. *James Dean Is Not Dead*. London: Babylon Books, 1983.

Pernice, Joe. *Meat Is Murder (33 1/3 #5)*. New York: Continuum International Publishing, 2003.

Robertson. *Morrissey, In His Own Words*. London: Omnibus, 1992.

Rogan, Johnny. *Morrissey and Marr: The Severed Alliance*. London: Omnibus, 1992.

Rogan, Johnny. *The Smiths: The Visual Documentary*. London: Omnibus, 1995.

Slee, Jo. *Peepholism: Into the Art of Morrissey*. London: Trafalgar Square Publishing, 1994.

Sterling, Linder. *Morrissey Shot*. London: Martin, Secker & Warburg Ltd., 1992.

Woods, Paul A. *Morrissey in Conversation: The Essential Interviews*. Medford, NJ: Plexus Publishing, 1992.

Music Magazines and Fanzines

Alternative Press

American Songwriter

BAM

Big Takeover

Bliss

Blitz

Bob

City Fun

Clash

Creem

Debris

Explicit

The Face

First and Last

Guitar Player

Guitarist

Guitarist & Bass

High Fidelity

Hit

Hot Press

i-D

iGuitar Interactive

International Musician

Jamming!

Loaded

Loud & Quiet

Magnet

Melody Maker

Mojo

The Mouth Magazine

Musician

NME

No. 1

Oor

Overground

Paste

Premier Guitar

Q

Record

Record Collector	Smash Hits	Uncut
Record Mirror	Sounds	Vice
Rolling Stone	Spin	Vintage Guitar
Rorschach Testing	Time Out	Viva La Rock!
Rox	Total Guitar	Vox
Select	Ultimate Guitar	Zig Zag

Other Newspapers and Magazines

Cambridge News	Observer
Guardian	Shortlist
Hollywood Reporter	Sun
Him	Telegraph
Irish Times	Time
People	Times (London)
Liverpool Echo	Travel Almanac
Manchester Evening News	Vegan
New Statesman	Wall Street Journal
New York Times	

Music Websites

A.V. Club	Death and Taxes	Pitchfork
The Autojubilator	Drowned in Sound	Popmatters
BBC Music	iHeartRADIO	Poweron
BillyDuffy.com	Ink 19	The Quietus
Consequence of Sound	miPRO	Spinner
Dazed Digital	MTV Hive	Stereoboard

Fan Sites

askmeaskmeask.me	plunderingdesire.com
askmeaskmeaskme.com	smithsonguitar.com
johnnymarrplaysguitar.com	thesmiths.cat
morrisseyscans.com	thesmiths-onion.org
morrissey-solo.com	vulgarpicture.com
passionsjustlikemine.com	

Official Websites

andyrourke.com	mikejoyce.com
johnny-marr.com	true-to-you.net (Morrissey's semi-
officialsmiths.co.uk	official website)

Index

THE FAQ SERIES

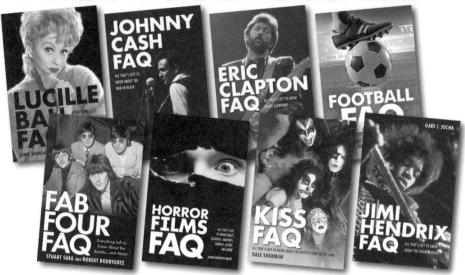

AC/DC FAQ
by Susan Masino
Backbeat Books
978-1-4803-9450-6 .... $24.99

Armageddon Films FAQ
by Dale Sherman
Applause Books
978-1-61713-119-6 .... $24.99

Lucille Ball FAQ
*by James Sheridan
and Barry Monush*
Applause Books
978-1-61774-082-4 .... $19.99

The Beach Boys FAQ
by Jon Stebbins
Backbeat Books
978-0-87930-987-9 .... $22.99

Black Sabbath FAQ
by Martin Popoff
Backbeat Books
978-0-87930-957-2 .... $19.99

Johnny Cash FAQ
by C. Eric Banister
Backbeat Books
978-1-4803-8540-5 .... $24.99

Eric Clapton FAQ
by David Bowling
Backbeat Books
978-1-61713-454-8 .... $22.99

Doctor Who FAQ
by Dave Thompson
Applause Books
978-1-55783-854-4 .... $22.99

The Doors FAQ
by Rich Weidman
Backbeat Books
978-1-61713-017-5 .... $24.99

The Eagles FAQ
by Andrew Vaughan
Backbeat Books
978-1-4803-8541-2 .... $24.99

Fab Four FAQ
*by Stuart Shea and
Robert Rodriguez*
Hal Leonard Books
978-1-4234-2138-2 .... $19.99

Fab Four FAQ 2.0
by Robert Rodriguez
Backbeat Books
978-0-87930-968-8 .... $19.99

Film Noir FAQ
by David J. Hogan
Applause Books
978-1-55783-855-1 .... $22.99

Football FAQ
by Dave Thompson
Backbeat Books
978-1-4950-0748-4 .... $24.99

The Grateful Dead FAQ
by Tony Sclafani
Backbeat Books
978-1-61713-086-1 .... $24.99

Prices, contents, and availability
subject to change without notice.

Jimi Hendrix FAQ
by Gary J. Jucha
Backbeat Books
978-1-61713-095-3 .... $22.99

Horror Films FAQ
by John Kenneth Muir
Applause Books
978-1-55783-950-3 .... $22.99

James Bond FAQ
by Tom DeMichael
Applause Books
978-1-55783-856-8 .... $22.99

Stephen King Films FAQ
by Scott Von Doviak
Applause Books
978-1-4803-5551-4 .... $24.99

KISS FAQ
by Dale Sherman
Backbeat Books
978-1-61713-091-5 .... $22.99

Led Zeppelin FAQ
by George Case
Backbeat Books
978-1-61713-025-0 .... $19.99

Modern Sci-Fi Films FAQ
by Tom DeMichael
Applause Books
978-1-4803-5061-8 .... $24.99

Morrissey FAQ
by D. McKinney
Backbeat Books
978-1-4803-9448-3 .... $24.99

Nirvana FAQ
by John D. Luerssen
Backbeat Books
978-1-61713-450-0.............$24.99

Pink Floyd FAQ
by Stuart Shea
Backbeat Books
978-0-87930-950-3.........$19.99

Elvis Films FAQ
by Paul Simpson
Applause Books
978-1-55783-858-2.............$24.99

Elvis Music FAQ
by Mike Eder
Backbeat Books
978-1-61713-049-6.............$24.99

Prog Rock FAQ
by Will Romano
Backbeat Books
978-1-61713-587-3...............$24.99

Pro Wrestling FAQ
by Brian Solomon
Backbeat Books
978-1-61713-599-6.............$29.99

Rush FAQ
by Max Mobley
Backbeat Books
978-1-61713-451-7................$24.99

Saturday Night Live FAQ
by Stephen Tropiano
Applause Books
978-1-55783-951-0.............$24.99

Prices, contents, and availability
subject to change without notice.

Seinfeld FAQ
by Nicholas Nigro
Applause Books
978-1-55783-857-5.............$24.99

Sherlock Holmes FAQ
by Dave Thompson
Applause Books
978-1-4803-3149-5.............$24.99

Soccer FAQ
by Dave Thompson
Backbeat Books
978-1-61713-598-9.............$24.99

The Sound of Music FAQ
by Barry Monush
Applause Books
978-1-4803-6043-3.........$27.99

South Park FAQ
by Dave Thompson
Applause Books
978-1-4803-5064-9.........$24.99

Bruce Springsteen FAQ
by John D. Luerssen
Backbeat Books
978-1-61713-093-9.............$22.99

Star Trek FAQ
(Unofficial and Unauthorized)
by Mark Clark
Applause Books
978-1-55783-792-9.............$19.99

Star Trek FAQ 2.0
(Unofficial and Unauthorized)
by Mark Clark
Applause Books
978-1-55783-793-6.............$22.99

Quentin Tarantino FAQ
by Dale Sherman
Applause Books
978-1-4803-5588-0 ....$24.99

Three Stooges FAQ
by David J. Hogan
Applause Books
978-1-55783-788-2.............$22.99

U2 FAQ
by John D. Luerssen
Backbeat Books
978-0-87930-997-8...........$19.99

The Who FAQ
by Mike Segretto
Backbeat Books
978-1-4803-6103-4 ....$24.99

The Wizard of Oz FAQ
by David J. Hogan
Applause Books
978-1-4803-5062-5...........$24.99

Neil Young FAQ
by Glen Boyd
Backbeat Books
978-1-61713-037-3.................$19.99

HAL•LEONARD®
PERFORMING ARTS
PUBLISHING GROUP

FAQ.halleonardbooks.com

0515